C000138111

Parenting Your Teen:
A Relationship Training Manual

DAVID UNGER, PHD, MFT

ISBN-10: 0996761330
ISBN-13: 978-0-9967613-3-8

DavidUngerPhD.com

"This is our first task—caring for our children."

Barack Obama

Spoken after the massacre of 20 elementary school students at Sandy Hook Elementary School
December 16, 2012

CONTENTS

FORWARD

Her voice sounded agitated. "I got a call from the mother of one of the other kids in my son Jack's carpool. She said that she thought I should know that Jack was bullying his older brother while his brother was driving. It was bad enough he was being a bully, but it was causing Lou to not fully attend to his driving. That lack of concentration was making this woman's son uncomfortable and she was considering having him leave the carpool."

She took a breath and continued: "I do think she is right. Jack does bully his brother. Lou has told me he does not want to talk to Jack anymore and does not want him in the car when he drives."

The mother paused for a moment before adding: "I have talked with him. I've grounded him. I've taken away his access to social media when he's home and I think he's getting better. But I am still worried. What do you think I should do?"

I have been a high school counselor long enough to know that navigating the teen years is challenging for all. There are so many responses this parent could have to her child's "bullying" behavior. Some of those responses might help improve his behavior, and some might even improve the parent's relationship with her child. Of course, some responses may exacerbate his behavior and make things worse for everyone. And, as many a parent can attest, many of our responses don't seem to matter much one way or another.

As frustrated and ineffective as you may sometimes feel, how you interact with your child will significantly shape his life. Sigmund Freud thought that by the time your child reaches adolescence, your job of influencing is mostly over. There is a good amount of truth to that, as you have probably observed your sphere of influence dwindling. Yet, while your role may be smaller, these are critical years in your child's development and your last, best chance to make a difference.

This mother was hearing from another parent that her child was being abusive. Not knowing the mother or the child, I needed to learn more before I could say anything other than, "I'm glad you called. I can hear the distress in your voice. Let's talk."

I don't get a lot of calls about bullying, but I do get some. More often calls come in about partying, grades dropping, stress increasing, social life increasing or decreasing, or any of the other myriad of issues families face as their child makes his way through adolescence. Unfortunately, there is not a one-size-fits-all remedy for adeptly navigating the teen years, but there are some skill-sets you can learn that will help you guide your child to a more rewarding existence.

You are reading this book because you would like to make things better with your teenager. Or your child is about to begin his teen years and you want to be prepared.

I am all for that.

How you do that is a process I would like to engage you in so you can make things better with yourself, your family, and your teenager. And we can throw in your friends as well, maybe even the world. But let's aim mostly to improve the relationship between you and your preteen or teenager.

At the school where I work, I hold the title Director of Counseling Services for the Upper School (9th-12th grades). I have spent a lot of time with students, parents, and teachers; students with their parents, parents with teachers, teachers with students, and all other manner of groupings. I provide whatever guidance, mediation, advice, empathy, commiseration, and hand-holding I can. I've been in the room when we counseled a student to leave the school and invited one to return. I give talks to the students and the parents. I write periodic letters to the parents and generally do my best to make their child's teenage years as fulfilling as they can be.

As for the mother on the phone, we spoke for the better part of an hour and came up with some strategies she could employ to reduce his "abusive "behavior. A more complete answer will come to you as you read the book, but for now here are two ideas I had her consider. I asked her what she thought prompted her son to be abusive. What purpose did his behavior serve? This is a good question to consider in most situations. What does the person want? If you can figure out their end goal, you usually can devise alternative ways to reach it.

I also asked her if she had spoken to her child about the phone call she received informing her that her son was being "abusive" to his brother. She told me she had and in no uncertain terms told him how upset she was, but wanted to speak with me before having a second conversation with him. I inquired if her son thought he was being abusive. She didn't know. I suggested that she ask him what he thinks and feels about the call and his being called abusive. If you want to help change your child's behavior, you need to not just tell him how you want him to behave—you also need to hear what he thinks, feels, and wants and work together to create those changes.

Even though at one level your teenage child is moving away from you, on another level this is an excellent time for you to be able to connect with him in more meaningful ways. He is more mature than he has ever been and more able to engage you in substantial ways. He may not be doing that so much, but that doesn't mean he isn't capable. He is able to forge a vibrant, honest, caring relationship with you. You and he just need to learn how to do it, but it isn't that hard. Even if he is not that interested.

I welcome you to the book and hope that reading will assist you in improving your relationship with your teen.

INTRODUCTION

This book is written as a manual. In my experience many people who read self-help books have specific interests and often look at the Table of Contents so they can go directly to the chapter of most interest to them. If that is true for you, by all means feel free to skip ahead to those chapters that seem most relevant to you. While I wrote the manual in some order and think it reads best to go from the beginning to the end, I am all for getting the information you need so that you can implement the kinds of changes you hope will make your family's life better.

If you are dealing with a substance abuse issue with your daughter you may not want to read the chapter about curfews. That is understandable and the manual was written so you can go directly to the issue of most concern to you. Yet, I do want to mention that when you deal with curfews you are dealing with issues of trust, responsibility, boundaries, and consequences. All of which are involved with issues surrounding substances. That is my way of saying you can go directly where your interests lead, but if you read from cover to cover you will see that the information builds upon itself.

I think you would be best served by at least reading a few more pages so you get a sense of who I am and my core beliefs. But, sometimes you just want to pick up a book and go directly to the part that most pertains to your current interest. No matter how you read this book, I hope its format as a manual will be helpful to you.

I had two important stylistic choices to make when writing this book. In the world of psychology both of these choices would be called avoid/avoid conflicts where you need to pick between two options you would just as soon not pick. Sort of like do I do my homework or do I do my chores? This is the opposite of an approach/approach conflict where you would have to choose between seeing your favorite band or going to your best friend's party.

The first choice was a grammatical avoid/avoid conflict. In referring to your teenage child do I say she or he or she/he or what? For the most part I have opted for switching genders with each chapter. As you read through the book please be aware that I am really saying your son or your daughter but I couldn't easily follow that option throughout the book. So, in this chapter I will use 'she' and in the following chapter I will use 'he'.

The other choice I had to make was what do I call parents who are married versus parents who are divorced and re-married or re-partnered and step-parenting? I couldn't find a satisfactory one-size-fits-all solution so throughout the book I use various terms to suggest you might want to discuss something with your partner, spouse, other parenting partner, or yourself if you are doing it alone.

One other thing you ought to know before we go any further: this manual is also written as a workbook. There are places for you to jot down your reactions and places for you to write your reflections upon questions I ask you to consider. And please feel free to engage in a discussion about any topic from the book at my website where I and other readers can respond to questions/ideas raised (http://relationshiptrainingmanuals.com).

Since I am a believer that you need to start your journey where you are and with yourself, I want you to think about this book as an invitation to take a more active role of parenting yourself. Yes, the book is about parenting your child. But before you make changes to how you parent your child, let's focus a bit on how you parent *you*. Once we get to adulthood we all unofficially take over our own parenting. So, let's see if you can help you out with your own self-management, then you can go forward and apply some of the concepts and see how they work for you and your child.

While you may want to improve your relationship with your teenager, there is no certainty that what you do will bring the desired results. You already know there is nothing I can provide you that will guarantee the results you may want. But, there is something I can offer that has a greater potential to make you happier. You can aim for making you feel better. That, at least, you have greater control over.

In psychology books we talk about interpersonal relationships and intrapersonal relationships. Which basically means your relationship with others and your relationship with you. While your relationship with you may not be ideal, it is the one where you have the most control. You can do your best to control how you interact with others; you can't control how they will react to you. You can try to get the odds in your favor, but that is about it.

If you can improve how you feel about you, that will also have an effect on those around you. In most situations your increased happiness will please those closest to you, but sometimes it won't. Not everyone is going to be happy just because you are happier. In fact, they may be envious, threatened, or suspicious. Your feeling better may cause others to react to you in somewhat different ways. Which, if you play your cards well, you will be able to use to help those others feel better about themselves as well.

So welcome to The Relationship Training Manual for Parents with Teenagers. I will do my best to make your relationship better—for you and for them. I can't promise results, but I am hopeful. Hope you are as well.

There are a few things you ought to know about hope. Research supports that hope is the best predictor of a meaningful existence; it fights depression and is a contributor to living a longer life. Hope comes in all shapes and sizes. Learning how to create it, in addition to receive it, will be discussed later. For now, let's just hope the book will be useful to you.

SECTION 1:

YOU AND YOUR RELATIONSHIP WITH YOUR TEEN

1

WHAT YOU BELIEVE, WHAT I BELIEVE, AND CAN WE AGREE?

I was driving to work one day and heard a newscaster say, "People like to believe what they believe and think what they think."

I got to thinking about that and asked myself if that was true for me. Do I like believing the things I believe and thinking the things I think?

Yes, I do.

I don't always like what I believe, but there is a certain comfort I have in what I think I know. If I believe good deeds reward the giver, I am more likely to do good deeds. That may not be entirely true, but I believe it and so it is true for me.

Until proven otherwise. Which occasionally it is, but not enough to change my point of view.

I know when someone agrees with what I think, it makes me happy. It confirms my worldview and reinforces my good feelings about my beliefs.

But what about when someone disagrees? Am I happy they disagree with me? Usually not.

Why not? I asked myself. What is the big deal if someone doesn't think like I think or believe what I believe?

As is true with most things, it depends on the circumstances. If you happen to disagree with what I think politically, we might get into a lively discussion about values and approaches to governing, but it is very unlikely that either of us will change the other's opinion. For many, political beliefs are firmly fixed. But if we have a difference of opinion about approaches to parenting, we might both be more willing to rethink our position and possibly alter our approach to being a parent. Most parents are less secure in their parenting approaches than they are in political affiliations.

If we happen to agree about politics, there is a shared comfort in the familiarity of our values. If we happen to agree about parenting approaches, we might feel reassured. And that might make us both feel comforted.

This agreement could be a positive or negative thing. Having your beliefs validated in accordance with someone you respect is reassuring. But if all you get is reassurance, it might disincline you to stay open-minded about all things parenting, which would be unfortunate.

So while I would like it if you agreed with my thoughts about parenting, I also would like it if you challenged them. Or at least run the ideas I present through your own value system and see if, where, and how they line up with who you are and how you want your children to be raised. Employ what fits and modify what you can to make it your own.

As parents we have a sacred duty to do our best to make our children's lives as good as they can be.

Parents everywhere will debate what it means to live a good life and I do not profess to know all the answers. I do know, however, that as parents it is our job to raise our children to be the kind of people we believe can live a fulfilling and meaningful life. While I might want to challenge some of your beliefs and you might want to challenge some of mine, I am going to support you living your life and raising your child within your own framework of what it means to have a life well lived. I might put some qualifiers on that as we go forward, but basically I am here to support you.

And, let's all keep an open mind about how best to live life.

I think all parents want their child to be able to look back over her childhood and offer a heartfelt thank-you. You want her to be proud of the life she has lived and able to acknowledge how your efforts contributed to her creating a life well lived.

I am not sure if we will agree some of the time, most of the time, or none of the time. In truth, I am less concerned about that than I am to have you think about the issues raised and challenge yourself to be the best parent you can be.

2

THE BASICS

If you think about the teenage years as ages 13 to 19 and fudge a little around the edges and make it 12 to 21, you know there is a lot of difference between a 12-year-old and a 21-year-old. Those years between 12 and 21 see many more changes than any other time span in our lives.

Typically children go from living at home to living outside of the home. They go from not being all that interested in romantic relationships to having a strong interest in them. They go from being financially dependent to hopefully making inroads to a living of their own. They go from having you guide and manage their decisions to mostly managing their own life.

Being a parent is a learn-as-you-go thing. You can try to study up on what might be coming your way, but we know the real learning is in the moment and in reflecting back upon our actions.

You learn how to change a diaper, hold a crying child, explain things you don't really understand, worry when he has his first sleepover, be disappointed when he doesn't do as well as you had hoped, and then you get to learn about his leaving home. You don't know how to do any of these things when you start out. You do some better than others. You have regrets about this and pride in that.

Many of the changes from age 12 to 21 result from your child pushing you. He wants more freedom, more space, and for you to be less involved in his life. Some parents are extremely skilled at knowing when their child is ready to go to another level of independence and they help facilitate that shift. Other parents try to hold the line as long as possible until eventually the child rebels.

Parents often don't know things have shifted until after the fact. When your child took his first steps you probably were there and eagerly cheering him on. When he sneaks his first drink you probably won't be there and may not be eagerly cheering him on if you hear about it.

Children need to learn to live within the boundaries and to push against them. They need to find what works for them and what doesn't.

It is helpful when a parent can smooth the way to independence, but it is also helpful when parents are steadfast in enforcing rules and boundaries so the child can learn patience, acceptance, persistence, and how to get around obstacles. While skill is necessary in all instances, I would imagine the part about obstacle clearance is not what you want to deal with on a frequent basis.

The bottom line is parenting a 12-year-old is different from parenting a 21-year-old. As he grows so too must your interactions with him. How you interact will always be fueled by love and concern, but today's guidelines will need to be adapted and usually before you are ready. Just like you need to buy back-to-school clothes each year, so too will you need to review last year's curfew, weeknight outings, and whatever other new freedoms your child seeks.

Your role as a parent evolves. As much as you would like to freeze moments in your child's life, it does not work that way. We all have to keep on moving on. The no-going-out-on-weeknights rule that was held pretty firmly in 9th grade is going to come under heavy attack as your child moves through high school. The more you can embrace or at least open your mind to those changes, the easier it is going to be for everyone.

I remember in graduate school a group of us students were sitting around talking about what specialty in psychology we wanted to pursue. Someone mentioned they had heard that adolescents were the least desirable group to work with. Not because they wouldn't be enjoyable, but because of economics. My classmate explained that most teenagers are not able to pay their way and their parents may be unwilling as well. While parents will spend any amount of money on their younger children, by the time their kids are teenagers they may no longer want to continue to invest in someone who has not demonstrated a positive return on their previous investments.

Needless to say if you bought this book you don't totally follow that belief. From my experience when parents have serious concerns about their teenager they want to spend the time, energy, and money to help. Maybe dollar for dollar they spend more on supportive services for their younger children. I don't know. I just know when things are not going well for a child, my phone rings.

As challenging as it may be to raise a teenager, it is way too early to throw in the towel. In fact, the teenage years are prime time to invest in the wellbeing of your child.

There is still time to be influential in your child's development. (My hope-inducing statement.)

But it is dwindling. (My anxiety-producing statement—sorry.)

However immature they may seem at times, teens have far greater insight into themselves and how the world works than their parents ever had at their age. Children now learn in vastly different ways than previous generations and are exposed to an influx of information from across the planet.

You still have a considerable advantage over all the other learning that he is engaged in. You live with him. You have more up-close and personal time even though you may be seeing him less than ever.

If you have read my other relationship manuals you already know I am a believer in the curative powers of relationships. Simply put, if you want to improve your child's teenage years, you need to improve your relationship with your child.

As you witness your influence over your child decline and his ability to stand his ground increase, you may be mourning your loss of control. Not that you ever had all that much, but I am sure all of us parents fondly look back to those days when our children looked up to us for guidance and approval with open, endearing eyes.

Those days may now seem like a distant memory. But don't despair, help is on the way. We are going to spend the rest of this book focusing on:

- How you can continue to be a positive influence on your child
- How you can help him to make sound decisions
- How you can help him to be more responsible
- How you can help him have greater enjoyment and fulfillment in life

All this can happen while you:

- Feel closer to him
- Respect him more
- Trust him more
- Enjoy him more

Resulting in:

- You feeling better
- Him feeling better

This is not an "in your dreams" promise. I write this with the firm belief that you have within you the ability to make all that happen.

Will life be perfect? Of course not.

Will everything you do and he does bring you high levels of satisfaction and gratitude? Of course not.

I imagine that by the time you have a teenager in your home, you would have learned that neither are you the perfect parent nor is he the perfect child. You both are perfectly imperfect.

You have seen your limitations and his.

You have been proud and pleased and disappointed and hurt. By yourself and him.

The longer you live the more you realize the hopes and aspirations you had for yourself when you were young have had to come face-to-face with reality. Hopefully in some ways you have exceeded your dreams for yourself. You have also probably seen some of your hopes go by the wayside. Life does that to us. However you look at your life, your child's life, and your relationship with your child, every day presents opportunity anew.

Six weeks ago I adopted a puppy. Four weeks ago I started going to puppy class. The instructor had some beliefs about dogs and how to train them that guided the classes. He told us his job was really to train the owners. Since the dogs were going to follow us and learn from us, we were the ones who needed training. We needed to learn what to do with the dog to get the dog to behave in desired ways.

The way to become the master of our dog was to control the resources. You want the dog to behave in a certain way—you give the dog a treat when he does what you want. He doesn't do what you want—you don't give him a treat. Dogs learn quickly.

Lest you think I am going to liken parenting a child to raising a dog and will want you to become the master of your child, let me tell you why I mention the puppy class. It was obvious to me and the other participants that our teacher knew how to establish a clear relationship with each dog. It didn't matter how unruly each puppy might be, he had the skills to get that puppy to behave the way he wanted. Even if we didn't.

I realized at that point that the quality of my parenting of the dog was going to go a long way towards having that dog become my best friend. If I didn't train the dog well and the dog ate my slippers, barked all night and pissed on the floor, I wasn't so sure how much I was going to want her as my best friend. I needed to do my best to help her be her best.

As the instructor taught us ways to communicate with the dog, it was apparent that some of us in the class had already taught our dogs behaviors that would need to be unlearned. We all had interacted with our dogs in some ways that did not promote the behaviors we desired.

Consistency was something none of us did consistently.

Which brings me to a truth the instructor taught us about dogs, and this one I do think directly applies to humans: dogs do what works. If they can yelp or beg for food and get you to come or feed them, they will continue to yelp and beg. As long as you eventually give in they will persist, having learned that the yelping/begging will sooner or later pay off. If you don't give in, they will get tired and give up. If you give in, they learn to wait you out.

Researchers do experiments with rats where they put them in a maze and when the rats find their way to a buzzer they get a yummy rat treat. The researchers reward the rats with a treat a few times in a row and then don't reward them for a few times. They alternate giving and not giving a treat and soon the rat is hooked. It will keep banging on that buzzer hoping that eventually the treat will come. The rat has learned that the reward is not consistent, but if they bang away long enough the reward will ultimately follow.

Since humans are mostly smarter than rats it does take a few more reinforcements to get them to keep coming back. I think we all know that slot machines are set up to eventually take all your money, but the possibility that maybe you would be the one who gets the big prize encourages people to keep on pushing the button.

Psychologists call this "intermittent reinforcement" and it is a very powerful way to affect someone's behavior. Later on we can consider some ways to intermittently reinforce some of your teen's desirable behaviors. For now I mention the yelping/begging dog and rat to suggest to you that most likely there are behaviors you have taught your child that you are going to have to undo. He likely has learned what works and what doesn't. He is not going to change what is working for him. You are the one who is going to have to change your approach and reconsider how you balance your reinforcements.

Reevaluating your parenting approach is on an ongoing task. Just like the dog owners who came to that puppy class with various less-than-desirable behaviors already in place, the instructor needed to start with each of us where we were and help us learn how to train our dogs and ourselves.

I am not implying that your child is an animal and that you need to train him. What I am saying is he has been trained and so have you. We all are shaped by our environment. There is nature and nurture, and both have had their way with us.

In order to improve the conditions of your life you may want to explore some new ways of doing things. You may want to reflect on how you are parenting and consider how your actions align with your values and desires. I learned in the puppy class that I needed to pay attention to how I was interacting with my dog. I also learned that as a parent it was incumbent upon me to attend to how I parent. Which is often easier to say than do.

So, let's start.

Whatever you are or are not doing with your child is what it is. It is not good or bad, right or wrong (unless it is, but that is another chapter). You don't need to judge, blame, or chastise yourself.

I know people feel guilty for actions taken or not taken. They feel remorse for how things have turned out. They wish they had chosen another path or been more of this or less of that. I don't want to take those feelings and thoughts away from you. But I do want to suggest that dwelling on those subjects does not guarantee future actions will be any different. Instead, look forward and plan actions that will likely yield better results, rather than just berating yourself.

3

A TEENAGER'S PRIMARY JOB

While you are learning new ways to interact with your teenager, they are immersed in all manner of learning. A teen's first and foremost task is to learn. These are their peak learning years. In fact, just between you and me, your teen's brain is actually working better than yours. Right now if we put you and her in a new learning situation, she would leave you in the dust.

Fortunately, as David Mamet wrote: "Old age and treachery will always beat youth and exuberance." I would substitute experience for treachery. Yet as your child hits her teenage years your ability to stay ahead of her diminishes. Parents have to stretch themselves to continue to find effective ways to parent.

Just as her job is to learn, your job is to continue to learn how best to be her parent. It is an evolving undertaking. Each day your child will be actively learning. She will be exposed to new subjects in school, interface with social media, and interact with actual friends. She will also be continuing to learn what your needs are, how to handle you, and how you relate to the world. As she gets older she will see you more clearly and gain a better understanding of how to handle herself around you.

Unfortunately, even though your child is heavily immersed in learning, her brain, as you may know, is the last organ to fully develop. She may be taller than you and look more mature than you did at her age, but her brain doesn't completely develop until she is in her late twenties to early thirties. About 80 percent of her brain function matures by the end of her teens.

That means that even though she thinks she knows more than you and she can learn faster and adapt quicker, you still need to be the parent. She needs your help and guidance regardless of how much she protests. The tricky part is for you to learn how to provide that guidance and support in ways she will value and pay attention to. You and I know she is not going to adhere completely to your wishes, but you want to hope you can keep her in the "A" range.

What you don't want to do is interact with her in such a way that you ignite her rebelliousness and she pushes against you in ways that are ultimately harmful to her. Sure, she needs to rebel in some ways. What you don't want to do is provide impetus for her to do something you are all going to regret.

Your children will want to try new things. This is actually something you taught her. As she grew up you exposed her to whole new worlds. It was exciting for you and her when she would encounter some new situation. You might remember taking her to a movie or someplace special, or introducing her to ice cream or a swimming pool.

As you have gotten older, while you still like going to new places and doing new things, you have most likely peaked in this arena. But she hasn't. She wants to go out and do new things more than you do. It is in her job description, as it is in yours to worry about her.

Frances E. Jensen, MD is a neurologist and mother as well as the author of *The Teenage Brain: A Neuroscientist's Survival Guide to Raising Adolescents and Young Adults*. Here is what she says which will help you understand more about your child: "Nothing—whether it's being with your friends, having sex, licking an ice cream cone, zipping along in a convertible on a warm summer evening, hearing your favorite music—will ever feel as good as it did when you were a teenager." The pleasure center of the brain peaks in the teen years which explains why teenagers often do things you cannot understand. It also explains why when we do something now it doesn't have the same level of enjoyment it once did. Ugh.

Here is one more thing you intuitively know, but let me confirm for you. Before I tell you, do you want to guess what is the last part of her brain to mature?

You may know it by its formal name: the prefrontal cortex. You may have heard it referred to as the part of the brain that is responsible for rational, executive functioning. That means it organizes your thoughts, weighs consequences, assumes responsibility, and interprets emotions.

I think we can agree that the sooner your child's prefrontal cortex develops, the better for all. Unfortunately, she thinks it is sufficiently developed already regardless of the fact that science says she still has a ways to go.

This is my best advice: tell her that while she thinks she knows all she needs to know to make sound decisions, she really is only operating at 80 percent of capacity, at best. She might want to consider letting you add that other 20-plus percent.

While you might wish she would consider your having 20 percent input, she would most likely want you less involved. When it comes to significant issues that will directly affect her life, aim for getting her to ask for your or someone else's consultation whose prefrontal cortex is more fully developed. Maybe there is a relative she admires or perhaps she would be willing to speak with a school counselor or a therapist. You can tell her that when it comes to making major decisions in life, it rarely hurts to get a second opinion. She can still do exactly what she wants to do, but at least she has opened herself up for some feedback and reflection before acting.

4

DRAMA

Drama is a phenomenon we experience a lot at school. We hear students use it to describe other students: "He is all about drama." We hear teachers use it to describe students: "Every time he gets a grade he doesn't like, there is drama." And we hear parents use it to describe their child: "I wish he would cut back on the drama."

As far as I can tell, drama is what we used to call "making a big deal out of something." It is okay if we ourselves exaggerate something but we would prefer others to put a lid on it. As a parent you don't want to reinforce exaggeration, but you don't want to neglect that your child is trying to get your attention.

I am sure, as a parent, you have seen your share of drama of all kinds. The good, the bad, and the ugly. What helps me and what might help you is putting the drama into context. Remember that teenagers are encountering many things for the first time. So, yes, teenagers have drama. They respond to situations in absolutes. I often hear the words "always" and "never." Exaggeration is central to their communication. They see things in black and white and nuance is a concept the younger ones won't pick up on for a while. Of course, your teenager will go to great lengths to tell you he does not see things in black and white and is keenly aware of nuance. And they are. 80 percent worth.

Teenagers for the most part are pack animals. Yes, you have loners and outsiders, but students tend to cluster together way more than adults do. That brief water cooler conversation you have with a few people at the office is duplicated from the moment your child arrives at school until he leaves. Then at home he continues the dialogues and gatherings on social media.

You may have noticed that when you are with others you tend to be more exuberant and expressive than when you are by yourself. Kids spend the day bombarded by each other's adrenaline and hormones. The interactions I witness are infused with dramatic tones. There is a lot of laughter and play. Those interactions prompt people to be spontaneous and try to engage the group. One way to get other people's attention is to take whatever was just said and try to outdo it, relate to it, or play off it. The holder of that sparked school-day energy is who comes home to you, ready to have a snack, a nap, and then get back to it. And, one hopes, do some homework along the way.

My office is next to a courtyard where seventh and eighth graders tend to hang out between classes. I cannot tell you how many shrieks and "Oh my Gods" I hear at top volume. I walk over to where the seniors hang out and the shrieks are fewer, the "Oh my Gods" toned down.

There are some teachers who will not teach middle school students because there is just too much energy in the room. Coupled with that energy is considerably less self-consciousness than they will have in the coming years. Seniors are too cool to shriek. Although, to be truthful, they still retain some of that enthusiasm and I do hear the occasional burst of joyful noise.

The trials and tribulations of your child's love life, friend life, school life, and the rest of life are experienced in profound ways. Some children hold their reactions in. Others want to share. Whether your child shares or not, please remember he is spending his day reacting and interacting with the world, if not with you. A good part of the drama you witness at home is because he is dealing with so many new things for the first time. As cool, calm, and collected as he may seem, he lives in the minefield of teenage life. Something usually explodes somewhere along the journey.

When your child tells you that you did something or somebody else did something and now his life is ruined, you need to remember he is seeing the world from a very different point of view. To dismiss it as exaggeration is to not understand and value his reality. The number one complaint I hear from teenagers is that their parents don't listen and understand them. Parents, students tell me, listen a little and lecture a lot.

While many parents like to end their "talks" with a lecture and some advice, it is important to remember to simply listen and validate. If you want to encourage him to share with you what is happening in his life, try not to devalue how he does it.

5

RETHINKING THE GOLDEN RULE

The Golden Rule suggests that we do unto others as we would have them do unto us. For the most part I have thought this a good basic guideline for all relationships. You treat other people with the kind of respect you would like to have and the world would be a better place for all of us.

As heartwarming and logical as the Golden Rule may be there are times when parents get frustrated and are not able to continue a disagreement. They close the door on discussion and say some version of, "Because I'm the parent."

That statement refers to the other version of the Golden Rule, "the one with the gold rules."

When you use a statement like "because I'm the parent," you are basically teaching your child that whomever has the most power is the one who gets their way. Certainly there is some wisdom to this principle. A child needs to learn that while "might" may not always make "right," it does hold the clout.

If "because I'm the parent" or words to that effect have come out of your mouth, I would like you to consider removing them from your vocabulary. If you have used them in the past, you have already taught your child the basics of the power dynamic and now it is time to move on. While this statement may have helped you end a discussion or put an argument to rest, it has done nothing to increase your child's opinion of you.

Your child is following orders because you have the power, not because she respects you. It is akin to what is taught in the military—you salute the uniform, not the person. Your child will salute you, but she won't necessarily like or respect you.

I have had enough adults in my therapy office tell me they did not value their parents' strong-arm maneuvers to be able to warn you about the long-range effects of "the one with the gold rules." When the time comes to move out she very well may be gone and you can only hope to forge any kind of meaningful relationship with her. At best, you will get a dutiful relationship.

That may sound harsh for I suspect most parents have played the power card at least once. The more you do it, the more you are trying to rule your family from a power position. While that might be okay for you, I would suggest that you add love, care, and respect as reasons why your child would follow your rules and guidance.

Try instead: "Because I love and care for you."

I imagine the rules you make are based on some thought/principle/belief that you hold. Why not share those? Your child may disagree, but at least she knows you are coming from a point of view that has a level of concern about her welfare. Even if she thinks your rule is misguided.

At one time or another almost all parents put their foot down. I don't have an issue with that. My concern is about the frequency of the use of power. If you use it too much it will cause your child to pull away from you because she doesn't feel you are really with her or in support of her. Your relationship becomes adversarial. If you do get frustrated and stop the conversation, you are basically choosing to disengage from her. That translates into you not truly caring about her welfare.

Sure, maybe later on she will come to understand that what you did came from your love and care, but it doesn't usually work that way. It usually works that when she gets older and moves out, she may choose to interact less and less with you. And when you get much older and the power has considerably shifted, she is not going to be any more inclined to be there for you than you were for her. Ouch.

When you had challenges when your child was younger it was easier for you to manage the situation. Sometimes you may have played the power card and sometimes you may have practiced the Golden Rule and found a more charitable resolution. You may have tried to empathize with her point of view. You may have thought back to how you wished your parents had treated you when you were in a similar circumstance.

As children push to open their universe and parents endeavor to keep them safe, there can often be differences of opinions. Issues have to be faced and decisions made. How those situations are dealt with is the topic of another chapter. Right now, the goal is to have a mindset of how to best help your child. Toward that end, many parents subscribe to the original Golden Rule of doing unto to others as you would have them do unto you.

However, there is a flaw with the Golden Rule.

Even though it has been around for centuries and is ingrained in many cultures, the rule has a self-centered tone to it. The idea is to treat others the way you would like to be treated, not the way *they* would like to be treated. There is an underlying assumption that what you would like is what others would like as well.

While it is certainly true that most of us would like to be treated respectfully, we might get to wrangling over how that plays out. I am sure you can think of instances where someone gave you a gift that was more a gift they would have wanted for themselves than one you would have wanted. Just because you want something does not mean others want the same thing. And indeed, their idea of respect may not entirely match your own.

I would prefer the rule said: "Do unto others as they would have you do unto them." That would be my New Golden Rule. While this may seem like a fine distinction, it does affect how we think about treating others.

Suppose your 16-year-old daughter has a midnight curfew and she comes home at 12:30 without having texted or responded to your calls. What would you do? Or more precisely, what have you done when something like this has happened?

If you applied the basic Golden Rule, you would handle the situation in the same way you would like it handled if you had broken curfew. In the case of a missed curfew, that might mean some understanding of the circumstances, a very short lecture, and a small consequence that could be satisfied quickly.

If you went with "the one with the gold rules," you might start with the lecture and end with your choosing the consequences. There would be little discussion.

If you opted for the New Golden Rule, you might start by asking your child what happened, accept her explanation, and ask her what she thinks the consequence ought to be.

When you ask your child how she would like to be treated, dealt with or responded to, it opens the door to greater understanding and connection. There is no power hierarchy. There is a one-person-to-another-person exchange. One of those people happens to be the child and one the adult. Sometimes these conversations can be among the most intimate and profound.

Yes, it is possible you won't agree with how she would like to be treated and a discussion may follow. On occasion things can devolve and you might have to employ a "the one with the gold rules" type of decision. But, hopefully by respecting her thinking and her point of view it will lead the way to a more mutually agreed-upon solution.

One rule, three views. All of which could be employed in different situations producing different results.

So what is the best response?

There is none; each situation warrants its own respective choice of response.

Your child will learn, as you have learned, that she can't always get what she wants. But she can be listened to, cared for and respected. In return, she will learn to listen, care for and respect *you*.

6

THE FIRST BOTTOM LINE

Your job as a parent is to raise your child so he can leave your home and build a meaningful, enjoyable, and rewarding life.

If you hold that to be true then your parenting actions ought to be geared toward supporting and helping your child build a wonderful life. In the strictest sense, every direct action you take that involves your child, and a lot of the actions you take that *indirectly* involve your child, need to fall into one of two categories:

You are either helping your child or you are not helping your child.

We can debate about what is helping and what is not. We all could probably debate both sides of whether it is better or not better for your teen to have a summer job, go to a concert on a school night, or take an additional AP course. There is merit on both sides of most parenting decisions. While I am certainly going to put forward my beliefs, I can probably support yours. Just as long as it comes from your heart and truly reflects your concern for your child's welfare.

The difficulty we all face is having our actions and interactions reflect our best selves. We have been grumpy, short-tempered, selfish, lazy, and unsure about what is the best thing to do—for our children, and ourselves.

Every parent I have spoken with wants to be the best parent. And they all worry at times that they may not be doing the best by their child. It is not always easy ascertaining what is the best thing to do as a parent. Should I be more lenient or more demanding? Should I let him do this or not? Often it is easy to know that what you are doing is not optimal, but hard to know what *would* be optimal.

I have an optimistic belief that everyone is always (and that is a word I don't use a lot) doing their best—even when by all appearances they are doing a lousy job. Let's take the teenager who barely speaks to his parents, skips school more than he attends, has a grade point average close to 0, apparently has no social life, and seemingly has no interests aside from getting high in his room.

A lot of people would not think that child is doing his best. But I do.

Here's why. I bet if we knew the history of what preceded this moment, we would understand how and why he is "choosing" to be where he is and doing what he is doing. We might not like or condone what he is doing. We might think he is capable of doing much better things. But if we were to talk with him, we would discover that right now he is doing what he thinks is the best thing for him in this moment. Perhaps escaping his reality is a better choice for him right now than trying to do something else to improve his situation.

Might he wish he were not in that situation? I hope so. But given the circumstances he is in, he is trying to do his best to cope with life as he knows it. Sure, we might and he might want him to have better relationships and a greater investment in life. But right now, as far as he can tell, he is doing his best to deal with his reality.

Let's look at an example somewhat closer to home. How about the extra helping of food you ate? The errand you are putting off running? How about the fact that you belittled your teen because you don't think he worked that hard on his history paper and got a less-than-desirable grade? Are you doing your best in those situations?

Certainly you can do better. But we are not talking about ability. If you had nothing else to do you might run that errand now or inquire more sensitively about his history class and paper. But there are other forces at play that are pulling you in different directions. Weighing all your options, you decide in the moment that you are going to feel better if you take that extra helping or not run the errand or criticize your child. You might regret it a moment later and maybe even in the moment, but for some reason you elected to choose that path to follow.

Why choose a path that is not optimal for you? Why do something you know is not your best? People have been grappling with those questions since self-reflection came into being. I am going to share my two cents later on, but for now, I would like you to consider that maybe we all are doing our best to do our best. Even if what we are doing is not the very best we are capable of.

There is a difference between what people are capable of accomplishing and what people are able to do in any given moment. I would like to think that boy in the room can do more with his life, but something is getting in the way. Teens are often quick to blame their parents and slow to take responsibility. If we are going to help that boy, we need to find a way to connect with him and engage him so we can move beyond the blame and onto the resolution.

I don't profess to know what is the optimal course of action to take at any given moment. I do think that if you are guided by your heart more often than not, you won't regret your choices. Certainly you will make mistakes. Hopefully reading this book will allow you some time to reflect on what being a loving, effective parent means to you and give you some tools for helping that boy find his way to a more rewarding life.

Having been a licensed therapist for most of my professional life, I have come to believe that taking the time to reflect on yourself and your life is a good thing in and of itself.

Plus it often leads to some action.

But, even without any action, there are a considerable number of therapists who believe therapy is about self-reflection and awareness. Those therapists guide you to focus on:

- How do you think/feel about that?

- Why do you think/feel the way you do?

- How do you think you learned that?

Therapists often throw in this question as well:

- What do you want to do about it?

Put that all together and you have your basic therapy session.

You may recall this chapter is titled "The First Bottom Line." The first bottom line is: your job as a parent is to raise your child so they can leave your home and build a meaningful, enjoyable, and rewarding life. To do that you are going to have to turn your attention to you, your child, and your parenting.

As you read, I suggest you focus on the topics presented in each chapter and see how they relate to what you think/feel. Rather than just read the book like a novel, stop and ask yourself what you think and feel about what you just read. Reflect on you, your life as a parent, your relationship with your child, family, friends, and anything else of importance to you. The more involved and interactive you are with someone or something, the more you are going to get out of it.

For the time being all you need to do is open those lines of internal communication. With that increased awareness you will find yourself attending more to your own core beliefs and values. Future actions will come from a more grounded place and you will, indeed, be more conscious of doing the best you can do.

Which is why people lie to themselves. When you have an honest conversation with yourself you may not like what you hear. If you don't like what you think/feel, you may stop looking inward. Or you may just go and do something about it.

Which leads us to the second bottom line...

7

THE SECOND BOTTOM LINE

People have mixed feelings about change. We want it when we want it, but not when we don't. We want it to be the way we want it to be, otherwise we don't want it at all.

Unfortunately, it doesn't work that way.

Since we can't know whether change will be for better or worse or make any real difference whatsoever, we often opt for complaining or procrastinating. And leaving it at that.

I once saw a cartoon in *The New Yorker* where these two guys were sitting at a bar in Heaven and one of them said, with a look of disappointment on his face, that he had never realized there would be nothing to complain about.

People like to complain. I don't have to tell you that. You probably like it too. Or at least do it often enough that it seems you like it.

Almost everyone utters a couple of complaints a day. Between work, politics, weather, traffic, and rising product costs, there is an endless supply of material to complain about.

Complaining is a form of bragging and mild protest. When you complain you really are pointing out how much you have to endure and how great you are for withstanding the suffering.

One thing people like about complaining is it usually does not evolve into an action plan. You can just complain and leave it at that.

Of course, if you complain too much about certain things the people around you will eventually want you to either shut up or do something about it. Stick to complaining about the weather and at most someone will suggest you move. If you hear yourself continually complaining about the weather you might even consider moving.

I have learned that when someone says you are doing something "too much," be it complaining about the weather, drinking, or anything else, it means you are doing it more than they are. We don't do something too much. Only others. And only in comparison to ourselves. If I drink the same as you, then you are not drinking too much, but if you are drinking more than I am you are doing it too much. "Too much" is very subjective.

When it comes to taking that "too much" thing and actively pursuing doing something different, people opt for:

a) Sticking with the status quo

b) Making small changes

c) The occasional major shift

Since change has to do with the unknown, it carries with it an element of fear along with an element of excitement. When the fear wins out, people try to put what is concerning them out of their minds and focus elsewhere.

That can work. For a while anyway. Holding on to the status quo will only work for so long because ultimately time changes everything. But for the short term parents can usually forestall making changes to how they interact with their teen. Yet the nagging issues will creep back into your awareness and you will have to struggle with it again until you shove it back to the corners of your mind. In psychology terms, that is called "repression." It is one of Freud's defense mechanisms that we all employ now and then.

If your relationship with your teen keeps coming into your thoughts and you are not pleased with how things are going, you may decide to make some changes. Maybe big ones, maybe small ones. Most parents start small, but some make wholesale changes.

Choosing to make small changes is less threatening and holds a greater likelihood for success. Many people have written about "small wins," which boils down to aiming for a 'first down' instead of a touchdown. Get enough first downs, you'll eventually score. Some people skip the small wins and just throw the ball downfield and try to score on one big play. That works too.

We will get into some of the possible changes you can make, but for now let's just remind ourselves that if something is going to change, you're the one who must initiate it. You're the one reading the book, after all.

If you want, right now you can put down the manual, sit quietly, and think about your life. How do you think/feel about making some changes in your parenting? What you would like to do differently?

_____

_____

SECTION 2:

HOW YOU REALLY CAN CHANGE & MAKE A DIFFERENCE IN YOU AND YOUR FAMILY'S LIFE

8

ACCEPTANCE

As much as you love your children, you, more than anyone, know they have strengths and areas where you wouldn't mind seeing some improvement. In that regard they are like everyone else. Except they are yours.

We all have things we like about ourselves and others. As well as things we are not that keen about. We have those things we do well and those things that challenge us. We wish we were more this and less like that.

What with all those pros and cons about us (and everyone else) we need to learn how to gracefully live with who we are and who we are not and who they are and who they are not.

Let's begin with you. What are the traits, characteristics, and things you do that make you feel best about yourself?

_____

_____

_____

What are the traits, characteristics, and things you do that make you feel the worst about yourself?

_____

_____

_____

Let's take a moment and reflect on what you just did. What did you just do with those two questions? Did you read them and move on?

Did you stop and reflect?

If you did stop what are you aware of in your response? Did you dwell on one question more than the other? Did you have an easier time with one or the other? What do you think/feel about your response?

If you didn't stop and kept reading what do you make of that response?

How is your response familiar to you?

How do you think/feel about that?

Whatever you think/feel about yourself and however you answered those questions, the more pressing question is what you do about those parts of you that you like and those parts that hold less appeal?

Take a step back from yourself and think about the people you know and your general sense of people as a whole. Do you think most every person on this planet ought to be able to come up with a list of things they like about themselves and things they wish were different?

I do.

From what I have observed people have mixed feelings about themselves. No one I have met hates themselves totally or loves everything about themselves. I am sure there are some out there who hit the extremes but I'd be surprised if we could find a person who truly logs in at 100% in either direction.

But maybe. You never know.

For the rest of us, we spend our lives coming to grips with who we are and who we are not. We bump into our limitations and navigate around, through, or away from them.

I am sure if you and I could speak with everyone about this we would discover that:

- Some people have qualities about themselves that they feel strongly about one way or the other that colors their overall satisfaction with their life.
- Some people are not that adamant about much of anything and have a general overall sense of liking themselves and their life or not liking themselves and their life.

We fill the spectrum of the continuum.

You can find people who have great success and seemingly ought to be happy but are miserable. And you can find people who live in poverty and extreme conditions that are making the best of their lot and enjoying their lives.

The cliché therapists and self-help groups advocate having an attitude of gratitude.

Easy to say. Hard to cultivate. But not impossible. We all can upgrade our gratitude. And our attitude.

But to do that you need to do something else first.

I find it amusing that in writing this book about parenting and relationship-building I keep going back to lessons I learned in graduate school. I went to graduate school to study psychology because I figured the more I knew about how people operate in the world the more I ought to able to digest that knowledge and put it to use in some way I had yet to discover. As I progressed through school I learned a lot of this and that, but it was hard to project how to put it all together and do something meaningful in the world with that information.

Most of my classmates wanted to be therapists. I had never been in therapy and while I was curious about it I didn't have any great desire to be in it or to do it. I just wanted to know how to help people get the most out of their lives. Myself included.

In school I didn't have any big "ah-ha" moments. I had quite a few "that's an interesting idea" moments. Some of those interesting ideas I tried to incorporate into my life.

I remember one day in class we were talking about our parents and if we had heard them say "I love you" to one another and to us. The teacher asked us if our parents hugged each other and us and how our parents physically demonstrated their love. I had never really thought about it before but I became aware that my parents rarely hugged or said "I love you." To each other or me. I always had felt totally loved and knew they loved each other but those overt actions had not been an active part of the equation.

One day I went to my parents' house and told them I loved them and hugged them. It was a bit weird and awkward but felt good. From that day on we increasingly said we loved one another and hugged each other and increasingly it became more comfortable. There wasn't more love, just other ways of sharing it.

I mention my graduate years to express how at different times in our lives we learn new ways of doing things. You can do something for years and years and then one day decide to do it differently.

In order to do something differently in an attempt to make things better for you there is one more thing you need to do.

It was expressed by one of my professors this way: "Acceptance is the key." I don't know if he made it up or heard it somewhere, but the phrase stuck with me.

Just the concept that something is THE key is pretty powerful.

I imagine a lot of people would have differing views on what is the key and is there a key and a key to what? But before you go off on that discussion let's just consider the fact that my graduate clinical psychology teacher imparted the belief that if you want to change your attitude about yourself or anything about you, acceptance is the key. It is a concept worth consideration and one I have carried forth to this day.

I will give you an example that supports his belief. If you ever go to an Alcoholics Anonymous meeting or any other self-help meeting that follows the writings of Bill Wilson you will hear that the first thing everyone says is, "Hello. My name is _____ and I am an alcoholic." That is a statement of acceptance.

Their belief is that if you can't accept that you are an alcoholic, you are not ready and able to quit drinking.

Certainly people have been able to quit drinking or moderate their drinking without going to AA. For those people to change their behavior they had to come to grips in one way or another with their behavior and consciously make an effort to change what they were doing.

The basic belief is if you want to change something you first need to accept that you want to change something. The reason you want to change what you are doing is because there is a preferable behavior that you want. You either want to reduce or eliminate something you are doing or increase or introduce yourself to a new behavior.

If you don't think you have a drinking issue or any other issue then there is no reason to change your behavior. Others may think you have an issue and they may say you are in denial, but until you can find your own dissatisfaction with what you are doing, you aren't going to change.

If you look at your list of things that you don't like all that much about yourself you very well may want to change some of those things. If you don't like your height that is going to be very difficult to change. But if you don't like your weight or your job or your relationship with your child, those things can change.

The first step toward change is admitting that you are not happy about certain things and would like to change some of your ways. Yes, some things are going to be easier to change than others and some things you may not be able to change. Or may just change a little.

You probably can't change your height. You might be able to stand up straighter and wear shoes with higher heels, but most likely you are going to remain about where you are. But one thing that can change is your attitude about your height or anything else that bothers you.

That change may very well set the stage for other changes.

But first things first.

Let's look at those things you like and those things you like less and see what we can do about your attitude about them. Go back a few pages and take the items off your list and one by one put them in the following sentences.

First take the traits, characteristics, and things you do that make you feel best about you and put them one by one after the "I am" statement.

I am _____

I am _____

I am _____

I am _____

I am _____

Now list the traits, characteristics, and things you do that you feel worst about and put them one by one after the "I am" statement.

I am _____

I am _____

I am _____

I am _____

I am _____

Acknowledging to yourself who you are is a viable first step towards making peace with yourself. Let's just say you wrote down that you are smart but you also wrote down that you are not happy with what you have made of your life. Perhaps you believe you have underachieved given your abilities. That is not uncommon in our culture, but that doesn't make it any easier for you.

So how do you make peace with that? And if you did find greater peace would it lead to an increase in your self-esteem and satisfaction?

Think about the things you are really good at and the things you are not so good at. If you think about subjects in school many people might say "I am not a math person" or "I am not a language person." Carol Dweck, PhD would want you to know that when you say those defining things you are operating on a fixed mindset instead of a growth mindset. Those people who say "I am not good at math" usually close the door on putting effort into getting better at it.

As one parent told me: "I am not good at math. I know how to balance my checkbook. That's all the math I want or need to know." While that parent may not want or need to know much more, his mind is closed to learning more. He isn't going to put effort into learning any more. On the one hand that is fine; there are way too many things in the world for you to be able to learn them all and certainly if you don't have to why invest your time in something you think you are not good at?

But, Dweck would want that parent to know that if he chose to put more effort towards math he would get better. She would want him to say: "I am not good at math—yet."

Yet. It is a word you might consider adding to some of your negative "I am" statements. If you wrote, "I am not as sensitive to my child as he would like," you could add a yet to it. That one word adds hope. You accept what is and yet hope for what might be. Especially if you put effort into it.

It is time now to speak about existentialism.

I have two favorite therapists. One is Carl Rogers, PhD who wrote about the necessary and sufficient conditions for therapy, and the other one is Irvin D. Yalom, M.D. who happens to practice Existential

Therapy. Yalom wrote my favorite therapy book titled, *Love's Executioner.* In it he talks about 10 of his cases and the book reads like a highbrow detective novel. If you ever wondered what goes on in the mind of a therapist this is a great book to read. But I am not here to sell his books, just some of his ideas.

A tenet of his—and he is not the originator of this thought—is that life is not fair.

We all know this.

We know you can inherit wealth and you can inherit limitations.

You can play by the rules and someone can cheat and beat you out of something.

You can be in the wrong place at the wrong time just as easily as you can be in the right place at the wrong time.

Shit happens. It does not get doled out equally.

You can be smart and not happy with what you have made of your life just as easily as you could be considerably less bright and be happy as a lark with your lot.

You can be an underachiever just as easily as an overachiever.

Regardless of how good you are and how hard you try, someone else might get the corner office and the boss's daughter.

Sometimes life can be great. And sometimes it sucks.

No matter what you do, whether you have the corner office and the boss's daughter or are panhandling down on the street corner, there is going to be this ache in your life. Whether it is dissatisfaction with your life or whether you are singing "Is This All There Is?", you are going to have this gnawing sensation.

The gnawing sensation is there because you know your life is finite. I remember talking to Dr. Stuart Bloom once and saying, "If I die," and he corrected me and said "When you die." I didn't particularly like hearing that, but I couldn't argue with it. We all know, whether we like to acknowledge it or not that sooner or later we are going to die. Not a lot of people like that reality.

The gnawing sensation is there because you could be doing something else in some other place and life could be better. It comes because you don't always win, not everyone likes you, and you can't always get what you want. It comes because not everything in your life is perfect.

If things get better now they will get worse later. As joyful as life can be it is also painful. Plain and simple. Pain is part of life.

Even in the best moment in your life you have an awareness that the moment is fleeting. As much as you want to freeze the frame you know that this too shall pass. Which is good for those moments of gloom, but not so much for those highlight-reel moments. Existentialists are not an overly happy lot. Existentialists believe the formula for life contains within it a level of discomfort. We all find different ways to deal with the discomfort. Some try to deny it. They put on a happy face and whenever discontent or anxiety shows up they find ways to ignore it. I have a colleague who, whenever I ask how he is, the reply is, "Wonderful." You know, and I know, and he knows he isn't always wonderful, but that is his story and he is sticking to it.

Other people look outside themselves for some relief. When you get a new job, new love, new car, that all helps lessen the pain. When you do some retail therapy or go on vacation or have a drink or two that helps. For a short time those things do make things better.

But they fade and the angst comes back.

So, you drink more or eat more or make more vacation plans. All in the hopes that there is something outside yourself that you can do or get or go to that will make you feel better.

Some people wise up and realize nothing outside them is really going to make things better on a long-term basis. They figure if things are going to get better they need to work on themselves. Maybe they go into therapy, join a gym, take up yoga, or eat more organic food.

Those things do help make them feel better. But they don't fully take away that ache. They may lessen it. Or alleviate it for a time, but the gnawing persists.

So what is a person to do?

Some people find a spiritual path that provides a greater level of comfort. They place their faith in sources outside themselves that provide guidance. Their pain is their cross to bear and their connection to a higher purpose helps ameliorate their angst.

Most people come to the realization that living gets increasingly difficult and they try to make the best of the deal they have been handed. That is called acceptance.

It does not really matter how you come to it, but the greater acceptance you can have that things are the way they are, the greater your chance to do something about them. Accepting precedes change.

I have another thing to share from Dr. Yalom that you might find interesting. He wrote a novel called *When Nietzsche Wept*, which imagines a meeting between Freud and Nietzsche and is full of brilliant insights about life. He was inspired to read the book when he saw a play in which the wife of a psychiatrist was concerned that her husband was becoming depressed. She knew he was too vain to go to a therapist so she hired another psychiatrist to present himself to her husband as a patient in need of help. The other psychiatrist's job was to heal her husband without him ever knowing he was actually the one in therapy.

I mention this because you may have a child or a partner who is resistant to therapy. Rather than force the issue you might see if you can turn the tables without them ever knowing. If you practice some of the techniques in this book I strongly believe it will affect the behavior of those around you without you ever having to say anything to them directly about their seeing a therapist. If you want additional help you might read one of Yalom's books.

In the meantime, see what you can do to accept those things in your life that are bothersome to you. If you can say, "I am not happy about my relationship with my teenager," you can begin to do something constructive about it.

9

BUILDING INTIMACY – THE NECESSARY AND SUFFICIENT CONDITIONS

I suppose if I had to prioritize interpersonal skills I would rate giving and taking feedback in the top three, the other two being sharing your thoughts/feelings and listening to theirs. If you want to get emotionally closer to someone a good place to begin is to consider how you respond to the things they do and say. We will get to sharing thoughts/feelings and listening later, but right now let's focus on how to give your child (or anyone else) feedback. Then we can focus on how you take feedback.

First let's do a bit of dissection. There was a landmark study conducted in the '60s about conversations. There were a lot of limitations to the study, but it paved the way for researchers to continue to look at what is important in conversations. The study was conducted by Albert Mehrabian at UCLA and what he found was when someone is sharing a topic that has an emotional component the listener responds 7% to the actual words, 38% to the tone, and 55% to body language. In the literature this has been called the 3 Vs—Verbal, Vocal, and Visual.

When listening to someone who is being emotional or is spiritedly sharing their values/concerns, people trust what they see and the level and modulation of the voice way more than they do what is actually being said.

I am sure we all can think of examples when someone said something and the look on their face had nothing to do with the words coming out of their mouth. We could tell they were unsettled even if they said everything was fine.

Over the years people have poked holes in the findings, but for the most part the fundamental truth of the study remains—if you want to be taken seriously, your words, tone, and body language need to be in sync.

Carl Rogers, PhD researched and wrote about person-centered therapy beginning in the 1950s and continuing into the 80s. At the time he began writing the medical model was the primary delivery system for therapy. As with medical doctors, the psychotherapist was the expert and with their guidance a patient could find their way to better mental health. Rogers saw things differently. He wanted the client to be the expert and the therapist to facilitate the client finding the answers within themselves. The idea that the client had the answers within them was a revolutionary thought at the time. His belief in the client's ability to heal herself was a considerable step toward the client's personal empowerment. It is akin to when a parent conveys their belief in their child's abilities.

Simply put, it feels good when someone believes in you. Especially if they are an authority figure.

Rogers researched how therapists conducted therapy and found there were three things a therapist needed to do in order "to create the necessary and sufficient conditions" for therapy to occur. The more he looked into what makes therapy work he discovered that the conditions really became a roadmap to creating intimacy. He found that the conditions that foster the exchange between a client and a therapist are the same conditions that bring all people closer together. What was true in the therapeutic relationship was true in all close relationships. The creation of these conditions was something everyone could do and you didn't need to go to graduate school to learn it.

You don't have to create these conditions to build a close relationship, but it sure helps. You certainly don't have to do them all the time. Once again, you might want to consider that 10%-20% bump up.

There is a good amount of research that supports the value of endeavoring to use the conditions to improve communication. So when you get stuck in a conversation and you are unsure about what to do you can refer back to them and see if they can help you out. When giving feedback and engaging in a back-and-forth intimate conversation, these conditions can serve as a baseline.

Let's start with congruence. Rogers' research underscored that in close relationships being congruent was one of the three necessary and sufficient conditions to building intimacy. Essentially, being 'congruent' means that how you are on the outside is consistent with how you are on the inside. In other words, if you were upset with someone you would not act like everything was fine. If you were happy you would share that. If you were sad you would act accordingly and so forth. What you feel is what others see. His research supported the findings of Albert Mehrabian's 3 Vs so you want to endeavor to keep your verbal, vocal, and visual in sync.

I think this quote from Mahatma Gandhi that is on Oprah's list of top ten happiness quotes sums it up quite well: "Happiness is when what you think, what you say, and what you do are in harmony." Who am I to argue with Gandhi and Oprah?

Needless to say this is not always desirable or easy. We don't always want those close to us to know what is going on. We like our privacy. Yet, it is one thing to tell people at work you are fine when you are not and quite another to tell someone close to you. Rogers would want us to endeavor for greater honesty with those we truly care about.

Of course, you can keep your mouth shut and not share. Or if you were aiming to keep some things private while at the same time being open you might say something like, "I am thinking something which right now I would rather keep to myself." That would be a congruent statement. It might get you off the hook from sharing. But if you are like most people, if you hear something like that you immediately want to know what the person is thinking. Which is why most people just keep their mouth shut.

Telling someone what you are truly thinking/feeling is not something most people do on a frequent basis. We rise to it now and then and share easier truths, but most people are not so sure that being congruent is such a good thing.

Knowing there is some good research to support that taking the chance to be a bit more honest with those you love may motivate you to take a few more risks. Which I encourage. You might consider taking small risks and the occasional big one. You can speak with your partner or child about how you think/feel about sharing more of your truths. See what they think/feel.

Often if you kind of want to have a more truthful relationship but want to tiptoe up to it you can just talk about how you want to say something but realize you are hesitant. You can share your own internal pros and cons about speaking. In the therapy world they call that a meta-disclosure—you don't really share something, but you share how you think/feel about sharing.

But there is a buyer beware I need to mention here.

Sharing how you think/feel about sharing more of your truth is going to pave the way for you to eventually spill the beans. Plus it is going to make them want to hear what you have to say.

It is a kind of foreplay. You may not immediately follow it up with more truth-telling, but chances are you will. You'll say a little something. They will say a little something and one thing will lead to another.

Certainly the other person ought to respect your desire for privacy and not bug you to open up .If you share what is making you hesitant perhaps they will be able to comfort you so that it will be easier for you to share. It can be important to test the waters before you plunge in. If there are assurances you need you can ask for them. You may not get them, but you can ask and depending on their response decide to go forward or not.

You can ask for her to quietly listen and not respond until you are finished. This is, in fact, the therapist's preferred model for conversation. You talk, she listens until you are done. She talks, you listen until she is done. No interrupting.

You can ask her to quietly listen. That doesn't mean you will get it, but it does mean she heard your wishes. How she honors them will remain to be seen.

The person you are speaking with may support, urge, nag, pester, demand, or whine that you say what you have to say.

I don't think you can ask her not to "overreact" to what you are saying, because she needs to be able to freely respond to you. You can let her know you want to discuss something and hope you both can talk about it in a respectful and honest way.

It gets dicey when people share their truths because you do not know exactly what is going to come out or how the other will react. People often start to talk about their hesitancy to share and if the other person doesn't blow it they usually just keep wading into the pool until they get in the deep end.

Speaking your truth is a critical component to building trust. Yet how you share your truth is as important as what you share. There is a phrase that therapists use that I would like to share with you—"Honesty can be a weapon." Telling someone what you really think/feel can be employed to purposefully hurt the person. Instead of saying something cruel or mean-spirited, just share the truth behind those statements and meta-disclose: "I am aware I want to say something hurtful to you."

Then if you are on top of your game you might add something along the lines of, "The reason I want to hurt you is…"

Why not share what is going on with you and place secondary value on that piece of truth that is only going to hurt her? If you can share why you want to hurt her and have a discussion about that the chances are you can take that hurtful piece of truth and find a less harmful and hopefully more productive way to share it.

Therapists spend a lot of time with their clients exploring what emotions are associated with their actions. When a therapist notices that the tone or content of what the person is saying has a cold nasty edge the therapist would have them delve into what is prompting that tone.

Usually when a person gains insight into the causes of what is provoking them, they become better able to share what is affecting them in such a way that the other person can actually hear, value, and support them. You could be reacting to words that have historical meaning to you or a reaction to one of those perpetual problems. Sharing what is sparking your reaction instead of the reaction itself can be helpful to both parties in putting the conversation into a clearer context.

Otherwise you just get into a nasty confrontation. Which may be what you think you want because your being hurt has prompted you to want to hurt back. But my guess is that is a knee-jerk reaction and not really what your heart desires.

Since self-reflection and truth-sharing are not things everyone likes to do all that often, it may help you when you do decide to share a truth to ask yourself why you want to share this item now. If you want to give someone some feedback about what they are doing or about something they did, it can assist you to clarify:

- What is your motivation?

- What are you hoping to gain from sharing it?

- What do you want to happen between you and the other person?

Answering those questions may lead you to want to share those answers as well. Or maybe not.

Depends what you want and how you want to try and get it.

I personally think sharing motives and what you want is often more important than sharing information and facts. I often find when something prompts an emotional reaction in me and I voice my reactions I am not only sharing my thoughts/feelings about the thing, but I am also exploring out loud my own process. If I am sharing something in hopes of getting closer, why not share that desire as well? If I am upset about something someone has done and want to get back at them I often put that out there first and see how they respond.

Being honest in relationships is not an easy thing. It requires an active attentiveness to how you are experiencing the world and a willingness to share your truth. Carl Rogers' research pointed out the value of our internal thoughts and feelings being shared in much the same way as we experience them. Being as congruent as you can be with yourself and others was one of the three elements that he discovered built intimacy.

Most of the time that will serve you very well. And when it doesn't you can rely on empathy.

Empathy is the second part of Rogers' "necessary and sufficient conditions." Sometimes people confuse empathy with sympathy, so let's start by defining the two.

Sympathy is when you feel sorry for someone. Perhaps they have lost a loved one, made a mess of something or generally feel lousy. You might say, "I am sorry for your loss," or "I am sorry things are messed up," or "I am sorry you are feeling lousy."

We all have times when the world is not treating us as we would like. Hearing people say they are sorry that you are experiencing what you are going through can help make you feel a little better. And when you are not feeling well every little bit helps.

Empathy is a little different.

It is not that you don't feel bad for what someone is going through, but rather it is an attempt on your part to understand how it might feel to actually be in his or her circumstances.

People can botch up empathy, because it is both a simple and complex thing to offer another. Simple in that often your attempt to understand can be easily expressed with a sigh or a "yuck" or "that must feel awful." Complex because it is not easy to grasp how someone else truly feels.

The redeeming part of empathy is in the attempt to understand. You don't need to really understand, because truthfully most of us think nobody really understands what our lives are like. If you have a 103 temperature and a stuffy nose and are spending more time in the bathroom than you would like that does not mean that when I have those exact same symptoms I experience them just like you.

People often get cranky when someone says "I understand" because at some level you know they don't. Maybe they are trying to be empathetic and commiserate with you, but that statement of understanding usually conveys a lack of wanting to truly understand. It is a shortcut akin to walking by someone and saying, "Hey, how are you?" and then keeping on walking. You don't really want to know. You just want to greet them, be friendly, and move on.

Saying "I understand" is sort of the fast-food version of empathy. It is quick, it suggests nourishment, but it isn't really fulfilling.

Most people just don't know how to react to another's misfortunes.

Do I engage them or leave them alone?

Do they want to talk about it or forget about it?

What exactly is the best thing to say when someone has lost someone close to them or is suffering through sickness?

Nobody knows the answer to those questions. It varies from moment to moment and person to person. Which is why when someone tells you about their pain a lot of people say "I understand" and hope that covers sufficient ground.

If your intention is to be polite and not get involved you can stick with the "I understand." If you want to be closer and perhaps more helpful to the person you can take a shot at saying something more empathic.

Keep in mind, the goal is not to perfectly capture how the person is feeling, but to convey to the other person your desire to understand how things are for them. Don't get tied up in trying to say the exact right thing.

A solid empathetic statement is akin to just asking, "How you doing—really, how are you?" But instead of asking that, which is a fine thing to do, you can try out something like this: "Ugh. I know when I have gone through somewhat similar circumstances I have felt horrible. How are you doing?"

You don't want to assume that just since you went through something similar your experiences would be the same.

Often we hear people ask, "How are you?" and we know they have no desire to know how we are doing. They are just exchanging pleasantries. If you actually told them how you were they would be caught off guard and probably want to get out of the way as quickly as possible. They would figure you did not know how to deal with social norms and would be afraid you would cross any number of decency boundaries.

If you do really want to know how someone is doing ask them how they are and when they say "Fine" say "No really, how are you doing?" When they begin to be evasive say something that lets them know you really do care about how life is treating them. Often you can let them know by your expressions, gestures, and the sounds you make. I probably have said "Ugh," "Ow," "Yikes," and frowned and grimaced to clients more than I have said or done much of anything else.

Attempting to be empathetic tells the other person you really do care how things are for them. That heightened lever of concern is what draws the other person closer.

The third condition is called Unconditional Positive Regard.

I think most of know our relationships are conditional. While we might aspire to not have conditions on them, most of us have seen our care and concern ebb and flow depending on how the other person is behaving.

Most parents would say their love for their child is unconditional and I agree with that. But our behavior towards our child is often conditional. She does something that tests our tolerance and pushes our patience to the brink and we may do or say something that would not easily fall into the unconditional love category.

Yet Rogers would like us to have Unconditional Positive Regard. What he was hoping for is that we would have a reverence of life. This comes from the writings of Albert Schweitzer who influenced Rogers. The general idea is we are all in this together. No one's life is any more valuable than anyone else's and we should endeavor to respect every living thing.

I have issues with mosquitoes and the ants that overrun the kitchen so I can honestly state that I am not going to get perfect scores in this department. And yes, people can annoy me too. I can get upset and I can be short-tempered and mean-spirited on occasion.

That said, I do try to respect the sanctity of life and be kindhearted. But I know I don't get perfect scores.

Life is challenging for everyone. In different ways at different times. Some people live in constant threat to their lives with bullets and bombs going off all around them. Some people live in quiet places where "things like that don't happen around here." Wherever you live and whatever your circumstances you deserve the respect of others and we all need to take care of the world within which we all live.

I see these conditions as I do most things: they exist on a continuum. Sometimes you hover around the middle, other times you lean one way or the other. I aim for the high end and know I won't always get there.

When it comes to communicating with those closest to us the vast majority of us want to be caring, respectful, and considerate. It is just that at times we are tired, grumpy, and not feeling our best. At those times when provoked we may not always come across as caring, respectful, and considerate as we might like to be. To which I say keep aiming toward being the person you want to be.

When you fall short, admit it. To yourself and those affected by you. Then pick up the ball and try again.

No one gets to have perfect relationships. With themselves or anyone else.

What you get is opportunity. Until you don't.

So, while you still do, keep opening your mind and heart to learning how to be a better parent, lover, and friend to you and everyone else.

10

NUMBER ONE THERAPEUTIC FACTOR

There is a realization most people discover early in life: life is unfair and it hurts at times. Everyone has to find their own way to deal with the pain that life hands out. Some people are their own worst enemy when they hit a bump in the road while others seem to more gracefully adapt.

While existentialists contend that life is filled with pain, they also acknowledge there are varying ways to respond. You know for yourself that you can react differently to events depending on the time, place, and circumstance. My mother always used to say it was best to avoid me when I was hungry. While I would like to think I can still positively interact when I am hungry I know it is not my prime time.

Today I was chatting with a colleague and someone walked by and my colleague asked the person to stop, introduced them to me, and we had a short pleasant conversation. Later another person walked by and my colleague did not introduce them to me. The person was emitting a "Do Not Disturb" vibe. My colleague told me the person was usually grumpy and best avoided.

Writing this today I think of those two people who walked by me. One I got to chat with and one I stayed away from. Now, we all have times when that "Do Not Disturb" sign goes up, but given what my colleague told me about the second person I suspect that sign is up most of the time. I thought about that guy and wondered how the pain that caused his grumpiness related to the pain he had carrying around all that grumpiness. He has to live with himself and I didn't think his life at home was that much jollier than it looked as he walked by.

It is too bad, I thought. Too bad for the pain that came his way and too bad that he is not able to carry himself in a less burdensome way. Some might say his demeanor is the way he has chosen to interact with life given the circumstances before him and maybe he is fine with the way he is. Certainly we all are ultimately responsible for our lives and if he chooses to live his life this way so be it. Who are we to judge his life?

But if he wanted some assistance I would offer this view:

- Something unwanted happens.

- You are hurt mentally, physically, spiritually, or any other way.

- As with any wound you go through a healing process.

- As you heal you endeavor to make the other parts of your life not fall apart.

- To quote Bob Dylan, "You keep on keeping on."

How you keep on keeping on, confront, and rebound from the challenges you face becomes a measure of your life.

I know when I am worn out and would prefer to stay in bed and yet manage to drag myself to work I consider myself a professional. Most everyone can go to work when they are feeling fine. When you are dragging and can motivate yourself to go I consider that being a professional worker.

Obviously the more challenging obstacles the world throws at you the more it is going to take for you to cope. It is one thing to go to work when you are worn out; it is another to go when you have suffered a significant loss. There are times when it is best to lick your wounds and let them heal before you head back out into the world. We all want to do our best to weather the storms that come our way and find safe harbor. Maybe even a better harbor. Before you head out searching for new harbors sometimes you just need to pull up the covers and rest.

In a psychology class I teach to high school seniors we read a book called *I Never Knew I Had a Choice* by Corey and Corey. I suspect the grumpy man that walked by did not spend a lot of time dwelling on his choice to be grumpy. He just is. But if a few pages back he wrote down "I am grumpy" and was able to acknowledge that to himself he might also acknowledge that he would prefer not to be. If he could accept that he is indeed grumpy and he would like not to be so grumpy, he might be able to reduce that grumpiness. Or maybe he would say he enjoys his grumpiness and even if he were given the opportunity to change it he might elect to keep it.

I don't profess to know why he is grumpy, but let me hazard a guess about his grumpiness. If given the chance to rid himself of it, while he might speak about wanting to change it, he might very well choose to keep it.

Because it serves him.

His grumpiness kept him from having to speak with me. It has probably kept him from having to deal with others. While I would like to think there are potential upsides to speaking with me and others I also know there are potential downsides. He is protecting himself from the hurt of those downsides.

He is choosing to miss out on the potential ups to avoid the potential downs. I can understand that. We all do that at times.

You and I might think he is getting the short end of the deal. But as we can attest those downsides can be pretty hurtful. If you get hurt one too many times the pain of isolation might be better to deal with than the pain of wounds inflicted by others. He might give lip service about wanting to change, but may opt for the safety of the familiar.

Playing the guessing game we could say he is choosing to be grumpy to avoid the pain that might come his way if he were more friendly and outgoing. If we spoke with him he might acknowledge that and say, maybe reluctantly, that is a choice that, given the options, he is willing to make.

But what if we said to him we might be able to help him better weather the pains that others inflict and build his skills to improve his odds of having more rewarding encounters and relationships?

He might not go for that because we can't provide a guarantee and he might be risk avoidant when there is the potential for more salt on his wounds. Let's pretend we could promise him that we could improve his relationship skills and give him solid tools to deal with the rejections and hurts that come his way while guaranteeing he would enjoy more positive results than negative ones.

Do you think he might take us up on that?

Would you?

If I could promise you that I can offer you a simple thing to do that will improve the quality of your relationship with your child (and partner) would you be willing to give it a shot?

Yes? No? Depends?

If you said "No" or "Depends," I would like to know why. Since I am not able to speak with you about this right now, why not just write it down? That way in case we do get to speak later you can show me what you thought. Why would you not take me up on my guarantee to share an easy thing to do that would improve your close relationships?

_____

_____

_____

I can understand hesitancy. I think we all have seen enough commercials and heard enough "money back guarantees" to have become suspicious of guarantees. I am sure we have all experienced enough promises broken to not fully believe them when we hear them.

I also believe each of us has broken a promise and might now be more hesitant about offering them because we know we haven't always backed them up.

But conversely, we probably all have promised someone something and been able to deliver on that promise. Some of us have better batting averages than others. (Want to guess yours?)

When we hear a promise or a guarantee it does get our attention. So, when I tell you that I will share with you something that I guarantee will make your relationship with your child (and partner) better it ought to at least get you to pay a bit more attention. Who knows? Maybe this guarantee will actually come true.

While you may be skeptical you can also be hopeful. After all, if something is guaranteed it ought to at least turn out to be pretty good. And hopefully real good.

So, let's review.

When I tell you that I guarantee I can share with you something that will make your relationships better you might pay a bit more attention. As skeptical as you may be, you may be hopeful that maybe, just maybe, I could really share something that would work for you.

Is that about where you are now?

If so, here goes.

Irvin D. Yalom, M.D. wrote a book titled *The Theory and Practice of Group Psychotherapy*. Many people in the profession consider it the best book written about group therapy. Others consider it one of the best books about therapy period. In the book he writes about therapeutic factors that make group therapy work. Just as Carl Rogers thought you needed to be congruent, empathetic, and have unconditional positive regard, Yalom thought there were eleven factors that made group therapy work.

Don't worry, I am not going to review them all. Just one.

Before I share what the number one factor is, let me also tell you that while he wrote about therapy groups, you can consider any time you are with someone else that you are in a group. You can apply his factors to the grouping you have with your child, family, partner, friends, and really to the relationship you have with yourself, since sometimes you can be of two or more minds.

After considerable research and experience Yalom found that the single most important healing element was the instillation of hope.

When people are hopeful they feel better.

When you lose hope it is hard to proceed.

If you go to your doctor and they tell you that you will get better, that in itself is healing. We all dread hearing bad news when we see a doctor. While some people are able to rally from bad news many more are able to rally around the good news.

Before I go any further I need to ask you something. Are you a little disappointed with this instillation of hope thing? Were you hoping for something a little better? Something that you would read and it would invigorate you?

Here I am talking about guaranteeing that I could make your life better and all I have to share is the instillation of hope? That is pretty weak.

I am guessing you hoped for more. I can't blame you.

But, perhaps you recognize that before I told you what the single most important healing element was, you might have been feeling better. Maybe a little skeptical, but also probably a little hopeful and that little hopefulness probably had you feeling better. Once you got the "answer" the hope was gone and you might have gotten a little deflated.

Which is why we have heard the slogan—"Keep hope alive."

Before we move on, let me point out a few more things.

You will feel better about your life if you inject more hope into it. We can talk about how to do that, but for the moment just hold on to the idea that bringing more hope into your life will make you feel better. Guaranteed.

Okay, that was a joke. I can't guarantee that kind of thing. I am sorry I misled you. I will endeavor not to mislead you again. But I couldn't think of a better way to illustrate the point.

To be congruent if I do mislead you again I will eventually cop to it because I really do believe in honesty. Sheldon Kopp, PhD wrote in his book *Back to One*, "Truth is subservient to honesty in my storytelling," and I will use that as my only defense.

If you reflect on the last couple of pages you have read and how you felt as you went along I am pretty sure you can attest that when you had a little hope instilled in you, you probably read a little faster, got a little more attentive, and for the moment, you felt better.

If that is true, then consider finding ways to instill more hope in your life and the lives of those around you.

It is somewhat akin to when you buy a lottery ticket. On the one hand you pretty much know you are not going to win. But you bought it in hopes that you would.

Until the winner is announced you can hope to win. Having that hope and dreaming what you would do with that money does make you feel a little better.

Of course, that can plummet when you lose. But there is always another ticket to buy.

Let's review some more:

1   I suggested that you ought to be able to bump up your lot in life by 10%-20%. You might very well do more, but if you want to make some changes in your life I think it best to aim for a little improvement. Anything else will be gravy.

That 10-20% percent may be harder for others to notice, but you will know. It may be discouraging that others may not notice right away. But remember you aren't doing this for them.

Sure, their recognition and appreciation might help out and they may even be a beneficiary of your changes. Still, you are doing this for you and you need to appreciate and value your efforts.

2   I asked you to write a list of some of your strengths and areas that could use some improvement. Then I asked if you could take ownership of those traits and accept them as your truths by saying: "I am ___." Acceptance is key.

3   I mentioned this grumpy guy who walked by me who maybe would just as soon stay exactly the way he is. But, if he wanted to consider improving his lot by 10%-20%, he could begin by acknowledging who he is and who he isn't and accepting those truths.

4   The next thing for him to do to make those changes is to instill some hope into the situation. In his case, he could skeptically and grumpily say to himself that maybe, just maybe, he would be able to improve the quality of his life.

If he (or you) could find that hope it would really help.

But let's say he (or you) is not able to do that. Hope is not always easy to find.

I think you and I can agree it is not always possible to fool ourselves. We may want to have hope, but finding that hope when things looks bleak requires an elusive skill set. If the doctor said that if you took these pills you would feel healthier, that ought to instill enough hope in you to swallow some. It would be harder to motivate yourself if the doctor said she didn't think the pills would help. Even if you find a glimmer of hope that does not always translate into forward action. Many people succumb to the long-shot odds.

There are times you need to dig deep within yourself and find some grit. You don't need a lot. Just enough to get the motor running in first gear. Even if the doctor said you only had a one percent chance, wouldn't you want to try to focus on the possibility instead of the probability? You may want to keep hope alive, but it could be flickering.

Let's just say you adopt that position that there is nothing you can do that will make your life better. That is a pretty extreme position, but let's just says you are that extreme person. I would like to believe that even if you are that "nothing can make my life better" person and you are reading this you aren't really as stuck as you put on. Why even read a book like this if you don't have some hope that reading it will make your life better?

But even if you are reading this because somebody told you that if you didn't read it they would leave you, even if you are that person, I still have hope for you.

Because I believe in osmosis.

If you keep reading, some of this stuff is going to rub off on you. Somehow, someway, there will be something you ingest from reading this that will change how you conduct your life. You will do something without thinking and it will turn out well. That little tweak will come with a concomitant rise in your level of hope. You will notice the improvement even if you don't think about it, because the next time something similar arises you will face it differently with a bit more hope. Of course, it could come crashing down and then you could scurry back to your previous position. But, according to the research, before you bombed out you were a little happier. And maybe you didn't bomb out. What then?

Let's see.

Pardon me, that just read like an infomercial.

I am sorry.

I just wanted to give a little shout-out to hope and encourage you to invest some time and energy in finding it. Even if you don't have much hope, that osmosis thing will seep its way into your actions.

Let me ask you something. Right now in your life, where would an infusion of hope help you out?

_____

_____

Remember we are not looking for a giant step forward in the hope department. We just want that 10%-20% bump up in your hope. So think about a place in your life where you would like to be more hopeful. And consider this—if you were more hopeful about this thing what would you do differently in your life right now?

_____

_____

Now comes an interesting intersection. If you were actually able to think about what you would do differently if you were more hopeful, you have a <u>Next Action Step</u>. Not that you are going to take it, but there it is.

Some people might actually put this book down now or very soon and take that bit of hopeful action and put it in motion. Some people might wait a bit. Others a bit longer.

Some might keep reading because there are still words to read and we haven't formally come to the end of the chapter. Maybe if you keep reading you will glean one more really solid idea that will be the catalyst that will start your engine and give you that injection of hope that will send you on your way.

Okay, I can offer a booster.

If you would like to be more hopeful about something and know what you would do if you were more hopeful, what do you think it is that keeps you where you are?

_____

_____

I don't know what your answer is. But unless you said fear in one way or the other I don't think you answered fully. More often than not what stands between us and what we want is fear.

Fear of this or fear of that. The list is pretty extensive.

If you can face that fear you usually can go forward.

Which is why hope can help. If you can be more hopeful about things turning out well or at least better it can bolster your courage. If there is a place in your life where you would like to be more hopeful, you might want to consider what you are afraid of and how that fear is getting in your way. To help with that you can read on to the next chapter which deals with fear and how to manage it.

Truthfully, there are situations in all our lives that don't provide much opportunity for hope.

You may own your fear and brainstorm ways to be more hopeful and come to the realization that there is no room for hope.

In those situations, acceptance is usually the key.

It doesn't necessarily bring you hope, but it may bring you peace.

Which is hopeful.

11

MANAGING FEAR AND RISK

There are those among us who are more risk takers and those who do what they can to minimize their exposure to risk. You can be a risk taker when it comes to climbing mountains, investing in stocks, or trying new things, but may be risk avoidant when it comes to being honest with others.

You could be willing to share your personal truths with others but afraid to be alone.

You could be afraid of heights, planes, snakes, spiders, or shadows in the night but willing to tell your child the truth about your adolescence.

We all are afraid of something. Sometime. Sooner or later something fearful will come your way.

We show it differently and handle it differently but we all get to deal with fear. Some know fear more than others, but no one gets to avoid it entirely.

There can be moments of fear in every day. You can hear a noise, have a meeting with the boss, not hear from your child, or feel something in your life is amiss. Small fears may register a 1 or 2 on your emotional Richter scale, some larger ones might come in at a 5 or 7, and the really big ones can take you right up to the top of the scale.

You never know what is going to cause those rumbles to become tumbles. There are things you wouldn't necessarily think would evoke a fearful reaction that could come along and catch you off guard. You could be thinking everything is fine and then the phone rings and you hear something that could significantly affect your life. You might get off that phone very afraid. Or elated. Or sad. Or mad. The phone rings and with it comes the unknown.

Let's just say you wanted to better handle the stressful, fearful times in your life. And let's just say you asked me what I thought you could do that would build up your navigation skills when fear crossed your path.

I wish there was a formula I could give you that could guarantee solid results. I wish I could provide that level of hope. Unfortunately, I can't point to any tried-and-true formula that has been time-tested and has glowing reviews.

What I can offer is an exercise regime which, like most regimes, is destined to not be fully followed. But see what you can do.

- Take small risks.
- Do little things that most probably will be of little consequence.

I am sorry to say this, but it is true. If you want to get better at dealing with fear you need to deal with more of it, not less. You are not going to build your skills without exercising them. There are plenty of unexpected tense situations that will come your way and fear will come with them. You can't control what the world deals you, so you might as well build your skills.

You can be proactive and choose to take small risks where you experience a low level of fear. You can build your confidence like any other muscle by starting small and building. Something happens and you feel that initial wave of fear in your body. You can ask yourself, what exactly is scaring you and what low-risk thing could you do to try to reduce that fear? Then you can choose to do it or not.

If you want to do some self-therapy you could pick a time during the day when you could take a few moments to reflect back on the day and scan for those fear/chance-taking moments. Think about the actions taken and not taken. See if you can acknowledge to yourself the efforts you made regardless of the results.

One time in the heyday of my bachelor life I saw a very attractive woman across the room and wanted to meet her. I didn't know anyone there and I knew if it was going to happen I would have to walk across the room and say hello.

I was too afraid to say hello, afraid of being awkward, her rejecting me, and me feeling not worthy enough to be with someone like that.

So I drove home in a funk. I was not happy with myself for not taking a chance and speaking with her. Sure, I could have fumbled my words and she might have laughed at me and told me to get lost. (I am a "think of the worst and hope for the best" kind of guy.)

But I didn't let that happen. I rejected myself. I didn't even give myself a chance.

I didn't like that and I told myself that from then on I was going to let other people reject me and not have me do it for them. I have not batted 100% with that decision, but I have upped my batting average. Even though it hurts when someone rejects me, I would rather they do it than I do it.

In many ways I now fear rejecting myself more than I do others rejecting me.

Fear takes many forms—fear of flying, failure, the list goes on. Fear can limit activity. My fear of rejection kept me from taking a chance and speaking with the woman across the room. Many of the things others do without much effort requires some people to scale a giant wall of fear.

Most children have a little anxiety when they first start school and have to leave their family. Most soon get comfortable and going to school is no big thing, except when there is a test or some other un-pleasantry waiting. Some children really don't want to go to school and going requires a lot of parental support and creates a high dose of anxiety all around.

Every year I receive at least one call from a parent who is having difficulty getting their child out of bed. They cajole, they bribe, they threaten, they withhold, then they call. Unfortunately there usually is not an easy fix. Working at a private school we have some leeway in how we approach these situations. Usually we set up some one-step-at-a-time kind of protocol where we have the student make small inroads into coming to school. If it is too much to do a whole day, how about part of a day? How about they come and visit school when no one is there? We have to tailor-make a plan with the child so she can take on her fear in bite size pieces.

Most parents have difficulty dealing with their child's fears because the child's fear activates the parent's fear. If their child won't go to school then they won't get into a good college and then their life will be ruined. Albert Ellis, PhD called this 'horribilizing'. We take one event and then run with it to its most horrible conclusion. He advises focusing at the moment at hand and not letting your fear run rampant.

Parents want to stabilize events to minimize their own fear. When your child's life is not going the way you want it to go, emotions get triggered. Parents get worried, they get angry, they blame themselves, they blame the child or the school, and they are afraid.

At first, they usually don't talk about their fear. They just act on it.

You might want to consider speaking about what you are concerned and worried about. At least initially to the other parent. Whether you are afraid that if your daughter doesn't go to school she will end up not having a valuable life or afraid that whatever caused her to do what she is doing is not reversible, your fear is going to prompt you to do something. Your child may not hear the cause of your fear, but she will sense your fear. Which then will make her afraid.

Parents are supposed to be fear soothers not fear enhancers. If you speak to your child about what you are afraid of it will allow your child to respond directly to your fear. If you just come at her with your consequence-laden emotional tirade it will only spawn an argument.

The more you know about what you are afraid of and can share it with others the more able they will be to assist you. While your child's response to your worry may not fully soothe you, you will at least have gotten the real issue on the table. Your daughter may think your fear is irrational and you may think her behavior is unacceptable, but at least now you are focused on the core of the issue.

Most people would rather not think about the things that provoke their fear. Thinking about scary things can scare you. Yet, avoiding your fear is not going to help you deal with it any better. You will be able to improve your ability to handle your own fears if you make an effort to think about yourself and fear every day. You don't have to do anything. Just reflect on the role of fear in your day and how you respond to it. As you get more comfortable acknowledging fear, you will also become aware of your responses to it and begin to explore other ways to manage those things that cause you worry.

Here is a two-part homework assignment:

1. Every day for the next week set aside 5 minutes to allow yourself time to quietly focus on how fear has involved itself in your day and how you have responded to it.

2. Every day for a week in some way do something you are fearful of, something that raises a small caution flag. Find small opportunities to stretch yourself. Just a little.

Regardless of how your risk-taking activity pans out you need to reward yourself for having taken the chance. The goal here is not so much to take chances and do fearful things so that you win prizes or praises— although you might.

The goal is to become more comfortable facing your fears. Whether you are just thinking about them or doing something about them. There will be fearful items that you think about that you will chose not to face. Okay, those items are too loaded to take on now. Instead of beating up on yourself for what you are not doing, consider rewarding yourself for what you *are* doing.

If I had made it a point to go up to an attractive women each day for a week and initiate a conversation I am sure it would have built up my courage and ability. Instead I took what I could have learned in a week and extended it over a year.

Sure there will be things that you remain fearful of. Jumping out of a burning building will probably always be fearful. But talking honestly with your child or facing some other less life-threatening fears ought to become easier as you allow yourself to attempt those things that give you a little fear. You can walk across the room and introduce yourself or go out to dinner alone or tackle something with less fear than you previously held.

Practice taking small risks. Reward yourself regardless of what you did and how you did it. Tomorrow will provide you more opportunities. You won't bat 1000, but don't let that stop you from coming to bat.

Try it for a week. Or two. Or as long as you like.

Of course if you focus on fear you will become more aware of it. This is a two-sided coin. You might be more blissfully unaware of how much fear you hold before you attend more to its presence. Yet that awareness will allow you to consciously put effort into reducing the fear. Just because you may not consciously be aware of how much fear you are holding does not mean it isn't there. Fear will motivate you whether it is conscious or not. You might as well know what it is triggering you and how it is affecting your life. With that increase in awareness you will gain the ability to make more conscious choices about how to proceed.

It is risky facing fear.

Almost as risky as not.

12

GETTING FROM HERE TO THERE

This is as good a time as any to address the issue of:

- What do you want?

- How you are going to get it?

- Or how are you going to deal with not getting it?

I would imagine part of the reason you are reading this book has to do with some interest you have in focusing on your relationship with your teenager. Maybe you want to improve your relationship with your child and/or his with you and/or parts of his overall behavior.

You don't have to do or change anything about how you relate to your child—all you have to do is read the book until you have had enough. Hopefully you will finish it, but many people don't finish self-help books. They read until they find what they wanted or didn't and then they put it away. Maybe they will revisit it later when they want a second opinion but more than likely it will sit on a shelf or rest in their Kindle library.

How you deal with what you are reading is entirely up to you.

I want to suggest something that is helpful to me and has been helpful to many others. Take a step back from what you are doing and quietly reflect on how you think/feel about what is going on in your relationship with your child. Or talk about it with someone close. Or both.

Therapists and their clients find that when you speak your thoughts and share your feelings, it can alter how you think and feel. The very act of saying something out loud helps define it for you and helps you more clearly understand what you have been silently thinking/feeling.

Plus the other person may chime in with their thoughts—which may be wanted or unwanted, liked or not liked, forgotten or remembered.

Whether you keep some thoughts/feelings to yourself or share the lot, the time you invest in reflection yields a high rate of return.

Throughout the book there are places where I leave space for you to write down your thoughts. I want to encourage you to take some time to reflect on the ideas presented and whatever random thoughts/feelings come your way. You can do it where I offer it and you can do it any time you like.

Since I am a teacher I encourage you to underline things, write in the margins, and interact with the book in whatever ways help you get the most out of it.

Now I want to ask you something. When I suggested ways you could interact with the book did it evoke any thoughts and/or feelings that you can identify? Maybe you read what I just wrote and had a moment where you thought about writing something down, but decided to keep reading and deal with it later. Maybe you thought you should write something down, but didn't.

People often think about things they should do. But they don't always do them. I should talk to someone. I should volunteer. I should write that thank-you note. I should try harder with my teenager. I should be writing down my thoughts in this book.

Albert Ellis, PhD, who wrote *A Guide to Rational Living*, created a word that I want to share with you. When you think about things you should be doing he called that "shoulding" on yourself. He (and I) would prefer you don't do much of that. When you aren't doing what you "should" be doing, you walk around feeling not so good about yourself. Yes, we all have to do certain things we don't want to do but should do anyway. We should take care of the items on our "to do" list that are mounting up. We should do this and we should do that.

A certain amount of shoulding comes with the territory of life. You just don't want to add unnecessary shoulds to an already over-burdened life.

I mention this because I don't want you shoulding on yourself. When I suggest things, I only do so because I think they might be helpful to you.

I don't believe one size fits all.

If something doesn't work for you—don't do it. When I ask you to reflect on something and you don't feel like doing it, don't.

And hopefully you won't should on yourself for it.

When you hear yourself saying you should be doing something, see if you can catch yourself. Ask yourself if there is any part of you that wants to do this. If there is, see if you can include that part of you that wants to do something into your self-talk. You can say something akin to: "I don't really feel like reflecting on this now, yet I know if I take some time to think more about it, I may be able to gain a greater sense of resolution." Having acknowledged both sides of the issue, if you still don't feel like doing it now, let it go. If it's important enough, it will come up again…and again.

If there is no part of you that wants to think about the issue now, ask yourself how important it is for you to do it. If it isn't that important, let it go.

If it *is* that important, just do it and complain about it later.

People opt to do things with and for other people often because they feel they should even though they would prefer not to. When someone calls you and asks a favor, it is not always easy to decline. You agree because you feel you should but you would prefer to do something else.

Therapists will line up to tell you to endeavor to do less of the things you should do and more of the things you want to do. They would also add some qualifiers such as ensuring it doesn't hurt others or yourself.

As people get older and time becomes a more precious commodity, they more often choose to do the things they want to do and feel less need to do things just because they "should." We are all older today than we have ever been while at the same time being younger than we will ever be again. I would like us all to follow our hearts as often as possible and enjoy what youth we have and what wisdom we have learned.

No one gets to live a perfect life.

No one is untouched by pain, disappointment, heartache, and the unfairness and harshness of life.

There is often an element in most everyone's life of "I wish I had done better" or "I'm not living as great a life as I had hoped."

Most people don't like feeling inadequate. But we all feel those things at different times. It is part of the human condition. I don't like it. You probably don't like it either. But we come to accept it.

That doesn't mean I don't whine and feel bad at times because of the hand life is dealing me. It just means I don't want to set you up for thinking this book, that new car, that vacation, drug, or yoga position is going to take away the pain of being alive.

The pain that life deals is there for all of us. In different ways and at different times, and unavoidable.

Hopefully we can all learn to navigate through life in ways that reward us—along with everyone we encounter—while sufficiently managing the challenges that come our way.

I think we all have heard a version of: 'The longest journey begins with a step.'

Or

'This is the first day of the rest of your life.'

Or

'Just do it.'

Pardon me for stating the obvious, but if you want to do things differently you need to do things differently. Not just think and maybe talk about it, but actually do it.

Yet for many of us changing how we interact with those around us is not that easy. Sure you can say to yourself that you are going to be more honest or kind or thoughtful or any number of things. But translating that thought into consistent action requires you do something different.

Therapists often ask clients:

- How do you feel about _____?
- What do you think about _____?
- How do you think/feel about how you are presently dealing with it?
- What do you want to do about it?

Therapists help their clients become more aware by simply asking those questions and doing their best not to be too judgmental about the response. You can save yourself some therapy dollars by asking yourself the questions and doing your best not to be too judgmental about your responses. Therapists basically repeat those questions until the session is over.

Of course they do more than that, but those are the basic exploratory questions—unless you have certain analytical beliefs, in which case you would throw in:

- How does this relate to your mother?

I am not going to go there with you now.

But if you have an analytical mind and like to mull these things over, you can always think back to your childhood and the lessons you learned. Figuring out your relationship with you parents and how your upbringing influences what you do with your life is a fascinating journey which many therapists encourage their clients to explore.

Let's say you are reading this because you are open to relating in a new way to your teenager. Perhaps you would also like to relate in new ways to others, but let's just stick with your teenager for now.

There are reasons you relate to him the way you do. For most parents how they relate to their children is heavily influenced by how their parents interacted with them. If you like how your parents treated you then you will do your best to parent in a similar fashion. Sure there will be some differences, but usually the sense of being loved will be the same. You might be more strict or liberal, more up-to-date and evolved, yet how your children feel about you will usually be similar to how you feel about your parents.

If there were aspects of how your parents treated each other and you that you did not like, then you are apt to not to repeat those things with your partner and children. Or at least you'll try.

For those people who were abused or raised by distant and/or critical parents, as much as they might want to not continue those behaviors, they often find themselves behaving in similar ways as their parents— which then invites a measure of self-disgust, resentment, or just plain disappointment in one's self.

Carl Jung, MD was an influential voice in the development of Psychology. He wrote: "The greatest harm to a child is the unlived life of the parent." I think we all know the example of the parent who was not able to fulfill his dreams and pushes his child to do what he could not do. What we probably see less clearly are our own interests that we didn't realize and how those affect our approach to our child. To be a better parent Jung would have you come to terms with your own realities and not impose them on your child. Parents who are unfulfilled or heavily damaged by their own parents are at risk for over-parenting their child to redress their own hurts.

We have all been exposed to positive and negative parenting role models. We have seen movies, read books, visited friends' homes, and watched our parents and others. We adopt some of what we have seen and experienced often without thinking. One day we hear ourselves saying something to our children and realize those were the exact words that came out of our parents' mouths. That can be a heartwarming or chilling moment.

The first time you want to cook something, you read a recipe and follow it. The second time, you look at the recipe and remember back to the last time you thought it would be improved if you added or subtracted an ingredient. The third time, you glance at the recipe and perhaps add or subtract something else. The fourth time, you barely look at the recipe and just cook it the way you want. By the fifth time, you no longer look at the recipe. The dish has now become your own.

The more we do something new, we continue to add our own touches to it. This is how it is with parenting. You are nervous at first and tend to follow closely what you have learned, but as the years go by you create your own parenting style. When you become a parent you realize that whatever you have observed, read, and tried to learn about parenting is not really as helpful as you might like it to be. Parenting tends to present numerous opportunities for you to fly by the seat of your pants. It is certainly a learn-on-the-job kind of job.

Situations are new and unique to you. Suddenly there is this person in your life who is dependent on you and your job is to raise him to be the best person he can be. Yet so little of what you do can guarantee results—good or bad. Each day presents numerous opportunities for you to interact with your child and you often won't know for a long time just how things will turn out. You can get positive or negative immediate results, but those don't necessarily foretell the future.

You do your best and hope for good things.

Whatever way you are parenting, let's explore some things you could do that would hopefully make you feel better and improve the quality of your relationship with your teen.

Trying out new ways to parent will be hit-and-miss. You can try something once and get satisfying results and the next day the same thing falls on its face. What you are aiming for is not so much day-to-day improvement but overall improvement. Don't should on yourself when things don't go perfectly. Just keep endeavoring to show your child how much you love and care about him.

13

THE WARNING

It is my ethical duty to provide a warning for you. It is one you already know, but one I think needs addressing:

Whenever you change one part of a system, it changes the system.

There is sufficient research in this area for me to comfortably tell you that if you start changing how you interact with your family, it will make a difference in how your family reacts and interacts with you and each other. It is akin to Newton's Law that for every action there is an equal and opposite reaction. While Newton was talking about the laws of physics, the fundamental rules apply. When you do something, others react.

Which is why people are reluctant to make changes. Change is risky.

Things may improve. Or not. What you may consider improvement others may not.

It is uncertainty that holds us back.

When I first became a therapist I had a client tell me a story about her high school experience. She hated high school. She felt like a social outcast and spent the majority of her days in the girls' bathroom. Her father came to her at the end of her sophomore year and told her that he was being transferred and over the summer the family would need to move.

She told me she loudly protested. While she was suffering at her school she knew how to work the system. She could get out of classes, sit alone in the bathroom, and manage to get through the day. She didn't want to move because she was "comfortable" and familiar with her circumstance.

Her father did not give in to her pleas and over the summer they moved. She told me that on the way to her new home she realized no one at her new school would know anything about her. For the rest of the summer she planned her reentry to high school. When she got her back-to-school-clothes, she bought what she thought the popular girls at her old school would have bought. When she arrived at the new school she introduced herself and said that at her previous school she had been one of the more popular girls.

Since no one knew any better, they accepted her as such. She acted as she had observed the more popular girls act and soon she had a solid group of friends. She ended up really enjoying her last two years of high school and only used the bathroom when nature called.

For most people, the discomfort experienced has to be significant enough to tackle the uncertainty of change. She told me that if she had not moved she would have continued high school as she had started it. She didn't really have to make the choice to change because her circumstances shifted beyond her control. While I don't recommend lying, I do recommend seizing the opportunities you have to make a difference in your life. You can wait until things get so bad you feel compelled to make changes, but why wait for the alarm to go off?

I want to help make the first steps simple enough so they won't rock the boat too much, but will hopefully help you feel better and avoid things getting worse.

Since the book is about relationships, part of our task is to focus on your happiness and how you communicate with yourself. What I am going to ask of you is your honesty. You don't have to be honest with me or anyone else. Just yourself.

If you can't be honest and clear with yourself, things are not going to be much better with anyone else. Even if your truths are not easy to bear, if you don't face them head-on you have little chance of becoming happier with yourself and improving the quality of your life.

In order to pursue being happier and improving your life, you need to:

- Begin where you are.

- Be honest with yourself about how you think/feel about your life.

- Be honest with yourself about you think/feel about your relationships with the people around you.

- Be honest with yourself about how you feel about your work, how you spend your free time, and what really makes you happy.

Nobody but you needs to know what you think/feel and do about these things. You can share what you want when you want. But first you need to spend some time with yourself and reflect. This would be a good time to put the book down and do just that.

Often when we are doing other things, we squeeze in moments to think about our life. Hey, we lead hectic lives. But let's be honest with one another; if you want to improve your relationship with your child or anyone else, it will help to give yourself time to stop doing other things for a few minutes and allow yourself the time and space to ask yourself how you are feeling and what you are thinking about your life.

Some people like to reflect in a free-association type of way and just quietly be by themselves and let their mind take them where it will while gently focusing on the question: How am I? Other people like specific questions to ponder. For those that like the questions, I have put together some that can serve as a catalyst for your thoughts.

Before you read the questions in the next chapter, I want to share something with you about self-help books.

For the most part they are not that helpful.

It is not that the ideas are poor or that there aren't stimulating items that spark your interest. It is just that most people read the books like any other book rather than read the book like they did back in school. Back then you had daily assignments and you would fill in the answers in the book. You did homework, which is the time-honored way teachers get you to think about the material when you are home and focus on it sufficiently so that hopefully you absorb it in some fundamental way. Then you would come back to class the next day and go over what you had done. The other thing teachers do, which you will find I am guilty of, is to repeat the same thing over and over until it is imprinted in your brain. Sorry.

If you want to try to get a bit more out of this self-help book, why not read the questions, reflect on them, and answer them as best you can? Don't just glance at the questions and then continue reading. Take some time to consider the questions and maybe even dwell on some before moving on. There is no reward for finishing the book quickly. Certainly every question is not going to engage you in a meaningful way and you may skip some. Some questions you may want to share so you can go over your thoughts/feelings with someone else.

Give yourself the gift of time to think/feel about the topics. You might even write down some thoughts. For example, you could write down something like: "Think about how to deal with the curfew situation." There is research that points out the value of writing down an unfinished thought.

Here is an excerpt from a *Scientific American* article by Maria Konnikova which neatly explains how this works:

In 1927, Gestalt psychologist Bluma Zeigarnik noticed a funny thing: waiters in a Vienna restaurant could only remember orders that were in progress. As soon as the order was sent out and complete, they seemed to wipe it from memory.

Zeigarnik then did what any good psychologist would: she went back to the lab and designed a study. A group of adults and children were given anywhere between 18 and 22 tasks to perform (both physical ones, like making clay figures, and mental ones, like solving puzzles)—only, half of those tasks were interrupted so that they couldn't be completed. At the end, the subjects remembered the interrupted tasks far better than the completed ones—over two times better, in fact.

The significance of the study is that if you have something unfinished, you will think more about it. You don't have to resolve everything right away. As you read through the book you can jot down to-do notes and incomplete thoughts and your mind will take over, keeping many of them alive while you carry on.

14

YOUR FIRST ASSIGNMENT

1.   Right now in your life, what is giving you the greatest happiness?

_____

_____

2.   What is it about the above mentioned that provides you that happiness? In other words, what are you doing that makes you so happy? (If you said your child gives you your greatest happiness, what exactly are you doing with your child that is providing that happiness?)

_____

_____

3.   What other things in your life make you truly happy?

_____

_____

4.   Any ideas of what you could realistically do to make those things even more prevalent in your life?

_____

_____

5.   What do you think would happen in your life if you were able to take one or more of these things that make you happy and do it 10% or 20% more?

_____

_____

15

PLEASE TURN IN YOUR HOMEWORK

Actually you don't need to turn it in to anybody but you. Hopefully you have spent some time thinking/feeling about the role of happiness in your life. Different things make different people happy.

While some philosophers and observers of life don't think it is important to be happy, I do. If being happier is not on your wish list then you can skip this whole section and just move ahead to other matters.

Some people hold the ethic that happiness is something you earn through hard work. For those people the idea of focusing on being happier without including the heavy lifting you need to do to get there is like putting Saturday night before the workweek. To those people I say work and happiness can be interwoven and benefit from each other's participation. And who says Saturday doesn't come before and after the workweek?

There is a whole branch of psychology called 'Positive Psychology', the basic tenet of which is the happier you are:

- The longer you live.
- The healthier you live.
- The more meaning and value you find in life.
- The greater appreciation you have for your life.

That works for me.

You may recall that the last question I asked you was what you think would happen if you could take one of those things that makes you happy and do it 10% or 20% more. While a lot of people desire big changes in their life, most therapists find that change usually happens incrementally and think it is best to aim for a 10% shift.

That is a realistic, obtainable shift. Once you have that 10% in place you can consider 10% more if you want.

But let's not sneer at 10%. Most people would gladly take a 10% raise, being 10% fitter, 10% smarter, and 10% happier.

If you want to aim higher, go for it. For this moment, however, please consider that if you did something that makes you happy 10% more, it might bump up your overall happiness quotient with your life.

I can't see much wrong with that.

I would venture to say that most of us if we really wanted to could:

- Eat 10% healthier.

- Exercise 10% more.

- Socialize with family and friends 10% more.

- Spend 10% less money on non-priorities.

- Interact 10% more lovingly with ourselves and others.

I think those 10% increases are, to use a baseball term, within most people's wheelhouses. For non-baseball fans a wheelhouse is that sweet spot for a batter where they have the most strength and power.

I think we all want to believe that if we really put our minds to it we could get into our own wheelhouse and improve our life batting average.

Maybe you don't improve your life 10% across the board. But doing those things that make you happiest is usually an easier path to self-improvement than engaging in some of the other activities you may need/want to employ.

So right now, why not consider bringing this thought into your life on a semi-regular basis: "I am going to consciously endeavor to do more of what makes me happiest."

Just carrying that thought around ought to improve how you feel about yourself and your life. Especially if you occasionally do something about it. But for now, let's not even focus on doing anything other than carrying around the thought to endeavor to do more of what makes you happiest. Holding the thought and not acting on it will actually help keep the thought in the forefront of your mind and will eventually kick-start you into action.

Once you start feeling a little better it is easier to apply energy in other arenas. You know how when you feel rotten you don't feel much like doing anything? So too is it when you feel better you are more likely to want to do more. You might want to do more physical and social activity. You might want to take better care of your body. You might find 10% not to be that elusive.

For now, don't worry about doing anything other than thinking more about what makes you happiest. Let's see what just thinking about creating more happiness on an ongoing basis does for you.

That's all.

For now.

16

YOUR FIRST POP QUIZ

Unfortunately that "now" that I referred to at the end of the last chapter has now become a then. This is the new now. Which if you happened to quickly go from one chapter to the next didn't give you much time to dwell in that "let's see what just thinking about creating more happiness on an ongoing basis does for you." Sorry, but we are moving on. If you aren't ready you might just want to stop here.

List some specific things you can do starting today to help make you 10% happier.

- _____
- _____
- _____
- _____
- _____

Take that list and pare it down to one thing you can actually do today that will make you happier.

- _____

List three things that are going to get in your way from making this happen.

- _____
- _____
- _____

What can you do to overcome those obstacles?

- _____

- _____

- _____

What can you do immediately when you finish reading this to put your "one thing to make you happier" item into motion?

- _____

Think about how you can make this a daily or more frequent part of your life. What can you do tomorrow and the next day and the next day until it morphs into its own active part of your life?

_____

_____

_____

_____

_____

_____

Bonus questions:

Can you think of someone with whom you can share your answers to this pop quiz?

- _____

If a name came up for you, when you stop reading why not make that the first thing you do? Tell that person what you are doing and how they can help you.

Really—reach out to someone. It may not be easy, but more than likely it will help.

If there is no one you can comfortably share this with, consider among your goals for your greater happiness creating a relationship that would allow, encourage, and support you so that you would want to share more.

In the meantime, go take that first step.

17

DOING THINGS DIFFERENTLY

There is no overriding reason to do anything differently if things are working fine the way they are. Making real changes is no easy matter. If you have ever tried to give up a bad habit you know it is not a painless process. We all can list New Year's resolutions that have come and gone. Good intentions only take us so far. Yet I imagine matters have gotten to a point with your teen where you are willing to consider other approaches.

There is an abundance of books, articles, and lectures on doing things differently. That is because there are a number of ways to get yourself to try something different. You have a heart attack and the fear of death prompts you to change your lifestyle. You watch an episode of a weight-loss program and get inspired to reinvigorate your life.

However one gets motivated to change their ways, there usually is one significant through-line. You need to want to change more than you want to stand pat. There is only one thing that is going to get the pendulum to swing to a place where you walk the walk and not just talk it. That one thing that will make the difference is your care, respect, and love for yourself. Maybe that is three things. Either way you need to mean enough to yourself for you to invest in the challenge of breaking the mold and doing things differently.

Erich Fromm, PhD, an early pioneer in psychological thinking, wrote a book called *The Art of Loving*. It was his contention that loving is an art and for love to fully flourish within us it needs to engage four elements. We need discipline, concentration, patience, and utmost concern. Basically he thought if you want to get the most out of your love life, you need to:

- Practice restraint and be disciplined in how you approach your partner.
- Make your love a high priority and focus on it in a concentrated manner.

- Be gracious with your time and exercise patience.

- Have your love be worthy of your utmost concern.

When you do these things, love flourishes. Be it with your partner, your child, or yourself.

Love is a matter of commitment. Having made the commitment to parent a child, you know that, like a marriage, at times you are going to face trials that will challenge your ability to love. Often when it comes to your teenager you need to recommit to supporting and loving her in the best ways possible. The love that flowed so easily when she was younger often is spoken more than it is felt. Ways of interacting evolve over time and you can find yourself falling into ruts that are not in anyone's best interest.

Deciding to break a habitual way of doing something is an act of love towards you. Be it quitting smoking, eating healthier, having more family meals, or talking with your child in a more engaging manner. Tackling these issues is a matter of choice. Some of them you can quietly embark on and see how they go. Others you may want to speak with someone else about before you take any action. Research says when you share a goal it increases the odds of obtaining it. It's up you, but why not play the odds?

One of the reasons we don't like to tell people when we decide to quit something or commit to do something is that it can be embarrassing if we fall back into our previous ways. As soon as we tell someone, the pressure is on us as well as the risk of humiliation if we don't achieve what we stated.

Which is also why it helps motivate us.

It's a double-edged sword.

Just because the research says that you increase the odds of following through when you share what you want to do with someone doesn't mean it is easy to do. There is often a fear of judgment and rejection. Sure, it may help to tell someone, but that doesn't mean they might not say and do things in return which will hurt your feelings. They might even say or do something that creates a rupture in your relationship or causes you to abandon or reevaluate your goals.

There is always uncertainty even with good odds. There is that chance things will turn out for the worse. Telling may very well have unforeseen consequences. You may regret telling them and believe their participation made things worse. Of course, what might not seem so good right now may turn out to be for the better in the long run.

There is no telling what will happen.

At least you are betting with the odds.

Optimism and chance-taking is often embraced more when you are younger. As people age, resignation and stagnation can zap that optimism. With decreasing optimism comes less willingness to take risks.

Misfortune can also wear you down, although many people are able to keep hope alive and believe in a better future even in the worst of times. The trick to being more hopeful is to not attach your hopes to a specific thing. Instead of hoping your child gets into an Ivy League school, hope your child gets into a college where she can enjoy herself and prosper. Hoping for the one specific outcome brings with it a bag of worry, which doesn't do much for being hopeful. Hoping for a more general outcome allows for variation in how it is attained.

It is never too late to believe you can improve your relationship with your child. Regardless of the severity of your relationship, there is always some available avenue toward improvement. The longer you endure the status quo the more challenging it can be to mobilize yourself to make changes. Which is why it helps to aim for that 10% improvement and not procrastinate too long.

There is one word I want to highlight now that will help you achieve that 10%.

The word is *will*. You need an act of will. You need to tap into your willpower.

Therapists call it volition: the process of making and acting on decisions.

You need to find within you the discipline to follow through on your resolutions. It is not always easy to will yourself to do something, but it is necessary.

You have done it before and you can do it again.

We get up and go to work when we would prefer to be at home. We can walk away from that extra helping and we can get our taxes done on time.

We all have willpower. It's like a muscle. Some people really develop it and others not so much.

Like any muscle, it needs exercise. You exercise it and it grows.

Like most everything else, if something is going to get done you are the one who is going to have to do it. If you don't do anything proactively, the odds are not stacked in your favor that anything will improve.

If you go back and look at your Pop Quiz answers, then take a chance and share your Pop Quiz with someone, you will have to deal with their reaction. And your reaction to their reaction. And so forth. They may say hurtful and/or helpful things. They may not react exactly as you would hope. You will need to interact with them. React to them. Be with them in a moment of truth-sharing.

(Later in the book we will get into the nitty-gritty of these kinds of intimate conversations, but for now let's just focus on what you want when you share with them.)

If you told another person that you were reading this book and there was a prompt for you to share what you would like to happen in your relationship with your child, what would you want from that conversation? How would you like the conversation to go? Ideally, what would the other person say or do?

_____

_____

How would you like that conversation to end?

_____

_____

I would hope that in your conversation with them there would be a level of caring, support, acceptance, and honesty—gently delivered and hopefully gently received.

When you share, you may not get that warm reception. That will make it harder for you to carry on. Regardless of how they respond, once you come forward and open up to someone it is incumbent upon you to respond to the situation with your A-game. If you don't model the kind of behavior you want, who will?

Mahatma Gandhi summed it up when he said, "Be the change you wish to see in the world."

If they say something hurtful to you, don't stop the conversation and walk away. Find a way to make this a valuable conversation for you The person has said something that touches a raw nerve for you. While that is not enjoyable, it is telling. If you can listen to them there is a good chance you can learn more about how to manage that hurt. People can assist you in changing your behavior if you let them.

Of course, they won't always assist you in the way you would like to be assisted.

If you tell them how you would like to be supported, it will increase the odds that they will help you in a way that is closer to the way you would like. But they are not going to be there for you perfectly. Just humanly.

If you tell someone you want to raise your voice less at your child and would be grateful for their help, think about what kind of help you would actually want. Do you want someone calling each day and asking how you are doing? Do you want someone to bring it up now and then? Do you want them to say nothing unless you bring it up? Do you want them to let you know when they hear you raise your voice?

What you want may evolve over time. Which would require you keeping them up to date. Which would involve communicating. Which might mean letting them know when you have done things you are proud of and when you have lost momentum.

Many years ago while waiting in a doctor's office, I read an article about romantic relationships in _Cosmopolitan_ which had a quote that has stayed with me over the years. It has comforted me and others and perhaps it will assist you as well.

The article contended that people break up an embarrassing number of times. We go back and forth in our own mind and then on and off with our partner. If you shared all your on-again/off-again, ups/downs, and frequent breakups and make-ups to a friend, it could easily become embarrassing. I realized that this start/stop process was not just true for romantic relationships but applied to many of our connections with others.

Being embarrassed is something many don't deal with easily. We often go out of our way not to publicly humiliate ourselves. Yet we can go back and forth on something an embarrassing number of times. Many people have started more diets, joined more gyms, and broken more resolutions than they care to share.

It is one thing when we keep these starts and stops to ourselves. It's another when we have a witness. Humiliation and embarrassment, if they need to be experienced at all, are usually preferred to be dealt with behind closed doors. Which is another reason people have difficulty sharing their goals and desires.

Most people share themselves a layer at a time. Having someone be privy to your daily fluctuations is not easy. People get afraid that if other people saw the real truth of their lives, their relationship would be compromised.

I want to encourage you to be brave and commit to letting those people closest to you know you more fully, to share your goals and the trials and tribulations on the path to achieving those goals.

Yes, you will be greeted in all manner of ways. Some responses will feel enthralling and nourishing. Other reactions will wound you. Don't let the wounds stop you from the greater good of reaching out for support and being known. Remember that even with all the possible downsides the statistics pretty solidly support the value of sharing your concerns with people close to you whom you trust.

The fate of not being known is isolation. The consequence of being rejected is hurt. It is a wound you can mend.

Let your shared embarrassment be a connector between you and others. I can assure you they have their own embarrassments and shortcomings. Your humanness is not much different from theirs. If you share yours, they will probably share theirs too.

Many people have relationships with friends, lovers, parents, and children that are not very intimate. People hide their truths and in doing so isolate themselves even though they may be surrounded by others. Sometimes the worst loneliness occurs when you are with people but not really connected with them. In order to build closer relationships, you will need to step into that space that separates you.

Deciding to do something, wavering in your decision, and taking two steps forward and three backward happens all the time. Everyone I have ever spoken to can speak to wanting something but faltering in making it happen. I mention this to alleviate any pressure you might put on yourself about improving your happiness quotient. Don't should on yourself and say you have to do something and have to do it now and you better not chicken out.

You can want to improve your relationships. Want to be closer with your teen, want to be happier, want to share, and want to have the willpower to affect changes in your life. Sometimes those wants dwell inside and you never take action. If that happens to be you, so be it. If this book doesn't get you mobilized now, I would like to believe it will take its place in your awareness, and when you are ready to take action you will.

However and whenever you start taking some actions, a day will come when for whatever reason you don't follow through. You may rationalize or deny or "should" on yourself. You may pass on another opportunity and perhaps one thing leads to another and soon you are back where you started.

People break up an embarrassing number of times. That doesn't mean you don't get back on course and do what is best for you. It just means the road curves and is bumpy.

But it is a road.

So get back on it.

18

INCREASING YOUR HAPPINESS – A SIMPLE GUIDE (SORT OF)

Happiness, according to the Merriam-Webster dictionary, is a state of "wellbeing or contentment." With that in mind, let me ask you:

- How important is being happy to you?
- Would you like to be happier?

What would you say if I told you I could share with you a solid research finding you could easily employ that would make you happier?

Interested?

This isn't me trying to be a cheerleader and get you pumped up to make changes. This is actual research that has been conducted regarding happiness. To make things even better, the research focuses on those things you really like about you and do well. This is not about taking on something fearful and feeling better for having conquered your fear—although pushing through fear does usually make you feel better.

This is about taking your strengths and joys and building on them. Plus, if implementing the research works for you, it very well may work for your teenager. I imagine if your teen is happier, most likely you will be too. Especially if he is happier because he is doing things you support.

While many people think having more money, better looks, greater intelligence, and a new car will make them happier, they are buying the wrong lottery ticket. Sure, any of those things may make your lot in life easier and provide some momentary improvement in your overall happiness, but they don't provide a sustainable foundation. Happiness revolves around relationships: the ones you have with those people closest to you and the one you have with yourself. The more you can improve those interactions, the happier you will be.

Professor Martin Seligman, PhD has devoted his professional career to studying happiness. Among his many projects he created a survey of character strengths. I recommend that you log on to the survey and take it. It's free. There are a fair number of questions that will take you about 30-45 minutes to complete. Once you are done you get a description of your core strengths. It will give you something to consider about the strongest positive aspects of your personality. If you take the description and share it with your teenager, it ought to make for a lively conversation and give you both some insight into making things better between you. It might even encourage him to take the survey as well, but let that idea come from him to avoid any pushback.

Here is the challenging but empowering part.

Seligman has found that if you take your top five strengths and utilize a different strength in a new way each day for a week you will experience improvement in your wellbeing. In his follow-up work he found the people who did this felt better after a month and then even better six months later. If you take the survey, you can read some of the new ways he suggests using your strengths.

What I find valuable about this approach is you get to improve your wellbeing by attending to your strengths. You don't have to conquer your lesser qualities; you get to add muscle where it already exists.

Some of the core strengths Seligman found involve creativity, curiosity, courage, kindness, honesty, perspective, humor, and self-regulation. Let's say kindness is one of your strengths. Seligman would have you reflect on how you demonstrate that kindness and have you think of other ways you might be able to express it. Taking something you are good at and finding ways to expand on your strengths will add to your own sense of accomplishment and happiness.

In the psychology class I teach for high school seniors, I ask them to take this survey and try their hand at utilizing a different strength in a new way each day. Finding those new ways can be a bit of a challenge, but they enjoy the exploration and the results. For once again, what you are doing is putting something into a conscious place in your life so you remember to focus on it. Having that awareness helps promote change.

So often we can put one foot in front of the other and get to the end of the day without having attended to some of those things on our to-do list. I am sure we all have experienced starting the day with good intentions and ending without having accomplished all we wanted.

Students have an advantage in these matters as they are used to having homework. Sure, they forget it from time to time, but they know it is lurking and usually each day they find time to focus on it. Adults often have more balls in the air and have to consciously move something into the priority category for it to get continued concentration.

If you can increase your happiness by taking your strengths and doing something new with them, you ought to feel better. At first it may be hard to let go of being self-conscious and you may not be able to get into the flow of the activity. The more you allow yourself to be a beginner, the easier it will be to find your own flow.

People tend to want to be proficient yet don't want to struggle with learning. Good luck. My suggestion is to continually remind yourself that you are learning, maybe slowly, maybe awkwardly, but you are learning. You can usually look back and see that you know more today than yesterday. Doing things differently means doing them not-so-well at times.

I had a colleague once tell me about being in a yoga class and looking around at others in the room who were so much more limber and experienced than she was. She told me she used a line from *Winnie the Pooh* that helped her. "Silly bear," she said to herself when she found herself being self-critical. I often hear myself uttering those words as I try to relax and let myself be less accomplished than I would like to be.

Mihaly Csikszentmihalyi, PhD, a professor and researcher at the University of Chicago, has determined that when people engage in something where they have a comfortable degree of proficiency, they can lose a sense of time and let go of being self-conscious. They get in the zone.

Getting into a zone often happens when one plays a sport or gets involved in a hobby. You get lost in the activity. That immersion in the activity is what makes us feel better.

When we get fully involved in something, our attention to our own life dissipates. That kind of engagement improves wellbeing. It is akin to what happens when you go to a movie, read a book, or get involved with your electronics.

The level of involvement you have with a book or an app is less than the involvement you have when you are more actively participating. Many people know that when you are stressed, doing a physical activity can relieve tension. When you exercise, you fire up your beta endorphins and that physical activity can engage your mind as well as your body. A basketball player is going to be more involved than someone playing an app for they are using their physical and mental energies. But even playing the app results in a lessening of your self-consciousness.

The more involved you get with something outside yourself, the happier you become. This is why people don't mind going to work when they are having problems at home—it takes your mind off of you and onto something else. The simple truth of involvement is most of the moments you are involved in an activity you aren't worrying about all the things you usually worry about.

Even if you sit in a lounge chair and do a crossword puzzle, you can experience getting lost in the activity. Whether you are fully engaged with your mind or your mind and body, the goal is to create more of those moments. Often when people are involved in creative endeavors they can get lost in the activity. Artists and musicians as well as architects and engineers often lose track of time. So too can an assembly worker as they focus on the task at hand and let go of other distractions.

In Csikszentmihalyi's research he found that 20% of Americans engage in flow activities several times a day. An almost equal amount report never having experienced flow. I don't know in which category you would list yourself, but I would imagine if you could bump up the time you spend in flow activities you probably wouldn't complain.

Parents often lament the time their kids devote to social media and playing apps. They wish their kids did something more "productive." Yet when their kids are spending time doing these things they don't have to worry about their homework or other things you want them to do that they would rather not do.

Teenagers today report having higher levels of stress than previous generations. We will discuss reducing their stress later on, but for now try to consider their hobbies as flow activities that reduce stress. Social media, listening to music, and playing games may not be your choice, but it is theirs. It may cause your stress level to go up but chances are it is reducing theirs. How you navigate that difference we will also address later. For now, keep an open mind about flow activities and what you can do to bring more of them to you and yours.

The way I look at history, people have always wanted to spend some amount of time escaping from their day-to-day realities. Whether it be going on a vacation, reading a book, or going to a movie, people want some time out from their lives.

We often judge how much "escape" is good for us. If your child plays video games into the wee hours, many parents consider that too much. If your child reads books under the covers, many parents kind of like that but eventually tell him to put the book away. If your son wears headphones much of the day and basically tunes you out, most parents wish it were otherwise.

Of course any of these behaviors may eventually become a positive thing in your child's life. That gamer kid may grow up and create story lines for other games. That reader might become a writer. And that kid with the headphones a music producer. You never know.

One thing I do know is most of the students I speak with multitask when they do most everything. They watch TV, text, do homework, snack, and do most things concurrently. Many have a hard time focusing on one thing for an extended time. I imagine that has pros and cons that we could discuss, but the bottom line is most teenagers multitask at levels their parents have a hard time valuing.

Even when I share with my students the research regarding the less effective outcome of doing more than one thing at a time, they still find pleasure in keeping many balls in the air. That doesn't mean they don't hunker down now and then and focus on one thing. It just means they like the stimulation that accompanies having more than one thing happening at a time. This is one of those battles you might consider not turning into a war because from where I sit, the tide has definitely turned. If you don't feel like conceding this issue, outlaw cell phones, computers, and television at meals. Some experts suggest no electronics an hour before going to bed.. That is, at least, something you can mostly monitor.

Regardless of how you judge your or your child's activities, we all need time to get out of ourselves. Television provides this for many people as does the Internet. Entertainment has always been about taking you to a different place, where you don't need to be concerned about the various aspects of your life. A place where you can forget you and focus on others.

We benefit from downtime. And we all need get-up time. The key is balance.

A lot of solid research supports that people who lead more physically-engaging lives tend to be happier. While going running and working out by yourself will provide a bump in your overall happiness, you could increase it even more if you exercised with others or tried to do an activity that had you moving, thinking, and interacting. The more of you that you can give to an activity, the greater your sense of flow. As much as all practitioners in the healing arts want you attend to yourself, they also want you attending outside yourself. It is in the company of others that we really discover ourselves.

There is a forced flow that happens when you "have to" deal with others. You need to communicate and connect in some way with each other. However minimal that connection and moment may be, it is an instance of flow. No matter how self-conscious you may be, your greater focus is on the moment at hand and not just your usual areas of concern.

While there are activities that garner lower flow streams than others, they are all good. The more flow, the happier you will be.

So said Mihaly Csikszentmihalyi and so shall I.

There is one more thing I want to share with you about happiness that you probably know, but just in case, I want to share the results of a study conducted in 2015 by Dan Carlson who is a sociologist at Georgia State University. Here is what he said: "When it comes to relationship satisfaction and couple conflict, the only arrangement that seems to be problematic is when the female is doing most or all of the work with the kids."

When the raising of a child is a shared responsibility, couples have less conflict and a more satisfying sex life. This is not earth-shattering news, but it does underscore the value to everyone of having the parenting of your child be a shared responsibility. The more lopsided the oversight and activity level with your child the greater the likelihood for dissatisfaction in your relationship with your partner.

Now, it is hard to determine which is the chicken and which is the egg. Did the lack of shared parenting drive couples further apart or did couples who were not that close together tend to not feel equally invested in the raising of their children? Whatever the cause, you would be well advised to try to get your parenting partner more involved in parenting activities.

Since you are the one reading the book, chances are you are the one with the greater immediate concern about the welfare of your child. Instead of you just focusing on upgrading your interactions, see if you can take various sections of the book that appeal to you and share them with your partner so that they too can take a more active role in their teenager's life.

I suggest you show the other parent a passage and ask what they think about it. Hear them out. Ask them to expand on something so you can understand their thinking more clearly. Be interested in fully getting their thoughts/feelings aired before you share your own. They may want you to share your thoughts first and if that is the case so be it. But, make sure you hear what they have to say. Aim to have a discussion about parenting and not try to win a debate about whose approach is best. Remember that parents that parent together have less conflict and more enjoyable sex lives.

Even if you are disagreeing about a point, you are gathering together in the best interests of your child. One thing affecting your child is how you discuss issues with the other parent. You are the model. Hold that thought while you navigate your way through the conversation.

Even if the other parent is not behaving in a way you would prefer, that does not mean you can waiver from your responsibility to behave in the ways you would like your child to behave. You cannot control how others will behave. But you can keep a close eye on yourself and endeavor to be the parent you want to be. The more you live up to your own values about parenting the happier you will be.

19

TWO HAPPINESS EXERCISES

I mentioned earlier that there is a relatively new field of psychology called Positive Psychology which basically focuses on wellness in your life and how to build on it. In this chapter, I'd like to pass along the two most studied and effective activities that Positive Psychology practitioners suggest to increase happiness.

The first is called Three Good Things.

- Every day for a week you write in a journal three "good things" that happened that day.
- Along with those three things you write why you think each "good thing" went well.

This improves your positive feelings because it demands that you take time each day to focus on the positive aspects of the day. It takes your focus away from the things that are not going well and puts an emphasis on the good things you might otherwise take for granted.

Research finds that most people really like doing this activity. Even though the overall increase in mood is not that significant, people continue to do the exercise. Some every day, others more erratically. At the end of one, three, and six months, people have an increase in their overall sense of wellbeing.

What I like about the exercise is that it encourages you to focus on the highlights of your life. It doesn't disavow the lowlights. You can reflect on what is troubling you and the "bad" things that happened in the day as much as you want. This exercise just asks you to not forget to enjoy the best of the day.

Whatever it was. Big, medium, or small.

Attending to the good portions of the day doesn't require much effort, and it doesn't have to involve anyone else. Just write three words, or three sentences, or whatever you want. Take time to think about the good things in your day.

Hard to argue with that.

If you want to add a layer to the exercise you can also take time to think about the good things in your life in general. They may not have had any action that day, but that doesn't mean certain people, places, and things don't play an important role in your wellbeing.

Most parents, regardless of the status of their relationship with their child, are grateful to have their child and know that much of their happiness (and other emotions) centers on their child.

Thinking about the good things, good people, good places, and good times helps you appreciate your life.

The second exercise is called the Gratitude Visit.

This activity has a few more steps and involves others which is why it is second. Usually things people can do alone and quickly have more of a chance of getting done than those activities that are more complicated and involve actually dealing with another person.

You can see if this has appeal to you or not.

- You write a short letter to a living person in your life who has done something significant for you but whom you have never fully thanked.

- The letter needs to tell the person what they have done for you and how it has contributed to where you are now in your life.

- When you have completed the letter, you contact the person and tell them you want to visit them but don't tell them about the letter.

- Then you go and read the letter to them.

Research says the positive afterglow of this meeting lasts a month. That may or may not seem like a long time to you. But when you compare it to the warm memories and feelings you have after most enjoyable activities, this tends to linger longer.

Doing this activity also paves the way for you to express your gratitude to others on a more informal and regular basis. It encourages you to take the time to think about someone you never thanked. If there are those people in your life—and there are in most people's lives—there may be a level of guilt you have about not having thanked them. If you can motivate yourself to write to them and speak with them, it relieves whatever burden you were carrying. That right there is a positive thing.

This activity does require more of you than the "Three Good Things" and as such is not as easy for people to do. So, do the first. But think about this one.

You don't even have to do the visit. Just write the letter. That could be a valuable gift to you in and of itself. Once you write it, you can decide what to do with it.

Therapists often suggest to clients that they write letters to people living or dead with the idea that they will never be sent. Just writing the letter is therapeutic.

You may have your own to-do or can-do list of things that would help you feel better. You might want to consider these two activities. They are not going to turn things around for you with the kind of instant big-time gratification we all desire, but they can start laying the groundwork for an ongoing increase in the positive feelings you have about yourself. Those feelings are going to help you with your teenager as well as everyone else in your life.

20

HOW TO PUT THEORY
INTO ACTION

There is reading about something and then there is doing something about what you are reading. Let me give you two relatively easy ways you can incorporate the Three Good Things into your daily life with your partner, close friends, and child.

When you take on a new activity sometimes you are met with instant success and gratification, other times instant failure and disappointment and everything in between. Needless to say if something works really well the first time you are more prone to want to do it again. If you get less-than-hoped-for results, it is more difficult to try again.

Sadly for many parents and teenagers there is not a lot of tolerance for not doing well at something. There is a lot of performance anxiety that goes into many of life's activities. Just about everyone wants good results and if they are not soon realized people often move on to other activities.

Accepting that you won't be as good at something when you first try can be elusive. I often find students come into class thinking they need to know what they have come to learn. When they don't know something they are reluctant to admit it.

We live in a time when it is increasingly difficult to work through the frustration of learning. So much of what we encounter in our daily lives comes to us quickly. Events happen around the world that we know about in minutes, if that. When we try to do things and they don't yield positive results in a short amount of time, we lose momentum. Reaching one's potential requires a level of effort that not everyone can sustain.

Rome may not have been built in a day, but teenagers see Rome—or an accomplished athlete or singer—

and want to emulate that outcome. Unfortunately they don't see the effort it took to make it happen. Supporting your teenager in being a gradual learner is a gift you might consider giving.

Sociologists and psychologists have observed that this generation of young adults often don't feel that good about themselves. It is not that they aren't doing well enough with their lives. It is more that they think they should be having a "special" experience with life. Growing up they were told how special they were so when special things are not happening in their lives, they feel badly about themselves.

Learning is a step-by-step by side-step and back-step and forward-step process. Hopefully we can teach our children these things, but according to observers we all struggle a bit with this.

I was watching a commercial the other day and realized that rarely did the camera stay focused on a single event for more than two seconds. The story was told in brief images. My take-away from that is our tolerance for lingering moments and slow-moving action isn't what it used to be. It is hard for a lot of people to sit comfortably through a 1940s movie. The action is too slow to unfold, and people get restless.

Social media and cruising the Internet keep us moving at a fast pace. A side effect of the blitz of images and stimuli is less time spent in the slow lane of learning. Learning to do something well not only takes time, it involves dealing with a lot of frustration, setbacks, hurdles, and a lack of speedily becoming as competent as you might hope to be.

Learning how we can best learn and techniques to improve our abilities is a course we all would have benefitted from taking.

We are asked from the beginning of our lives to learn new things. Yet how we best learn and how to be the best learner we can be is something very few ever get taught. So learning becomes a haphazard activity. Parents and teachers try a myriad of ways to help children grow. Some methods work better than others. Some don't work now but might later. Others work now but won't later.

As we grow we become aware of which study habits work for us and which don't. We learn where we stand compared to our classmates when it comes to memorizing, speaking in front of the class, time spent doing homework. You can ask pretty much any student in any class to rank their classmates in terms of grades, brains, and amount of time they spend doing homework. Kids know this about their peers and then they compare and contrast.

Most students I know readily admit they could apply themselves more.

Most students are aware of what they need to do in order to get better grades.

Many parents get exasperated by their child not applying himself more.

Most parents try to motivate their child to apply himself more. They use all manner of ploys. They threaten, take away things, they guilt-trip, they plead, they go to therapy, and they talk with me.

I usually tell them to back off.

I also add a few other things for them to consider to make life better.

When I inquire why it is so important for them to have their child achieve more, I often hear that if they had only applied themselves a little more along the way and if they knew then what they know now, things might have turned out better for them. Since they want better for their children, they want their children to be better teenagers than they were. Or if their child is acting out more than they did, they would like their child to at least get within their ballpark.

If you happen to think anything like that let me suggest that it is never too late to learn something new that can help you manage your life in a more rewarding fashion.

Yes, it might have been nice to have been savvier about life earlier and pushed yourself to greater heights. Aside from bemoaning that fact, there is not much you can do about it. Go ahead and continue to bemoan it, but let's also do something on the other side of the ledger.

I mention this because whatever you take away from this book and try to apply to your life will have varying degrees of success. You might take a shot at the Three Good Things exercise and only come up with two or as soon as you think of a good thing you will think of three bad. If something like that happens, you might decide to abandon the exercise all together.

That is an option.

But if you had felt that way the first time you tried to walk you would still be crawling around. Consider cutting yourself some slack as you learn new ways of doing things.

Since I know that if you try something and it goes well you have a greater likelihood of wanting to try it again, I am going to throw out a first step that might yield some decent initial results.

Think about the living people you consider closest to you. With whom do you have the most honest, caring relationship? There may be many people on your list or perhaps none. For the purposes of this exercise I am going to hope you have at least one. Even if you don't think you have anyone that is really close to you, pick the person who has the closest, if not a close relationship, with you. For those who do have more than two people with whom they have honest, caring relationships, please list the top two.

_____

_____

Ideally you want to speak to one of those people face-to-face, but if that is not possible a phone call, an email, or a text will do in descending order. I know some people think anything worth doing is worth doing right. I believe that, yet I also believe in doing things one step at a time. Instead of waiting for the "perfect" time to start, it is usually better to just start now or pretty close to it.

You don't need to make a big deal about this exercise. In fact, initially it is better to make a small deal of it. The next time you are talking or writing to this person, throw into the conversation that you are grateful to have this person in your life. Say something akin to: "I have been thinking about things I am grateful for in my life and I wanted you to know that you are definitely one person I am very grateful to have in my life."

Or

"I have been reading this book about improving relationships with teenagers and it starts off by suggesting we ought to think about the things in our life for which we are grateful. I know you know this, but I wanted to say it out loud—I am grateful to have you in my life."

If those are too touchy-feely for you, try something like: "It's good to see you."

Or

"That was fun."

That's it. Just say something simple and true.

Then, and this may be even harder, close your mouth and silently and slowly count to 10.

When I used to train therapists I would speak with them about money and telling their clients about their fees. Most therapists, and especially those at the beginning of their career, know they are not providing much more of a service than what they dole out for free to those close to them. To charge for something they give away for free is very challenging. When I would go around the room and ask students how much they would charge, most of them were hesitant to speak and for the most part they came up with a figure that was way under the norm.

I told them when they finally got to work with a client to double their number and say, "My fee is $____," and then shut up and count to 10.

They usually wanted to follow their statement with, "But I work on a sliding scale." Their anxiety about asking for their fee prompted them to respond to the number instead of letting the client respond. If the client said, "What?! That is outrageous!" they could always add, "I do work on a sliding scale."

When people say something that makes them feel uncomfortable they often respond to what they are saying instead of letting the other person respond first. That is why I suggest that when you say what you are grateful for, don't follow it up with more words. Let the other person react to what you are saying.

If you don't do this kind of thing often, yes, it will be uncomfortable. When you share your honest feelings about someone else you have taken a risk and exposed yourself. That is unnerving. Yet, this is the positive kind of discomfort. The kind you know is in your best interest. Even if it takes you out of your comfort zone.

When you share, don't do it in hopes that the other person will respond in kind. Yes, that might feel validating, but you are not doing this for them to share with you. You are doing this so you can feel better. Sure, it will be icing on the cake if they meet you in kind, but even if they don't say anything, your task is to share your gratitude.

The research and common sense happen to agree that if you attend to what you are grateful for it will become more present in your awareness. You will notice more things for which you are thankful. That alone will help you feel better about your life. And hopefully you will start to share more of your gratitude. Whether it be a beautiful sunset or a kind act of another.

I am a believer in preparing for the worst and hoping for the best.

So, what are the worst things that could happen if you share your gratitude to another?

This might be one of them—you share with this person that you are thankful to have them in your life and they tell you that in truth they are not really grateful to have you in their life. In fact, you are extra baggage and since you brought it up they don't really want to carry on anymore so this will be the last conversation you will have with them.

That would be pretty bad.

So, what would you do if that happened?

Let's be honest here. Would you be so hurt and despondent that you would kill yourself? If that is a real possibility you have every reason to be hesitant and every reason to go see a therapist right away. If your life is on the line then you really need to get more help than this book can provide. I would like to see you find someone who could work with you to find more reasons to live and help you find ways to make your life more meaningful and fulfilling. Let's not have your wellbeing dependent on anyone else's acceptance or rejection of you.

If your life is not on the line, and my example is extreme, then the worst thing that could happen would involve a fair amount of emotional pain and personal wear and tear.

I certainly can see that if I were sharing with my teenage daughter my gratitude for having her in my life and she told me she didn't want me to be involved in her life, I would be extremely hurt. I would carry that hurt until I died. I might not kill myself, but life would be a lot less meaningful to me.

Which is why sharing truths is risky. It's much easier to talk about the weather.

Research says that if you share personal information about yourself, others usually respond with something personal of their own. The odds are with you that you will get something in kind back, but there is no guarantee.

You are doing this for you. Sure it will hurt if your child or anyone does not emotionally embrace what you share, which is why you consider the worst case. What really is the most likely worst response you will get? Usually if you can picture that response and find a way to deal with it, anything else is going to be easier. Not easy, but easier.

If someone does come back at you in a hurtful way, that will inform you about that person and influence the likelihood of you reaching out to them again. Which is why I suggest having two people on the list.

It is good to have a second option if the first doesn't work out so well. I would save the sharing with your child for down the road after you have had some practice with others.

I was taught long ago that if you were looking for work and had five places you wanted to interview, go to number five first and work your way to the top of your list. You want to build your skills so by the time you get to the place it really counts you have worked on your delivery.

If you do take a chance to share some gratitude, take some time later in the day to revisit the experience. Many people take up journaling, some like to sit quietly. Whatever you do, here are some things to consider:

- How do I think/feel about my sharing?

- What did I do that I feel good about?

- How do I think the other person thought/felt?

- If I were to do this again is there anything I would like to do differently?

- Even if things did not go well can I find the good in what I did?

In the therapy world, therapists focus on:
- How you feel

- What you think

- What you do

Asking yourself how you feel about something, how you think about it, and what you can do about it can become an endless feedback loop and drive you crazy if you don't call a timeout now and then.

But as Socrates said: "The unexamined life is not worth living."

So maybe you did the exercise or maybe you didn't and maybe it went well or maybe it didn't. The point is that if you want to feel better about your life you need to get your gratitude muscle in better shape. Regardless of how much gratitude you have or don't have, I am betting it wouldn't hurt to have more.

And how do you get more gratitude?

By accepting that you will be a gradual learner and searching for the things in life for which you are grateful. Think about them. Maybe draw them or sing about them or write about them or talk about them. It doesn't matter so much how you experience your gratitude, just that you find your own ways to do it.

Nike had it right.

Life is so much about the continuum. We all live on it.

If you think about your age, weight, values, income, style, and most anything else, you are on this end of the continuum or that end or somewhere in between. Wherever you are there are people to the left of you and people to the right of you. You can almost always count on there being people who have it better and people who have it worse than you.

So it is with gratitude. There are people who have less gratitude than you and people who have more. There are people who have less of something than you and are more grateful and people who have more of something and are less grateful. The person who earns a minimum wage may be more grateful to be earning their salary than the executive whose year-end bonus wasn't big enough.

How grateful you are for what you have is about your attitude.

We aren't always aware of the attitude we have or are projecting. We do know when we see someone else who has a lot of attitude. Often when we say someone has "attitude" it is a negative thing, but, like most everything else, attitude lives on a continuum. Often when you see someone who is grateful it is illuminating. Especially when you realize you have more of the thing they are grateful for than they do, but aren't feeling the same way. Some not so much.

You might want to make a mental note to pay attention to how people around you show their gratitude. See how they express what they are thankful for. Becoming more aware of how people express any gratitude they have will open your eyes to how others see and appreciate the world. You don't have to see things their way, but it can help broaden your horizons.

And if you happen to see someone doing something that touches you, you might even share a little gratitude about what they did.

It's a sentiment from a 1944 song by Johnny Mercer and Harold Arlen: "You've got to accentuate the positive. Eliminate the negative." Therapists call it positive reinforcement. It rarely hurts to acknowledge the positive things that those around you are doing. It is another one of those things that increases the odds of it happening again.

If you are willing to accept the idea that gratitude is a central component to living a more valued life, then encourage yourself to look at life through the lens of gratitude. See what is before you that you are grateful for. Maybe a little. Maybe a lot.

Consider this exercise. The next time you have dinner with your family or a friend, tell them something about themselves that you are thankful for.

That's it. Just say one thing. Then shut up. Count to 10.

If they don't say anything, move on. If they do say something, respond. Try to avoid allowing the conversation to go into unpleasantness. And if you can't, well, at least you got some gratitude in there.

Remember that the point of fumbling around, being awkward, and doing these exercises is to develop your skills as a gradual learner and to strengthen your gratitude muscles.

21

PRAISE AND SELF-ESTEEM

Research conducted at Columbia University by Carol Dweck and her associates found that 85% of American parents think it is important to tell their children they are smart. However, if you don't mix in some other messages, telling them they are smart might actually be causing them to underperform.

"When we praise children for their intelligence," Dweck said, "we tell them that this is the name of the game. Look smart, don't risk making mistakes."

I can tell you from having taught in schools for most of my career, students do not like to take risks and they certainly do not want to make mistakes. As a culture we have created a generation of risk- and mistake-avoidant children.

But there is hope.

Dweck ran a bunch of experiments. In one group she had an examiner give this feedback after students worked on a puzzle: "You must be smart at this." In another group the examiner told the students: "You must have worked really hard."

Dweck and her researchers performed numerous follow-up experiments with these groups and found that the "you must be smart" group were less inclined to take chances and expose their lack of knowledge while the other group was happy to experiment and fail. Over time the smart group did worse in school and the "worked really hard" group considerably improved.

To quote Dweck again: "Emphasizing effort gives a child a variable they can control. They come to see themselves as in control of their success. Emphasizing natural intelligence takes it out of the child's control, and it provides no good recipe for responding to failure."

Other terms for effort are 'grit' or 'stamina.' You want to encourage your child to persevere.

Many children get frustrated when they don't have instant gratification and success. They don't value toiling to get results. They want the touchdown without the sustained drive.

If you have told your child she is smart, do not despair. Those statements help build her self-esteem and are necessary. But to maximize your child's intelligence and engagement, you also need to emphasize effort.

Parents often come to me worried that their child is not doing as well as they think she could. I encourage them to notice any time their child is studying and working on projects and say something short and sweet, like, "Hey, it's great to see you focused on your work," then walk away.

You can still sing her smart praises, just include some praises for the effort she is showing.

While telling your child how smart or creative she is does build self-esteem, it does not improve grades or career achievement.

Dr. Roy Baumeister reviewed thousands of research experiments on self-esteem and had this to say: "I am smart, the kid's reasoning goes; I don't need to put out effort. Expending effort becomes stigmatized—it is public proof that you can't cut it with your natural gifts."

As a parent you need to strike a blow against whatever peer and personal pressure your child faces. Support and encourage your child to work at something in order to learn it. If you acknowledge when your child is trying something, even if she is not doing it perfectly, it reinforces her belief in the value of trying.

When you are with your child and you are watching a movie or sporting event or concert, throw in a line about how much the performer must have worked to be as accomplished as they now are. Children and teens often see the ease that a professional has acquired without acknowledging the effort it took to get there. You can be the person who points out the effort and praises it. They will get the message.

Here is a disturbing fact about praise: only children under seven take praise at face value. Older children, like adults, view it suspiciously. By the time they are teenagers they discount praise and actually tend to see criticism as a more accurate description of their aptitude.

While I don't want you to start criticizing your teen, I do want you to consider reserving your praise for when she truly earns it. Teenagers become distrustful of praise because they often think it is disingenuous. Many parents think they need to be cheerleaders and believe they need to extol many things a child does that don't really need that level of attention.

Earlier I wrote about how young adults (today's Millennials) often don't feel that good about their lives. They grew up being told how special they are, then when they get out into the workforce and life is not all that special they feel as if they have failed in some way. As a parent of a teen, you can help your child by acknowledging her specialness when she truly is special, and acknowledging the effort it takes to bring success to fruition in her adult life.

We all need positive attention. Very few people get an overabundance of it. Please continue to praise your child and let her know if you think she is smart, funny, creative, or has any other positive attributes. Just endeavor to keep your praise in line with your actual thoughts.

We will focus on how to give constructive criticism later on, but for now see if you can shift some of your praise toward her efforts.

If you think you might have invested too much energy into building your child's self-esteem and not enough focus on building her desire to achieve through effort, you might want to read Carol Dweck's book, *Mindset: The New Psychology of Success*. There is a wealth of information there that can help you out.

I had a client once who told me she came home from school with a report card that had all A's and one A-. Her father's response when she showed him the card was, "What is this A- about?". Ouch. Twenty years later this client is in my office because no matter what she does she doesn't feel good enough about herself. Now I am sure many parents would be happy with that report card, but may find other places where they point out a child's failure to meet their expectations.

Self-esteem is a fragile thing. I would have preferred that parent asked his child what she thought about the card. Or he could have said something about the A's before focusing on the A-. Your opinion of your child's achievements are going to play a large role in her self-esteem. See if you can find a way to applaud her achievements before you focus on her lack of perfection.

SECTION 3:

COMMUNICATION SKILLS

22

OVERVIEW

Even though conversations involve you and others, we are going to start with you. That probably comes as no surprise.

Like everything else in life you need to take 100% responsibility for making things better and that includes how you communicate with others and with yourself. Yes, it would be nice if other people would share the load and sometimes they do. But if you want to ensure something is going to get done you need to take full responsibility for it happening. Sorry.

Like they said in *Field of Dreams*: "If you build it they will come."

Research was done by UCLA professor Gerald Goodman, PhD on the different actions you can take in a conversation. His findings indicated that there were 6 response modes that we all use when we communicate. Basically he thought you could break down what goes on when people interact into 6 different categories. He thought we all would benefit if we could improve our skill set in each area. See what you think.

I will share with you my synthesis of his findings along with my own add-ons. The 6 modes are Disclosures, Questions, Advice, Interpretations, Reflections, and Silence. While we all know what these words mean, when it comes to conversation there are different ways to use each one. The next 6 chapters are going to be devoted to each mode so you can get a full understanding of how to employ each.

23

DISCLOSURE

Basically anything you say or do is a disclosure. You are pretty much always disclosing something about yourself. Whether you are telling a story or sitting quietly, you are disclosing. People see, hear, and maybe touch and smell you. They respond to what they sense from you. It is almost as if we each have our own odor/aura that we give off whether we want to or not that gets those around us to respond in different ways.

There are times you have a "No Trespassing" sign on your face or a look of dismay or joy. The tone of your voice may be weary, excited, flat, or authoritative. Your nonverbal language speaks out to others and they respond to what their antennae pick up.

Those closest to us tend to have a pretty good read into what we are thinking and feeling. Sure we can keep some things to ourselves, but overall those we are close to know our emotional state and a good part of what we are thinking. Sure, we all can fool some of the people some of the time.

You can try to act cool, calm, and collected when you are not and sometimes others won't see through it. Hiding your thoughts/feelings is a necessary skill to have, although one I would hope doesn't get employed all that often. You need to be careful because withholding your truth too much may result in both you and others feeling a level of estrangement/distance from each other.

How you disclose and present yourself to the world is something you want to monitor well. Especially when it comes to interacting with your children. But we all know our emotions can get the better of us. Even if we want to interact in calm, level-headed ways, our attempt to speak calm words may be undermined by the tenseness we and those around us are experiencing.

I am one of those people who thinks being a parent is a sacred duty and you need to do your best to do your best. Some may argue that the teen years are the lean years for appreciating your children and it gets challenging to maintain your best behavior. Yet even the parents I speak with who are having major issues with their teens still believe they are fortunate to have their child in their lives. Although certainly there are those times they don't feel all that fortunate.

But the bottom line is children are the best gift that life can give you. Maybe you have discovered a better gift, but I never have gotten a better one. Even though there may be moments parents would like to return the gift, being a parent is the bounty of life.

There will be times when your teenager wants something that you are not entirely sure you want him to have right now. Could be a body piercing, tattoo, sex, drugs, or a sleepover at someone's house that you are not so sure about. Could be anything. At some point in his teenage years he is going to want to do something that is going to be conflictual for you. Sooner or later you are going to want to talk about it.

If you want to have a "serious" discussion with your teenager about something it helps to first do a self-check about how you think/feel about the topic and what you want/hope to get out of the conversation. Usually there is something that is emotionally triggering your wanting to "have a talk," and if you can sort out your feelings before you interact, it might help you both out.

It could be something he did or didn't do or it could be you're just missing him in some way and want to talk about it. Once your emotions get revved up enough, it usually prompts you to want to get that emotion out of you. Sometimes you act out and sometimes you talk things out. When it comes to parenting I am more of a "think before you act" kind of person. Every now and then spontaneous is a good thing, but I endeavor to save that for the happier moments. That is not to say that when you want to have a serious talk it can't involve happiness. It is just that those talks usually don't start that way. But we can hope they end that way.

You could be happy or upset or afraid or any number of things. Since having a bit of an emotional change usually primes the pump, you might want to consider how you want to bring that emotion to your child. If there is going to be an abundance of your emotion you might want to run it by someone else first and let them receive the initial wave. When you do talk:

- Share what is bothering you and why it is bothering you.
- Ask him what he thinks/feels.
- Ask what he wants to do about it.

Then I would take what he wants into consideration and tell him what I would like to do about it. And go from there. That is my basic "let's talk" format.

When you arrive at the point where you need, want, and are going to talk with your child, keep this in mind. Whatever is troubling you and affecting you is really about how you think/feel about being his parent at this moment. You are welcome to share that and your child needs to respectfully listen to what you have to say. He can endeavor to be understanding and empathetic.

But he doesn't need to take care of you.

He needs to decide for himself how he wants to respond to your concerns. He may need time to be with that before he initiates any action. Or maybe he will respond right away.

Whether you are talking with him because of a concern you have about his behavior or because you have something happening in your life, he is not your emotional confidant. He does not need to take care of your emotions. Yes, he needs to respectfully listen and do his best to understand and empathize, but making you feel better is not at the top of his job description now. It may move up, but right now your job is to take care of you and him and his job is to take care of him. Yes, that is unbalanced, but time very well may even things out.

For the time being you can be your child's emotional confidant—if he will let you. But he is not supposed to be yours. As he has gotten older he has probably reduced the amount of emotional comfort he seeks from you. Let that be a model for you as well.

While certain children get thrust into the role of being the care provider it is not something I encourage. Unless you are seriously laid out and out of resources let your child be a child.

When you are emotionally triggered by some action and feel a need to address it with you child there are some items to consider before you react to your immediate impulses. Don't let your emotional urgency prompt you to act if you don't have to take action right away. Taking time to think things over usually helps. As does spending a moment on your own therapist's couch and asking yourself, how come you are having such a reaction to this? What is all that emotion about?

Once you can get a grasp of the historical antecedents or fear centers that are evoking the degree of your response it can help you deal with what is happening now in a more present fashion. You want to be dealing with the issue at hand and not off-loading some old material.

Having decided to go ahead and speak with your child, you might scan for a good time to have this discussion. While you are the one with the issue, once you share it there is a good likelihood that your child will be thrown off course for some time. The night before a test or a big paper is due is probably not an ideal time for a heavy conversation. There is no "good" time for a difficult conversation. Some times may be better, but if you are spending too much time thinking about when to talk, you probably are procrastinating. You might be better served focusing on what you are afraid of and dealing with that first.

Once you are ready here are a few tips for sharing difficult or challenging matters:

- Let your child know the reason you want to speak with him is because you want to improve matters.

- Use the word "I" as often as possible and "you" as little as possible.

- Tell him what is going on with you.

You can begin with a headline: "This is about _____."

- If there is a story involved don't go on and on.

Keep it under 5 minutes.

But make sure you don't leave out important elements.

Get the whole story on the table with no surprises coming later.

- Let him know how you think/feel and what you would like.

- When you want to hear from him tell him you would like to hear from him and then be quiet.

- Do not interrupt him. Listen to him with the same respect you would like him to have towards you.

While it may seem stilted and unnatural at first, conversations work better when one person talks and the other person listens and doesn't talk until the other person is finished.

Some therapists say to take an object and whoever is holding it gets to speak until they pass it to the other person. I think that is a bit much, but if it helps you, go for it. Sometimes it can be helpful to start with something like that to get into the flow of going back and forth and then you can let it go. The important skill to learn is to let each person have a turn. You don't have to do this 100% of the time, but I think you will find it really helps.

Maybe you like to be interrupted, in which case you might enjoy interrupting others. Most people don't enjoy being interrupted so why cut someone off unless you ask and get permission first? If you step on someone's toes because you are trying to expedite a conversation you probably have just extended the conversation. Not only are they not finished, but now they are upset with you for interrupting. Instead of having one thing to deal with you have now compounded matters. But, you probably have already learned that the hard way.

24

QUESTIONS

There are two kinds of questions: closed-ended and open-ended. Closed-ended questions ask for short answers. "Where did you grow up?" gets a brief reply. "Did you like the movie?" begets a "Yes" or "No." Open-ended questions create space to roam. "What was it like growing up there?" ought to provide more information. "What was the movie about?" could spoil it for you but give you a sense if it is your kind of movie.

There is a time and a place for each kind of question but usually when you are opting for a conversation open-ended questions are more likely to get the other person talking. If you ask close-ended questions and get short replies you often are left needing to ask another question and then another and then another. The onus is on you to keep the questions coming as opposed to putting the onus on them to more fully answer.

Of course I am a therapist so I am used to getting the other person to talk and I put myself more in a responding mode. The therapist's stock in trade question—"How do you feel and what do you think about that?"—can be answered succinctly but usually they encourage the other person to explore and share how they think/feel at a deeper less superficial level. Especially if they are paying big bucks for the experience.

Certainly parents have many questions about their teenagers' lives. At one point you knew everything and as she has gotten older you know less and less. That lack of knowledge affects parents differently.

There are the times you are worried about your child's wellbeing and you want to ask her questions so you can understand more fully what is going on with her. When she tells you she is feeling sick your parental instincts kick in and you want to know the symptoms so you can access what to do.

Then there are the times you think she may have done or be planning on doing something that does not meet with your approval and you want to know just exactly what is going on. In those instances the warmth you exhibited when she was sick may take a backseat to your anxiety over what she's up to.

Later in the book we will talk about substance use/abuse, partying, discipline and the nitty-gritty issues that parents encounter. But for right now let's focus on having a generic conversation with your child and how you can ask questions that will elicit a more forthcoming response.

Even if you ask an excellent question that does not mean you will get an equal return. It just increases the odds. Some teens who are going through their identity searching/rebellious years just want to keep you out so they can find their own way. Others are more prone to be introverts and want a higher degree of privacy. It is not so much that they are excluding you from their lives as they are including more things just for them.

Many a parent has known the frustration of not having as truthful and open a relationship with their teenager as they would like. If parenting were easy you wouldn't be reading this book. There are many unanswered questions parents have about their teens. Part of the challenge of raising a teen is learning how to comfortably evolve with your child's increasing independence.

Since you are probably going to have to learn to deal with knowing less, the least you can do is sharpen your skills so you can get the most out of the opportunities you have.

 Most parents enjoy hearing and responding to something their child is sharing about their day. Especially if what she is sharing is something you both feel good about. If she comes home from school and says something wonderful happened you probably will say some version of: "That's great. What happened?" Your enthusiastic response will prompt her to want to share.

When she comes home and tells you that something happened at school and she doesn't want you to get too upset, you might say, "What happened?" The encouragement that was in your voice before has been replaced by wariness. In the first situation, she wants to tell you. In the other, she thinks she has to tell you. One conversation calls for you to lovingly linger while the other could get horribly prolonged.

Either way, you want to hear the story.

How you respond to her telling the story will dictate how much more she will tell you.

Good listening begets good speaking.

The more supportive job you do of responding to what your child shares, the safer she will feel about sharing with you. Which is why you might want to hold off on the criticism, dirty looks, and other non-approving actions.

Those can and will come, but try to save them for after you hear all of what happened and how she's doing. Better to get the whole story on the table before you react. .

You can always respond in a heavy-handed manner, but once you offer a disapproving look or comment, the less of a back and forth, open and honest conversation and relationship you will have. In the one case she is anticipating your disapproving response and will be hesitant to tell you everything. While you cannot undo her fear of your response, you can mitigate her fear by listening to her side of the story and holding off your judgment until all the facts are in.

There is a word that therapists are encouraged to incorporate in their thinking, which I believe would be good for you as well.

The word is curiosity. Be curious.

Let your child know you want to understand.

Try not to make your questioning as if your child is on trial and you are giving her the third degree. Consider an attitude of genuine interest in who she is, how she thinks, and what she feels. Rather than give primary attention to your reaction, try to have your curiosity to know and understand her take precedence. How she thinks/feels about matters is critical for you to know, for it will guide how you and her manage the aftermath.

Your questions can convey your interest, as will your facial gestures, body language, grunts, and sighs. You can even give quizzical looks that ask the question without you having to say anything out loud. Having a look of concern and curiosity often can supplant having to ask a question. Your demeanor will disclose your interest and if she feels your desire for her wellbeing she will be more disposed to continue to share.

Yes, you can ask the probing questions. But save them until you have heard everything she has to say. Remember your job is not to play detective and find her guilty of a crime. Your job is to help her find her way so that she can build a rewarding and meaningful life. If she has stumbled along the way, while it may concern and upset you, how you tend to her will lay the groundwork for how she will tend to herself in the future.

There are questions you ask where you really are curious and want to know more about your child's life. "How was school today?" and "How do you feel and what do you think about what the teacher said?" Then there are the questions where you are curious about other matters: "Did you drink tonight?" or, "What the hell were you thinking?"

Often when children are younger they are eager to share their day with their parents. As children grow parents often lament that their children share so little. Parents ask how school was and they get a "Fine" for a response along with a clear message that their child does not want to speak to them about it.

What is a parent to do?

Parents often ask me how to get their child to open up more to them. I ask if it is a boy. Not just because more often than not boys, like men, share less than women. But because there has been some research into differing ways to engage boys and girls. I'll share some of that research, but I will also preface it by saying the fundamental rules apply. The more kind, curious, and supportive you are, the more your children will share with you. The more judgmental, critical, and withholding of positive feedback the less likely they (or anyone) will be to share with you.

Boys have an easier time talking when they are doing something. They are less comfortable when they are asked to sit down and talk. If you watch a game together or play something together or do pretty much anything together they are more able to talk about school or life while they also have something else to attend to.

Needless to say this is not true for all boys. Some boys are happy to sit down and talk and go over the events of the day. I have even had parents tell me that they think their son shares too much. Everyone's situation is different, yet for most men and boys it is easier to have a conversation if they also have their focus on something else. As much as you might want their full attention, you are often better off at least starting with sharing their attention with some other activity.

There is usually a lot more conversation that happens in the kitchen and in front of the TV than any other room. In the kitchen and in front of the TV there is usually other activity going on so the discussion can wrap around what else is happening in the room and not be the sole focus. This is one of those places where multitasking can be of assistance. Until someone says: "You're not listening to me." Then you need to mostly stop everything and pay attention.

There are times for having full on concentrated talks and there are times for partial attention talks. If you are having a partial attention talk and say "You're not listening to me" it will get the other person's attention and most likely you will get more if not all their attention. But be aware, you are also getting their irritation at having to give up the other activity. Since often it is hard enough to talk about something without adding some unnecessary irritation into the mix, I suggest you say, "When you are done with doing such and such I would like to finish this discussion." Then smile, tell them to enjoy what they're doing, and to come find you when they are ready. If you can do that, the other person is likely to appreciate your supportive attitude and with any luck some of that will come back to you.

Girls, the research says, are more approachable at bedtime. I think most of us have fond memories of having a sleepover or being away on a trip when the lights went out but the talk went on. Those can be special moments of truth sharing. You don't even have to turn the lights out. Just be in their bedroom at bedtime some nights.

Being in the bedroom at bedtime also works for boys. I am sure we have all seen enough movies where a parent sits on the child's bed and tells a story or reads a book and then kisses goodnight. While that is the Hallmark version, many parents can fondly recall similar moments. So can your children. Which is why bedtime chats work well.

Sitting on the side of the bed and chatting about the variety of subjects that living presents usually bring a parent and child closer. Until they don't.

There comes a time when most children no longer want you to be with them on their bed. This often happens with teenage girls and their dads and teenage boys and their moms. But it can happen with either parent, stepparent, relative, or friend. When this happens it is often accompanied by a desire for more privacy. It also can correlate with the desire not to be kissed in public and soon thereafter not to be seen together in public.

Parents need to be sensitive to their child's desire for independence and privacy. If there are times when your child does not want you to "put them to sleep" or say "goodnight," I think it is best to give them their space. Say goodnight from the hallway and don't make a big deal of it. Then, if you need to, go cry in your bedroom because your little child is growing up.

Hopefully there will be nights when you can knock on their door and ask if you can come in and chat. Then ask if it is okay to sit on the bed or sit down somewhere and tell them you just want to chat and spend some time before they fall asleep. It is okay if that is your full agenda. It is better to save your "I need to know" questions for another time. This is your hanging out together time. Enjoy it.

There are couples that don't like to argue in the bedroom as they like to keep that space excluded from the frictions that arise in the relationship. Certainly they can have squabbles and minor brushes that come up while they are in the bedroom, but they commit to not bringing their unresolved disputes into the bedroom. In much the same way, I think you want to limit the amount of skirmishes you have in your child's room. You want that to be a sanctuary for them. Don't fill it with your vitriol.

Often parents don't know what to talk about with their teenager. I like the "Would you rather…?" game. You can always ask your child would they rather be a movie star or a rock star, a circus performer or a rodeo star, a parent or a child. The lists are endless and they often bring about unexpected information that will help you and your child understand each other more. I would answer the questions as well as ask them.

We all need to learn how to make and handle mistakes.

Schools often discourage children from making mistakes. Students don't like to raise their hands unless they know the answer. Teachers often praise those that get it "right" while giving minimal credit to those who try hard.

Many people are mistake avoidant. They don't want to put themselves in situations where they can make a mistake and be embarrassed. For those teenagers who received the parental message that they were smart, there is a reluctance to demonstrate to themselves and others evidence to the contrary. In order to maintain their belief in their intelligence they often refrain from extending themselves and thus end up underachieving.

Help your child (and yourself) by rewarding effort. In the therapy world they encourage you to have a mistake and then a retake.

It is not easy to make peace with mistakes, let alone embrace them. If you can learn to more gracefully accept and see mistakes as an active ingredient in the learning process, it will make life much easier. Yes, not a lot of people enjoy making mistakes. It is how you hold your mistakes and deal with them that really matters.

I wouldn't make the reduction of mistakes a goal. I would aim for more mistakes equaling more learning. Yes, there are show-and-tell moments in life when you really don't want to make mistakes. But more often than not it is through our efforts and the mistakes we make that we learn and grow. Many people get stressed because they are afraid to make a mistake. It is often that added stress that can compromise our efforts. You might want to consider finding ways to acknowledge the efforts and mistakes that are made around the house and in your life so your child can come to value them more and not be so mistake-avoidant. The more you focus on effort and that old "try try again" motto, the better the chance your child will not become easily discouraged and will do that retake.

Some people think if their child makes a mistake a harsh consequence is what will get their attention and focus. Others believe some TLC will soothe the wound and the natural desire to not want to make a mistake again can come from within and does not need to be yelled from afar. Others believe valid criticism from the parent along with the child's self-assessment is the way to go. I think you can certainly say, "I wish this hadn't happened, here is what I would have liked to see you do, and I hope you will learn from this." But before I said that, I would want to know how they thought/felt about it and what they learned and want to do. Often if you ask that you don't have to say much of anything aside from, "Well done."

Your child will make mistakes. Sometimes you will get upset just like you do when you make mistakes. You may want to raise your voice and say mean and hurtful things. You may do that to yourself as well. Later on I would hope you can chalk it up as one of your mistakes and not be so heavy-handed on you or her. If you make the mistake of behaving poorly toward your child you can model apologizing. That is something she is going to have to learn to do as well when she makes mistakes.

Let's say it is 2:30am. Your child has a midnight curfew and you have not heard from her since she left the house at 7:00pm. You have texted her, called her, and gotten no response. You are in bed. You are tossing and turning. Then you hear the front door open.

What would you do? What have you done?

You may not have had a scenario exactly like that, but if you have a teenager you might recall some time when you were worried and upset about something. If you can remember a time like that, think back about how you handled yourself.

Any feedback you would like to give yourself? Anything you would like to do differently if something like this were to happen again?

Whatever you did or would like to do I want to suggest that before you share your anger and upset, why not share your relief that she is okay? You very well may have done that because the bottom line is always her health and safety.

Then be curious and ask what happened. Once you have heard her story, share your reaction. But let her go first.

It is almost always better when you are having emotional issues to let the other person go first.

"Honey, are you okay? What happened?" That is usually a good place to start.

This is a closed-ended and an open-ended question which often is a good combo. Starting a conversation on a factual plane is usually an easier way to begin. Then you can get into some version of, "Please tell me how come you are so late and didn't call and didn't pick up my texts and calls."

I would do my best to say that in a curious, inviting way and keep my upset in the background. Of course, that is not always an easy thing to do. But it is something to aim for.

Ever watch a newscast when the reporter is interviewing someone? They don't show a lot of footage of the reporter but you usually get some quick shots. They look like Bobble Heads. They are going up and down and doing their best to non-verbally encourage the other person to keep talking.

Be that Bobble Head.

Nod up and down, convey your understanding, and let her know you want to hear what she has to say. It won't kill you. It might help her open up.

Of course if you don't want to hear what she has to say then you can do whatever you want. But I will warn you that if you don't want to hear what she says, why would she want to hear what you say? Respect is a two-way street. If you don't show it, other people are not going to be eager to give it to you. You might be able to rule your nest through power and intimidation, but that has a much shorter shelf life than you might want. And when the shelf life is gone they are gone as well.

If your child is coming home noticeably late you know she either has a story to tell or she is in the midst of some large scale rebellion. If she has a story you want to hear it. If she is being rebellious you might want to consider that for someone to rebel they need to have someone or something to rebel against.

To quote one of my favorite '60s slogans, "If you are not part of the solution you are part of the problem." If you want to work on solving the problem ask her what she thinks the resolution ought to be and listen. She has as much insight into what she is rebelling against as you do and probably more. If she thinks you are being too restrictive see if you can get her to suggest some compromises that she thinks would be acceptable to both her and you. Getting a teenager involved in problem solving goes a long way towards getting your problems solved.

Nod, listen, encourage, and ask questions until she is done telling her story and you have no more questions to ask about what happened.

One last question you can ask: "Is there anything else you want to tell me or I ought to hear?"

Once you get finished with that, you can share what you need to share.

And wait for the next mistake.

25

ADVICE

Research says of all the interventions a therapist can utilize, giving advice is the least useful. Want to take a stab at why that is?

Certainly we have all received valuable advice. Someone has told us something that had a significant impact on our lives. There is no argument that the right piece of advice at the right time can be invaluable. Heck, this whole book is my advice to you about parenting your teenager so obviously I believe in it.

It is just that the batting average for advice is real low. Not quite as low as the odds of winning the lottery, but the kind of low that you wouldn't want to bet a lot on. But there are some things you can do to improve the likelihood of your advice being followed.

Here is a piece of advice we have all heard and mostly agree on: eat better and exercise more.

How are you doing on that advice?

How about "do unto others as you would have them do unto you"? You batting 1,000 there?

There is a lot of advice we hear that sounds good to us but for a myriad of reasons we are not able to fully follow. We often wish we could, but for somewhat unknown reasons we just don't follow the advice quite as much as we might like. As Oscar Wilde quipped, "The only thing to do with good advice is to pass it on. It is never of any use to oneself."

If you are going to give advice you want to aim for something within the person's reasonable ability. Of course, your perception of their abilities and their own self-evaluation might not always match up. While sometimes generic advice is valuable (like telling your child to say 'thank you' when someone gives him something), if you can give specific examples of the advice in action it can be more helpful. You could say, "When a teacher gives you back a paper you have written with their comments on it, thank them for taking the time to read and give you feedback on it."

Advice with an example often provides a concrete item that children can more readily grasp. Yet you don't want your examples to provide a limiting structure as younger children tend to be more concrete in their thinking. If you tell them to thank their teacher they may do that, but not generalize the suggestion to thanking others. Sometimes you need to add a second more generic piece of advice to assist your child in looking at the larger picture.

Even when delivered and received well, advice is still the least useful communication technique for therapists. I will tell you why.

Let's say you were my client and you asked me, "David, how do you think I should handle this situation with my teenager? What advice do you have for me?"

I could answer by saying, "You could do such and such…"

But by answering that question I am also saying I know the answer better than you. While I may sometimes think I do, and sometimes maybe I do, my job as a therapist is to empower my client.

Sure, my answer might help empower you. But so too would this reply: "What advice would you give yourself?"

Asking your child for his thoughts tells him you are interested in what he thinks. Maybe you agree. Maybe it was something you never considered. Maybe you don't agree. Maybe it was what you were going to say. Asking his advice to himself empowers him and gets him thinking about what is best for him. While that empowerment might make him a formidable force when you interact with him, you do want him to be empowered in life. And life starts at home.

It is helpful for you in learning about your child to hear how he would like to handle various situations. It is also helpful for him to reflect on his values and beliefs and be able to share them and have them respected if not agreed with completely.

If you want to empower someone you need to let them know that you respect what they have to say. Which is why a good part of parenting is listening to your child and supporting his thoughts/feelings, if not his judgment.

You won't always agree with him and you may make decisions that do not line up with his beliefs. Parenting requires you to make unpopular decisions. Listening and incorporating his point of view to whatever degree you can will help him be more engaged and invested in the situation.

As a general guideline when there are problem situations that need solving it is often wise to ask the "offender" what their advice is for solving matters. You want to teach your child about taking responsibility, making mistakes, forging solutions, and cooperative problem-solving. Many of the work conditions he will find himself in as he enters the workforce are going to involve problem solving and working with others. He might as well get an opportunity to exercise these muscles while he still is safe in the sanctity of his home.

Advice we give ourselves has a better chance of being followed than the advice of others. If you happen to agree with your child's advice you can say as much. If you don't agree you can ask him what advice he thinks you would offer and ask for his advice in resolving those differences.

26

INTERPRETATION

If you ask most people what they think an interpretation is in the therapy world, you might get something along the lines of it being when the therapist tells you that your inability to fully feel good about yourself centers on your unresolved issues with your mother. While there are some therapists who do a fair amount of interpretation, that is not the kind of highfalutin interpretation we are talking about here.

In day-to-day conversations there are different kinds of interpretations that frequently happen. The first is when you watch and listen to what the other person is saying and then you break down for them what you really think is going on with them. They may be telling you about one thing, but you may be thinking something else entirely is going on with them. They can be talking about worrying that their child is drinking and suddenly you blurt out, "This isn't about your child's drinking, this is about your fear of her not getting into a good college and getting a good job and having a good life."

Friends can say those things now and then. Usually that means they are trying to help get to the root of the concern. Instead of focusing on strategies concerning how to deal with their child's drinking, they might be better served coming to grips with their fear about their child's future. That is not to minimize the drinking issue, but rather to point out that the mother's fear may be exacerbating her ability to really help her child.

Whether we share what we think is going on or not, it is important for us to be able to read into what someone is saying and try to discern their bottom line truth. Understanding what is going on around us and what other people are really saying/thinking/doing helps us navigate our passage through life. We learn by trial and error when something is bothering someone and how best to approach them.

When you want to get a better understanding of what is happening with another person, using an interpretation can help you. You can say what you really think is going on with them and encourage them to take some time to reflect on themselves and probe a little deeper. Or not.

Your interpretation, after all, is your way of seeing their life. You may think they are doing this because of that, and while you may be right, you may also be saying something about you as well. The fact that you thought what you thought, given a world of thoughts, does say something about you. You might want to dwell on that. If you think their talking about their child's drinking is really an overall concern about their child's future you may be on the money or you may be saying more about what is on your mind. If you do decide to share an interpretation do it as a suggestion of what you think might be going on. If they shrug it off, let it go.

If it is important it will come up again.

There are a few observational skills that can assist you in building your interpretation abilities. They have to do with body language and nonverbal behavior. A lot of people take more stock in nonverbal behavior than they do in the words they hear.

People can lie a lot easier with words than they can with their body. Poker players are always looking for their opponents' tells. They look for those signs that let them know if the person really has a good hand or not.

We all look for tells. We look to see what the other person's face is telling us.

While someone's face is the biggest tell, the body has its own story. You see someone standing with their arms crossed in front of them, you may assume they are not feeling open. You see someone fidgeting, you figure they are nervous.

You may not be consciously aware of what the other person's face and body are telling you, but it is information your brain is processing. What you do with it, how you interpret it—well, that is something we can talk about.

If you don't pay much attention to what people are saying nonverbally you might want to give it a little conscious effort the next time you are around people. Just observe. Watch people in a public place who are interacting and try to guess how they are feeling. You may not know what they are talking about but you ought to get a feel for how their conversation is going.

The more aware you become of observing people the more able you will be to "read" what they are saying. Experience is a great teacher. The more you do this the better skilled you will become. Sure, some people can fool some of the people some of the time, but the more you consciously focus on what the other person's body is telling you the better a detective you will be.

If you see someone fidgeting when they speak with you at first you can just note it. It is hard to know what it means for that person until you have more experience with them. Maybe they always fidget, maybe only when they are very nervous. Maybe when they lie.

Observe and collect data. Don't jump to conclusions; jump to awareness. And if you want to ask them if what you think their body is saying is true, do it in a tentative way: "I see your toe tapping and I wonder if you are in a hurry or if it is something else entirely?"

Nonverbal behavior is usually easier to understand than verbal behavior. You see that guy you just cut off on the freeway giving you the finger, you pretty well know how he is feeling. He doesn't have to tell you with his words. Although he might. "Actions speak louder than words" is a cliché we all have heard and that guy's actions speak loud and clear. You don't have to use a lot of brainpower to try to figure out what is going on with him.

You do need to use more brainpower when you listen to the words. People tend to be very careful when they speak and often shade their thoughts. Certainly there are times without hesitation when we all blurt out in a clear and direct way what we are thinking. Yet often if someone feels strongly about a topic they will share something less direct and see how you respond before they focus in on what they really think. If you don't respond encouragingly to their first remarks you may not get to hear what really is going on with them. You might hear the milder opening statement and interpret their thoughts one way, but without hearing the follow-up statements your interpretation could be off.

Reading and understanding people is more art than science. Interpreting what someone truly feels and means is an ongoing learning process. If people are more congruent it is a lot easier, but still most people hedge their comments until they feel comfortable enough to let their fuller truths out. To you and them.

I encourage you to use a variation of this statement: "What do you mean? I don't fully get what you are saying. Help me understand."

If you say that in a supportive, encouraging way, you ought to get more information. If you say it in a threatening way, you are liable to see their withdrawal.

Which you then can interpret. Alone.

When your teenager is unusually nasty to you, it could have something to do with what is happening in her world or it could be some residue of some history between you. You can never fully know why someone is doing what they are doing which is why it behooves you to use a tentative voice: "Does your demeanor now have something to do with other matters in your life or has this got something to do with the disagreement we had last week? Or something else entirely?" This interpretation is your idea about what might be prompting her actions and she may agree completely, partially, or not at all. Either way, say it once then don't mention it again for some time and only when you think it might really be of value to your child. As I mentioned earlier if something is truly important it will come up again and again until it is satisfactorily handled.

I don't do a lot of interpreting of what people are saying/doing but when I think something is incongruous I am apt to speak out. If I think something is going on with the person that does not seem congruent with what they are expressing I usually say some version of: "I hear you saying such and such, but it looks like something else is going on."

Therapists are tasked with making the unknown known. Not everyone needs to do that. Sometimes it is best to let things lay low. You don't have time to talk about everything that happens during the day, but when you have a higher degree of thoughts/emotions it is usually a good time for some honest conversation. Chances are if something is bothering you, it is going to come out sooner or later and most of the time it is better to nip things in the bud before they fester.

There is another kind of interpretation that happens frequently. Someone says to you, "I had a great time at that party," and you reply, "Sounds like you had a lot of fun."

What you have done there is take their words and put your own interpretation on them. They said they had a "great" time at the party and you interpreted that to mean they had "fun." You take what others say and put it in your own words. As with many things there are positive and negative aspects to this.

The positive is you are connecting to them. You are taking what they said and relating to it in your own way. This can relay to the person that you are listening and get what they are saying. They might feel understood and be encouraged to continue.

On the negative end when they say "great" and you say "fun" you aren't really 100% getting them. You could be off a little or a lot. They might feel that you understand them or they might feel that you have no clue and have taken what they said and made it about you.

It is safer to use their words, but if you do it all the time it is annoying and people look at you funny. So sometimes reflect their words and sometimes interpret them with your understanding of what they mean.

As you know, communication is a dicey thing. You could be trying to be attentive and they might think you are missing the boat. You could interpret something and think it is on the money and helpful and the other person thinks it is hurtful and insensitive. You could put what they say in your own words and they might think you nailed it better than they did and feel even better understood.

You don't know how the other person will receive what you say. You hope that if it comes with good intentions that will ameliorate any missteps. But you never know. As Lyle Lovett sang: "She wasn't good but she had good intentions." Good intentions take you only so far. We tend to judge ourselves well if our intentions are good, but others judge us less on our intention and more on our behavior. She may have had good intentions, but that didn't seem to sway Lyle.

Nobody communicates perfectly.

People get misunderstood and feelings get hurt. If you are genuinely trying to understand someone, though, they will usually have a positive response to your attempt. They might think you have no clue, but at least they see you looking for clues.

27

REFLECTION

Here is how I teach reflection to my students: I stand up and move to the left and talk and then I move to the right and talk. Quickly they grasp that two people are talking and I am not just talking to myself.

I move to the left and say, "I was going to a party where I didn't know anyone and I was standing outside the door feeling very nervous."

Then I move to the right and say, "You were going to a party where you didn't know anyone and were standing outside the door feeling very nervous."

Then I move left: "Yes, I was going to a party where I didn't know anyone and I was standing outside the door feeling very nervous."

Then right: "You were going to a party where you didn't know anyone and were standing outside the door feeling very nervous."

Left: "Exactly, but it is very annoying when you repeat everything I say."

Right: "It is annoying when I repeat everything you say."

Left: "Yes, it is extremely annoying when you repeat what I say."

Right: "It is extremely annoying."

Left: "Yes."

That is reflection at its most annoying.

By definition, a reflection is a mirror image. If one person says something, the other reflects it back pretty much verbatim. You may notice as I went through it I didn't repeat everything exactly, but I was close to it and the critical part was to repeat the key words.

Repeat the key words.

Yes, repeat the key words.

Unlike interpretation where you might substitute "scared" for "nervous", here you would reply, "You were nervous."

Now, I know this sounds horrible. It is the most contrived, phony, cheap therapist kind of thing.

Yes, it is the most contrived, cheap therapist kind of thing.

It is also the most effective thing therapists do.

Before you say, "Well that settles it, no therapy for me," let me explain.

Two of the main complaints people have in relationships is that they don't feel listened to and they don't feel understood. Reflection lets the other person know you are hearing exactly what they are saying. Since you are not adding your own words the person feels more precisely understood.

Understanding does not mean agreeing. It simply means I fully hear what you are saying. Now just since you echo the words does not mean you understand the depth of emotion that goes with it, but at least you let the other person know you are closely listening. If you throw in an empathic look on your face that might help them know that you more fully understand.

Now, of course if you go around reflecting what people say all the time eventually someone will hurt you. It can be obnoxious if overused because it just parrots what the person is saying. Sooner or later they will want more from you.

But, slip it in now and then, especially when you really do want to hear more about what is going on with the other person. I think you will find the person feels more connected to you and keeps talking.

Try it out.

When I teach this to my students I follow it up with a little challenge. I tell them for the rest of the class I will reflect things they say and they won't even be able to know when I am doing it.

How can that be? How can I teach them about reflection and then do it and they not know it?

Indeed, how can something so blatantly annoying be so invisible?

And truthfully, this is a challenge I do lose. But I pretty much fool everyone in the class at least once if not multiple times. It is not because I am a magician, but because all you need to do is speak a few key words now and then and nod your head like you understand; most people will keep talking and not really even register that you said anything.

I believe that when you try it you will find most people just keep talking with the comforting knowledge that you are listening. Which is what allows for greater intimacy. Which is why it is used so much by therapists. It conveys understanding and encourages the person to keep talking.

Of course, when you first do it, you will think you are doing something so transparent and gimmicky that the person will give you a nasty stare. They might. It has happened to me. But once you practice it a few times, I think you will find you can get away unnoticed and it will easily fit into your communication skill toolbox.

There is an interesting finding about therapy that I thought you might enjoy and which may have bearing on your life. I mentioned that often therapists use reflection and clients hardly notice. It turns out that the clients of those therapists think of the therapy as being very effective, but not so much the therapist. The therapist that gives more advice and is more active is considered the better therapist, yet the therapy is not considered to be as effective.

It puts therapists in an interesting dilemma. Do I do more so clients think better of me or do I do less and have them think better of the therapy? I mention this not because you may be considering being a therapist or going into therapy, but because when it comes to your child you might want to consider using some understated methods to get him to open up to you. Now, I can't point to any research to back me here, but I am guessing that while you want to be considered the best parent, you also want your child to consider himself to have the best life. If there is a way to blend your involvement so that you get the recognition you want and he gets the empowerment he needs you can go the head of the class.

28

SILENCE

Being silent with another comes easily to some and not so easily to others.

You know which one you are.

If you happen to be mostly comfortable with silence, I have a few things I want to point out to you. If you are not so comfortable with silence, maybe I can help build up your enjoyment of it or at least your tolerance.

Conversations are not tennis matches where one person says one thing and then hits the ball over to the other. They are more like football games where one person might have possession for a long drive and the other may run one play and turn it over. Discussions can go back and forth in rapid bursts or there can be pronounced silences between comments. Eventually you need to hear what everyone has to say, but getting there requires travelling a new path every time.

If you are one of those people who mostly feels a need to fill the quiet spaces, what do you think prompts you to want there to be continuous conversation?

_____

_____

What are you concerned would happen if there was silence for 30 seconds, a minute, or a couple of minutes?

_____

_____

What do you think the silence says about you?

_____

_____

Why do you think that?

_____

_____

In a conversation when there is a silence it is considered a "shared silence." Even though the other person may have been the last to speak and theoretically it is your turn, it is still considered a shared silence. Yes, for the first moments the onus is on you, but once you get past a few seconds the ball is in both your courts.

Often people who are uncomfortable with silence think it reflects on them. It is as if the silence means they have nothing of merit to contribute. Other people might think they are lacking or not fully able to put together something worthwhile to add to the conversation. Of course, the other person could be experiencing the same thing or just be patiently sitting in the silence waiting for inspiration.

I am sure we have all experienced those times when we have wanted to say something but we couldn't find the words. If you are talking with someone who you hold in high esteem or are trying to impress someone, many people often stumble over what to say and end up saying nothing or blurting out something they wished they had not said. We all can empathize with that.

While I don't wish those moments on any of us, I am more concerned with the day-to-day conversations you have. Is there room for silence when you talk with your family and friends? That can be a place where you could more easily practice being silent. Doesn't have to be a long silence, just a little longer than you currently allow.

When you have those moments when you want to impress and it doesn't feel like it is happening you can always revert to congruence and state the obvious: "I am having trouble saying anything profound/funny and I sure wish I could because I would like you to think there is more to me than just this pretty face." Or you could just reflect the last thing they said and hope to get the ball back to them.

As a therapist I would encourage you to see if you could extend the amount of time you can be in silence. We call it stretching yourself and just like the stretching of your body, stretching your communication skills is also a healthy activity. If you are good for 5 seconds now, see if you can add to it. Sort of like holding your breath, which is something some people do to remind themselves to slowly breathe before they talk again. There is no ideal amount of time to be comfortable with silence. The goal is to learn how to be comfortable for longer periods of time. Hopefully you will discover that the time you spend in silence does not affect the other person's opinion of you—heck, they might even think you are more thoughtful.

You want to get to a place where you don't feel like you need to break the silence because of your discomfort in it. You want to break it because you have something to add to the conversation. And sure, most everyone breaks silences because they feel socially awkward after a point. So be it. Just see if you can stretch that point.

We have all heard the proverb, "Silence is golden." What with the price of gold these days it might be something worth investing in.

I want to share with you something that therapists learn that I think will help you. It is not that I think that you ought to do what therapists do. More that therapists talk all day with people and we do learn certain things about communication just by doing it so much. Plus most of us read a fair share of research on the subject.

One thing we learn is that silences that are broken by the client are more beneficial to the client than silences broken by the therapist.

If a client has been speaking about something and then pauses, certainly a therapist could say any number of things. But if a therapist remains silent, the client will eventually continue. When they do continue, what they say will be more connected to where they left off than anything the therapist could say. That's why a lot of therapists endeavor to say considerably less than their clients. Where the client goes tends to be more useful to the client than where the therapist thinks they ought to go. Not 100% of the time, but more often than not.

There are some implications for all intimate relationships in these findings. If you want the other person to delve more deeply into what they are saying, leave room for them to do so. You could reflect what they last said or you could be quiet and do your best just to be with them. If they are telling you something important to them, most likely they will continue with an encouraging look from you.

Being silent does not mean that you are partially listening to someone and watching the game. It means distractions are limited and the focus is on talking together. Being silent means you are listening to them. Yes, you could be multitasking in the kitchen and conversing at the same time. Having a shared silence with someone means you are not being silent because you are paying attention elsewhere. You can chop vegetables and talk, but don't get so lost in the chopping that you are not attending to the conversation.

You talk, you listen, you reflect, you listen, you disclose, you listen, you interpret, you listen, you ask questions, you listen, give advice, listen, disclose, and sometimes you are silent. You blend those response modes into your intimate conversations. Some more than others, but they are all at your disposal.

While you are doing that you might also want to follow these basic guidelines that therapists use when working with couples, families or groups:

- One person speaks at a time.

- Share until you are done, but don't monopolize.

- Listen without making faces or emitting negative sounds or turning away.

- No interrupting.

- No name-calling.

- No raised voices.

- No threats.

The better job you can do of following those basic guidelines, the better off your conversations will be. We will get into using these skills when dealing directly with your child, but for now just remember the basic components of communication are disclosing, questioning, interpreting, advising, reflecting, and being silent.

That's it.

29

A PRIMER ON EMOTIONS

Now is as good a time as any to give a brief overview of emotions. There are so many valid and useful theories concerning the nature of our emotions, I could write a whole other book on the topic. And even then, I would likely leave out some valuable information.

For the purpose of *this* book, I will stick with the simplest model I know. Plenty of people have added on to it, and you can too. People have said it is too simplistic, and you can too. People have used it effectively, and you can too.

I think this model is worth your consideration because it takes a subject as complex as human emotions and gives you an easy way to conceptualize it. Whether dealing with your emotional life comes easily to you or not, having a roadmap will help you navigate your way through the maze.

Often, when people are emotional they say things they otherwise might not say. Some people believe that is where the truth lies. Other people think that while what you say may be truthful, it doesn't accurately reflect *all* that you feel. The words you blurt out when you are angry may represent an unguarded feeling, but it lives next door to a host of other thoughts and feelings.

You can feel this. And you can feel that. Just like you can think this and you can think that. You can have mixed thoughts and feelings. In fact, you often do.

In search of a clearer understanding of emotions many people have created theories and diagrams to explain them. I wish I could give someone credit for the theory I am going to share, but no one has been able to determine who actually came up with the idea. There are a bunch of claimants, but I have yet to find an agreed-upon creator. So, whoever you are, thank you.

Here it is:

The four basic emotions are mad, sad, glad, and scared.

If you ask yourself how you feel about something, it ought to fall into one of those four general areas.

You could be mad, furious, irked, annoyed, or any number of other mad-like feelings.

You could be glad, euphoric, pleased, happy, or have some other feeling in that area code.

You could be distraught, depressed, sad, or just not feeling good—all feelings that leave you down and gloomy.

You could be scared, and may describe that feeling as terrified, afraid, worried, or fearful.

That is the model. The next time you are feeling something, you can ask yourself, "Am I mad, glad, sad, or scared?" That is a good place to start exploring how you really feel about something.

Here are my add-ons.

Feelings live on a continuum.

If 10 was the maddest you have ever felt and 1 is the least angry you have felt, if 10 was the happiest you have ever felt and 1 the least happy, if 10 was the saddest you have ever felt and 1 the least sad, and if 10 was the most scared you have ever felt and 1 was the least afraid, where are you in each category at this exact moment?

Right now I am this mad: ____. This glad: ____. This sad: ____. This scared: ____.

You can ask yourself these questions about anything going on in your life and you ought to get answers. Some things won't register because you are just not that consciously invested or aware of it. Other things will clearly stand out.

Getting in touch with your feelings is a matter of following this four-lane road.

You can think of mad, glad, sad, and scared as lanes on a highway or places on a map. This way, attending to how you feel is akin to asking for directions. It is as if you have a map but you can't quite find your way. Ask yourself: "Am I mad about this? How so?", "Am I glad about this? In what way?", "Am I sad about this? Anything there?", or "Am I scared about this? Why?" Asking these kinds of questions helps you find your way and the lanes open up.

And you know all roads eventually lead to Rome.

Exploring how you feel and think is a lifelong quest. Each moment brings a new set of reactions. Some you are aware of, and others you may not be aware of at all.

You might find that you have more than one feeling about something, just as you might have more than one thought. You might feel angry that your teenager is mad at you while at the same time glad he is sharing with you and not shutting you out. You might also discover that you are sad because you do not want him to be upset with you. And you might even be scared that this is going to harm your relationship with him.

You can have a range of emotions and thoughts about those emotions. It can go on and on until you call a timeout.

When it comes to sharing emotions, it can be helpful to remember that you want your thoughts and feelings to be respected and understood just as your child wants his to be honored. Make it easier for both him and you by expressing yours in ways you know he can hear. Not because you are speaking loudly, but because you are not blaming, raising your voice, or being demeaning to him. You are sharing your feelings and thoughts because you love him and want to have a close, meaningful, truthful, and enjoyable relationship with him. Which, like any close relationship, will not always be ideal for both of you.

I am not naive. Well, maybe a little. I know when someone is angry with you that the knee-jerk response is to fight back or shut them out. Fight-or-flight is an ingrained response. When something frightens us, attacks us, or hurts us, we either want to fight back or take off. All animals have this primal response, including humans.

When emotions are triggered, people often want to jump into them or run away. We have our own fight/flight with ourselves although I prefer to think of it as engage/disengage. When our emotions are triggered, we have to decide if we are going to engage or disengage. When your child is upset with you, try to listen and not fight back. Engage with him in a manner that shows your concern, compassion, and desire to understand and support him.

Hold that mindset somewhere in your head while you share from your heart.

While I advocate for engagement, there is also a need for disengagement at times. We all need time alone to be with ourselves, to quietly reflect on how our life is going and how we want to deal with the present situation.

Most of the time when your child is engaging you, it is not the time for you to disengage. You very well may not want to hear, put up with, or attend to what your child is saying, but this is not the time to walk out, slam doors, raise the drama level, make threats, or otherwise aggravate the situation. Try not to add fuel to the fire—instead, see if you can put this one out before it spreads. If you have issues you need to share, save them for another time. If your child has brought you something that is upsetting him, you need to pay attention to his issue and not all the other ones related to it.

Consider making a commitment to yourself to work through difficulty as best you can and to not leave a disagreement until some mutually acceptable resolution or timeout can be agreed upon, more or less.

If someone is being abusive or threatening or intimidating, it may be necessary to walk away. We all have a level of respect and appreciation we need in order to willingly engage in a conversation. If you do not feel safe and respected, it may be necessary to leave or bring in someone else.

If you have to leave a conversation, so be it. But if you are the one that has opted to end the conversation, you are obliged to be the one who initiates a follow-up conversation in the near future. You can leave the conversation, but not the discussion or relationship. Do not threaten to leave the family. If that is a conversation you want to have, save it for another time when that can be the whole focus of the discussion and not an add-on to what your child is bringing to you.

Anyone can feel threatened when someone else raises their voice or gets angry. You can fear that the other person will hate you, hurt you, leave you, or be dissatisfied with you. You can worry that the relationship is "up for grabs."

All those feelings are often felt when an argument gets intense. There is no right or wrong way to feel during these moments, and if you feel those things, so be it. Just don't walk out unless you really need to for your own safety and wellbeing. And if you do walk away, be sure to take a return slip with you.

If you think your child is being abusive to you, there could be valid reasons to take a timeout, if for no other reason than to show that abusive behavior will not be tolerated. But before you walk away, tell him it is not acceptable for him to speak to you the way he is, and if he wants to continue the discussion you would like him to be more respectful with his language. He can feel what he feels and you do want to hear about it, but you want to hear it spoken in a respectful manner.

If he continues, tell him you are going to leave now and will return shortly when hopefully you can resume the conversation in a mutually acceptable manner.

If you are not able to have emotionally-charged conversations without someone walking away feeling disgruntled, hurt, shamed, or devalued, then it is time to call your therapist. You need help outside of the relationship.

When someone walks out on an argument, the person left may experience a range of emotions, very few of them on the positive side of the continuum. Whatever upset them in the first place has now been surpassed by the thoughts/feelings associated with the other person leaving. They are left to stew, wait, and cope with having no control over the situation. Any resolution to the initial concern is now on hold, accompanied by a new set of emotions.

While I do support walking away from abusive or threatening situations, I also encourage you to get another person in the conversation who can help keep the back-and-forth from being spoken or heard in abusive tones—a moderator of sorts. One thing I have learned as a therapist is that someone may hear something as abusive but the speaker may not see it that way. Sometimes things are clearly abusive and other times it is…iffy. In those gray areas, it can help to have another person in the room. Usually it is the other parent or a sibling who could endeavor to be open-minded, although to be truthful that is not always easy to do and comes with its own set of consequences. Ideally, if the conflict is significant enough and not resolvable relatively quickly and painlessly, you ought to call a therapist who works with families.

One aside here. If you think your family would benefit from seeing a therapist but others don't want to go, you go. Don't let their resistance get in the way of you getting the help you need.

If you do think you are being disrespected or abused and you decide to stop the conversation, be aware that walking out creates a level of anger as well as fear. People get upset with you for not working things through, and they start to feel afraid. Afraid that if they say or do the "wrong" thing, you will leave. This puts them in a difficult bind—they want to be honest with you but if they tell you their truth you may walk away. Out of the room, or worse, out of the home.

You may very well want them to feel that way to prevent them from voicing their anger at you. But, just because they are afraid to voice it does not mean they don't feel it. They are only keeping it from you, along with other aspects of their love.

Withholding their ability to be honest with you will cause them to feel less connected with you and as they grow up they will have less interest in being around you.

When emotions are not flaring, focus some conversations on how to talk with each other. Discuss what feels out of bounds for you and what you need to be able to work through these discussions in a way that is more beneficial for all.

People in your family may not want to engage in meaningful, emotionally-laden conversations. They are not easy for everyone. If you think your family discussions need an upgrade then you might want to have a family meeting to talk about having family meetings. You can share your wishes and concerns and open the floor to others to share as well. The goal is to have some mostly agreed-upon guidelines for having emotionally-charged discussions. Well, that's the goal, but sometimes you have to settle for close enough.

We have all walked away from challenging moments in relationships. You may not leave the room, but you may find a way to shift the conversation so it doesn't get too close to you. We all want to dodge a bullet when we see one.

While you may not be the one who gets up, walks away, and slams the door, you may be the one who craftily moves the conversation along so that it doesn't dwell on issues you would prefer not to address. Or you may react so negatively when conflicts arise that others choose to walk away from *you*.

We all do the conflict in/conflict out dance. Engage and disengage.

My goal is to make those conflicts run smoother so you don't have to get into that much of an emotional state when you enter them. Sort of like going into an elevator on the ground floor of a very tall skyscraper. You may be a little scared, but you know the odds are good that you are going to get off that elevator and be on a floor that has a very different view, and probably a better one.

The trick to not having to disengage is to learn how to be with another person's emotion. It helps to remember that this is what they are thinking/feeling. While it may not bode well for you, it is really about them.

You just need to respectfully listen.

You don't have to do or say anything.

99% of the time you don't have to take any action in the moment.

You can listen, speak, or not speak and consider what she said, then say you will get back to her as soon as you can. You need time to sort through everything. This will allow you to extricate yourself a little more gracefully and mutually.

If listening is unbearable and you know that if you speak it is going to challenge your vulnerability, you can share those thoughts/feelings and then say you need a timeout. Just remember, with every timeout comes a time in.

When you do share how you think/feel, remember you are talking about you. Not him.

Do not use sentences that sound like "You are..." or "You make me feel…"

Those "you" statements are not going to help.

Here is how to translate a "you" statement into an "I" statement. Most people, myself included, don't do this perfectly, but again the goal is improvement, not perfection.

"You are inconsiderate" can translate to "I like it when I am taken into consideration."

Instead of saying, "You are mean," you might simply say, "Ouch."

"You only think of yourself" could come out as "I like it when I can tell you have thought about me."

It is not easy doing these translations. Usually people use disguised "you" messages. "You're mean" becomes "I think you are mean." This is not a true "I" statement, because while there is an added "I" in there, the message is the same as before.

The focus needs to be on you, not them.

Here is a blend of "you" and "I" messages which a lot of people use: "I like it when you take me into consideration." I think that is fine. You are speaking about what is important to you and it lets the other person know what they do that you like.

Just try to stay away from the "You are _____" model. Those statements tend to be incendiary.

While name-calling can be cathartic, it is best left for when you are watching a sitcom or other forms of entertainment. They get paid; you don't know them and hopefully will never meet them. Call them what you will.

When it comes to the people you love, call them by their name or one of the mutually acceptable nicknames you have for them. Leave out the invectives you might want to hurl impulsively.

Needless to say there are numerous times when parents use "you" messages with their children. Not all of them have a negative twist.

"You are smart," "You are lovely," and "You are funny" are also "you" messages.

While they may burden a child and have some unforeseen repercussions, even if they are intended to be positive, most people would say those are acceptable and maybe even gift-bearing "you" messages. I certainly have handed out my share. I like to tell students or anyone if I think they are smart, creative, thoughtful, sensitive, funny, or anything else that comes to mind in the moment. For the most part, people like hearing those things and they may even provide a boost that someone else recognizes something about them. Of course, you never know how people will take things and what they will do with them.

"You" messages are a bit like headlines; they condense the story, but they don't tell the whole story. It is usually more informative and useful to hear what got the person to come up with the "you" statement. If they think you are an asshole that may be all you need to know. But you might have an interest in what exactly you did that made them think you were an asshole. Once you hear the story from their point of view, you may or may not agree. But at least you know how you earned the name they gave you.

Even "you" messages with the sole intention to support can have unforeseen negative consequences. I mentioned earlier that parents who say "You are so smart" may be building their child's esteem, but you also want to pair that with, "When you work hard I see how you can teach yourself and learn from your mistakes." Without the pairing, that well-intended "You are so smart" may actually inhibit your child's development.

Riding out conflict can be bumpy as emotions get thrown all over. Sometimes you will manage yourself and the conversation in ways that you can tell make everyone feel better. And sometimes you won't. You will use "you" messages that make you wince and ones that bring you closer. You will use "I" messages that upset the other person, and ones that will touch their heart.

You do your best to do your best and accept what you can.

Throughout our lives we are exposed to opportunities found and opportunities lost.

We have moments of great joy and great sorrow.

We have wins.

We have losses.

We like certain things about ourselves and not others.

We like certain things about those around us and not others.

Life is a mixed bag. We don't always get what we want. Maybe we get what we need.

And maybe we don't.

We fail and make mistakes.

We learn and adapt and take new steps.

Like it or not.

People evolve.

SECTION 4:

PASSING THE STRESS TEST

30

STRESS

Most of us carry around more stress than we would like. For the most part, the amount of stress teenagers endure is substantially more than their parents had to contend with during their teen years. We all know a small level of stress can have some beneficial effects. It can be a good motivator and help you focus and get through projects. We all also know too much stress will kill you. Like most things it exists on a continuum.

I have not yet seen the teenager who dies from stress. But I have seen a lot get sick, stay away from school, get cranky, and manage their stress in what I would consider less than optimal ways. I would like to see if we could lower your child's and your own stress level down that 10%-20% (or more).

If you go with the generic definition that stress is mental or emotional strain, there are a lot of things that fit into those categories. Usually people talk about being under stress when it starts to feel like there is "too much" worry and/or pressure than you really want. "Too much" is not a very scientific word, but it is one of those things that you know when you feel it.

The "too much" pressure that teenagers usually feel is a combination of some traditional stressors and one big more recent stressor. The traditional struggles that teenagers have that invoke stress include, "I want to be liked," "I want to be independent," "I want to do what I want to do," "I don't know what I want to do," and "I want to figure out what to do about my evolving sexuality."

While certainly a teen's social life is a continual subject of self-examination and exploration, high school juniors and seniors come to my office about one time for every twenty they go talk to the college counselor. Teens are feeling more stress in this generation than in their parents' generation when it comes to what college they are going to apply to, get into, and be able to go to. Career/college and all its attendant issues are far and away the number one stressor. For students and parents.

Here is your primer on stress.

We all walk around with stress. It could be related to our health, our wealth, or any number of things that cause worry. Usually whatever load of daily stress we are carrying is relatively easily or at least functionally managed and we can go on about our business and still enjoy our lives. Other times the pressures mount and start to undermine our happiness and sense of wellbeing. Sometimes something unexpected comes our way. It could be a positive or negative thing. Even if we are excited about a new development, the newness of it brings with it a measure of stress. Stress comes in all shapes and sizes from all directions and we never know when it will start and/or stop. In other words, to be alive is to know stress.

According to Corey and Corey, the authors of *I Never Knew I Had a Choice*, there are four primary ways stress comes our way. They are frustration, conflict, change, and pressure.

- Frustration—We all know this one. You need to be someplace at a certain time and something happens to delay you and you start to stress about getting there on time.
- Conflict—We all know this one too. Conflict, as you will read about later, also comes in many shapes and sizes, but as soon as it comes your way, your blood pressure goes up along with your stress level.
- Change—Doesn't matter whether it is welcome or not, it still comes with a stress attachment.
- Pressure—I am sure we all can relate to this. Sometimes it is self-imposed, other times it is the real world telling you that you need to do this and that by such and such time along with these multiple other things.

Adolescence is all about change, conflict, frustration, and pressure. It's no wonder they are stressed.

But so too did you have to deal with change, conflict, frustration, and pressure when you were a teenager. And like your child you still need to deal with social pressures, trends, desires, and your evolving sexuality. Not to mention money, health, and your teenager.

I know there are readers whose children may have no desire to go to college and certainly the road to a fulfilling life does not rely solely on college. But where I work almost everybody is taking that path. I don't think it is the best path for everyone, it is just that where I work most everyone has college in their sights.

Even if you and your child are not thinking about college, there is this looming reality that all children face. At the end of their childhood comes the responsibility of taking care of themselves. College is often a good way to postpone that reality. Although it does come with costs.

No matter how lousy a job of parenting your child thinks you are doing there is a contribution you are making to her life circumstances that one day she is going to have to carry herself. Your child knows that not that far down the road the expectation is she will be taking financial care of herself. She also knows, perhaps from first-hand experience, that financial issues cause a lot of stress. And she knows she does not know how good a job she is going to do at providing for herself. Most teenagers try not to think about that too much and focus on the moment. But it still lurks somewhere in the background.

Teenagers know that even if you go to the best colleges it does not guarantee a good life, but they believe it increases the odds. So do their parents. Which puts added pressure on everybody.

Most people know that college graduates make more money than non-college graduates. Most people believe that the more money you make the happier you can be. People know money doesn't buy happiness. They also know they wouldn't mind having more money.

Most parents want their children to go to college. Many kids do as well. Many kids also just want to go do their thing and trust that it will all work out. Sooner or later they will all test the "real world" waters, but college keeps them out of the deep end for awhile. Although, more and more students now have to work to help pay their way through school, and even then they come out in debt. But that is another horrible stress story that is best addressed elsewhere. For now, we will stick with the fact that whether you go to college or not, the pendulum is shifting toward becoming financially independent.

At the same time she is stressed about college and life in general, she is also counting the days until she moves out. Maybe he doesn't have a calendar on the wall to mark off each passing day, but she does have a calendar in her mind. So do you.

Moving out may be a long-desired emancipation, but it still comes with the stress of the unknown. Moving itself is on everyone's Top 5 Stressors List (rounding out the list is death, divorce, major illness, and job loss). You child may be mostly excited about leaving home or mostly scared or have any number of thoughts and feelings about the subject. Whatever she thinks/feels about the next stage of her life, it too comes with a level of stress. Change is stressful. All those Top 5 stressors are built on change.

Teenagers are usually excited about the future. They tend to be eager to move from childhood to being an emerging adult, scary as it may be. Parents may be excited to witness their child growing up, but a lot also would just as soon time slowed down and their child got to be a child longer. Be it excited or scared, the unknown future carries worry, doubt, and stress.

Whether your child is headed into adolescence with a strong desire to get out of school and into the "real" world or your child is fretting about her GPA and test scores, there is going to be stress. As I read history, adolescence has always been a stressful period for parents and children. Some families gracefully glide through those years, others have a bumpy ride. Most families have periods of both.

When something stressful happens to one family member it can often become a shared experience. There is the tension/worry/drama surrounding the incident that evoked the stress. There can be the added tension/worry/drama that arises from how you handle the stressor. And then there is how your behavior and everyone else's rubs one another. While you often cannot control the catalyst that prompts a stressful reaction, you can manage the way your family addresses the situation.

Here is a pop quiz:

On a scale of 1-100, with 100 being the most stressed you have ever felt, where are you in this moment? ____

How do you think/feel about that?

_____

_____

_____

What are you doing to assist you in responding to that stress? What strategies/skills/techniques are you consciously employing to help you keep that stress at a manageable level?

_____

_____

_____

Are there things you are doing now that on some level you know are flaming the stress?

_____

_____

_____

What do you do when your stress level increases? How do you ultimately find relief? Any thoughts about that?

_____

_____

_____

Since I work at a school where the students and their parents tend to be very interested in grades, let me ask you, what grade would you give yourself on how well you manage stress? _____

Whatever score you gave yourself, if you are like most parents of teens you wouldn't mind improving your GPA. Unfortunately, I am only going to remind you of what you already know. I have no magic to do here.

But I do want to remind you of the simple things you can do every day to reduce stress that take anywhere from one minute to however long you want. It is hard to use the excuse of "I didn't have enough time" when some of the techniques you can utilize can take only a minute. Of course, you might get more out of it if you give a bit more time than that.

What I like about some of these techniques is they don't have to take long and you can pretty much do them anywhere and with anybody and never have anyone know you are doing anything special at all. Sure, you can grab a yoga mat and spend an hour helping lift the stress out of your body or you could run or bike or do any number of physical/spiritual/intellectual activities that can involve you to such a degree that your attention to the stressor(s) is reduced and you feel relief. Those are all on the A list of stress-reducing activities.

Devoting conscious time to directly doing something that will help alleviate stress is almost always a good thing for your mind, body, and soul. Stress does not always wait until you have time to go the gym. Sometimes it sneaks up on you, grabs your attention, and affects you to such a degree that your usual level of functioning is difficult to maintain. In those moments it is good to have something at your disposal to help calm you down.

I remember a scene in a movie where a couple was testing out a mattress in a department store and one of them had an anxiety attack. They yelled out, "Does anyone have a valium?" and a hoard of people came running forth. While certainly seeing your doctor and asking if they thought it would be a good idea for you to have some medication to help you with your anxiety is an option, that isn't exactly the direction I was going. I want to suggest that it is good to have something readily available to help you lessen the stress you are experiencing. Medication is an option and one you can speak to your doctor about.

Marsha Marcoe, a licensed Marriage, Family, and Child therapist, focuses much of her work on helping people cope with their own anxiety. There are numerous strategies that she has her clients employ as what works for one does not always work for the other. Anxiety can undermine your enjoyment of life, and finding workable measures to reduce it will serve you and those close to you.

What I am going to suggest are simple things, most of which you hopefully know already. They are simple, but they help. Not a lot, but a little. Sometimes a little is enough. Especially if you add this little to that little and get more than a little. The goal is to take whatever spike your stress level is feeling and get it back to a more workable range. If you usually are feeling about a 30 on the stress scale and you spike up to 80, you want to find a way to get back down closer to that base level.

Whether you are alone or with other people you can use this technique:

Breathe.

Deeply.

Slowly.

Hold it a moment.

Let it go.

Hold it a moment.

Breathe.

Repeat.

Do it until your mind takes you elsewhere.

One minute of that breathing exercise is not going to get you down from an 80 to a 30. Three minutes might get you closer. But the goal isn't to get to 30 right away; the goal is to steadily and gradually get back to holding your usual level of stress. If you can breathe deeply and slowly and get that 80 to a 60, that alone will make you feel better. Then you can work on getting that 60 down to 40 and so on.

When your stress level shoots up there is a fear of loss of control. Certainly you don't want to be more stressed, but more stressed is what you are becoming. You need to stem that tide. Doing a simple breathing meditation ought to take the edge off your stress and help you move to calmer regions.

Of course if the stressful situation is unresolved you are going to continue to have a higher level of stress. That is unavoidable. What hopefully you can avoid is having that stress build upon itself till it becomes very uncomfortable and perhaps debilitating. Focusing on your breathing and refreshing your system is something you can control. In those times when you feel like you are losing control, it is helpful to have some anchors and activities that you can do that will help you feel more in control.

There are all kinds of breathing meditations you can learn. The one I offered is a more basic self-guided model. If stress is an ongoing issue in your life, my best understanding of the research on meditation is that pretty much everyone who practices frequent meditation reports positive results. Once again, don't look at any one thing as the cure-all. Think of doing something that will take the edge off of your anxiety and help you go forward in a more managed way.

Before you think that must mean hours of meditation a day in the company of monks, there is one other thing I understand from the research on meditation. While you could join the monks and reap the benefits, you can also practice mediation alone in the comforting knowledge that no one meditates all that well. Not even the monks. Meditation could just as easily be called Meditation & Distraction.

Which is part of its gift to you.

I have a class of seniors in a class simply titled 'Psychology'. We mostly talk about life and life skills.

We read and talk about stress and its causes as well as how to deal with it. We also do some different kinds of meditations. They like the short ones. Although they wouldn't mind a long lay on the floor with eyes closed. I have learned not to do that one so much anymore as the snoring added to the distractions.

We do a twenty-minute guided meditation where I ask them to sit up straight and close their eyes. I start them breathing slowly and ask them to follow their breath as it comes in and out. Every few minutes I remind them to attend to the breath going in and the breath going out. After twenty minutes I tell them to open their eyes when they are ready and come back into the room.

They all have a different story to tell. Some were thinking about this or that and then something else. Some zoomed in on the breathing and then went off to parts known and unknown. Others dozed off. Most find they can attend to the in and out of their breath for a brief time and then their minds go racing, only to be brought back by either my prompts or a jolt of awareness that reminds them they are supposed to focus on their breathing alone.

Some think they are not doing it right. They ought to be able to still their minds and be at rest. I tell them that would be nice. Some people can even do that for longer times. But once you discover consciously thinking about something, your mind tends to enjoy the activity and wants to be talking in your ear a good part of the day. It is not easy to get your thoughts to quiet down and go to their room.

I tell my students there is not really a right or wrong way to mediate. While the goals of Buddhist meditation are lofty, they also encompass the best of the human spirit and qualities worthy of our attention. Buddhists, along with some pretty valid research, believe stilling your mind and allowing yourself to just be is a path to enlightenment and nirvana which are considered to include mindfulness, concentration, supra-mundane powers, tranquility, and insight.

Just thinking that a little breathing could get you some of those things might be a good enough motivator to give it a try now and then. Being more mindful, concentrated, tranquil, and insightful along with the possible enhancement of your own superhero qualities, are not really subject to judgment. As you go through life you continue to learn how best to hold on to those higher human values. You don't really do them in a right or wrong way, good or bad. You do them as best you can.

And, if a little concentrated breathing can help, why not?

Sanjay Gupta, CNN's chief medical correspondent and a highly respected physician, tries to meditate by focusing on one word. He uses a word that I think we could sit quietly and reflect upon. Gentle.

Sometimes I am in a meeting or talking with someone or just out in public somewhere when I do some gentle deep breathing. Not so much because I am stressed, although that can happen too, but I deep breathe just to remind myself to relax and take in the moment. Other people don't know the difference between my regular breathing and my deep breathing. I also often flex my muscles. I usually opt for my legs, my butt, and whatever else I think I can do without them noticing.

When I am with close friends I don't mind if they know I am flexing and deep breathing to relax myself. They might even offer their help or encourage me to talk about it which for me usually leads to tension reduction. (Yes, most of my friends are therapists and/or teachers.) Although to be truthful, the talking it out path often starts with more awareness of my anxiety which tends to bump up the anxiety. Then when I talk more about it I find that sharing what is bothering me usually lightens the load.

Other times I prefer to be more discrete. Often I just don't want to get into it. There is a time and place for everything. Usually more than one more time and place. There are times to open up and times to shut it down; just do your best to manage the stress and get home and to bed.

I often opt for keeping my stress to myself when I am at work. Some days I will share with colleagues; other days I walk around and say "Fine" when asked how I'm doing. As a school counselor a good part of my job is to help de-stress others. While it can help them to know that they aren't the only one stressed, they usually prefer that I listen to what's going on with them. So I mostly listen and breathe and flex and try to concentrate on what they are telling me.

If you want to do something more proactive to reduce the stress you need to break it down in pieces. It is a divide-and-conquer thing.

If you are feeling that your stress is "more than I want to handle" and you are getting close to "too much" you need to move out of the reaction mode and into the action mode.

I would break it down like this:

- What is the main thing I am stressed about?
- What has to happen so I won't be so stressed?
- What can I realistically do about that *now*?
- What are the next steps I need to take to resolve this?

If you were in my office I would also ask you, "What is getting in the way of you doing those things now?" Then we would talk about what you think might be holding you back and what you think/feel about that. Then we would talk about what you want to do. Hopefully talking about these things would help clear the way for you to have a greater degree of motivation and conviction. If that didn't help clear the way to you taking some actions, I would venture that this might not be the moment for action and the time might best be spent in meditation and reflection. I would also urge you to keep focusing on what is getting in the way of that clarity and motivation and what can you do about it.

When we had exhausted that, I would add one more thing. I would then say, "Whatever you do, let's talk about it soon and see how things are going. Whether you have done nothing or many things I want to keep in contact and help you get to the other side of this." Sometimes the challenges that life presents are not easily handled. There can be layers and layers of issues that keep assaulting you. Some you can dodge, some you can fend off easily, and some are a big pain in the ass that you need to deal with your entire life. Whatever the challenges that come your way, it helps to have something in your pocket to help you out. Even if you only reduce your stress 1% that is a step in a healthier direction.

Let's add it up.

There is your own stress about what is happening in your life.

There is your child's stress with what is happening in her life and your stress about her stress.

There is your stress with what is happening in her life that you don't know about.

There is her added stress dealing with your stress.

There is your added stress dealing with her stressing behavior with you.

And the beat goes on.

I hear this all the time from students: "My parents are stressing me out." They tell me how their parents are overreacting to what is going on with them. I have had students tell me something painful that happened in their life that they were mostly managing only to have their parents find out and now the child has to handle his parents' emotional reaction too. Her stressful issue is now compounded. Too often I hear it became more about her parent's reaction than it was about her.

Some students tell me about the pressure they feel from their parents and how their parents are micromanaging them. Other students tell me their parents aren't putting as much pressure on them as they put on themselves.

I hear from parents: "My child is not doing what I tell her or want her to do." I ask how they tell their child what they want. They often say they started very politely and nicely to inquire about what their child was doing at school or in her social life, then they started to nag, argue, take privileges away and do whatever they could to get their child to behave in the way they wanted When that isn't getting the job done they call me.

I am sort of like a plumber that way. I don't get a lot of calls when things are flowing smoothly. When things get backed up or clogged, the phone rings.

Usually what I need to do is help parents back off. Their nervousness has gotten so that their household has become infected with a worry illness which manifests itself in chilly relationships. Things don't feel so good between people. They've lost that loving feeling.

I work with parents and students to bring it back. I aim to get the parents and the child more aligned. I think the role of parents evolves and by the time your child is in their mid-teens you have moved over to the passenger seat. Certainly, legally you are the driver, but by the time your child is getting his driver's license you ought to sharing the driving duties. Soon they will be on their own and driving alone. You need to help her get there safely. You can't do that if you don't let her drive before she leaves your home.

Michael Riera, PhD wrote *Uncommon Sense for Parents with Teenagers* and speaks about how a parent needs to move from being a manager in their child's life to a consultant. Often that shift in role is harder for the parent than the child. It is hard to let go of control and decision-making. Learning to trust your child to make those decisions is a state of mind many parents never fully achieve. Being more on the sidelines as they make their life mistakes is stressful.

Parents want to help their child manage their stress as they take on more responsibility. Parents don't want to inflict their child with their own worries, but just like when someone has a cold and one-by-one everyone else gets it, so too does stress spread from one to the other. As much as a parent might say that they don't want their child to be stressed about their stress, they also tend not to mind too much if that added stress yields some positive results. When it doesn't help, they would like everyone to take a moment.

The better a job you can do of helping your child with their stress the less stressed you will be. Channeling your stress into action steps you can take with your child ought to help reduce your stress as well as theirs. You can ask them what you can do to help reduce their stress. When they tell you to back off, try to do that. See if their remedy is any better than yours.

When your child is stressed and she asks you for help, "How can I help you?" is a really solid way to reply. Right after, respond with, "Ugh. I am sorry you are so stressed. I hate it when I am. How can I help you? What's going on?" Once you hear what she said and have commiserated, you will want to know what you could do to help her. Try to do that.

Often children don't know what would help them, to which I tell you that talking to you is helping her. Just because she might say you are not helping her, doesn't fully mean you aren't being useful. She can vent some steam at you and even though it is disappointing that you couldn't make things better, you at least tried which lets her know you care. Sure, you hope you can come up with the cure-all solution, but you can't always solve every problem and take away her pain. But she learned that long ago when she got her first cold and you couldn't make it all better then, either. But she knows you did what you could and just having you there was comforting. Still is.

Just don't go and blame her, shame her, or otherwise stray from being a loving, supportive parent. Save the "you should have" or "you should" for another time. When your child opens up a wound to you, you need to heal it first.

When I finished my first draft of this book and started to edit, I wanted to look over the book and see how often I had spoken about college. I went to *find* and typed in the word "college" and went looking for where I had used the word. I quickly discovered I had used "college" a lot. A whole lot. Then it dawned on me that I am writing a lot about college because students are thinking about it way more than they would like and thinking about it is causing way more stress than it ever did for their parents.

I was talking this morning with a teacher and asked him how often he had conversations about college when he was in high school. He thought for some time and came back with, "Hardly ever." Times have changed. I don't have to tell you that. I also don't need to tell you that talking about anything related to college can be a walk on an ice field.

There is stress for everyone around the college application process that we will go into in greater detail in subsequent chapters, but for right now let me say that for most students, the whole subject can easily get overwhelming and quickly inflammatory. When you throw in all their relatives asking them about what they are doing and where they are going, your friends and their friends asking, and the fact that they have never done this before, it all adds up to boatloads of stress. "Proceed with caution" is written all over the word "college" and all its associates until the day they get into a school of their choice.

You have or will probably hear versions of "Go away," "Leave me alone," and "Can we please talk about something else?" While I don't think you have to have 100% adherence to those requests, I would aim for coming close to that. When she says, "Enough," I think you are best served by stepping away.

For how long? We can talk about later.

A big part of the college process has your child going through a maze of activity where she often feels powerless. Yes, she can study, work on her grades, her essay, and all those things. But she can't control whether a school says yes or no. All the steps which add up to that decision can easily engulf her and make her want to go hide or vent that frustration at someone she feels safe with and knows loves her.

We all need to get under the covers now and then. Let her go there when she needs. It gives her a sense of control and power in her out-of-control world. Her hiding out and avoidance will seem too much to you and barely sufficient for her.

Even though you may not trust that your child will come out and take care of business, the heavy odds are on her. And if she doesn't come out soon enough for you, call your school counselor or therapist.

Sometimes we all need to take a timeout from stress and the tried-and-true escape for many is going to sleep. It isn't always peaceful, but often it is a more restful place.

We all know the research that says teenagers need more sleep than they get. There is not a lot a parent can do as social media seems to spring to life as the evening wears on. Yet, I would be remiss if I did not encourage you to encourage your child to get at least 8 if not 9 hours of sleep each night. You can also consider a blackout of electronics a couple of hours before she ought to be asleep. Recent research would suggest that 30 minutes would be enough to allow her to sufficiently unwind so that she can get a good night's sleep.

Even if you could pull that off, she won't get 8-9 hours of sleep every night. Teenagers really don't need a full night's sleep all the time to function at a high level, but the deprivation does take a toll over time. Most teenagers, as most adults, would be better served (and less stressed it turns out) if they had a better night's sleep.

Throw in a nap and you are actively reducing stress while basically doing nothing.

Hard to beat that.

31

KEEP IT IN PERSPECTIVE

I got the title of this chapter from Daniel H. Pink, the best-selling author of *Drive: The Surprising Truth About What Motivates Us.* I attended a speech he gave at a Challenge Success conference where he was speaking about our overscheduled, highly-stressed adolescents. The Challenge Success program is a research-based organization out of Stanford that develops curriculum, conferences, and other programs for parents, schools, and kids looking for a healthier and more effective path to success in the 21st century. You might want to look them up (http://www.challengesuccess.org).

Basically Daniel Pink says that parents need to keep things in perspective. Parents tend to get overly involved in their children's lives and log in too many hours reading books on parenting, questioning their parenting, and anguishing over their parenting. Those weren't his exact words, but you get the drift. He would like you to take a break from books on parenting and trust that you know enough to parent well. I echo his advice and suggest you consider it right after you finish this book.

If you have had a conflict with your child, chances are he will be over it long before you. You will replay it, rethink it and want to reboot it. He will sulk for a little bit and then get on with his life.

Madeline Levine, PhD, another best-selling author at the conference, wrote *Teach Your Children Well: Why Values and Coping Skills Matter More Than Grades, Trophies or "Fat Envelopes".* You may have heard of her as she wrote the most responded-to editorial in *The New York Times* about raising successful children. Levine thinks parents do their children a disservice when they don't allow them to learn more on their own. She spoke about 3 interventions parents make:

1. Doing What They Can—This happens when a child is basically doing something well and the parent hovers over the few mistakes he makes. More often than not if they backed off he would learn on his own and end up feeling better about himself.

2. Doing What They Can Almost Do—This time the parent doesn't support their child being average in the activity. Heck, Madeline Levine said we are all average at most things. Let your child excel where he wants to and be average or below average elsewhere. We all do some things well and some things okay and some things not so well at all.

3. Confusing Parent Needs With Kids Needs—This is what happens when you wanted to do something in your life or something happened to you that now you are going to try to resolve with your child. If you didn't make the most out of high school don't push your child to make up for your losses. Let him have his own life. Not yours and his.

I work at a school where there are a lot of stressed parents and children. The Challenge Success program is trying to work with educators, parents, and students to make school more engaging and less stressful for all. It is an uphill issue filled with small wins and steep cliffs.

Parents want their child to sleep more, be more engaged, and enjoy school. They want the best for their child but best means many things to many people. Where I work it usually includes getting a high GPA, high test scores, a well-rounded resume, and getting into a good college. That is the common perspective. Even though pretty much everyone will also say life is not all about what college you attend, it is challenging to embrace a wider perspective when it comes to junior and senior year. Although, to be truthful, many parents just want their kids to enjoy themselves and do well. And for many children that is the path they mostly take.

In an ideal world grades wouldn't matter so much and college wouldn't matter so much. In fact, that ideal world exists for most people. Once your child is out of college it becomes much easier to embrace a wider perspective and support your child pursuing his own dreams. (At least for a few years, but that is another book.)

I had a student in my office yesterday tell me how hard it was for him to motivate himself to study for classes he thought were useless. I am sure most of us can relate to that in some way and we have all had to find a way to deal with those aspects of our life that feel useless, a waste of time, boring, and annoying. He told me was fully aware that he was being self-destructive but he just could not push himself to do more than the absolute bare minimum and sometimes not that.

I knew he had an interest in business so I asked him who his favorite business person was. He quickly replied, "Larry Page. CEO of Google." So, I asked him if he thought that in any part of Larry Page's day he had to do things he didn't like and thought were useless, bothersome, and just not what he wanted to be doing. He conceded that might still be possible and he did know we all have to find ways to deal with things we would rather not deal with. I asked him what Larry Page would tell him and he said, "Suck it up." He looked at me. I looked at him. We nodded in agreement.

Students, like their parents, need to learn how to navigate their way through life. You need to know how to make the best of what you have. You need to learn how to excel in your areas of interest. You need to learn how to take care of yourself and those you love. And you need to learn how to do what is asked of you in a satisfactory enough way so that you can move on. You need to learn how to suck it up.

I often get students in my office who are not doing well in a class and blame the teacher. We all know that certain teachers are very skilled and others less so. I am sure there are teachers who make life unnecessarily hard for their students. Just like there are bosses and managers that do that for their employees. Yes, we all ultimately have to find our way around the obstacles we encounter, but that doesn't mean the obstacles don't share the blame for making things so difficult. It is just that it doesn't matter how thwarting the teacher/boss may be, you still need to find a way to handle matters. Because it is your life we are talking about.

I tell these students there is something I really don't like. I tell them it is bad enough when someone I like does something that hurts me, but it is so much worse when someone I don't like, don't respect, and don't care for hurts me. I don't want to give those people the power to harm me. I urge these students not to let this teacher that they don't like cause them to suffer. When the time comes to add up their GPA and they see that lousy grade they got from that lousy teacher they are going to be extremely upset. Especially when they think maybe that grade caused them to not to get into the college of their choice. Don't give the person you don't respect that power, is what I tell them.

Don't let this person who is looming large in the moment play an even greater role in your future. Keep this grade and this class in perspective. Get through it with minimum damage. Suck it up.

Take care of the things that don't really interest you but need to be done to complete school so that you can focus on the things that really interest you. Do the things you like doing. The research says if we did more of what we liked we would probably feel and be more successful and happier. Do more of what you like and then take the time to adequately handle the things you don't like.

Build on strength. That was the concept Madeline Levine was extolling. Let your child be average in some places and help him engage in the areas where his strengths and interests lay.

Students in high school have decisions to make about how much effort to put into doing well. Parents have to decide how much effort to put in to having their child do well. How much do you push? How much do you stay back? When do you get a tutor, a therapist, or a vacation? The more effort your child puts in the greater the likelihood he will enjoy the rewards of his effort. The more effort you put into managing his life the less chance he has to learn those skills.

Go talk with other people who you think are successful in their lives both personally and professionally and ask them how they got to where they are today. Chances are they will tell you it was not a straight ascent, but one full of ups and downs and a few arounds. That might be true as well for you.

While none of us like to see our children hurting, we all want them to be successful. Knowing the path to success is usually not the straight and narrow one may help you allow your child to find his own path and him to believe in the value of his own mistakes and retakes.

Let me leave this chapter with this quote from Madeline Levine which I think sums it all up: "While we all hope our children will do well in school, we hope with even greater fervor that they will do well in life. Our job is to help them know and appreciate themselves deeply, to be resilient in the face of adversity, to approach the world with zest, to find work that is satisfying, friends and spouses who are living and loyal, and to hold a deep belief that they have something meaningful to contribute to the world."

32

THE PRIMARY TASK OF PARENTING

This could easily be a one-sentence chapter, but if you have not learned by now, I take my time getting to the point. So, let me mix things up and get to the point early. The main task of parenting is to raise your children so they can leave your home and be responsible, caring adults who can build their own meaningful lives.

The job of a parent is much like that of a consultant. The goal is to be unneeded. Not because you did a poor job, but because you have set things in place so she can thrive without you.

The question becomes, "How do I take this totally dependent infant and help make her become this totally independent adult who still calls me now and then and wants to visit on holidays?"

Most parents aim to accomplish the goal of independence some time after high school or college graduation, but don't really have a set structure to get there. They figure nature will take its course and sooner or later their child will become self-sustaining and hopefully responsible enough to make a decent life for herself.

I don't think it much matters when this occurs, just that it occurs. Ideally it overlaps with the time you want her to be generating enough income to financially support herself and your financial resources have not been overly drained.. With the ebbs and flows of the economy, many families find themselves living together beyond the time they had initially thought. Even those children that move out and have jobs often have to rely on some financial aid from their parents before they can fully make it on their own. It is not easy to support yourself financially, as we have all come to know. For most people it takes a good deal of effort and we still live paycheck to paycheck.

If your grown child needs to continue to live with you or have a degree of financial support after you had thought she would be moving out and supporting herself, it can create a whole new set of challenges for you.

That money you hoped would be spent on you and your future plans now needs to go to her and her present circumstances. Or not. Legally you don't have to help her out after she is 18, but legal and moral obligations are not always the same.

Given that room and board and financial obligation are no longer legal, the level of support you provide is now a different kind of choice. Many parents feel a moral responsibility to help out their children until they are on firmer footing. Of course, feeling that responsibility and being able to afford it are two different things. Since money is the primary conflict area in people's lives, you can anticipate a range of feelings about how you continue to financially support your child.

I was taught in graduate school that for people to be fully independent they need to be emotionally, financially, and physically independent. If emotional, financial, and physical independence is the working definition of what it means to be independent, you can tell a lot of people have not fully gotten there.

How well do you think you meet the three criteria? If you had to rate yourself on a scale of 1-100, with 1 being 'not at all' and 100 being 'completely', what numbers would you give yourself?

Are you emotionally independent? Are you able to make decisions for yourself while weighing the voices of others, but not being overly influenced by them? _____

Are you financially independent? Are you able to generate enough income to provide for yourself? Your family? Your retirement? Your old age? Your child? _____

Are you physically independent? Are you able to take care of yourself? Are you healthy enough in body, mind, and soul that you can feed, dress, and make your way through life? _____

When you look at those numbers you either feel pretty good about yourself or not. It depends on what you consider a healthy number.

When you look at your child and rate her you either feel pretty good about her independence or not. You might feel good about her physical and emotional independence and less so about her financial independence. After all, for most teenagers their peak earning years are still in front of them.

However you score your child it would be nice if you could help boost her score. And while you are at it, you might want to work on yours as well.

If part of the task of parenting is to teach your child how to be independent, having her living at home after you had hoped she would leave can wreak havoc with your own sense of being a "good parent". Parents often see their child's "successes" as a reflection of their parenting skills. They also see their child's "failures" as a reflection of their parenting skills. No one likes to be reminded of their failures. Jackson Browne sums it up nicely: "Don't confront me with my failures, I have not forgotten them."

Unfortunately, when your adult child is living at home at a time you and she both thought she would be living elsewhere, you both are confronted with your own failures. Failure is a harsh word to apply here. I only use it because I heard it once from a parent and I thought it echoed a common worry. Most people hopefully would not view their child returning home as a failure as we all know life has its ups and downs. Sometimes we all need some shelter from the storm. Yet parents so often align their evaluation of their parenting with the behavior of their child. The child gets an A, they are a good parent. The child comes home after their schooling and is unemployed or underemployed and you find yourself not looking forward to people asking you how your child is doing.

Parents are usually grateful that they can take their child in and help him out. Most don't want the circumstance to last that long. Some wish it were shorter and some would be happy to have it last longer. Most parents enjoy having their grown children living with them even if it means at some level they are not as independent as they ultimately will need to be. Gaining independence takes time and often when children set out to make their way in the world they need various levels of support from their parents. Some give it and some don't. Some give more and some give less. Some would argue giving less is giving more. These are personal value decisions that can cause a lot of conflict while creating a rationale for actions.

There are families that hold the value that their children ought to live with their parents until such a time as they marry. Certainly that is a valid point of view, and if it is yours, then having your child return home after college or stay with you during college is as you would want it to be. My only concern here is that your child shares this value. If they do, fine. If not, I would recommend asking for some assistance outside your family.

We all know the story of the college graduate who comes home after graduation and instead of being there for a brief transitional period ends up staying for years. There are also those children who didn't go to college and went to work and have not been able to earn enough to be able to live outside their parents' home. There are any number of reasons that grown children return to their family home.

No matter how old the child is it is hard for parents not to parent. We all have heard if not uttered the phrase, "As long as you are living in my house…"

Just because your child is now an adult doesn't stop you from having house rules and personal opinions. It just can make some of the rules and opinions less welcome. What prompts that "as long as you live in my house" lecture is usually the adult child has not followed the younger child's rules of the house that were in play while she was previously living at home. Once a child lives out of the home for some time it is very challenging for her to abide by the restrictions that were in place before she left. It is hard to put a curfew on a 21-year-old, but it still can get under your skin when she comes home at 4am.

When children leave home and are away from the watchful eye of their parents they often use recreational drugs, drink more, and stay out and up later. Without their parents there to monitor their behavior they are free to set their own guidelines. However, once they are back in their parents' home there can often be clashes just as if they never left. Not too many parents like to see their child taking hits on the bong in the middle of the afternoon while watching reruns.

What might have worked fine at college or at a friend's apartment doesn't always play so well at home.

Adjustments on both sides need to be made. On the one hand your parenting job was to help her be independent and she certainly is demonstrating that on one level. Yet watching your child relaxing when you want her to be job hunting can test your tolerance. Just like in high school when you weren't exactly sure how/when she did her homework, you may not be seeing her job-hunting skills on display. She may be relaxing in the midday because she was networking at night and connecting with people in her way may very well get her employed. You never know. Most jobs are found through referrals. You just know it is hard to walk into the living room and see her getting high or drinking or behaving in any way that doesn't fit within your comfort zone.

So parents enforce the fundamental rule—when you are in my home you follow my house rules. Of course, that also implies that the home isn't their child's home, or if it is, it is one where they still don't have voting privileges.

I have a twist on this dynamic that you might find interesting. A friend of mine had his parents visiting his house and he told his parents that in his house certain rules applied. One of his parents was a smoker, but in my friend's house his parent was not allowed to smoke. If you believe that the primary dweller of the house establishes the house rules then it is only fair that this apply both ways. Fair, but not easy to enforce.

It's just not always easy to determine whose house it is and how much each vote counts.

I think most people would agree that if it is your home you can set the rules. If you visit a friend's house and they request that you take off your shoes, you take off your shoes. You may not do that at your house, but if that's the way they do it at their house most people follow along.

If someone—be it a friend, child, or parent—does not want to abide by the rules, they can choose not to stay. I think in general terms that is fair and most people play by those rules of conduct.

It is when you get to specifics that it can get dicey. Especially when you are dealing with your own grown children.

If your grown child does recreational drugs and you do not, you can stand by the rules of your home that there will be no use of drugs in your home. Or you can say, "You can do what you want in your room, but I would prefer if you did it elsewhere, or even better, not at all. And remember, no driving under the influence."

If your child wants to stay out till the early hours and your last curfew was 2am, you may try to hold the line or just let her do her thing. Or maybe you both can consider some concessions.

Which brings us to the fine art of compromise.

Parenting a teenager carries with it the task of modeling adult behavior. Yes, your child is not quite an adult, but they are starting to flex those muscles and they are looking at how you handle yourself much more closely than they used to. When you have disagreements and conflicts, the way you manage your end will be a model for her about how to handle hers. Of course, to your joy or dismay, she won't totally follow in your footsteps now. She is still a teenager and needs to find her own voice.

Unless somebody horribly screwed up and you want them to feel miserable for a while, most people would prefer that the members of their family felt good. If you hold that value, then when it comes time to work out a compromise you will want to arrive at a place where everyone feels good enough.

"Good enough" is a term many therapists use. I like it because we can't always feel good about what is happening but we can feel good enough. It isn't first class travel, but it isn't steerage either. When it comes to compromise the general consensus is all parties have to give some to get some. If you are willing to give up some of what you want then "good enough" may very well be the best you can hope for.

Some people hold the idea that compromise means they give up as little as possible and get the other person to give up as much as possible. That might work in the business world, but it is not solid groundwork for loving relationships, and I am not that sure it is good for business either.

Often you can just ask yourself, "What do I really want here? What is a good enough solution for me so I can move towards resolving this thing in the best way possible for all?"

Let's use the example of having your grown child staying in your home after college and how you work out his comings and goings. I recommend you set up a time to talk about the issue and each person begins with a statement of what they want. Since there is a bit of car sales in compromise, not everyone has to start with their "good enough" solution. Begin with what you really want, and be open to discovering a good enough solution if what you ideally want is not agreed upon.

Before any comments and editorials are made it is best if each person states what they heard the other person wanted. Just utter this statement: "You said you would like total freedom to come and go as you see fit. Is that right?"

She will either confirm that or modify it.

Before you get into any back-and-forthing you need to agree that everyone understands each other's positions.

Once there is agreed upon understanding, it helps to offer some understanding of why your child would want what he wants. For instance: "I can understand that coming back from college where you had total freedom to come and go as you wish, it would be undesirable to have to be constrained by your parents' rule book."

Avoid adding a "but" to this point. Just convey understanding.

Do not denigrate her position. Do not name-call. Don't even try to poke holes in it.

Do say something akin to: "So what you want is total freedom to come and go and I want you home at 2am. How can we come to a good enough solution? Any ideas?"

I like putting this question on the floor rather than you answering it. You are empowering her to come up with a resolution. You may not agree to it, but the fact that you earnestly ask her to help find a solution will not go unnoticed.

When you ask your child to solve an impasse you are hoping that she can offer something that you can readily agree to. That can happen. In which case, you can say yes and stop at that. Or maybe she will stand her ground. Children usually do for awhile. They don't like to easily give up. Which in the long run may be a good thing, but sometimes it is annoying to have to continually face.

Coming to a compromise is similar to wheeling and dealing with a car dealer. You know you are not going to pay the sticker price and they know you are not going to pay the sticker price. But how much off you are going to get depends on your bargaining skills. You don't want your heavy-handedness in your negotiations to cause the other person to want to fight you more. Car dealers may want to laugh behind your back about how much more you could have gotten from them, but to your face they want to make sure you feel good about the deal.

The same goes for you. You want your child to feel good, or good enough, about the compromise. Asking, "How can we find a win-win solution?" puts the other person in the position of needing to solve the impasses in the most positive way for both parties.

Sometimes the good enough solution is doing it your way. Modeling taking a stand and holding your ground is important; just as you want to teach your children to compromise, you want to teach her leadership and how to flex her power. I would just caution you not to have that be the only resolution. More and more as your children age the balance of power shifts.

No parent fully knows when to hold the line and when to give some. It is an intuitive decision that evolves. As a parent you want to honor your child's ability to make sound decisions and to forge creative, mutually-acceptable solutions. To help build your child's skills, you need to give her opportunities to learn.

By the time your child nears the end of her high school career, she is most likely less than a year away from living away from home. She needs to be exercising her independence—with you there to back her up when needed.

33

HOW TO TACKLE FEAR

I could make this simple and fast and just say, "Face it and deal with it."

We all know that to get through fear at some point we have to take a chance. We either stick our necks out or we don't.

It is as simple and fast as that. Eventually you know you are going to have to do something and whatever you do it will be chancy. Even if you do nothing and choose to avoid engaging the thing that is making you afraid you are going to have unknown consequences. Perhaps safer ones in the moment, but you don't know the full price you will have to pay until later.

You can do your best to minimize your losses and maximize your gains, but in the end whatever you do is a move towards the unknown. Which means, you never know. Which is why you are afraid. The unknown, as exciting as it can be, is also our greatest source of fear.

For most parents, as soon as you know your child is alive in the womb you start to worry. Many parents start worrying while they are trying to get pregnant. It is hard to keep things in perspective when you have a child as your emotions awaken and expand in previously unknown ways. You worry about getting pregnant, you worry about being pregnant, you worry about the health of the embryo, you worry about the birth, the cough, the grades, the friends, the school, the drugs, the job, the spouse, the grandchildren, the whole process.

Needless to say some worry more and some worry less. However much you are inclined to be a worrier, you don't get through parenthood without bouts of worry. Did I do the right thing? Will he be okay? How do I handle this?

We don't want harm to come to our children—harm from others or harm from himself.

As your child grows he will have to take steps out into the world that require risk. Unless he stays home and never leaves, he is going to be doing new things, going to new places, and facing a lot of unfamiliar and unknown events. If he is holed up in his room, you are going to worry about that. It is always something.

According to research done at Yale in 2012 by Tylula, Belmaker, Roy, Ruderman, Manson, Glimcher and Levy:

Perhaps surprisingly, we found that adolescents were, if anything, more averse to clearly stated risks than their older peers. What distinguished adolescents was their willingness to accept ambiguous conditions... This finding suggests that the higher level of risk-taking observed among adolescents may reflect a higher tolerance for the unknown. Biologically, such a tolerance may make sense, because it would allow young organisms to take better advantage of learning opportunities...

Your child's aversion to stated risks may give you some peace of mind, yet his willingness to pursue more ambiguous conditions may take it away. As people age they become more risk-adverse. I saw a joke in *the New Yorker* where the parents were leaving their child at college and their final words were: "Be afraid to try new things." I am sure many parents can relate to the sentiments that prompted those words of discouragement.

The push within you is between your need for the comfort of knowing your child is okay and his need to explore the world. You want both. Yet it is hard to get both those items on the same page at the same time all the time.

So you worry.

You see something as risky and your child thinks it is no big deal. You want him to be cautious. While he doesn't want to get hurt and will utter some partially reassuring words of caution, you know his definition of caution does not always match as close to yours as you would like.

Intellectually we can grasp that for our species to survive we need the next generation to push past its predecessors. But that doesn't mean they need to speed down the highway or split up from their friends when they are in that haunted house.

Kids do risky things in part because it is exciting and in part because they don't realize the ramifications the way you do. Plus, they have seen you speeding down the highway countless times and if you can do that why can't they? You can rationalize your speeding and tell your child not to follow your example and speed. But once he is alone in the car, goes faster than the speed limit and realizes nothing bad happened, he is inclined to do it again. And again, until perhaps something bad does happen. But hopefully not. But maybe. So you worry.

There is a lot of inherent drama in raising children. I am not using the word 'drama' here in a judgmental way. I use it to underscore that when emotions get provoked situations can get tense. And I don't have to tell you that a good percentage of the drama in your life involves your child.

When drama erupts, outcomes are unknown and fear sets in. Fear of failure, rejection, and humiliation as well as fear of fear keep us in our restraints.

As I said at the beginning of the chapter sooner or later you will need to deal with something that creates fear for you. Trying to break it up into bite-sized pieces will make it easier, but walking through fear is not easy or comfortable. You do what you can to minimize the fear and maximize your chances, and then like Butch Cassidy and the Sundance Kid, you jump off the cliff.

34

SUICIDE

Fear and worry accompany you throughout your child's life. They ebb and flow. You have days with no conscious worries and days when your worries consume your life.

Not a lot of people speak up on behalf of the value of worry. Most people would like to worry less. Many people don't know how to worry less without subscribing to various forms of medication or denial. Once you start worrying, it is akin to winding up a watch. The worrying is going to keep ticking till the mechanism comes to a halt. Finding ways to bring worry to a more comfortable level has kept many a pharmaceutical company happy. It is not easy turning off your worry until something gets satisfactorily resolved. Which doesn't happen all the time.

Let's consider one of parents' biggest worries. This is a big worry because the possible outcome is usually a parent's worst nightmare

I am talking about the pain of having your child kill herself. No parent wants that. Parents tell me that if their child were to kill herself, they would be condemned to live the rest of their life with unbearable pain. They also tell me that they might not want to live anymore themselves.

Hopefully this is a pain you will never have to encounter. But given that you may worry about it there are things you can do to help you and your child reduce the possibility of it happening.

Here are some statistics and ideas to consider. While the research may initially cause you some degree of worry, hopefully we can put that worry to productive use.

According to Boston Children's Hospital website in 2015:

- Suicide is the third leading cause of death in 15-24 year olds in the United States.

- Suicide is the fourth leading cause of death in 10-14 year olds.

- Suicide is contemplated by up to 25% of children and adolescents at some time.

You may not want to know this, but suicide is a viable option for pain reduction for teenagers. Children at the greatest risk are those with depression, substance abuse issues, and/or problems with disruptive or aggressive behavior. That doesn't mean other children are not at risk, just that if your child is dealing with one of those issues you might want to take some extra precautionary actions. I would also add that children who have little impulse control are also candidates to be upset about something and react hastily.

I have either amped up your worry or calmed you down. Either way, the steps to take are mostly the same. If you child meets none of those criteria you can probably turn down the volume on your worry. But keep an eye out for warning signs which will amp you back up.

Helpguide.org, which collaborates with Harvard Health Publications, has this information on their website:

Major warning signs for suicide include talking about killing or harming oneself, talking or writing a lot about death or dying, and seeking out things that could be used in a suicide attempt, such as weapons and drugs. These signals are even more dangerous if the person has a mood disorder such as depression or bipolar disorder, suffers from alcohol dependence, has previously attempted suicide, or has a family history of suicide.

Take any suicidal talk or behavior seriously. It's not just a warning sign that the person is thinking about suicide—it's a cry for help.

A more subtle but equally dangerous warning sign of suicide is hopelessness. Studies have found that hopelessness is a strong predictor of suicide. People who feel hopeless may talk about "unbearable" feelings, predict a bleak future, and state that they have nothing to look forward to.

Other warning signs that point to a suicidal mind frame include dramatic mood swings or sudden personality changes, such as going from outgoing to withdrawn or well-behaved to rebellious. A suicidal person may also lose interest in day-to-day activities, neglect his or her appearance, and show big changes in eating or sleeping habits.

This is a lot of information to take into account. I want to underscore a couple of points. If your child talks about suicide you need to pay attention. I would suggest the first time you hear that word coming out of her mouth you need to accompany her and talk with a therapist. You want an ounce of prevention to provide that pound of cure.

You can ask your family doctor for help or a referral, but this is not really their expertise. Get your child to someone who has experience working with teenagers. While I do consider going to a therapist immediately a possible over-reaction, I do not want you to mishandle the situation and make it worse. Of course, the therapist can do that as well, so make sure you get a good referral from someone you know well and trust and keep a close eye on your child. Later I am going to share with you how I would address the issue before you get to the therapist and general guidelines for talking about suicide. But for now I would say if you hear your child talking about something that sounds like she has suicide in her thoughts you ought to address it in the moment and then call a therapist.

Let your child know by your actions that you are taking her words seriously.

I had a student once tell me that she told her mother she was suicidal and wanted to see a therapist and the mother said she would find one. A month later the mother had yet to find a therapist. The student told me she lost all respect for her mother. While there may be some exaggeration in what that teenager said, you would not want her to get so mad at her mother that she would kill herself to show her how serious she was. Better to just get her some help, especially if she asks for it.

I know some parents are reluctant to reach out for help because they think they will be harshly judged. I can't do much for your own self-judgment, but I can tell you therapists, while not perfect, are both trained to not be judgmental and come to learn it isn't really helpful. If someone is hurting instead of playing the blame game, therapists focus on how you feel, what you think, and what you want to do. Even if a therapist told you they thought you were doing a lousy job, don't let others' condemnation of what you do stop you from getting help. Find another therapist. Whatever judgments you might receive it is probably better to hear them now than hear them later. Of course, one of their judgments might be that you're so concerned for the welfare of your family that you reached out for help even when it wasn't easy to do.

From the interviews collected of people who tried to kill themselves and the notes people leave behind many of them were not 100% positive they wanted to die. They were more sure that they wanted the pain to end and didn't know a better way. Your job is to help your child find another way, a better way, to manage her pain.

Here are some things I tell teenagers who are thinking about suicide:

- It is fine to think about suicide. It is not fine to do it. Many people think about it and only a few do it. Thinking about it means you are searching for ways to get rid of the pain. That is good. Unfortunately, suicide is a long-term solution to a short-term problem.

- People think about suicide because they are in a lot of pain. Something does need to die. The pain needs to die. Let's aim to get rid of the pain and not get rid of the rest.

- It is not okay to kill yourself. Period. If you think there is a real chance you might harm yourself you need to talk to your parents, me, your therapist if you have one, your close friends, and anyone else of importance. Tell us loud and clear and demand we help you.

Sometimes an incident happens that thrusts someone into considering suicide. A loved one dies, a heart is broken, or a rejection occurs. Dr. Steven Roth hypothesized that rejection is often the trigger that catapults you to another level of consciousness. Other times it is a slow burn. Just like bills can pile up so can an emotional slump extend itself. You may wake up with some hope and find by the end of the day that you feel worse than the day before. It gets harder and harder to put yourself out there. The possibility of ending the pain going forward diminishes and the possibility of just ending it all creeps into the chasm.

However it arrives, the thought of ending your life takes on active consideration. People start to think about what it would be like to be dead; how would I do it, could I do it, and what would others say? Thinking about both the pros and cons of taking your life fills your imagination. Instead of thinking about the possibilities of things getting better the pendulum shifts. Now, you have something proactive to think about that can take over your thoughts and allow you not to focus on the issues that prompted your feeling this way.

For many people, those are acceptable thoughts, as long as they don't happen too often and don't really rise to a threatening level. Others have the thoughts come to mind and they quickly push them away. For others, once they have broken the barrier to considering suicide, the amount of time they dwell on it may be more than most parents want to know. Dwelling on suicide allows a person to find some peace as it becomes something they can control in a world that is not working the way they would like.

When a teenager tells you they have been thinking about suicide, it is a cry for help. It may not sound like a cry for help, you may not be sure it is a cry for help, but if your child is talking suicide they are telling you their world is not going well. When they tell you, they are basically asking you to help. If she didn't want your help she wouldn't tell you. So, even though it may not sound like she is wanting you to do something, at minimum you ought to pay more attention and engage her frequently in how her life is going. You can talk with her about what is making her want to kill herself and what you can do to help.

Most times you are not going to come up with any really good answers, but you want to get on the same page with your child. Check in with her, throw out lame ideas, ask her to tell you something she learned in a class, ask her to watch TV with you, anything. She probably won't want to do that much, but she likes being asked. Even if she doesn't act like she does.

The research clearly has found a relationship between suicide and hope. If your child loses hope that things will be better, she figures what is the point? The point for you is to not let her get to that point.

Many people feel suicidal but know at some level they won't attempt it. Yet the option to just let everything go is usually something people think about at least once in their life. It is sort of parallel with thinking about what you would do if you won a 100 million dollar lottery. You know you aren't going to win, but it is fun to think about what you would do if you did win. People can think about how others would feel, what would happen, how would it be if they decided to end their life? Not exactly as much fun as daydreaming about winning the lottery, but many people do it at least once in their life.

Let me be honest. I don't really know how many people think about suicide because a lot of people are not honest about it. I couldn't find any viable research about what percent of the overall population have thought about suicide at one time or another. There is a fair amount of research that says suicide is in the top 10 causes of death and over 30,000 annually die from suicide. But just how many think about it is harder to ascertain. From my experience if you have felt suicidal at some point you don't need to feel so alone. Someone you know has probably also had those thoughts.

Once the idea that you could kill yourself and put an end to what you are enduring enters your arena, you are in crisis. Not the capital letter crisis, but a mini one with the potential to become a big nasty one. I Googled the word 'crisis' and one of the definitions that came up was this: "a time when a difficult or important decision must be made." When you think about suicide, you need to decide if you are going to allow yourself to continue to think about it, put your thoughts elsewhere, or attempt it.

Just as your child needs to decide if she is going to end her life or reinvest her energy in living, you need to make decisions about how involved you want to be with your child and what you are going to do about her being at risk to kill herself.

I would hope you would decide to go talk to a therapist or at least someone you trust to be able to help you out. When you are walking on a tightrope and life is hanging in the balance, you want to do what you can to build a solid safety net.

There is one fact about suicide which at first glance may seem surprising. If you could pinpoint the worst day of someone's life, you might guess that close to that day is when they would be most likely to kill themselves.

Some people do kill themselves on that very day. But most don't.

Most people weather that storm and start to pick up the pieces. It is on this ascent back up when most people kill themselves.

What is surprising is they are starting to feel better and the worst is behind them. It is when things are picking up that they kill themselves. That doesn't make sense—they are feeling better so why kill themselves then? There is hope and hope is supposed to invigorate the will to live.

Here is how it works:

Let's use an example of a widow whose spouse has just died. This can be devastating and extremely painful and some people might kill themselves right then. Yet, for most people, when something horrible happens other people come and offer support and there is a level of attention that the person receives from the world. But as time goes by those people's attentions shift elsewhere and the loneliness takes hold. The widow starts to get used to the absence of her spouse and realizes things are a little better, but they still are horribly empty. The hope is that the worst is over, but the road ahead does not look that bright. It is at this point that many people give up. They realize things are better, but that better is just not good enough.

What is important to grasp is that if your child is depressed you need to be vigilant. Not just when you first get wind of it, but past the time when you initially think you have weathered the storm. Better to be extra vigilant than extra upset at yourself for not being more on top of things.

Part of the usual rationale for attempting suicide is that people don't really understand. And the ones that should understand the most aren't trying hard enough to make things better. You don't need to feed that rationalization. To whatever degree your loving attention is not helping her feel better, less of it is only going to do more harm. Your presence may not be the cure-all, but your absence certainly isn't. This is one of those times when over-parenting or at least close attention is needed. Stay connected, concerned, and supportive. Don't cut back on the attention until you are more than assured the crisis has passed and thoughts of suicide are no longer viable. Then continue for a little bit longer until she assures you there is no need to worry and asks you to please give her some space.

I am not saying you need to be eternally vigilant, although many parents do this naturally. But I am saying, you want to talk with your child about suicide. You want to use the word. You want to ask her how she is feeling. You want to ask her directly if she is feeling suicidal. You don't want to be shy about speaking directly about this.

Often parents are reluctant to talk with their child about suicide for fear that bringing it up will put it more in the forefront. If your child is thinking about suicide it often becomes her secret world and she is reluctant to share it. You do not want her to dwell alone in that world. Enter it with her. Allow her to talk about it with you. Don't make her hide her thoughts away.

You will know you don't have to worry when you ask your child if there is any chance whatsoever of her killing herself now or in the foreseeable future. If she answers that satisfactorily to you then you can move your heightened worry back to its normal range.

She may bark at you for thinking she is suicidal. To which you can reply: "I was. Now I am just checking because I want to do everything I can to help you have a wonderful life. If that means I ought to back off now I am happy to do that. Just promise me that you won't hurt yourself and if you start to feel like ending your life you will talk with me first and not do it."

Just like you need to be able to hold your child's anger, you need to be able to hold her thoughts/fears/concerns about suicide. Many therapists consider suicide an act of anger towards yourself. You hate what has become of your life so you punish yourself in the worst way possible.

I can see some truth in this. I am sure there are many reasons people think about ending their lives and most of us can probably support some people taking their lives.

Just not our children.

Certainly in extreme situations, some parents consider letting their child die. The pain and the path they are on are not enhanced by more time on this earth. Those are horrible situations to be in and certainly I would hope if you are in a situation like that you get as much support for yourself as you can get.

For most parents, having their child consider, let alone try to kill themselves is a frightening thought. Not only would it take a love of your life away from you, but it would cause you to carry an unfathomable sorrow for the rest of your life.

Having a child die is a parent's worst nightmare. Having your child choose to die affects you on a whole other level. Parents often have recriminations and carry levels of guilt, shame, and anger. It is hard enough being a parent and having oversight of a teenager who is taking more control of her life. It is devastating when a child does not have a chance to be an adult.

When you suspect that your child might want to hurt herself, you need to engage her in your most thoughtful caring manner. No shaming, no raising voices. Just your concern for her wellbeing. Remember, as nervous as you might be to talk about suicide, you want to know what is going on with your child. She will appreciate that you do not sugarcoat things and speak directly with her.

Your child may want to isolate herself. Like most animals when we are wounded we want to retreat. Don't let her. Well, let her a little because she needs her privacy and space. But keep plugging away at talking with her. As annoying as she thinks you will be for bringing up the subject it is imperative that you periodically directly discuss with her how life is going and if there is any need to be concerned about her hurting herself. Make sure you also ask a host of other questions to let her know you are interested in learning more about her life. She may not let you in, but keep knocking on that door. Maybe not so loud and so often, but often enough that she knows you love her, care about her, and are there for her.

As much as you don't want to hear about what your child is saying it is critical to her continued wellbeing that she can speak to you about anything and you can listen to her. To whatever degree you want to consider yourself partly to blame for her life not being more than it is, your engagement in knowing more about her and partaking in her life in a more involved and active way might be a good thing for you both. You are going to have to find what you can do with each other. Maybe it is just talking or watching TV or taking a walk. Whatever you can do with her, do it. She needs you in her life now. Not to be all of her life, but more of it.

If she won't talk to you, have her talk to a therapist. That therapist has a duty to warn you if they think she is a threat to herself or others. You can have some degree of comfort in knowing she is talking to someone in whatever meaningful ways she can about her life.

Suicide is about ending pain. You can help your child end her pain and provide some comfort and joy in her life. The first step is to tell yourself you are going to do that, then go tell your child.

SECTION 5:

CONFLICT

35

INTRODUCTION TO CONFLICT

A basic truth in relationships is that people need to mean enough to one another to go through the discomfort of conflict. If you don't care that much about someone, why bother going through all the emotional trouble to quarrel/argue/fight and be upset with them? Unless, of course, you enjoy conflict and seek it out. If you are that person, I want to suggest you read one of my relationship books and consider therapy. Relationships are hard enough without having a tendency to promote conflict.

Most people are conflict-avoidant. They would prefer not to argue. The emotional upheaval is something many people would rather not go through.

If you have a teenager, you are probably experiencing conflict whether you want to or not.

Since you are going to be involved in conflicts you might as well learn more about how to conflict in a more caring, effective, and relationship-enhancing way while mostly telling the truth.

Anger has been called the gift of love. I know that sounds strange but it is because those who get the majority of our anger are usually those we love the most. Lucky them.

People need to feel safe enough with someone to let their true feelings out. The reason people are conflict-avoidant is because it is risky to get upset and argue with someone. You never know how they will react and what will come of what you share.

Getting into a disagreement with someone can escalate and people can easily get their feelings hurt, get angry, and say things they may later regret. Given the stakes that can be involved when strong emotions are expressed it is no wonder why people choose to vent with those they feel they have the biggest safety net with.

Being on the receiving end of this "gift of love" does not always feel that great. The fact that it is being given because the person feels safe with you does not mitigate the discomfort that comes with it. Yes, it can be helpful to remember the anger would not be coming your way if the person didn't feel comfortable enough with you to share it. But that doesn't alleviate the emotional upheaval.

Anger, when managed well, can lead to an even closer relationship. But while anger may be a gift, it can cause a lot of pain. Conflict and anger are danger zones in relationships. They present opportunities for any number of things to happen in any number of ways, many of which can damage relationships. Issues can be minor and easily handled and issues can be major and escalate to a point where the advancement of the relationship is in jeopardy. With such high stakes it behooves us all to continue to learn how to improve our skills in managing conflict.

It is not of primary concern that conflicts occur. In fact, if disagreements are not present somewhere in your close relationships that can even be more troubling. Of course, if screaming, yelling, and threatening are involved that is another matter which we will address later.

Most of the time the primary concern for therapists is how anger and conflict are handled.

- Few people learned from their parents how to conflict well. A lot of the verbal messages parents got from their parents, while instructive, were often not fully modeled. Many of today's parents heard some version of, "Say you are sorry, shake hands, and make up."

- Many of those same parents saw their parents argue, cold-shoulder each other, and never shake hands or kiss and make up.

There wasn't a course we took in school about how to conflict well. Many of the messages schools did provide involved not conflicting, and if you did, the school would discipline you. I never had a course that outlined how to deal with emotions until I went to graduate school.

How to navigate our way through and around conflict is a skill we informally learn and modify along the way. Our conflictual style is shaped by the conflicts we have witnessed and the ones we've participated in.

Sometimes we initiated. Sometimes we responded. Some we watched. Some we remember to this day.

All affected us.

If you want to do a little self-therapy, you could reflect on this:

- Where and how do you express your anger?

- Who gets the most of it?

- Why them?

- How would you evaluate and rate your skill at expressing your anger and annoyance?

- How would those close to you rate your skill at expressing your anger and annoyance (bonus points if you ask them)?
- What could you be doing better?

I don't know if it helps you to think about these points, but if you are into it here are some other things you could reflect on:

- How you learned to express your anger
- How your mother expressed hers to your father, to you, your siblings, and the world
- How your father expressed his anger to your mother, you, your siblings, and the world

And if you want to go the full nine yards, reflect on:

- How you express(ed) your anger to your mother
- How you express(ed) your anger to your father
- How you express(ed) your anger to your siblings
- How you express(ed) your anger to your friends
- How you express(ed) your anger to your romantic partners
- How you express your anger to each of your children

Since this is a self-help book and I believe in the value of self-reflection, I like to throw in an occasional "take a moment." This is a good time to stop, look, and listen to yourself. You might want to pause here and go over some of those prompts.

Before we talk about conflicting in healthier ways let's focus a bit on avoiding conflict altogether. As I already mentioned, the discomfort of going through conflict causes many people to avoid speaking up or telling the truth. Many would rather avoid the situation than deal directly with it.

We have all tried to dodge some bullets and hope we can get away with not having to deal with something directly. I certainly don't advocate speaking the truth, the whole truth and nothing but the truth 100% of the time. I do advocate moving in that direction. 100% does not need to be the goal. Maybe because I work in a school I would encourage you to go for that 90% plus range and get an A. But, I also know not everybody gets A's in everything all the time. So aim for pushing yourself to consciously endeavor to do better.

I tend to believe that most of the time avoidance or misrepresenting yourself is penny smart and pound foolish. You avoid the difficulty in the moment but if something actually matters to you it will come back up again and again. Until you get some better resolution, the item that is nagging you is going to come back and bother you. It often comes out at a time and place and way you might not like.

Whether the upset, frustration, and/or anger is yours or theirs or a combination, it usually works out best to bite the bullet and deal with it sooner rather than later.

Let me point out something I have already pointed out to you: any change that is going to happen in your relationship with your child or anyone else is going to involve you.

- Whether you initiate it or respond to it, situations are going to involve you.

- Whether you want it or not, situations are going to evolve and eventually resolve.

In graduate school they reminded us about something that is both infuriating and liberating. We are all going to have to take responsibility for ourselves.

As much as we might like to blame our parents, our socioeconomic inheritance, our children, the government, and anything or anybody else, it doesn't change the fact that if something is going to get done, you are going to have to do it.

The reason your life is the way it is may be entirely someone else's fault and we could sit down together and bemoan your fate till the cows come home. That might even make you feel a little better. It usually does help to share your woes.

But if you want to change things you are going to have to do it.

Yes, if those around you would just shape up, your life would be better. But they aren't shaping up. At least not now or not enough.

In the meantime, even though ultimately you are going to have to focus and take care of business, it does not mean that you ought not to let off some steam about your circumstances. Please feel free to complain about:

- The cards you were dealt
- The people you have to deal with
- The tasks you have to do
- And anything else that weighs on you

Whine, complain, hit the pillow, yell out the window, or jump up and down. However your valve releases. Allow yourself the space to feel bad about your life. Just don't overindulge this hurtful part of the total picture. Recognize it, respect it, allow it time and space. Yet also know your healing depends on having that hurt become a smaller part of your life.

Just make sure when you are venting you aren't targeting those around you. In fact, it is often best to do a good portion of letting off steam when you are alone. Waiting until the rawness of your pain is less on the surface often makes your sharing easier on everyone.

Certainly, despite your best efforts, some of that stream you blow off is going to land on someone. Many people are familiar with the traditional description of how anger gets passed along. Your boss yells at you. You go home and yell at your partner. Your partner yells at your child. Your child yells at his sibling. The sibling yells at the dog. The dog chases the cat. The cat pisses on your bed.

Whether you plan to share your upset overtly or it comes out covertly, sooner or later if you are sufficiently upset about something it is going to come out.

So let's move on to helping you deal with conflict.

If you think about your life now, what are the top three things that cause you the most upset (financial issues, teenager-related issues, relationship issues...)?

1. _____

2. _____

3. _____

Do you have any observations about that list? Are there people on it? Things? Your behavior? Others' behavior?

_____

_____

_____

Now let's break this list down to two categories:

People and the things they do that upset you.

Things you do that upset you.

It is possible your list had neither of those, but I am going to guess that for most people one or both of these areas are major contributors to the conflict-laden portion of your life.

Let's say you wrote down "My child's laziness" or "My husband's stubbornness." Both are valid arenas for conflict.

So, what is it about your child's laziness or your husband's stubbornness that is so infuriating for you?

See if you can look beyond the obvious and figure out just what it is about these occurrences that upsets you so much.

Insight is one of those things that therapists like to promote. We want you to try to figure out the "why" of your behavior. Who did what to whom and when and how that affected you are avenues of exploration that take up many therapy hours. Insight into why you do the things you do won't automatically result in you doing things differently. But it will give you a greater understanding and appreciation of why you do the things you do and open the door to you making more conscious choices. With that awareness, perhaps you can gain a toehold into changing those behaviors you would just as soon leave behind.

In any basic psychology textbook, you will be introduced to the concept of fight-or-flight. As mentioned earlier, when faced with something that is threatening, people either want to get away from it or take it on. This is a survival instinct. You either run for the hills and disengage, or you step forward and engage.

When a conflict occurs, your fight-or-flight response is activated. Someone says something that triggers your emotional antenna and you either want to step away from it or respond to it.

Ideally both people want to engage in a discussion, albeit most likely an uncomfortable one. Often one wants in and the other wants out. Which then presents its own conflict. People often quarrel about whether they are going to talk about the conflictual thing that is happening.

"I don't want to talk about it" is not an altogether uncommon response. Or "Let's forget about it" or "Can we deal with this later?"

"We need to talk about this now" is not an uncommon counter-response. Or "No, I don't want to forget about it. I want to talk about it."

People often skirmish about whether to talk about what is really the issue. Coming to agreement about how/when/if something is to be discussed can be a protracted process. Or not.

Sometimes people bring up other issues to distract you from dealing with your issue. In the therapy world we would call this stalling tactic a 'red herring.' Someone brings up something to distract you from the thing you want to discuss so now you are focused elsewhere. It is not that their issue may not have merit. It is just that they are trying to trump your concern with their concern and not have to deal directly with what is bothering you.

Oh the tangled webs we weave.

Conflicts and arguments are back-and-forth events. One person says or does something and the other reacts in such a way that the first person feels compelled to say something pointed back, then that thrust is met with an equal or greater thrust and soon you have tempers flaring, blood pressures rising, and something more on your hands than you wanted. Which, once again, is why people are conflict-avoidant. Who needs all that hassle?

We all do.

Sorry.

Many arguments start about one thing and end up being about another. Along the way many provocative statements may be put on the table. What started out being about one issue has now opened up a whole other can of worms.

Of course, that doesn't need to happen, but it often does for one of two reasons:

1. The person who has the finger pointed at them does not want to deal with the original issue.

2. People warehouse their conflicts.

Little annoyances and irritating things go unspoken. Even though they are bothersome, people decide to hold back sharing because they know the other person is not going to like hearing what they have to say and then there is going to be a whole prolonged drama.

When one person does bring up something of concern, the discussion may become uncomfortable. There may be disagreements, feelings may be hurt, and that fight-or-flight response may trigger one to aggressively engage. Maybe the recipient doesn't want to deal with the issue at hand so they bring up something that has been bothering them.

These discussions can easily become arguments. Like a flash mob they start slowly and then more and more is added. These kinds of conflicts are not easy to navigate as you have a lot of balls in the air and usually people leave them wounded.

Often without the catalyst of a conflictual discussion people withhold sharing their grievances/concerns/annoyances which might create drama. Many people are drama-avoidant, but once the conversation heats up, they figure what the hell? As long as you are arguing, that thing that was nagging them might as well see the light.

It is no wonder that many people are conflict- and drama-avoidant. The buildup of pent-up emotions causes these discussions/arguments when they do happen to escalate and expand beyond the initial issue. Instead of having the challenge of dealing with one possibly small conflict, these events often turn out to be bigger deals than you want or need them to be. Thus rendering you more conflict- and drama-avoidant.

A cycle you might enjoy breaking.

Let's consider a scale of 1-10, 1 being your own personal lowest level of annoyance (when something annoys you just a little) and 10 being the most mad you have ever been in your life.

If you use this scale you can approximately rate how annoying/maddening something is for you. For instance, if you are stuck in traffic and have to be somewhere and know you now are going to be late you might rate that experience a _____. Of course it matters where you are going and what is causing the slowdown, but you probably have a general sense of how annoying that might be.

You probably also have a range for the time you are on hold and the bad service you receive as well as that one particular thing your partner does. You know if something annoys you a little you will probably put up with it, but the higher up the scale you go the more prompted you will be to say something.

If someone does something that gives you a 2's worth of annoyance, you figure why bother sharing? You deal with it by yourself and the moment passes. Then down the road another 2 happens and once again you think the pain of going through the drama of sharing is not worth it. Then a 1 happens and you swallow that. But then another 2 happens or maybe a 3 and you lose it. Those numbers add up until they come tumbling out.

You may have noticed when you have been on the receiving end of someone else's wrath that what they were upset about really was only a 2, but they hit you with an 8. That is because they didn't bring it to you when it was just a 2. They waited until that 2 met another 2 and a couple of 1s and maybe a 3 or 4 and then when one of those 2s happened again you got visited by the sum total.

I don't know about you, but personally I would have preferred to hear about that 2 when it first happened. Then that next 2 when it happened. Along with those 1s and 3s and 4s. I am sure if you share every 1 and 2 your partner might come to experience this as nagging. Yet in my experience the more you share the little irritations the less of them you have. If you are bringing 1s and 2s daily to your partner you might want to consider a therapist because larger issues may be at play.

I am an advocate for more small-scale conflicts than fewer big-time ones; they are less destructive and easier to manage. While I would prefer to avoid conflict and drama altogether I would rather deal with more small-scale ones than those big blowouts that can leave nasty scars. If you deal with the small ones as they come up you won't have those arguments where your partner is throwing in things you did weeks, months, and years ago.

John Gottman, PhD is one of the foremost researchers on couples and has found that close to 70% of all couples have something he calls "perpetual problems." These problems continue on and on throughout a relationship and are never fully resolved. They are just avoided or managed for the moment only to reappear later. I am sure if you reflect on your relationship with your child's other parent as well as your child, you can probably identify the perpetual problems in play.

Since the problem is perpetual it probably is something you can live with, but every now and then it annoys you to such a degree that you have to say something. If the problem were actually that horrific, it usually would not become perpetual because hopefully you got yourself out the door.

Unless, of course, you are the bigger part of the problem.

36

EMOTIONAL URGENCY AND TIMEOUTS

Some years ago, when I worked at Antioch University, I was promoted to be the Chair of a graduate psychology program. I was sent to Denver to take a week-long course on how to be a Chair. There were about 50 educators present representing a lot of colleges. One morning when we arrived we were given a stack of papers and told that this represented some of the mail and notes we might find on our desk on any given day. We were told to go off on our own for the morning and prioritize the pile and, if we had time, to handle as many of the tasks as possible. We would meet after lunch and go over what we had done and see what we could learn.

In each of our stack of papers was a series of notes back and forth between "you" and a certain faculty person. As the notes progressed the teacher got more and more aggressive. The notes were filled with belittling comments and unreasonable requests punctuated with veiled threats. In the afternoon when we debriefed, all of us reported being upset at the faculty person. Every one of us had written back to him. While we had put some other items on the back burner to deal with later, we all had something to say to the teacher right away.

What, we were asked by the trainers, prompted us to write back to the teacher? Of all the items we had been given to go through this was not something that needed to be dealt with right away. We could have chosen to wait a day or more before replying. But we all had an irresistible urge to respond. Nobody liked the faculty person and we were all irritated by his behavior towards us. Our annoyance pushed us into action.

I now call that need to respond "emotional urgency." There was no real urgency, but we all felt the desire to do something right away.

What was it that so beckoned us to respond so quickly? We all felt varying degrees of anger. For some it was a 2 or 3 and for others 6, 7, or 8. Even those that were only a little upset still wanted to get back to the person right away. No one wanted to disengage. We all wanted to engage.

The workshop leaders pointed out to us that if we had slept on it our response the next day may have been more measured. In fact, when we spoke about it again the next day most of us acknowledged that we would have toned down our reply. By delaying the necessity of our emotional urgency our 6 or 7 had reduced itself to a 3 or 4. The 2s and 3s were down to a 1. We all knew our reply the second day would have had a softer tone. Maybe one that would not have ignited the tension any more. Maybe even one that moved towards a consensual resolution.

"Act in haste, repent at leisure" was the quote we were all sharing with each other that evening. That lesson we all learned in the workshop is why I suggest that when you can, when your emotions get triggered consider giving yourself a timeout. Not everything needs to be resolved in the moment.

Your emotional urgency will want you to engage and discharge your upset. Yet, if your calmer waters can dampen your emotions you likely will find the delay brings you a more level and less inflammatory approach.

I am not advocating stuffing things away. I am suggesting that there are times when you may be better served saying to the person, "I would like to take a step back and be with this for a day. Can we get back together tomorrow at this time and pick it up?"

While that sounds simple, I know it is not easy taking a timeout.

Just like they do in sports, some people wait till the tide has turned too much before they ask for one. I recommend not waiting till things escalate and your timeout seems more like a maneuver to stop the other person than a step towards your peacemaking.

If you know something is upsetting you and you also know there is no real need to deal with it in the moment, you might want to give yourself some time to be with the upset before you publicly react to it. Could be a minute, an hour, a day. Just time to collect your thoughts/feelings and reflect on what you want to do.

There are plenty of ways of saying "that's enough for now" that can put a conflict on hold until everyone calms down. I recommend a simple "I" statement such as: "I don't want to talk about this right now unless we take it down a notch or two. Myself included. Let's all be quiet for a few moments, breathe, and try to continue in a less contentious way."

Then be quiet. If others are not being quiet, give them a pleading look and don't say anything. If no one else is going to take a moment at least you can. If you don't want to say anything out loud you can take some moments of silence just to be still and consider how you want to proceed.

Usually when people are conflicting they don't want to stop. Adrenaline is flowing and it is hard to walk away.

If you are at a point where you no longer believe the conversation can be constructive it is often best to call for a break in the action. It is better to end too soon than too late.

I know parents do not like it when their children walk away from a discussion and often want their child to stick it out until a resolution is reached. Certainly as often as possible it is best to start a conversation and come to a resolution before you take a break. This is a worthwhile model, but don't be restricted by it.

Unless there is an immediate time necessity, many issues can be put on hold and returned to in a couple of hours or a day or two. I wouldn't wait too long as the uncertainty can build anxiety. The reason to take a break is to let things simmer down in hopes that when everyone is calmer you can all come to a resolution. If the anxiety goes up in the interim, you defeat the purpose of the break.

Timing is everything. But one person's good timing may not be another's. Which is why you might want to consider saying something like: "I would like to take a break as I don't think I am in the best place to resolve this right now. I hope everyone will be okay enough with that. I know it isn't ideal to stop before we resolve this issue, but I really have reached the point where it is best for me to take a break. When would be a good time for us to get back together?"

While most people won't be happy with you calling time out, they will at least be included in the decision-making loop about when to resume. When you pull power plays it helps to distribute some influence while you take the lion's share.

When you are calling for a break and asking them when to reconvene, there is a balancing of power. Of course, you may not be available when they want to follow up or you may not want to follow up when they want to follow up, but allowing them a voice in the decision-making shows respect and concern. Two things a teenager, or anyone for that matter, appreciates.

In calling for the timeout you are not saying the reason you want a timeout is because other people are being unreasonable. You are recognizing the fact that you don't see a positive way to resolve this right now and are concerned that if things continue, they are headed south with you leading the parade.

While I prefer being able to talk things out in the first go-round, I think you (and everyone else) need to take good care of yourself. If you are at a point in a discussion where you honestly feel you cannot manage yourself well enough and you are at risk for doing something you might regret later—call a timeout.

You are creating a model for how to deal with conflict. If it is acceptable for you to call a timeout so must it be for others. Which is why you don't want to use it unless you really need it.

Often something happens that upsets you and the other person doesn't even know. In those cases you can take a timeout without ever asking for it. Just go take some time alone, think about it, and sleep on it before you share it.

Other times the other person will know and they may not want you to walk away. In these cases it is hard to ask for timeout. Your desire for a timeout can become embroiled in a power struggle over whose will shall triumph. In those battles of the wills here is something you can do. Earmark this page and if you find yourself in one of these situations ask them to wait a minute, go drag this book out, open to this page, and have them read this:

There are many advantages to taking something that just upset you and taking some time before you talk to the other person. Your initial upset is going to thrust aggression into the conversation that might easily be quelled by time.

Sure, the other person is not going to like it as they want to resolve the conflict now. But if there is no real need to take action now, please consider the mutual benefits of a timeout. You may have even told your child to take one now and then just to cool down and give herself some perspective. The fundamental rules apply.

When things get too heated for one person and they think they might say or do something they could regret later, take a break. If the issue is still troublesome later, the emotion will be right there. But with distance people often gain a better perspective: a sense of how others think/feel and more understanding of what is bothering them. When they do reengage they are usually are able to do so in a more empathetic and reasonable manner.

Sometimes you need to take another break when you pick things up as it is easy for feelings to get reignited and escalate. While I would prefer you hang in there and work things out, I also think if you are getting emotionally flooded and need some time to settle down, take it. Just endeavor to have your timeouts be at most a day or two.

If you decide you want a timeout, it is best to set up a time in. Pick a specific day and time and make sure you make that date. If the other person needs to break the date that is fine, but reschedule on the spot. If you call the timeout it is incumbent upon you to not avoid the follow-up. Make it your responsibility to ensure the talk gets to happen.

If you prefer to avoid the whole thing then please don't ask for a timeout. Keep those for when you really need a break and plan on returning to the discussion soon. If you want to avoid the whole thing altogether:

a) Tell the other person that you are not going to have this discussion with them. Period.

Or

b) Tell the other person the issue is off the table for now and you will let them know when it is up for discussion again, but most likely it is not going to be any time soon.

Or

b) Just avoid it altogether.

I don't need to tell you that I don't endorse avoidance, especially for extended periods of time. I am sure we all have our good reasons for wanting to avoid things and maybe some of them are valid. I would prefer you take an extended break over taking a subject out of the conversation entirely. That can be hard on the other person. But if something is so emotionally fraught that you can't speak about it with someone close, off to therapy you ought to go. If you are in therapy already, consider another therapist. And if two therapists agree with your reason for avoiding something, I can live with it.

Unless, of course, we talk and I don't agree with the other two.

But, I might. You never know. We all have unique circumstances. And I am mostly talking in generalities.

If those closest to you are not able to share in your truths, it is bound to create an emotional barrier that will only cause you pain. If your secrets are so severe that you fear their being known would destroy your life, please consider professional help. At least then someone will share your secret.

I am not a purist; I don't think those closest to you need to know everything. I do think they need to know the feelings you have about the things they do. Chances are if you don't tell them directly you will act out indirectly. We will get more into that shortly. For now, let's just leave it at this: if you are withholding thoughts/feelings and deeds done from your closest partner, you would be well served by talking things over with a therapist.

37

CRITICISM

There are a fair amount of techniques you can learn to help you navigate conflict better. We will go over the ones I think will be most useful to you, but first I would like you to dissect some of those major conflicts you have with you and others.

There are interpersonal and intrapersonal issues here: how you deal with others and how you deal with you. By now you know that I believe that in order to improve how you interact with others it is helpful to upgrade your relationship with yourself.

Let's start with this—when you make a mistake, forget something important, or just generally screw up in some noticeable yet not catastrophic way, how do you handle yourself? Do you:

- Berate yourself?
- Gently criticize yourself?
- Get despondent?
- Move on?
- Other?

Needless to say different circumstances evoke different responses and mistakes live on a continuum as well. Generally when you consider the more frequent kinds of mistakes you make how would you describe your reaction?

_____

_____

How does your reaction compare to how your father reacted to you when you made a similar mistake?

_____

_____

_____

How does your reaction compare to how your mother reacted to you when you made a similar mistake?

_____

_____

_____

Any observations you want to make about that?

_____

_____

_____

If you are like most people how you react to yourself has some resemblance to how your parents reacted to you. How you react to your child's mistakes usually is not too different than how you react to your own. Our parents' behavior is the primary influence on us. When the model is a positive one we add our own nuances but basically follow suit. When the model is not so positive we try to behave differently but often find ourselves following suit. Abused children too often become abusive parents. Most of us treat others in a similar fashion as we treat ourselves—give or take.

If you tend to be critical of others you probably are critical of yourself as well. The negative statements you make to others are usually matched by the ones you aim towards yourself. Your mistakes get your own share of your criticism just like the shortcomings, failures, and mistakes of others. How much you focus on your downside is most likely close to equal to how much you attend to others' less-than-stellar attributes. Although we all know the saying that we are more critical of ourselves than others, I have not found enough solid research to fully sign on to that.

Many people are critical and judgmental to the point that it inhibits their intimacy with both themselves and those closest to them. When you are heavily criticizing actions it makes it difficult to want to take any actions. Although that too will warrant criticism.

Ideally, critical comments serve the purpose of guiding the other person (or yourself) towards a better way of doing things. I am sure we all have benefitted from someone's criticism of us and we have been hurt by someone's criticism. Sometimes those overlap.

Criticism at its best is framed and delivered as "constructive feedback." People are more receptive if they think it is being spoken in hopes of helping the other. Even the criticism you level at yourself has a better chance of being of assistance if it is not packaged in belittling barbs. If a mistake is made or someone (including yourself) does something you don't like, you can tell them (or yourself) without resorting to shaming and degrading.

Criticism delivered at high volumes with name-calling attached usually has little chance of being incorporated. Certainly if your child is afraid of your wrath they may do things to keep you from being upset, but that doesn't mean they have found a better way. It just means they are behaving so that they can avoid you.

Criticism at its worst is aimed to hurt the other person. There may be some suggestion or implied suggestion about how to do things "better," but the primary intent is to hurt the other's feelings. That kind of criticism is more an expression of the person's frustration and anger than it is a valuable piece of critical feedback that might actually be of help.

As with many things there are different opinions about criticism. People who are highly critical tend to believe those that are less critical are not serious enough and don't work as hard. Those that are less critical tend to think those who criticize more are too demanding and demeaning.

Your child could do something that another parent thought was no big deal and best left alone. You, on the other hand, may think what happened is a big deal and certainly worth addressing. Are they too easygoing and you too strict? Are they under-reacting and you overreacting?

Suppose I could provide you with the exact balance of easygoingness and criticism. Suppose there was a simple formula to follow that significant amounts of research had found to yield the best results in terms of positively affecting behavior, quality of work, tasks accomplished, and the self-esteem of all—would you want to know that formula?

I would think most people would want to know the formula.

No matter how critical or easygoing you are if there is some tried and true formula you might want to at least check it out. Some people would learn the formula and do their best to incorporate it. Others would read about the formula, give it a little thought, and pretty much adhere to what they already were doing. I mentioned early in the book the newscaster who said people like to believe what they believe. However critical or easygoing you are most likely you think that is the best approach. And maybe every now and then a little doubt creeps in.

To which I say, let's see if you buy into the formula sufficiently to consider aiming for utilizing it now and then—say 10% more of the time than you do now. If the formula doesn't sound solid to you, you can always adopt a different formula. This is the best one I have for you.

The first part of the formula is easy for those that are critical to follow. And exasperating for everyone else. It simply says you can keep on being exactly as critical as you are. You don't have to change anything about how often and how scathing the criticism comes out.

Of course, the law says you cannot be emotionally abusive. We can argue long and hard about what is and what is not emotionally abusive—but for simplicity's sake let's look where most people look first—Wikipedia. Here is the Department of Justice's definition:

The U.S. Department of Justice defines emotionally abusive traits as including causing fear by: "intimidating, threatening physical harm to self, partner, children, or partner's family or friends, destruction of pets and property, forcing isolation from family, friends, or school or work."

Even with this definition there is still a lot of interpretation involved in abuse. Often the abuser doesn't see their behavior as abusive and the abused does.

I think when you are dealing with interpersonal relationships and you want to make them more fulfilling and rewarding you need to honor the one who thinks they are being abused. If a family member tells another they think they are being abused, it is incumbent on the "abuser" to find another way to handle the situation.

Surely someone will read this and perhaps take advantage of the situation by crying wolf. I would rather have someone call something abusive than not speak up.

I believe it is a fundamental cornerstone of relationships to respect another person's truth even if it is not yours. If someone tells you to stop, you need to stop. If you can't find another mutually acceptable way to deal with the situation, find someone who can help you.

If you think you are being abused, you need to tell the other person to stop and how you would like them to behave towards you. If they cannot stop the abusive action, find a safe place and call 9-1-1.

Relationships hinge on trust. If you are engaging with someone and they tell you that they think you are being abusive you need to stop what you are doing. It is your duty to interact with your child in a way that honors and respects his personhood. If you are unable to do that, you need to reach out. Remember, you are not the one who gets to define what is and what is not abusive. If your child lets you know he experiences you as abusive you need to get professional assistance. Whatever you are doing with your child needs attention. Ideally the whole family goes to therapy, puts their cards on the table, and lets the therapist help them straighten things out before they get worse.

A lot of criticalness comes out of having high standards and not liking it when they are not attained.

Fair enough.

It is okay to have high standards and it is okay to be upset when those standards are not met. It is not the being upset that is the issue, it is how you manage yourself when you are upset that is up for discussion.

As long as you are not being abusive with your criticism you can keep it up. (Although I will have more to say about that later, for now let's just say you don't have to alter the quantity of your criticism.)

If you happen to be a perfectionist you know that the majority of time, life does not measure up to your standards. Frustration and criticism are a daily part of your experience.

I don't think this will help much, but perhaps it will. Please consider that perfectionism is not a goal. It is a direction. It is not often attainable, just desirable. Be happy when you or others attain it. Even when you do it will fade and new arenas will open up where, once again, perfection is rarely attainable and sustainable. At your very best it is still not possible to be anything but perfectly yourself. You have no more claim on perfection than anyone else.

You might want to drop the goal of perfection and see if you can aim for close enough.

Continuing to berate yourself and others is not a useful activity. It might help you to vent some frustration but whatever gains you get by blowing off some stream to another are usually more than equaled by the damage of your assault. If you want to blow off some steam, go find a private space.

Let me assure those among you who worry that if you spare the rod you spoil the child. Or if you worry that if you don't set high standards and inflict pain when those standards are not achieved your child will not continue to strive for excellence.

Berating, blaming, and raising one's voice are motivators for the person to want to have less to do with you. Demeaning someone or challenging them to do better may work on an athletic field, but it will not serve your child. Especially when there are more effective techniques that will help everyone.

Even though I am raising concerns about how you criticize, you may remember that I said you don't really need to change how often you criticize people (including yourself). If you are abusive (in their eyes) then you need to tone down the abusive part but you can keep the critical part. I am going to come back to this later and make a pitch for reducing your criticism, but for now, let's let it be what it is.

People are critical because something is not measuring up to their standards. Regardless of whether the standards are unrealistic, the basic truth of criticism is that it is based on wanting things to be better. The vast majority of us would like to improve how others do things as well as how we do things. We want to feel good about what other people are doing and what we are doing, but lo and behold, people fall short.

While voicing your objection to how things are going is an option, so too is the option of learning how to tolerate life's imperfections. Greater acceptance of the foibles and frustrations of life can lower your blood pressure. Instead of focusing on criticism, try upgrading your level of praise. If you do this, you may think you are not really being honest. Yet, what makes you think when you are focusing on the criticism you are being any more honest than when you are focusing on the praise? Fully honest or not, you will find yourself feeling better when you let go of some of your critical nature and adopt a more gracious approach to life.

Let me show you how it works.

Research was done with teenagers who were having school or behavioral difficulties, substance abuse problems, and/or home difficulties. They were compared with teens who were not in trouble, not abusing substances, and whose home life was basically peaceful. When school administrators, parents, and other people in the community were interviewed about both groups, the researchers found that all the children had received about the same amount of criticism from parents and other significant people in their lives.

The difference in the two groups was the amount of positive feedback they received. The group without difficulties received significantly more praise. For every one negative response they received they had gotten at least five positives.

Many parents already praise their children a considerable amount. But a lot don't. And most tend to not praise those things that are best praised.

Parents tend to praise their younger children when they accomplish even the smallest thing. First steps and first words get lots of "oohs" and "aahs." Older children get good grades or do something special athletically or creatively and receive praise, yet the amount of positive feedback tends to dwindle when children become teenagers.

Parents want to encourage their children so they applaud their accomplishments. We all like to be seen, appreciated, and occasionally applauded for our actions so for the most part the positive acknowledgement reinforces behaviors and encourages children. Yet as children age, the balance of criticism and praise shifts. Everyone talks about how difficult the teen years can be. You would think that might be a good time to raise the praise, not cut back. As Carol Dweck pointed out, praising effort is an effective tool in your parenting toolbox.

Since parents spend less time with their growing children they see fewer actions that they can praise. Instead of speaking with their child about how the day has gone and finding something to underscore, a parent will often just throw in a line when passing their child in the hall. "Remember to take the trash out" and "Did you do your homework?" are not uncommon comments. While you might not call those overtly critical, there is an implication that something that ought to have been done has not been done.

Like most parenting actions there is more art involved than science. I think the formula of five praises to one criticism is a worthy goal. We all know that if someone tells us five things they like about us and one they don't, we are certainly going to remember the one. Negative comments have a longer shelf life than positive comments.

The balance between criticism and praise is ever adjusting. Learning how to do each more effectively will certainly improve your relationship with your teen and might even get you some praise in return. If not from him, at least from you. Finding things to praise is akin to thinking of three good things that happened during the day. Focusing on the positives does not take away from the negatives, it just makes sure there is emphasis on the behaviors that you value.

As your child grows try to keep that 5:1 ratio in mind. Even if you don't upgrade your skills, just aiming for that ratio ought to improve relationships with everyone at home.

38

CURFEW

In all close relationships there will be conflict. The goal is not to avoid it, but to deal with it, resolve it, and move on.

Sometimes that moving on doesn't last as long as you would like, but the better job you can do of conflicting the better chance you have of finding a mutually agreeable resolution. That's the goal of almost all conflict in relationships—finding a mutually agreeable solution.

Win-Win. Not Win-Lose.

If you are aiming for Win-Lose, you are fighting a losing battle. You can have winners and losers when you play competitive games, but differences of opinion and conflicts in relationships are best anchored in cooperative problem solving.

There is not a lot of upside in being the winner in a conflict with your partner or child if you know they are leaving the disagreement feeling like a loser.

When you love someone you want the best for them. Couples can be competitive about who wins a game and at the same time want the best for their partner. Just because one doesn't want the other to beat them at the game, it doesn't mean they want ill for the person or to have that person walk around and feel badly about themselves.

If you really are one of those people who want to win win win, maybe you can redefine your definition of winning so it is more inclusive, especially when it comes to people you love. Maybe you can consider yourself a winner if everyone walks away feeling better.

Teenagers are in that stage in their lives when they are emotionally and physically growing the most. There is a biological imperative to extend their boundaries and develop. Along the way they need to learn how to be responsible and independent. That road to responsibility is one we all must travel and I think it is fair to say most of us have had some less-than-stellar moments on the journey.

How well your child manages the transition from dependence to independence depends a lot on you. Your child is learning as she goes, and so are you. Even if you are on your fifth child, how you parent number five is going to be different than how you handled number one. The majority of parents tend to treat their firstborn with a greater degree of attention than the rest of their children. Parents gain confidence from experience and their degree of nervousness more often than not lessens with each child. Certainly each child brings her own unique circumstances and challenges, but as a general rule the anxiety you had coming home from the hospital with child number one is greater than you felt leaving the hospital with number five.

You can feel like you've got the parenting thing down with the first child and totally lose that confidence when number two comes along and is not as easily parented. One child won't conflict with you at all and another may challenge everything you say. You go from thinking you are the best parent to having no idea what to do.

While you may have a midnight curfew with all your children at a certain age, how long they have it and how you handle matters when they break the curfew probably has shifted as you have aged and have had different children to parent.

Parenting is an evolving process. It is a series of interactions that have no script. Just when you think you may have grasped the way to handle things your child does something that takes things to another level. Learning how to respond to their growing need for independence plays havoc with a parent's desire for harmony.

When it comes to curfews it is your teenager's job to push for more freedom. Your job is to decide when and how to give it to her. Up until a certain age parents usually have the final say. Most teenagers will abide by that final say especially if they can appreciate the reasoning behind the decision.

Usually when a parent resorts to a power statement it comes out of frustration. Teenagers are good at pushing back and challenging authority until the parent can't take it anymore. Frustration, like most things, exists on a continuum so once again I am going to suggest trying to nip it in the bud and not let it grow to the point of exasperation.

We all know negotiating differences is not an easy task. Sometimes you need to bring in a mediator to help, but there are steps you can take before you reach that point. The easiest way to limit the frustration that comes from going round and round in a disagreement is to realize that once you have gotten to the point where you are frustrated, you have passed the point to have a resolution where everyone will feel good. You just want to get to place where you can resolve things well enough.

To do that you are going to have to allow your child to be upset with you and for you to be disappointed in them. Once you have arrived at a solid impasse the only way to resolve it is by someone having to give more than they want to give. And usually, that is going to be your child. Not always, as there will be times you will give in, but very often it is the child who feels they got the short end of the negotiation.

But let's see if we can find a better way to resolve these conflicts.

Certainly you need to find a curfew that works for you.

You are the parent in charge of raising your child and you have to live with your conscience. You don't want to go too much against your grain because if something goes wrong you are going to beat yourself up for not sticking with what you believed.

Hopefully you can reach a decision that can be agreed upon even if she is happy with it. But your decisions need to be based on your own convictions/values/beliefs. The clearer you can be about them, the easier it will be for you to honor them and for your child to respect you, if not agree with or like.

Parents are called upon every day to react to their children's actions. They do this and you do that. You don't have time in the moment to understand why you said/did what you did and if it truly represents your core values. Most of the time parents react without giving things much thought. There is an action and right away there is a reaction.

Awareness of self is something that can come to light after the events of the moment are handled and there is time to reflect upon what occurred. Sometimes a light bulb goes off in the midst of something and you can have one of those "ah-ha" moments, but most people act/react all day without much reflection and consideration. Which is why it helps when parents spend time talking with each other about how their days have gone and their interactions with their child. Those conversations engage couples in discussing their parenting and gives them time to reflect on why they did what they did, how they feel about it, and what they might want to do going forward.

There are a number of topics parents can speak about at the end of the day that concern their child. Everything from schooling, socializing, partying, dating, eating, exercising, social media, and the ups and downs of relating to her. There is also the issue of curfew and whether to have one or not, and if so, when and how.

Here are some things you could think/talk about with your parenting partner that might help clarify your beliefs and help you set a path for future actions.

What is the purpose of a curfew?

You know some families don't have them. Some families have stricter ones than you and others have more lenient ones. Everyone has an opinion. What's yours?

Do you think teenagers who have later curfews are more or less likely to live valuable, meaningful, and enjoyable lives?

Do you think teenagers with earlier curfews are more or less likely to live valuable, meaningful, and enjoyable lives?

What exactly do you personally think is the value to your child in having a curfew?

What is the difference between having your child at home by 10:00, 11:00, 12:00, 1:00 or 2:00?

What are your child's peers doing?

What do you think your child wants and why does she want it?

Curfews are usually something parents can discuss with themselves first and then their children before it becomes a big issue and "has" to be discussed. It is a lot easier to initiate a discussion with your child than it is to be compelled to respond to something they did that "forces" you to have a discussion.

You may or may not already have had a series of curfew discussions or drug ones or school ones. It doesn't matter. Chances are, to most everyone's chagrin, you will be having more. Which is why it helps to touch base with your partner about how the day has gone as well as any concerns or thoughts you have about any subject having to do with parenting. Sometimes you hear or think something during the day but you don't have time to really consider it and it gets pushed into the background. Taking the time daily or almost every day to touch base with your parenting partner about common concerns regarding your child often provides that ounce of prevention.

If you happen to live with the other parent it really can be helpful to take a few minutes every day when there are no distractions and you can talk about your lives. Certainly your own work and personal issues as well as the status of your relationship need to be part of that discussion. Some days there is more to talk about and other days you just want to relax and not be bothered. That is fine, but see if you can make a point to frequently check in with your partner about your lives and the life of your child.

If you do not live with your parenting partner, you do need to make a point to confer with them regularly so you both are aware of what is happening in your child's life. Whatever differences you have, you share a bottom line commitment to the welfare of your child. If you do not have a parenting partner, you need to find someone you trust with whom you can honestly discuss your concerns.

Having these mostly regular discussions allows you to be more integrated with your life. When the next thing pops up you have a better chance of dealing with it from a more grounded, balanced way. You may not be aware of something happening with your child that the other parent has observed. Having them share that information will assist you both in planning the parameters you want to establish.

When I speak with teenagers about their curfews, I get an array of responses. Most teenagers acknowledge that curfews are established with their safety in mind. They realize the intent, but don't always agree with the need. Most think their curfew time is fair, but would like it to be later. Some think it is abusively early and others think their parents are too lenient, although they wouldn't want it any other way.

I had one high school senior tell me her parents varied their curfew for her when they knew what her schedule looked like the following day. She said she realized they were looking out for her and it taught her to think ahead.

A junior told me that his parents had a curfew for him when he started driving and while he didn't particularly like it he knew that if he could demonstrate to them his ability to be responsible about the curfew they would give him more freedom. I like this model as it teaches responsibility and rewards the child when he is able over time to show his ability to do as requested.

Most children want greater independence and they know they can earn it by being more responsible. It is a pretty simple equation. Demonstrate being responsible and be rewarded with greater freedom.

Of course, parents and children often disagree on the exact meaning of these concepts. Parents like to see their child being responsible over extended periods of time and children think that duration is longer than necessary. It may help you to remember that time holds a very different meaning to you than to your child. A month to a 15-year-old is $1/170$ of her life. To a 45-year-old parent it is $1/540$ of theirs. A parent may not think imposing an early curfew for a month is that big a deal and it might not be to them, but to their 15-year-old it is a significant amount of time.

Teenagers usually function better when they have shorter-term specific goals. Instead of saying, "If you let us know where you are and come home on time we will move your curfew back," I would say, "If you let us know when you go out at night where you are and come home on time we will move your curfew back thirty minutes in three months." If you make it six months or more that is probably too far off in a teenager's mind and won't be as effective. Of course, as a parent you want to see responsible behavior over a longer time period, which is why I would opt for more than a month or two.

Here is a simple tried-and-true formula: have shorter periods for your child to achieve smaller goals and longer timetables to achieve larger goals.

I have had teenagers tell me they have no curfew. Just expectations to act responsibly.

I like this model as well as it comes from a given. The given is "I trust you." If you expect people to behave responsibly they tend to be responsible. If you expect them to misbehave they are more likely to do so.

They call this a self-fulfilling fantasy. Your expectations influence behavior. Not 100% time, but more so than not. Unfortunately it doesn't work with your fantasies about winning the lottery, but it does work with your expectations about others.

Research does support that students who think they mostly meet their parent's expectations have better physical and mental health. While you might want to keep your expectations high so your child pushes herself to succeed you want to make them realistic enough so that she feels that she is behaving within the range of your expectations.

Trusting that your child will be responsible and do the "right thing" is an act of faith, because at some level you know she won't do everything just as you hope. She will make mistakes. Yet you believe in her ability to basically make good judgments and land on her feet.

It helps to have a bottom line trust that whatever happens things will work out okay. That kind of half-full optimism that your child will basically behave well will be transmitted to her and be incorporated by her.

Yes, your teenager will stay out too late at some point. She won't call exactly when you want her to. She will go to a party and not tell you. She will have a drink and not tell you. She will experiment. She will hope she doesn't get caught.

She is a teenager after all.

Not everyone can hold the belief that everything will work out okay. Those that can aren't always able to keep the faith 100% of the time.

So be it. We are what we are. Imperfect, not fully-evolved people who used to be children, and now find ourselves in the position of being parents without having mastered all the "best practices" of parenting, nor ever will.

It does help when interacting with your child if you can hold the belief that she will find a successful way to work things out. Even if you don't have 100% conviction. Save the part that is worried for your talks with your partner and convey your trust and belief to your child.

A curfew is often a parent's attempt to limit the amount of trouble their child will get into. Certainly if she is home at 10:00 there is less chance for trouble than if she was out till 1:00. But if you think that way too much, you will never let her out.

Not everyone is going to agree what time they should be home on a Friday or Saturday night let alone a Tuesday or Thursday. It does help to have a talk and ask your child what she thinks her curfew should be on a school night, weekend, and vacation. When you have this talk remember it truly is a talk and don't set any firm guidelines. Go into the talk with whatever ideas you have, but also with an open mind to hear your child's points of view, then evaluate the situation before you make a final decision. A consensual guideline may come up during the discussion, but if there is not general agreement you may want to hold off making a decision till you have time to sleep on it and talk it over with the other parent.

When you do reach a decision that is not good news for your teenager you can offer some empathy as you know if you were in her shoes you would be upset as well. Maybe you even were with your parents. You can have a time trial and revisit matters in a month or three or whatever. Remember it is good to provide hope that desired behavior will be rewarded.

If I made an unpopular decision or even if I made a mostly agreed upon one I would offer my child the opportunity to have the last word. Now that you have demonstrated your power it is time to give her the respect of the final word: "You can have the last word for now and then let's move on." Then let her say what she will and your only reply is basically, "Okay. I heard you. Now let's move on."

And move on.

As with the rest of the world, decisions that teenagers have a voice in have a better chance of being followed than decisions that are imposed upon them. It is harder to rebel when you get to vote.

Not that you don't rebel, but there isn't the same outrage. Unless you go back on your word.

I don't think families are a democracy. But as often as you can, if you can be democratic, it does build family cohesiveness. Giving your child a chance to speak about the guidelines for her life helps her stick to those guidelines.

Ask your teenager what the consequence ought to be if she comes home an hour over curfew and hasn't contacted you and doesn't have a good reason for not being in touch. She will think this will never happen and often you will find her consequences to be greater than what you would impose. Most teenagers think they will not cross over the parameters (especially if they think they are mostly reasonable) so the consequence doesn't really matter because they won't have to face it.

You can still ask her what the consequences ought to be if she came home 30 minutes after curfew and she didn't call. I would also suggest you let her know you value her thoughts and you can tell her if there are parts of her position you easily support. You may need to suggest tempering the consequences if you think they are too punitive and raising them if they seem too permissive. In creating consequences before the act, you can't fully anticipate the circumstances but you can create a mostly agreed upon principle that can be applied to forthcoming situations.

Once you have thought about curfews and discussed it with others, it is best to convey to your child your expectations for her behavior—before she goes out.

Consider telling her your expectations:

- Before she goes out you expect her to tell you when she anticipates being home.
- You expect her to call if she is going to be late.

- You expect her not to drink/do drugs and drive or be in a car with anyone who has had even one drink or one hit. (We will get into this later in more detail, but that is good for now.)
- You expect her to continue to be responsible and exercise good judgment.
- You expect her to have fun.

You will have your own expectations. Those are mine. I am sure other people have some good ones to add to the list. Whatever your expectations are I think it is important that your child knows them. That probably means you will lecture her too many times about them. She will roll her eyes and not listen. Still, it is important that she clearly knows your expectations for her.

If you just went through that list with your child most likely she will have something to say about some of your expectations. She might even have expectations for you—like not texting or calling her unless she has missed curfew.

You probably noticed I didn't have an expectation of her not drinking or doing some illegal substance. That is because I expect that in their teens children will try these things. Most kids do. I try to keep my expectations reasonable.

I would certainly tell my child that my hope would be that she would wait till she is out of high school to experiment with these things as her mind and body are still developing and it isn't in her best health interests. But who among us can say they haven't done something that is not in their best health interests? We all (or at least most of us) occasionally cheat on our health interests and hope we don't get caught. We say things like "moderation in all things," "everyone needs to be a little naughty now and then," or to quote Bruce Springsteen, "It is hard to be a saint in the city."

Some parents subscribe to the idea that since their child most likely is going to drink, they will let her drink in their home so at least they can keep an eye on her. While this is probably a safer route than doing it outside the home, it is easy for the child to infer their parents' general consent to drinking. That is a consent that I would prefer not be given. For me I would rather she had a sleepover at someone else's home, had a drink and threw up there.

Curfews are a parent's defense against alcohol/drugs and getting in trouble. There is not a lot a parent can do to prevent this and certainly having a curfew allows a parent to have a sense of partial control. Of course, we all know it is just as easy to get drunk at 5:00pm as it is at midnight.

If your child is going to do something they are going to try no matter what the curfew.

Sharing expectations, setting curfews, and handing out disciplinary actions are a parent's tools. But so are encouraging statements, affection, and your own modeling behavior. If you drink a fair amount what makes you think your child won't? If you are passing out in front of the TV and acting in sloppy ways, your kids may be repulsed and not want to follow in your path. That happens too.

For the most part children drink and do drugs in the approximate range of their parent's behavior. If you manage your life in a moderate way so most likely will they. For the most part it is a "Do as I do" world, not a "Do as I say" world.

Parents may have moderate behavior and their child as well, but that doesn't exclude anyone from getting in trouble. Teenagers have many ways to get in trouble with you, the law, and other authorities. They are prone to more spontaneous, less well thought-out actions. They could have one drink, feel good but not drunk, so they think they are fine. Then they could do something mildly thoughtless that becomes significantly thoughtless if they get caught.

Early in my career I was the co-director of a drug program where people who had been arrested for driving under the influence had to come for a number of sessions. Most of them would say they did not have a drinking or drug problem. I told them I had no way of knowing that, but one thing I knew is their drinking had gotten them in trouble with the police and if it were me I would find that problematic.

Parents send their kids out in hopes they won't do anything too stupid and there will be no call from the police or a hospital. Parents worry about those things. Probably more than they need to, and probably more than they want.

When it comes to worrying about your children the degree of worry is in proportion to the love you feel. So even though the worry is bothersome it is an indicator of love. You don't worry about things you don't care about, so worry is an act of love. That isn't going to make it easier to enjoy, but maybe it will frame it differently for you. Lest those of you who are not worriers think the worriers love their child more, please remember there are countless ways we show our love.

I remember once hearing a woman complain that her husband never told her he loved her. He told her he washed her car; if that wasn't saying he loved her he didn't know what was. He certainly wasn't washing anyone else's.

Parents lecture and establish curfews to minimize their own worry. They push kids to study more, be better citizens, and write those thank-you notes to help their child learn social skills and gain credentials to carry them to "successful" lives so their parents don't have to worry so much.

I am sure all parents will be able to list a host of other reasons why they want the best for their child and they all add up to wanting your child to be safe, live an enjoyable meaningful life, and continue to be a pleasure for their parents. The more they do that the less you need to worry and the more time you have to wash the car.

Certain municipalities have curfews for teenagers. In terms of teenager illegal activity, there doesn't seem to be much difference between those towns that have an earlier curfew and those that have a later one. Curfews do seem to protect teenagers from violence against them, especially if they live in cities where there is a fairly high crime rate.

The curfews in municipalities usually pertain to hanging out in public places. As long as your child is at a particular place or traveling between places they usually are not breaking the law. The laws aim to keep teens from lingering in public places after certain hours. Many parents use their local restrictions as guidelines for establishing their own rules.

Parents ask me if it really makes a difference if their 16-year-old has a curfew of 11:00, 12:00, 1:00, or 2:00. I have done a fair amount of searching for answers to this and can't find any solid proof that one of those times is any better than the other in terms of the mischief you child will get into and their overall behavior. There is just not a lot of good research to help you out.

This is one of those issues where you have to go with your gut and speak with the parents of your child's friends to get a better sense of how her peer group is handling the issue. Not that their guidelines will need to be yours, but the information ought to be helpful to you. There is a lot of social discomfort teenagers feel when they have significantly different curfews than their friends. It excludes them from building relationships and may cause unanticipated consequences.

Here is something I speak to parents about when it comes to giving teenagers more responsibility and allowing them to be more independent. Whatever their curfew is and however restrictive you are as a parent you need to remember that your child is going to leave home and have as much freedom of choice about her curfew as you do about yours. The better job you do of preparing her for having that freedom, the better she will deal with that freedom when she has more of it.

If you have a midnight curfew for your high school senior and she goes from midnight one month to no curfew the next, there is a good chance she will stumble. You need to get her from wherever she is now to where she is going to be when she moves out. To that end I would use a systematic approach.

If my child was going to move out or go to college after high school I would want her to have at least the last six months of her living with me with no curfew. If you have a 16-year-old with a 10:00 curfew you need to figure out how you are going to go from 10:00 to zero in whatever amount of time she has before she takes her next step. You might break down the time left before she moves out into segments and, provided she manages herself well enough, you can bit by bit loosen the reins.

The kids that have the most difficulty leaving home are the ones who have had the most restrictive homes. The more authoritarian and rule-laden parents are, the more challenging it is going to be for their children to take on being more independent and responsible. They need to be able to adjust to that freedom before they move out. I would prefer they went through the beginning stages of that transition while they lived in my home so if they stumbled I would be there to help them out.

Usually when teenagers get in trouble at the school where I work they end up in my office with their worried and upset parents. Among the many things I speak with the parents about is that even though it is unfortunate that this is happening, it is much better that it happened now than when their child moves out.

Parents know they have limited control/influence of their teen, certainly less than they had five years ago. They also know that once their child moves out that control/influence significantly decreases. If there are actions to take and monitoring to follow, those are best accomplished while your child still lives with you.

So, when it comes to curfews and other matters of independence, consider loosening the reins and let her stumble while you are still able to help her get back up.

Let me give you a piece of advice. If it is 2:30am and your child just got home and you're upset, limit yourself to "Let's all go to sleep and talk about this tomorrow." Reprimands, restrictions, resolutions, consequences, and threats are best dealt out after you have had some rest and some distance. 99% of the time there is no need to take any action steps in the middle of the night. Pronouncements are usually best left for the day after. The emotional urgency you experience in the moment may propel you to want to say or do something. Something you may regret the next day.

Certainly you may want to know what happened.

You probably are going to want to say something about how her not being in communication and coming in late affected you.

You will probably have something to say about what she has to say.

You will probably want to have the last word.

Okay, listen and talk and talk and listen. But hold the advice and consequences for later. You can sleep on what you heard and come back to it tomorrow. The facts will not have changed but the perspective/fear/anxiety might have.

If you feel the need to give some advice try suggesting that everyone go reflect on what they have heard and said and later on when we are all more rested we will discuss this some more.

I realize that for some people this is going to be impossible. Those people who like to have the last word and want to have a sense of control will probably need to have their thoughts be heard as well as their position on how things ought to be.

Do us all a favor: don't raise your voice, and keep it short.

Often when it comes time to deal with one of those moments when your child has veered off the path you were hoping she would travel your frustration and emotions will be like gasoline on a fire. There is just as good a chance that what you do will make things worse as it is you will make things better.

Anything you can say now can probably be better said tomorrow. Maybe not 100% of the time but probably sufficient enough amounts of time that you would want to try sleeping on it now and then.

Some people *like* conflict and don't mind throwing some gasoline into the fire. Often they think the real truth comes out when people are upset and unguarded so it is worth getting into noisy conflict as you get a good reading on what is really going on with the other person.

I think there is some truth to that. When people are upset they are less guarded and they tend to speak more honestly. But they are also more mean spirited in that moment. And that blurted statement while true in the moment may not be representative of how someone feels overall. If you want to get to the truth of things there are other roads you can travel that are more scenic and more revealing.

For those that still want to provoke conflict, let's see if reading this book doesn't upgrade your conflictual skills and allow you to create win/win resolutions. For those that insist on win/lose scenarios I am going to suggest you take that one to your therapist. I don't think I can get you to stop being attracted to conflict. But maybe I can help you get out what you need to get out of those situations without causing damage that is hard to repair.

So your child does something you did not want her to do. Could be a small thing. Could be a big thing. You know as a parent that sooner or later your child will do something that you do not fully want her to do.

No matter who you are in a relationship with, they will do things you do not want them to do. When it comes to your child there is usually a more emotional investment in having her learn how to do things in your perceived "best way." You may wish your partner did things differently. Your partner's behavior can annoy and frustrate you, but you usually don't feel quite the level of responsibility to change it as you do with your child. As a parent you have a sense of obligation to teach your children the best ways to be in the world so not only is she going off course troublesome to you but it causes a level of worry you would rather not have.

Since I would like to help you reduce unnecessary stress and worry, who says your way of wanting things done is the best way?

You do.

But you know you didn't exactly follow 100% of the prescription your parents had for you. Like you, your parents thought they knew what was best. Maybe if you had followed their guidelines your life would be better, but then again, going your own way helped make you who you are today. For better and for worse.

Your parents probably got caught up in what to do when you did something they would have preferred you didn't do. You might even remember how they reacted to you when you did something they did not like. It might be helpful to you to reflect on this: How is your handling of disappointment in your child similar and different than how your parents managed their disappointment with you? Some people find it helpful to observe how the parenting they received has affected them and how their behavior reflects or diverges from when they were on the receiving end.

I think all families need to sit down and talk about how they are going to handle letting others know where they are when they are out of the house and when they will be home. Everyone ought to be able to answer how they will inform others. This is akin to having an emergency contact list of people to call if something goes wrong.

Families can quibble over whether you let people know if you are going to be 15 minutes, 30 minutes, or an hour late and whether everyone needs to know your complete itinerary every time you leave the house. The goal is not to micromanage everyone's life, but to make sure someone knows approximately where you are and when you will be home.

Families need to create an emergency phone line. Who calls who and who do you call if you can't reach the person who is first or second on your list? Everyone needs to know who to call if there is some kind of emergency. And everyone needs to have the list of people to call so you can keep calling till you reach someone who answers the phone.

Everyone needs everyone's contact information.

Everyone needs to know who is out of state that can be called to be a point person if things get really bad.

Everyone needs to call at least one parent when they are not going to be home when they said they would.

Everyone needs to know if it is okay to leave a message or if they have to keep calling until they reach someone.

Every parent needs to let their children know where they are and how to reach them.

Most everyone ought to agree to those items or at least something close to it. You can add more, but the idea is to get people thinking about their responsibility to others when it comes to staying connected.

39

INTRAPERSONAL CONFLICT

In the world of psychology they talk about intrapersonal and interpersonal conflict. The 'intra' is the conflict you have within yourself—do I eat that dessert or not? The 'inter' is between you and them—are you sure you really want to eat that dessert?

Usually the better job you do of handling your own conflicts the better job you will have with others. So let's first focus on you and your conflicts and how you manage them. Most internal conflicts center around "do I or don't I" and "shoulds."

Do I or don't I:

- Eat that dessert?
- Tell them what I really think?
- Buy this item or not?
- Go here or there?
- Do this or do that?

Should I:

- Exercise more?
- Eat healthier?
- Do more meaningful things?
- Be more grateful?
- Call this person, write that person, and get together with these people?

Most people can put together a fairly substantial "should" list. If you spend any amount of time actually thinking about an item on the list it won't be long before you feel guilty. Once you start to feel guilty you either motivate yourself to take action or just feel worse until your defense mechanisms kick in and you are able to push the item out of your thoughts. Until it pops up again

We all have "should" lists and we all "should" on ourselves. Albert Ellis, PhD suggested trying to turn that should into a "want." That is not always easy to do. Sometimes the only "want" you may be able to find is the want to be on the other side of having done it. The want of the feeling of "accomplishment" and "done with it" can be an influencing motivation. Seeing the other side can assist you in getting there.

We each have different internal conflicts and deal with them in our own ways. There is not much to be gained from beating up on yourself for being internally conflicted and procrastinating. That is akin to berating yourself for being human. Yet most people can get frustrated and upset with themselves and do some name calling. Just try to limit it. Get your aggravation with you out and give yourself a talking to if you need to, but then let go of your anger at yourself and focus on moving forward.

Do your best to accept that you have a conflict and that you would rather not have it and would prefer to avoid the whole thing entirely. Say something to yourself along the lines of: "I am not happy about this, but I don't want to continue to fret about it so I am going to move on." Then force yourself to think about something else. Repeat as needed.

Sooner or later you know you will need to deal with it.

You have the choice about when and how to deal with it. Certainly the world may provide you deadlines, but you have the choice about how to respond to those deadlines. Some people pay their taxes early, others right around the 15th, others get extensions, and others don't pay. Whichever path you take there is a price you are going to pay.

Choices you make in life are accompanied by choices you are not making. If you choose to do your taxes early there is something else you are foregoing. If you choose to wait till the last minute you get to do other things while the clock ticks down.

Every "Yes" is accompanied by a "No."

Doing this means you are not doing that. As of yet we can't be in two places at once. If you are reading this you are not reading that. You are here not there.

Often the concern about the "No" is what is causing conflict over the declaring of the "Yes."

Finding a comfortable resolution to the inter conflicts that permeate our life can be time consuming and stressful. People easily get upset with themselves for not resolving things quicker and better. When it comes to our internal struggles we often are assisted by our internal critic who is happy to remind us that we are not handling our life well enough.

It is challenging enough living life without having to do battle with our own internal voices, yet we all have them. In cartoons you see the image of the angel over one shoulder and the devil over the other. I imagine we all have our own version of those entities who pull us in different directions. I don't know if it is the angel or the devil who is producing the criticism, but I can tell you that when we criticize ourselves we can get mired in our own despair. It is a losing proposition.

If you were criticized a lot growing up you might think criticism is a sign of concern and affection. Many children come to think the criticism they receive is real and the praise is not to be trusted. They come to see their parents pointing out their shortcomings as indicators that they're not living life well enough. Often these people end up being involved with critical partners who continue to point out their failings. When they are with someone who is complimentary, they tend to not believe them. They have a trust and comfort in criticism.

I tend to believe that if someone cares for your wellbeing they will tell you what they admire about you and enjoy about you. They will also tell you when you do things that hurt, distress, or concern them. They will give you this feedback in a respectful and loving way.

Whether you trust and believe in the value of criticism or not, you are going to get it and give it. I am going to offer some ways to conflict and bring your critical comments to light that might be of greater benefit to the recipient. How you express yourself and how you respond to others are the cornerstones of relationships. It is not so much that you are or are not a critical person; it is more how you deal with it that matters.

When dealing with internal conflicts I recommend that you don't repress them. When we repress something from our thoughts we are attempting to put it in the back of the drawer to be dealt with later. Sometimes we have to prioritize what we can deal with and in those circumstances you may choose to deal with this before that. But that doesn't mean you forget about the other thing. It just means you are not dwelling on it until you have more time to focus on it.

Repressed items have a tendency to fester. You may think you have neatly tucked it into the back of the drawer, but while it is there it often creeps its way into other parts of the drawer and begins to affect you in indirect ways. You may choose not to tell someone that you didn't like something they said to you, but you may find yourself taking little jabs at things they say.

As your internal conflicts come to your attention you can opt to put them on your "To Do Later" list, but at least make sure you keep that list present in your awareness. You can update and rearrange items as often as you like, but you will be better served by having the list and reflecting on it often. Which means you ought to actually write down your list of present internal conflicts you are having and update it as you go along. You may not have time to think about and do everything on the list, but just looking at it periodically will allow your unconscious mind to take a photograph and do some background mulling.

When you have internal conflicts, just as is with the case of interpersonal conflicts, they are usually better dealt with sooner than later. Since most people are conflict-avoidant, many would prefer to put off till another time what they don't have to struggle with today. We can all list good reasons for waiting to do something. Sometimes it is considerably better to wait. But I would wager that is not the case most of the time.

Let's focus on those times when at some level you know it would be better to deal with something now but your wariness keeps you from taking direct action. Maybe you hope it will go away. Maybe you think time will make it better or it will be easier to deal with when you don't have other things on your plate.

In the therapy world, they call those 'rationalizations': your mind's way of protecting you from doing something you don't want to do. I suggest you acknowledge and accept that you just don't want to do something now. You can dole out the truth to others, but don't fool yourself. There is not much long-range upside to that.

If you are hemming and hawing about talking to your teenager about your wanting him to apply himself more I am sure you can find reasons to delay the discussion. It will just set him off. It won't really help. Maybe he will change… While you are deliberating and putting off the conversation, consider acknowledging to yourself that:

- You do have an interest in taking care of this issue.
- You do want to get on the other side of the issue.
- There probably are more good reasons for approaching this sooner than later.

This is as good a time as any to introduce the 80/20 Decision Matrix. When it comes to making major decisions, whether it be moving to another city or having a serious sit-down conversation with your child, consider using a 1-100 scale. Out of 100, with 100 being completely 100% wanting to do something and 0 no interest whatsoever, you can approximate each decision you have to make. You may be 100% certain that your son could apply himself more. But you may only be 10% certain that approaching him will help.

Consider the example of moving to another city. If every time you think about moving you are only 20% sure you want to do it, you probably aren't going to move. But if most days when you think about it you are about 80% certain you want to move, you ought to just move. If you can think about something and consistently get to that 80% certain point that usually is good enough to go. It is hard to be 100% certain about many things. I am sure we have all had the experience of going back and forth about what to wear and what to order off the menu. Sometimes these decisions are crystal clear and other times we are not sure. When it comes to those issues of greater concern for you, it is often hard to be completely sure. There can be valid points on both sides of an issue. If you hold out for being 100% certain you may find the moment has passed.

When you're hovering on the 50/50 line it is hard to get much done. You can often go along if someone else has a lot of conviction, but still 50% of you isn't sure. When you have those close-call situations it is best to focus on what you can do to move it to 60/40, then 70/30, and then 80/20. Most likely you won't get to 100%. You are welcome to try. But as a general rule when you ask yourself about some matter and time and again you are coming out at 80% confident, that is sufficient to move forward.

While I would prefer that as often as possible you push yourself to resolution I also want you to give yourself a break if you aren't in a place to move forward. Procrastination has some benefits. It does give you time to be more thoughtful and sometimes you can come up with better solutions. But in those cases where you are conflicted about how to proceed with something, why not find someone and talk it over with them? You don't have to take any action, but often just sounding it out with someone will help you get the added clarity and oomph to move ahead.

Being honest with yourself about what you are doing and not doing and why you are and aren't doing it is worth your effort.

Know thyself. Accept thyself. Encourage yourself to explore what is holding you back from taking action. Perhaps if you understood your reluctance you might be able to find ways to provide yourself the necessary support to move through your resistance.

The more you find out, the more you pay attention to you, the more you will want to attend to the choices you make. While they won't all be grand and glorious, they will all be of your conscious choosing.

Trust yourself to know what is best for you.

You may not always make the best choices. Sometimes people like to opt for the easiest option and just do the minimum—which I would argue is the best you can do in the moment.

What you can do now or what you think is best in this moment may change in the next moment. As time moves on, life shifts and priorities change. Sometimes there come moments that require you to be diligent about what you are feeling, thinking, and doing with your life. Other times you can glide along.

When it comes to your own intrapersonal conflicts I suggest you be honest with yourself as often as you can, as long as you can. When you find yourself turning away from facing your truths, admit that to yourself. We all need to give things a rest at times. Gently acknowledge to yourself that there are places in your own self awareness that you do not want to go to yet. So be it.

I can't promise you that everyone will benefit from opening those doors, but I can tell you many have. You have the choice. You might want to talk to someone about that choice and your concerns so you can learn more about you, which may or may not encourage you to explore more. Whatever you decide you want to feel comfortable in your choice even if it is only 80% solid. Many times that is as much certainty as we are going to get.

40

INTERPERSONAL CONFLICT

Now about those conflicts with others.

Conflict is a part of any close relationship. Don't judge the quality of your relationships by the absence of conflict but rather by the quality of the conflicts.

If you are not having conflicts in your close relationships it most likely means the level of truth and intimacy is lower. Some people choose to forego degrees of intimacy if in return they get less conflict. I can appreciate that, as conflict is rarely a joyful thing.

But what if the tradeoff comes at the price of higher blood pressure, more internal stress, and less joy? You are increasing the internal conflict in order to decrease the external. Which is okay, but let's see if we can upgrade your external conflicts so you aren't so hesitant to get into them.

Here is how.

First, accept that there will be more open conflict in your relationships.

Second, accept that you can learn how to conflict in a healthier, more respectful and positive resolution-focused manner. You can learn to be more caring to them and you, more assertive, more empathic, and have greater effectiveness.

It doesn't matter how horrible the other person is at conflict. There are skills you can learn that not only will help you feel better but which also improve the other person's skills. Whether they want to improve or not. You will be able to influence them so they too will upgrade their skills.

See if you can allow yourself to believe that conflict can be a viable part of your close relationships and you can learn to be better at it. Conflict can become such a feasible avenue for connecting, focusing, healing, and moving forward, you may actually want to have more of them. Well, maybe not.

If you notice that your conflicts are becoming less of a big deal and more of an opportunity for creative problem-solving, you may actually want to speak more about those things you are less-than-pleased about. Conflict is a part of any relationship, but it is only a part. In order to minimize the damage conflicts can inflict, you need to make sure your relationship also includes actions to balance things out. One thing you can do right now is affective affirmations.

Affective affirmations are those things people say to one another that affirm their valuing of the other person. Whether you say "I love you" or "You're so thoughtful," conveying your appreciation to those you care about balances out most hurts that conflict may cause. Especially if you stick to that 5:1 ratio and make sure those you care about are not starved for your affection and attention.

Yes, conflict can hurt. That is because what is prompting the conflict is that you or they are hurt about something and often in the sharing that hurt gets wrapped in barbed comments It is one thing to say, "I am upset about how things went last night. I was thinking you were going to be home at midnight and not only did you not come home on time, but you never called." It is another thing to say, "I am upset about your behavior last night. You are inconsiderate and not trustworthy and I have lost respect for you."

You child is not going to want to hear either of those statements, but when you throw in name calling you are liable to cause more harm. Name-calling is destructive and does not have a valued place in communication, as the sentiments behind those words can be expressed in other less harmful ways. I basically think that when someone is name-calling they are in the fight mode and are not interested in resolving matters and connecting. They need to get their anger out. I would just prefer they did it without using name calling. That is a language skill people can learn.

So, what are these miracle skills that you need to bone up on?

Remember the last time you had good intentions to not lose your cool and things did not work out quite the way you wanted? Keeping your composure when things heat up is a skill most people have to learn and develop. It requires willpower and focus. The temporary satisfaction you might have by letting someone have it full blast may not feel so satisfying when things have simmered down. Restraint for the greater good is a worthy goal. And certainly obtainable in that 10-20% range.

Conflict arises because your emotions have been triggered. Once you engage someone, their emotions will be triggered as well. When walking an emotional landscape it is easy to trip. Especially when those who know you best know which buttons to push to upset your balance. Learning how to modulate your emotions to reduce your outbursts and inflammatory comments will serve you well.

You know how mean and nasty you can be when you are upset. You have seen you in action and you know how low you can go. You may have said mean things to hurt the other person. We all do it. Some more often and overtly than others, but we all have pushed back hard. The skill to acquire is to continue to push back, but to do it in a constructive well-meaning way instead of a hurtful one.

People in couples' therapy are often asked this question: "Would you rather be loved or right?"

In other words, do you want to continue to argue or do you want to find a way to connect in a loving way that might actually bring you closer instead of perpetuating the argument?

How important is it to be right? Why this time does it matter to you? How much does it matter?

Sometimes it matters a lot. Other times not so much. It helps to know why you are pushing your point of view so you aren't always arguing about things that really do not matter. Lawyers, who are versed in debate, often find their relationships to be adversarial because the skill set that serves them at work comes home with them and often does not serve them so well at home.

Sometimes being right matters because other things going on in the relationship prompted you to want to one up the other. Perhaps you are upset about something else that is unresolved and you are taking this opportunity to extract revenge. Or maybe this time it is about something really important where the right answer carries with it a significant consequence that the wrong answer does not. So, you continue to conflict to prove your point and argue for what you believe is really important.

When things are of significant concern to you it is important to stand up for them. Just do it in a respectful and caring manner and know when enough is enough. If you don't know, ask.

Do you think that for the most part you are able to monitor your tone, volume, and content so you mostly can engage in conflictual discussions with respect and caring and a desire to find a workable resolution?

Yes? No? Depends?

Do you think you are able to guide the tone and emotion of the argument so there is mostly caring, empathy, and a mutual desire for win/win resolutions?

Yes? No? Depends?

If you answered yes to those questions, congratulations. Those are not the easiest accomplishments to sustain when the going gets rough.

If you don't feel able yet to sustain those higher-ground practices, read on.

What do you need to do to practice the belief that relationships are about common concerns and blend them together with equal respect for you, them, and the relationship you share? In most interpersonal matters there really is no right/wrong or good/bad, but instead there is you, me, and us, and a common need to create a viable and hopefully enhancing resolution. Joe Noel, PhD often spoke about I, Thou and We. In relationships each of those points of view need to considered.

Yes, there is a right or wrong about whether you agreed to meet at 7:00 or 8:00 and you can argue about it back and forth. But if they think 7:00 and you know it was 8:00 how do you resolve that? You can't prove it was 8:00 and they can't prove it was 7:00. It boils down to he said/she said. You can call them names, makes exasperated sounds, and look at them like they are stupid, but what does that get you?

There's no harm in saying, "Obviously we remember this differently. Let's make sure in the future to really be clear with each other so this does not happen again." That statement moves away from the right/wrong and into the common ground resolution.

Which brings us to this.

If we are talking about serious conflicts you have then we are primarily talking about the people closest to you, the ones you love the most. Yes, you can have serious conflicts in the workplace and those stakes can get high. Yet how you manage your work conflicts—while similar to how you manage your personal conflicts—does have a different set of guideline, which if you want we can chat about on the blog, but for now I am focusing on you and your child and the people you call family.

There really aren't a lot of reasons to get into emotionally-laden conflicts with people who don't mean that much to you. You can argue over a movie or sport with anyone. But when it comes to things that have real meaning and value in our life, we are talking about sharing your truth with those who mean the most to you. Remember people have to mean enough to you that you are willing to go through the discomfort involved in conflicting. Otherwise you can just stuff it and move on.

So you have something that is bothering you and you may not want to share it but you know that it is something that is of sufficient concern to you to warrant sharing. Or you have something that you have no qualms about sharing and are eager to do so. Or they have something bothering them and they share it and that bothers you. Or your child just came home inebriated or you got a call from the school or the bill just came in the mail.

Regardless of how bothered you are, do you really want to hurt this other person? Randy Newman wrote a song titled, "I Want You to Hurt Like I Do." While I think that sentiment is alive in many people now and then, I would like to think that intentionally hurting the people you love is not on anyone's list of things they like about themselves.

Sure, they may have done or said something that hurt you and now you want to hurt them back. That is understandable. A lot people might feel that way. But feeling that way and doing it are two different things. This is where that modulation needs to come in. It is okay to want to hurt them or raise your voice or jump up and down. It is less okay to do it.

But certainly you can express the desire to want to do it. That is the preferred route. Get the impulse out there and acknowledge that bit of your emotional response.

You can say: "I am extremely upset. I want to scream, swear at you, and just blow off this anger."

And then say, "But I am not going to do that. I am going to do my best to as respectfully as possible let you know what is going on with me. But first, it would probably be best for me to be quiet and have you to tell me exactly what is going on with you."

Even people who have high expectations for their behavior sometimes say or do hurtful things to those they love. Why is that? Can you explain to yourself why you say hurtful things or do hurtful things to people you love?

_____

_____

_____

I don't know what you think. Perhaps it is similar to what I think. I think we hurt people we love because we have been hurt by them or someone up the line hurt us and the only place to let off some steam is with those who are around us. Most of the time we hurt those close to us because they have said or done something that was hurtful to us. It could have been any number of things. Perhaps we are too sensitive or overreacting. Whatever the motivation, something hurtful came out of our mouths aimed at someone we love because we were hurt or afraid or angry or all three.

How about we focus on stopping that "You hit me, I hit you back" behavior?

Instead consider this word: Ouch.

When someone says something that hurts you why not just say "Ouch"? Instead of verbally hitting them back and escalating the fight why not just let them know they landed a good punch?

Many people answer that by saying they don't want the other person to know they are hurt. To which I say, why wouldn't you want someone you love to know when they have done something to hurt you? Don't you want them to do less of that?

I get that telling someone that you are hurt exposes you. They will hear you say the things they do that hurt you and that may give them an avenue to do it again. But, wait, if you tell someone you love that there is something they do that hurts you and they continue to do that—well, there is something greater that needs attention. For my money, you need to get into therapy. Preferably with them, but if not with them then just you. Exploiting someone's vulnerability is not what I would want for you in your close relationships. I would like to think the person would endeavor not to do that hurtful thing and if they kept doing it, I would be sitting down with a third party and talking it out.

You want to be able to tell someone what they do that hurts you and you want that person to endeavor not to do that. This may need to be a discussion item as there are I, Thou and We points of view to take into consideration. But how that matter gets discussed and attended to needs to be guided by the principle of doing the least amount of harm.

Parents model behavior.

Kids are going to do as you do more often than not. You argue with them. They will argue with you. You say hurtful things to them. They will say hurtful things to you. You start letting them know how you feel and how their behavior affects you, they will start to do the same.

Not right away. Not just like you. But not that far away either, and not all that differently.

If you don't act the way you would like to act how are you going to get your children to act the way you want them to act? What is going to happen to change anything?

Nothing.

Well, maybe some chance event will come along that sweeps you all up in gratitude and respect and you start behaving differently toward one another. But why wait for that long shot to happen when you can build your skills and help make it happen?

Instead of meeting fire with fire, consider meeting any incoming hurt with an acknowledgement that what they said touched you. You could say something simple like, "What you said hurt me. It makes me want to hurt you back, but I don't really want to do that. I would like to talk about this in some way that is not as hurtful. I hope we can do that."

Certainly in the moment it would come out differently, but I would think that is the general sentiment you want to convey. Maybe the other person would be okay with it or maybe not. They may still be upset with you and want to continue to express what is going on with them in barbed tones. If they throw in something hurtful so be it. But you don't have to get involved in that exchange. They can express their upset in ways that do not aggress against you. That is a learnable skill.

If someone is strongly upset they are going to want to vent. Often once they get started it is hard to slow down. And, in truth, you want them to completely get whatever is concerning them off their chests and out into the open. Even if it comes out in terms that are difficult to hear.

You don't want to cut someone off. That will only upset them more and prolong their need to vent. While it is uncomfortable hearing them out, you will find that giving them the space to fully vent will get all the air out of the balloon and you will have less need to worry about it getting inflated again anytime soon.

- You do want to let them know when things are hard to hear and hurtful.
- You do want to ask them to continue to speak their truth and to try to do it in some way that is not purposefully provocative, threatening, or demeaning.

If it is you who is blowing off steam remember no name-calling, no bullying, and no belittling. Just honest, caring, respectful sharing of what is concerning you.

Okay, you say, *I will do my best to mind my manners. But it is not that easy. Especially when the other person is angry with me.*

I will remind you that if all this stuff were easy you wouldn't be reading this book. Relationships are a live organism that you can't control. You can only endeavor to make them as loving, encouraging, supportive, and engaging as possible.

I am sure there are qualities/beliefs/values you have tried to instill in your children and you've done your best to model them. And I am sure some have stuck more than others.

Usually when your child is upset with you it is not comfortable listening to her when she is letting you have it. Sometimes it comes in softer more indirect ways, other times it comes yelling at you full of the vocabulary you were hoping she would avoid using until she was older, if at all.

When those you love are upset with you it presents an opportunity to model how you would like them to behave when someone is upset at them. I suppose if you value raising your voice, swearing, name-calling, and/or verbal/physical abuse you will model that. I am advocating a different path. An honest, caring path that leaves room for difference and creative win-win resolutions. That's the goal. And, once again, no one scores 100% all the time.

A lot of people are reluctant to bring things that anger them into a relationship because conflict is so hard to resolve. People sit on their anger; they repress it, deny it, and often do their best not to have to deal with it. That is unfortunate.

A lot of therapists are going to tell you that it seeps out. You may think you are fooling some of the people all of the time, but even if they don't know the exact content they usually are feeling the anger in some indirect way. Many people opt for being passive-aggressive where you take small actions against the person without ever directly telling them you are angry. Most of us have chosen this path more than once. You arrive late because you are upset at something they did, or you "forget" to do something you were supposed to do to help the other person.

There are plenty of books on being passive-aggressive. For now, just consider yourself mature enough to not have to act out in this way too often and seriously ready to deal with your emotions more directly.

Let's see if we can make that happen.

First and foremost, when someone is angry with you, let them be angry. Don't try to change their mind, tell them they shouldn't be angry, interrupt them, or otherwise get in the way of the flow of their anger. It will do you no good to try to get them to stop, to try to tone them down, or to otherwise derail them. I am not saying it will be pleasant to hear what they have to say, but the sooner you let them get it out the sooner you will be able to resolve the issue. Besides, whatever is on your mind will eventually be spoken. Just hold off until they are done.

No faces, no noises, no demeaning looks. Just respectful listening. When you think they are done instead of launching into your own defense or anger tell them you get that they are angry with you and you want to make sure you hear everything that is bothering them. Ask them if there is anything else they want to tell you.

Your initial goal is to empty their tank. As long as there is fuel in there, things will be combustible. As much as you want to have your turn, the more they get out during their turn the easier your turn will be.

Now, many therapists would have you repeat back the major points the person has made to let them know you understand them. For most people that is too awkward and contrived. I would say if there is anything you are not sure about, ask them for clarification.

I did not say if there is anything you *disagree* about.

If there is something in what they said that you don't understand it is important that you fully get what they are saying before you respond. This is a critical point; before you launch into whatever you are going to say you need to make sure you clearly understand what they are upset about. A healthy portion of people's anger derives from their not feeling understood. The better job you do of understanding their point of view the greater the likelihood their anger will lessen. The more you refute and put down their point of view the longer the anger will fester. Their truth is their truth and needs to be respected as such. You don't have to agree with it or like it, but you need to honor it because that is what they think. Remember your ability to let them know you understand their point of view is going to go a long way towards resolving this conflict.

If people do not feel understood and appreciated you first order of business is to let them know you understand them. Sooner or later you are going to need to bring in the appreciation but when conflict is happening I would opt for understanding first with appreciation a close second.

If you want to get a really good grade at this you can say something akin to: "Let me be sure I understand what you are saying. You are upset with me because I _____."

That might be a little too much of a textbook therapy statement, but you can put what you understand in your own words.

Sure, they are still going to be angry at you for what you did or didn't do, but your interest in understanding why/how this upset them is calming. That is not going to get you completely off the hook, but it ought to bring the temperature down so you can discuss what happened instead of arguing about it.

Let's consider an example in two different ways: one where you screwed up and one where you didn't. In both cases your teenager is mad at you, but in one you are guilty as charged and in the other you are not. Let's also add that in both cases the degree of anger that your child has is more than you think your action deserves.

Whether I was at fault or not I would handle the conversation the same. If I were not guilty as charged I would at the very end point out that I understood things differently and that going forward we need to work on making sure we both understand the guidelines for the evening. Guilty or not the initial goal is the same— letting your child express herself and doing your best to understand her.

Her: "You are such a loser. You were supposed to pick me up at midnight and you came to the party at 11:30 and instead of waiting outside you came in and totally embarrassed me. I hate you."

You: "I get why you are mad at me. I got there earlier than we agreed to and I wasn't supposed to come in but I did anyway."

Her: "Yes, you completely embarrassed me and I don't want to talk to you anymore."

You: "I am sorry I embarrassed you. That doesn't feel good to hear. I don't want to stop talking right now. Can we discuss it a little longer?"

Her: "Why? You screwed up again and I should know better than to trust you. Why bother talking?"

You: "I get that you are frustrated with me. Is there anything else you are upset about? As long as we are talking we might as well get it all out on the table."

Her: "I could go on and on. You just don't get it. You are never there for me when I need you to be. And when you are you do it all wrong."

You: "Yikes. I am sorry to hear that you think I am not there for you when you need me to be. That doesn't feel good to hear."

Her: "How do you think it feels for me? This isn't about you and your feelings. This is about me and how you are ruining my life."

You: "You think I am ruining your life?"

Her: "Yes. Completely."

You: "Wow. I didn't know you were that upset with me. It is not easy to hear this, but I'm glad you are telling me."

The point I want you to get is that you have not defended yourself. You have just listened to her and let her know you are hearing her. It sounds a bit stiff to read, but the essence is to try to understand what she is experiencing and how that is for her. This is not your time to voice your opinions. Just hear hers. Your turn will come.

Yes, there are points in there that you could easily disagree with and argue that she is wrong and you are right. But resist the temptation. The first goal is to listen and help your child get out the pain she is experiencing. You job is not to get in the way or be right, but to help her find her way. We will get to your further response later. But first help her get her upset out so you can more fully understand what is upsetting her.

You may disagree with the time you arrived at the party and what exactly the agreement was for picking her up. But before you launch into that, you want to hear her out.

Obviously in this case your daughter has some built-up resentment and is exaggerating. Something that most teenagers do and which you as a parent need to ultimately help her with, but not while you are arguing. Save the discussion about how exaggerating won't serve her well for another time when you see someone on TV exaggerating and you can have a sidebar conversation and not a lecture. It is usually easier to point out something someone else is doing and voice your disapproval than to aim it directly at your child.

You can share with her how most people will know if you are exaggerating and then point out that what you are saying is not totally true. Then the conversation gets diverted into one about your exaggerating and the issue at hand either gets avoided or delayed.

If a parent was late picking up their child one time, the child could say, "One time." If their parent did it again she could say, "Twice." If they picked their child up late three times she could say, "A few times." If they have done it more than five times she would be justified in saying, "Too many times." If they did it more times than she can count, she could say, "Way too many times."

Here is a language tip for you and your child: don't say "always." And while you are at it leave out "never" too. Unless something actually happens always or never, refrain from using those words. Whatever the number is will be justification for you thinking/feeling what you do. Something does not have to happen always or never for you to justify your reaction. You feel what you feel. Period.

If you are the only one who feels a certain way, don't say "everyone." Your voice alone is enough. If you think/feel something, that is your truth. How many people agree or don't agree with you is considerably less important. People often think they can gain clout by ascribing their feelings to other people as well. Whether other people feel the same way or not is not of primary relevance right now. If something is important to you that makes it sufficiently important to those around you.

It doesn't matter if people think you are being "too sensitive" or "too picky." What matters is that it is important to you.

Of course once you are done expressing yourself you will need to hear if the other person thinks you are too sensitive or too picky That is their truth and when it comes around to their time to talk you need to give them the respect and support that they want.

When the teenager says, "You are never there for me," you know that is not true. Instead of paying attention to the sentiment that caused those words the parent might just want to argue about whether or not they have been there and not deal with the real issue that is bothering their child.

Your child can head off other people sidetracking them by saying, "Sometimes you are not there for me when I want you to be." That is probably a true statement most of us can make about the people in our lives.

There is no real argument there. Just a sad truth about life. If you child says "always" or "never" instead of "sometimes," put yourself in her shoes and see how that might feel if you thought your parents were never there for you in the way you wanted. It cannot feel good to think your parent is never there for you. That feeling is what needs attention, not the use of language.

Remember the first order of business when someone is mad at you is to hear them out and understand why they are upset. Once you understand what is bothering the other person the next thing to do is to validate that is the way they think/feel. Instead of saying, "You shouldn't feel that way," see if you can't find your way to saying something close to: "That can't feel good. I wouldn't like it either if I thought my father/mother was never there for me."

I would imagine that many of us would not be all that happy if our parents came in to a party unexpectedly when we were teenagers. Some might be mildly upset and others more so. Some wouldn't make much of a deal of it and others would crank it up. There is no correct way for your child to feel about things when they are provoked. You may have preferences about how she handles her emotions, but unfortunately while you might prefer someone else behave in the way you like, you don't have those controls. Just the desire for them.

When your child decides to let you know she is upset you can view this in many different ways. You may be upset if you think she is not being respectful. You may be hurt that she is choosing to focus on this one thing and not other things. You may get upset at her for being upset with you. Or you may think/feel all those things and more and yet have an entirely different reaction.

Since her sharing her anger is a statement of her comfort with you if not her pleasure, you can turn this emotional exchange into an opportunity to improve your relationship.

Why make things worse? Why not let your child get mad at you and in doing so also let her know you can hold her anger? You want her to know her emotions are not too much for you to handle. Many people are reluctant to share the depth of their emotions for fear they will be "too much" for the other person. While you don't welcome her anger, you want her to share it, and you want her to know it won't drive you away or make you love her any less.

How she lets you know when she is upset with you could probably use some upgrading and hearing what she is saying is going to test your resolve, but take a moment to be thankful she is telling you. Because if she is not telling you, you have worse problems.

Okay, you say. I let my child get mad at me and tell me what a disappointment I am or what a shoddy job

I am doing as a parent. I asked her if there was anything more and she threw some more stuff in and basically reiterated the lousy job I am doing as a parent. I asked for more and she said that was everything. Now can't I defend myself, get mad at her for speaking to me this way, or otherwise come back at her?

Yes, you can. But you need to be a role model here. Remember it is your task to help develop your child into an adult you can be thankful for and proud of. At this moment you are the teacher and you are teaching her how to deal with things when someone is upset at you.

Respond to her anger in such a way as you would like her to respond to yours or anyone else's. You want to honor and respect her telling you while you share your truths as well. Speak as one of the people who loves this child the very most and is invested in her welfare.

Don't let your anger trump your love. Of course, every now and then your hurt, frustration, annoyance, and disappointment will get the better of you. But hopefully those times are few and far between. It is not that you won't have those emotions. It is just that you don't want to share those feelings when you are very upset. Those sentiments are going to be difficult enough for your child to hear without you wrapping them up in anger. You want to get some distance and sort through why you are so upset and what would be the best way to deal with it and not necessarily the emotionally expedient way.

You can give out tough love, hard love, soft love, or good love. It matters less which version you subscribe to and more how you get your point across. You need to respond to your child in a similar way as you did when she was a year old and fell and hurt herself. You can't pick her up and hold her to help the sore go away, but you can talk with her in an effort to make her wounds heal sooner. Your baby cried when she was hungry or got hurt. Your teenager is doing the same thing. Her anger at you has within it a cry for help. What is bothering her needs to be attended to for her to feel better.

Attend.

If you read enough self-help books you will have learned that when someone tells you how they think/feel there is a preferred step to take before you tell them what you think/feel. That step is basically one of empathy. You first let your child know that you know she is upset and you are sorry she is feeling that way. You hear what a lousy job you are doing and tell her that while it doesn't feel good to hear, you know it must be even worse to have to experience. You would be upset too if you felt that way about your parents.

That would be the empathy step. If you do a semi-decent job of it you might be able to cool down the fire and she might open up a little more and start to give you avenues to explore to make things better. Or maybe it won't make any apparent difference. Either way, letting the other person know you have heard her concern and are trying to understand is a basic key to meaningful conversation. It will pay off in the long run if not the short.

I would like to think most of us would have an empathic response first before jumping in to our own reactions. Not just because empathy is healing, but because when someone is upset you want to be careful about launching into your own thoughts/feelings and taking the focus away from the person who is hurt. They are the one who is upset and initiated this interaction. You really do not want to take focus away from them until it is clear they are done talking. As much as you want to share what is being triggered within you, at the moment that is of secondary importance. Focus first on the priority at hand—attending to the healing of your child.

When your child (or anyone) is upset at you, there is a simple "Rule of the Game" that I follow.

My basic rule, aside from being respectful and caring, is when someone starts a conversation the ball is in their court. They get to express themselves until they are done. Do not hijack the conversation.

Their issue trumps yours. Just because they started to speak with you about *this* does not mean you now get to speak to them about *that*. If you want to speak to them about something that is evoked in you, bring it up another time or at least later in the conversation. This discussion is about the issue they brought up. Focus on it, don't change the subject, and don't make it about you.

Like a lot of rules this is a hard one to follow. Sometimes our emotions get triggered and there is some issue that was lurking below the surface that comes rushing out. So be it. Sometimes you will muddy the waters. Just try to remember she initiated the discussion and there is something that is out of balance for her and you need to pay attention. There are times we need to be the dutiful adult. This is one of those times. If you have moved the subject away from what was bothering her, make sure you circle back.

Remember the premise that in relationships there rarely is a right or wrong, good or bad. When you get into arguments about who is right, you have lost. There is no right way for your child to think/feel about you showing up at the party. There are preferable ways of expressing yourself and that is what you will model.

When the time comes to express what you think/feel about the issue at hand, a good place to start is with how you feel.

- What do you feel about having this discussion? (Hopefully happy she is telling you and not holding it in, but you could also be angry or worried that she is bringing up whatever she is bringing up.)
- Are you upset/disappointed/surprised that she is upset with you?
- What do you think about what she is saying? (Can you find the truth in her experience and validate it while also having your own point of view?)
- What do you want? (Hopefully something for her as well as you.)

If you can share some of those thoughts/feelings it ought to help bridge the space between you. Even though she is upset at you doesn't mean you don't want to be able to see eye-to-eye on many things that might require some movement on both your parts.

Once you have heard her reactions to your reaction, you can give your lecture about how you see the whole thing. But remember this is her issue. She brought it to you and it is not your time to grandstand and make pronouncements. It is your time to tend to your child's wounds. You will have many opportunities to speak with her about your concerns about what she spoke about. That might come in this discussion or another time. Just make sure that the issue that she brought up gets fully addressed to whatever "good enough" settlement you can reach in the moment before you bring another issue to the table. And remember, dealing with conflict is hard enough, you don't need to end one and start another.

Just like you didn't lecture her when she tripped and fell as an infant, your initial responsibility is to care for the wellbeing of your child. When she fell you did not lecture her about keeping her balance and tell her about the inconvenience to you to have to take care of her when you had other things to do. Now is not the time to tell her that if she had done this instead of that you would not have to sit here now hashing it out. Save that for your therapist. Be glad she is talking with you about her life—even if it is to tell you how you are ruining it.

Just keep reminding yourself that her speaking to you is a testament to the trust she has in your ability to handle her. That ability means a lot, especially when your child does not think she is able to handle her life as well as she would like.

SECTION 6:

THE DAY-TO-DAY

AND THEN SOME

41

WHAT YOUR CHILD NEEDS FROM YOU AND VICE VERSA

This will be a short chapter. What you child needs from you will evolve as she ages as will what you need from her. The one main through-line that we all need is to feel loved. Another is to love.

I don't know if these qualify a gifts per se, but I think the best gift a parent can give a child is for that child to know that she is truly valued. It helps when you can point out to her the things you like about her. While you might like that grade she got in her science class, you might also like the effort and focus she put in to making that grade happen, along with her analytical mind and ability to discern what is truly important. Try to find the qualities she possesses that you like and when you see them in action let her know.

You might not like her stubbornness when it comes to arguing with you. Yet I imagine there will be times in her life that her stubbornness will serve her well. See if you can let her know that while occasionally it may be frustrating for you to bump up against her willpower you know that is a good tool for her to have in her toolbox. She just needs some other ones to help balance things out. I might save pointing that out for when I saw those other qualities on display.

Everyone has insecurities. We are hesitant and afraid to do certain things. We often restrict ourselves when we don't have sufficient confidence that we will be able to work out things in a good enough way. We become afraid of making mistakes, failing, and being foolish.

The more a child believes her parents are on her side and believe in her the easier it is for her to take forward steps into the world. Those steps will sometimes be missteps. Knowing your love is solidly there for her allows her to feel more comfortable about trying new things, making mistakes, and continuing the effort to build a rewarding life. You believe in her and so will she.

I don't know how this worked for you, but I remember when my daughter took her first steps down a hallway. She was so excited as she kept her balance and made those first few steps away from me on her own. She hadn't gone far when she stopped, looked over her shoulder and made sure I was still there. Reassured that I was, she took a few more steps.

Being a solid fixture in your child's life allows her to explore the world with the knowledge that there is a safety net there for her when and if needed. When she was little and stumbled you picked her up and soothed her boo-boos and sent her on her way. That was a winning formula then and it still is now.

You won't always be able to be that solid fixture as life can be destabilizing. When your life gets on thin ice you will need some backup. Just as your child will. Reaching out for help when times are tough is a skill you can teach your child. Teach her how to ask for it. You do not have to be all things for your child. But you do need to teach her how to navigate her way to safety when necessary

I suppose we all could create a list of things a parent needs from their child. Certainly what parents want from a one-year-old is considerably different than what they want from a 15-year-old. Or is it?

Yes, parents want their older child to shoulder a greater range of responsibilities, but the basic truth is that what a parent needs from a child is to know that she is okay. A one-year-old may cry out when she needs attention and so too might a 15-year-old. The cry is different but the need is the same: I need help.

Your teenager needs you to be there for her when she needs you to be there for her and usually would prefer you weren't around when she doesn't need you. You just need to know she is okay. You need to trust she will reach out when need be and that no news is good news. Both of those do not come easily which is why I would want to let my child know what I need from her and ask what she needs from me. Sharing this information will be helpful to all. It won't guarantee results but it might help you sleep a little better at night.

When you can't sleep well, ask her how she is doing and when she says, "Fine" say, "No, really, how are things going? I want to know." If you are not comforted call the school, her friend's parents, and your therapist. You need to know she is okay and if you don't know that you need to do something so that you can be reassured.

42

SECURITY

A sense of security is something we all need. When we feel safe in our home, our work, and our world, we rarely think about how good it feels to be safe. We just comfortably accept that we don't have to worry about something. Sadly, we don't always get to feel safe. When our own sense of security is threatened it adds a lot of stress to our lives.

When parents are struggling with their relationship, finances, health or anything else that might dislodge the structure of the home, children get anxious. As do parents. That stress is not healthy for anyone and the longer it invades a home the less secure everyone will feel. Uncertainty, while it can have its moments, can also add layers of stress to a situation.

Ideally we are secure about ourselves and our ability to make a "successful", meaningful, valuable life. But most of us have some insecurity about that. We do not know the future. We can have hopes and beliefs and good odds. But with that we also have uncertainty, human frailty and no guarantees aside from taxes and death.

Many of the people I know are a few paydays away from having considerable financial unrest. We manage our lives as best we can, but there are a lot of people who have worried at one time or another about whether they might be homeless or underemployed. Many people are homeless or underemployed. Many people are one doctor visit away from disturbing news that could disrupt their life. Many couples are one good argument away from ending their partnership.

Security, as important as it is, is temporary.

We know life is not fair and shit happens. We just hope not too much of it comes our way and what does come we can resolve relatively easily.

A parent wants their child to not have to worry about the roof over his head or the food in his stomach.

But there is a distressing amount of people in the world that worry about these things every day. The more difficult your financial, health, or other destabilizing situation, the more you need to let your child know you:

a) Love him.

b) Want the best for him.

c) Believe in his ability to better his circumstances.

You don't ever want your discomfort with the turn your life has taken to cause you to lash out at your child and say "You will never be any good" or "You will never amount to anything."

Those kinds of comments are not good motivators for most people. They do get some children to rise up and prove you wrong, but statistically they become better predictors than motivators. If your life is not going the way you would like, it does not mean you need to curse your child with the same affliction. If you are disappointed in your life, spend time coming to your own place of acceptance and work on managing your life in more rewarding ways.

Hurting and handicapping your child because you're hurt is not a model for making the world a better place. Deal with your own situation in your own way, but deal with the parenting of your child in a way that is best for your child.

If your life is unstable then your child will adapt and learn to live in that instability. I had a sophomore tell me that this was the tenth school he had been to and as a consequence he was very able to make new friends. Keeping them, he told me, was something he didn't know much about, but by necessity he had learned how to reach out to others.

While learning how to deal with instability is a life skill we all need to learn, I think people get plenty of that in their lifetime and you don't need to add to it if you don't have to. If you are in the midst of a divorce or health/financial issues, everyone in the family will need to learn how to handle it. So be it. It is hard enough dealing with those kinds of issues; please don't beat up on yourself or others for being in the situation. Save your energy for figuring how to best resolve the situation.

While shit happens that you often cannot control, you are the model for how to handle it. The better a job you do of dealing with whatever happens, the easier it will be for everyone else. I don't want to make you feel guilty if you are not managing your life so well at the moment. I do know life can deal out some extreme blows that do humble us and our bouncing back resiliency is not always as robust as we would like.

I am a believer that if something big is going on it is best to tell your children. He will pick up on the felt change in things and will react but not understand why. Putting a name and a story to what is happening helps a family share and support each other. Being open eliminates some secrets and allows people to more openly share their experience. Which usually brings people closer. We have all witnessed horrible catastrophes and seen people come together in ways they would not have done if events were more usual. Invest in the power of your family and sharing together the truth of your life.

Sharing with your children that your relationship with your partner is challenging right now or your money situation is not as you would like it to be or your health is not in good shape is not an easy conversation to have. You want to be in as calm a place as you can be, because once you start talking emotions are likely to start flaring up. For you and everyone else.

Feelings are going to come out sooner or later. It is a good idea when you decide to speak with your child about something that is liable to be unsettling to start by saying, "There is something we all need to talk about. I want to make sure we all talk about this and join together in dealing with it." Then I would lead with the facts and the emotions will follow.

A loud family shouting match can send everyone to their corners. A good family cry will bring everyone closer. Sometimes you have one before the other. Ideally I would prefer you keep the shouting and name-calling for when you are alone. Then go ahead and vent away.

When you share something, others want to know how you are dealing with it and what you are going to do. Children especially want to know how their parents are going to deal with a destabilizing event. They want to know that everything is going to be okay. It is hard to give that reassurance when you are not sure yourself. I encourage you to seek out within yourself the belief that no matter how badly things turn out, ultimately everything comes to homeostasis.

I don't like to give this example but it is a worst case scenario that underscores this point. If you are not well and don't have long to live, that certainly is destabilizing for everyone. Your family will be operating in crisis mode and it will be hard for you to give the message that ultimately everything will be all right. And yet, even though you will not be present and you do know at some level there will be a great loss for your family and the wounds of that loss may last a lifetime, everyone will eventually find their way to laughter and joy and the ability to make their lives happy and meaningful. I don't know if your death will be comforting for you or not. It depends on a lot of matters, but as sad as it may be there may be some comfort for you in knowing your children will survive and ultimately be okay. You can give them that reassurance.

That is a worst case scenario and hopefully you are not facing that. Pretty much everything will in due course resolve itself and a new status quo will evolve. I would want my child to know that while things are not as I would want them in this moment, I believe in our family's ability to navigate these waters and arrive at safer, calmer shores.

Knowledge is calming. Even if it is alarming.

Uncertainty is more nerve wracking.

Having a plan, even one that may need to be reevaluated right away, gives a sense of security in uncertain times. We all like to have control. Plans, even plans you may not fully believe in, usually lessen anxiety. Less anxiety, more security.

My bottom line is this:

Do your best to make your children feel as secure as possible, as loved as possible, as believed in as possible and as trusted as possible.

And enjoy him and your time with him. For many people the years raising their children are considered the best years of their lives. Strife and all.

43

LYING

I would be lying if I said I didn't believe everyone lies. Some more than others. Some bigger than others. Sometimes to others and sometimes to ourselves.

Lying is a life skill. You need it to survive in this world. I am not happy about that, but as far as I can tell it is a necessity.

Of course there are all manner of lies.

There are the ones you tell your kids when they ask about Santa Claus, your sexual and drug history, and the truth about what really happened before and after you met their other parent.

There are the ones your child tells you when you ask where she went, what she was doing, and if she was drinking or doing drugs.

Parents have a low tolerance for the lies their children tell and high tolerance for their own. Most everyone has more tolerance for their own lies than they do for anyone else's. We usually can find the justification for our lies, and while we may understand the reasoning behind our child's lie, we still would prefer she tell the truth.

Children grow up to be able to discern most of the lies their parents tell. Yes, we all want to believe we can fool some of the people some of the time and indeed we can. If you happen to be charged to teaching your child that honesty is most usually the best policy you will need to model that value. The double standard you might hold about withholding your personal history, while it may get supporters when your child is young, loses importance as your child grows up. It may be okay and advisable to not tell your budding teenager about your misbegotten youth. You might want to save that for when she has established stronger connections to her own values about how to live her life.

I am sure most parents don't always walk the walk they are talking to their child. You may not be that into physical fitness for yourself but you may be encouraging and supporting your child to stay fit. Certainly she will realize sooner or later that your words and actions don't always go hand-in-hand. You may talk the talk but get caught not walking the walk. While that may not be your proudest moment as a parent, you are teaching her a lesson that she will run into time and again in the world. Might as well start to get used to it with you. But hopefully not too often.

If you are going to be extolling something to your child that you do not do you might as well come clean and share that with your child. You have reasons why you do and don't do what you do and don't do. They may not be the best reasons, but they are yours. They may be illogical or they may make perfect sense. Sharing why you do what you do and being willing to talk about it are the kinds of conversations you might want your child to have with you.

I know there are lies that are best kept to yourself. Or so it seems to you. It very well may be for the best to keep your truth to yourself. Or not. It is not always easy to predict what will be for the best in the moment and in the long run. Which is why people withhold the truth. Still, despite the possible advantages to lying, most parents say they want their child to grow up to be honest.

But do they really?

Parents want their children to learn how to tell small social lies that are commonplace in our society. When someone asks us how we are we know they don't really want to know so we lie and say, "Fine." Children learn the socially polite things to say. They even get rewarded for it. When your child thanks her grandmother for the generous and thoughtful gift that has everyone smirking, the parents slip a nod of approval to the child.

Most parents want their child to learn how to be polite and respectful even if it means leaving the truth behind. They just don't want their children to lie to them about the things that are important to them. Things that have to do with school, drugs, sex, and saying she is fine when she is not even close.

The "I did my homework" when she didn't is a lie most parents don't like to hear.

Since we all want to believe we can fool some of the people some of the time, and would prefer some of our behaviors go unnoticed, we gauge the risk/reward and at times choose to lay low and hope we get away with it.

Your child wants to be able to fool you. You want to be able to fool her.

You also want to be able to catch her most (if not all) of the time when she is fooling you. I am sure there are some advantages to occasionally letting her slip something by you. Especially if it is not a big ticket item. But, I would prefer she learn that it isn't all that worth it to withhold the truth and carry the burden of lying.

What do you think your fielding percentage is on catching the lies your child tells? _____

I would imagine most parents have a good sense of the degree to which their child lies to them. I have yet to meet the parent who thought their child was 100% honest about everything in their life. Well, that is not true. I have met those parents. But their kids were not yet in their teens.

From listening to students I have come to believe that once you get to be 13 you have a pretty good understanding of what you need to lie about to your parents. Your child will see how you react to certain events and if she suspects she is not going to get a positive reception she may choose to bend the truth, omit the truth, or clam up.

As your child grows up and develops her own sense of self, she will want to retain certain things just for herself. Keeping a part of her day or life to herself empowers her, while at the same time it disengages her from you. Her quest for autonomy will prompt her to want to keep certain things from you. It is not so much lying to you as being her own counsel. When she figures she can handle something, whatever it is, she might opt for taking care of the situation without you ever knowing. As we all know, sometimes that works out okay and sometimes it doesn't.

Some things you will never know, some you will suspect and some you might be better off not knowing. I would prefer your child tell you she does not want to share something with you than lie to you about it. While you might not be happy to hear this, your acceptance of her desire to withhold some truth lets her know you trust her ability to take care of matters. Your actions demonstrate faith in her, even though you might prefer knowing everything. That is the kind of endorsement teenagers need.

Certainly if things go south there will need to be a follow-up discussion where you will hopefully endeavor to keep your "I told you so" to yourself. You can be empathetic, disappointed, and full of questions and, if asked, ideas about how to proceed. When things don't work out for your child, you usually don't need to rub it in too much.

I tell students and parents that the contract I would want between a parent and their child is for everyone to share the significant truths in their lives with the family. I would want everyone to be forthcoming about those matters that they know are of considerable concern to others. It is okay to keep some truths to yourself, but the ones you know would affect others are the ones that need to be shared.

It is akin to when a parent needs to have surgery and they debate whether to tell their child before or after or never. Most children I have spoken with have told me they would want to know. Yes, they don't really want to know and worry, but if something is happening that could potentially be life threatening they wanted to know sooner than later. Of course, some children would rather not know. You might want to have a family discussion and ask what everyone thinks and wants.

I would want my child to tell me when she was more than the usual amount of afraid or anxious and the circumstances in her life were starting to shift not for the better. I would also want to know when things were picking up. I don't need to know the day-to-day although I would like to, but I really would like to know about any shifts. I would offer to provide that for her as well if she would like.

When parents discover their child has lied to them it does bring with it a shadow. There is a tendency to be a little more distrusting. If she lied about this one thing perhaps she is lying about something else as well.

Getting back the trust to a pre-lie state in which your child was held in higher trust can take time. Some relationships never get back there. Others can get back to an even higher level.

It is a funny thing about trust. Some people are more trusting and others not so much. Some people can easily brush off a lie and others are deeply impacted. There are many variables at play. Most parents start off fully trusting their child and over time learn what to trust and what to not ask about. Of course, your child started off fully trusting you and has had to learn to live with your imperfections.

Regardless of your fielding average catching her in the lies she tries to get past you, you are better served trusting that she will tell you the truth. That alone will not decrease her lying. But it won't increase it either. If you can combine that trust with a general trust in her ability to manage her life then her need to lie diminishes even more. She knows you believe that even if she screwed up big time, you believe in her ability to clean it up. She also knows you would prefer she didn't screw things up that much.

Regardless of how much you trust or don't trust your child, I am going to try to raise that level.

Let's once again start with you. If you want your child to be more truthful with you there are two things to consider:

1.   Are you willing to raise your own level of honesty?

2.   How do you reward her honesty and discipline her lies?

How honest are you with your child about:

- Your hopes for her?
- Your feelings/thoughts about her accomplishments?
- Your feelings/thoughts about her disappointments?
- Your hopes for your life and what has happened to them?
- Your feelings/thoughts about your accomplishments & disappointments?
- Your beliefs about lying?
- Your experiences with lying when you were on the giving and receiving end?

- Your experiences with lying when you chose to lie to someone you cared about?
- Your experiences of lying to your parents?
- Your experiences of lying to your child?

Would you be willing to initiate a discussion with your teenager about those items? If not all, some?

What do you think would be the upside and the downside?

_____

_____

If you decide to initiate a discussion don't deluge her with your truths. I would have them come out in bits and pieces over time. Even if you shared all your truths about those items, she may not share anything. While you are hoping you can create an ongoing discussion about these items, there is no telling if she will want to participate.

If she elects not to share her own truths what will you do?

Will you share your disappointment with her not sharing? Will you say something provocative to get her talking? Will you cop an attitude and say something to end the moment with a bad taste in everyone's mouth? Or will you let her know that you are pleased that you shared more of your truths and she listened and anytime she wants to pick up the conversation you are happy to do so?

Whenever you disclose something you are going to have a reaction to the other person's reaction. Sometimes you share it and sometimes you don't. If you were being completely honest about everything all the time your reaction to their reaction to your reaction to their reaction could keep you on a treadmill you can't get out of fast enough.

Honestly you could be mad, sad, glad, and scared. And honestly you might want to share some of that, none of that, or all of that.

When you are being honest you do it because it makes you feel good about you. Don't do something in expectation of the response. Sure, you can hope your modeling will be inspiring to her, but how your sharing affects her is up to her.

You model the behavior you believe in and leave it at that. A step at a time. And remember, this is the time in her life that she needs to disengage from you so she is liable to share less with you than you might like.

Let me introduce you to the concept of Successive Approximation.

If you wanted to teach your young child to memorize the alphabet you probably would not expect her to be able to hear it once and repeat it back correctly. You might hope she got the ABC part and yet whenever she veered off course you would either say nothing or gently remind her what came next. You might even do this for a few minutes one day and then again another. You might even sing it along with her until one day she gets the whole thing and you might say, "You really worked hard on that to learn it. Well done."

Each time your child tries to recite the alphabet and doesn't get it perfectly right it is called an approximation. She is approximating the desired final behavior. If she tries more than once it is called a successive approximation.

In the psychology research labs they run various experiments that basically prove if you reward the approximations it hastens the arrival at the goal. If you only reward the accomplishment of the final goal it decreases the odds of getting to the final goal.

People need encouragement along the way. Here is the example I often share with parents:

You want your child to keep her room tidy because you no longer can stand not seeing her floor. You buy her a laundry hamper and put it in her room and ask her to please put her dirty clothes in the hamper.

You walk in the next day and the floor looks a lot like it did the day before. But you notice there is a sock that must have been thrown in the general direction of the hamper as it is now resting half on the floor and half on the side of the hamper.

You say, "I'm glad to see the sock almost made it to the hamper. Well done."

Then you leave.

I know you could be having a fair amount of reactions to that approach and I wouldn't argue with most of them. Yet if you go into her room every day and point at something that almost made it to the hamper or made it in the hamper or was at least in the vicinity, it will, according to the research, yield you significant positive results. If you wait for the day that all the clothes are in the hamper the research would have you believe you will get to that day a lot faster if you acknowledge the steps along the way.

To be truthful, I don't know any specific research about the laundry hamper in the room since I made that up. That was my example of finding a quick easy way to acknowledge her successive approximation. Hopefully by acknowledging her improvement it motivates her to continue to improve. I know it is lame, but truthfully, giving positive attention to those efforts that approximate the desired behavior does significantly improve your odds of helping her meet the goal.

At some point in most every parent's life they think their child lied to them. Some parents choose to say nothing. Others want to talk about it.

Certainly I am in the "let's talk about it" camp, but I know parents differ on how best to respond to a lie. Rather than debate the issue, I will just share with you a way to approach the issue if you so choose.

I might say, "I need to talk about my concern that I think you may have lied to me. I don't know if you did and if you did I am not sure why you did. I just know it seems to me like you lied and that feels really bad to me. I would hope that whatever was going on with you, you would be able to speak with me about it.

"If you didn't lie I apologize and I know it probably hurts you to think that I believe you might have lied. I would totally get that. Yet if you did lie to me I would hope sometime that you would feel comfortable enough to tell me the truth. Either way I love you. I just feel bad about feeling bad."

I would like to think that I would say some version of that. I am sure others can find their own ways and point out things that I might well have wished I had said. I don't think you get to do these things perfectly. You just model the desire to be in loving truth with your child. She will do with it what she will.

If I shared my thoughts/feelings with my child and she basically just listened and then got restless and I could sense she had enough I might say, "I know this is uncomfortable to talk about, yet I am glad I shared this with you. I don't like feelings things are not straightforward between us. Let's drop it for now, unless you have something you want to share with me." Then I would let it go.

I mentioned earlier that sometimes honesty can be a weapon. There are many truths we think/feel which if shared we can pretty well guess would be quite hurtful to the other person.

Some of those truths need to be aired. Others can be left to oneself.

It is not always easy to determine if you are just being honest or if you are "sharing your truth" just to hurt the other person. While you might consider it lying to withhold the truth, you might also want to consider what is prompting your truth-sharing.

I am an advocate of being open and honest with those closest to you. I am also an advocate of self-reflection and checking out one's motives. I value getting as much clarity as possible about what is going on with me before I decide to tell someone something that I imagine will hurt them.

Of course things can get blurted out in the moment that have unforeseen reactions. Sure we have all blurted out hurtful comments that we thought we had tucked away. And we all have said something that we didn't intend to be hurtful and seen the other person get upset. We have said something that just slipped out and we wished we hadn't said it the moment it passed our lips.

Those things happen and while some self and impulse control might help you, those are not the kind of truths I am focusing on here. I am talking about something you think/feel about your partner or child that you have thought about sharing but you suspect would cause significant hurt. You have also hopefully thought about whether it really is necessary for this person to know this. Will sharing what you think/feel help them out?

If it can't pass the "I think it will be benefit them to know this" bar, it is better left unsaid.

You need to have a check-in with yourself about why you want to share something and if there is any part of you that is sharing it to hurt that person. If there is even a kernel of truth to your desire to hurt the other person, find a more direct way to deal with what is bothering you rather than throwing emotional darts. Those barbed truths are weapons and best checked at the door.

Here is a word I would like you to check at the door. It is a very potent word and while it may have done some good now and then it has caused a lot more broken spirits.

Disappointment.

As in: "You have been a disappointment to me" or "You disappoint me" or "I am disappointed in you."

I would like to take those phrases out of your vocabulary. Here's why. Children want to please parents. When your child does something displeasing to you, you might think it would motivate her if you told her you were disappointed. It does motivate some people some of the time. It may have motivated you when your parents said it. But it does other things as well.

But David, you say, sharing my disappointment is just me speaking my truth and not lying to my child about how I feel. I get that, yet saying you are disappointed in your child puts a focus on pleasing you and how important that is to you. While something may be personally important to you, it is not something you need to put on your child's shoulders. You can place a high degree of assurance on the fact that she knows when you are pleased with her and when you are not. You don't need to say a thing.

You want to build her self-esteem by having her do those things that are important to her. You don't want to overly reinforce the pleasing of others. Even if it is you.

Sure, what others think is important and what your parents think is often most important to a child. But, ultimately when she moves out of the house, she needs to build a life that pleases her. As she goes through her teen years her self-satisfaction needs to be more important than yours. While I always want my child to have an interest in pleasing me, I want her to know that what pleases me most is that she is able to build a life that pleases her.

If your child lied to you and you want to tell her that you are disappointed, not a lot of people are going to argue with that. I probably wouldn't either as your disappointment is your truth.

Yet, those words of disappointment have a long shelf-life. You might even be able to remember the things your mother and father were disappointed in about you. You might also be able to see how their disappointment shaped your life. Parental disappointment lingers in the psyche.

Rather than say, "I am disappointed in you," why not say, "Next time I hope you would…" and then fill in the desired behavior. Put the emphasis on the desired behavior, not the undesired one.

44

REGRETS, I'VE HAD A FEW

We have all heard that no one at the end of their life regrets the time they spent with family. Very few people say, "I wish I had spent more time at work." Some say they wish they had worked harder or better. Most say the time with family and friends is the most meaningful to them.

I often ask seniors where I work if they have any regrets. Turns out they have a lot.

The one I hear most often is they wish they had focused on doing better sooner and worked a little harder. I also hear they regret they didn't get to go to Coachella sooner and didn't get to be with so-and-so and occasionally I hear, "I wish I had partied more." We each get to have our own regrets.

Parents have regrets about their parenting. The common ones I hear are "I wish I had spent more time with my child," "I wish I had gone to Coachella with him," and "I wish I had put more effort into connecting with him more." One of the other frequent regrets I hear is from parents who wish they had been more helpful to their child throughout the college application process.

Parents ask me all the time, "Am I doing this (whatever this is) too much or too little?"

Parents talk with other parents and in those conversations they come across the parents who are doing something more than them and the ones doing less than them. They worry if they should be doing more or less or if they are doing well enough.

"What should I be doing?" and "When should I be doing it?" are questions parents are continually asking. When I speak with them and ask them what they are doing and what they want to be doing they often express regret that their relationship with their child is not as close and meaningful as they would like it to be. I usually tell them they are not alone. Many families become more estranged during the teen years than the years that come before and after. Adolescence is a tough course for everyone to navigate smoothly.

Parents want to be able to make meaningful contributions to their teen's life, but often don't know the best ways to be of assistance. As with most things there is no right/wrong or proper way to parent, yet we can't help believe there must be better ways. The parents that ask me about helping with the college process often don't know if it would be more or less helpful to increase their involvement. (More on the college process in the chapters ahead.)

What you are doing is both good enough and maybe not that good enough. No one raises the perfectly balanced ideal child. Some children are born with more skills and abilities. Plenty a parent has had one child who was easy to raise followed by one that was not. Whatever pride and assuredness they had with the first one is replaced by what follows.

There is always someone who is better than you at something. Other parents have children that are better students, better looking, smarter, more athletic, funnier, kinder, or happier to name a few of the categories parents use to compare themselves.

You can look around the world or even the parent body at your child's school and see richer, better dressed, more "successful" and happier-looking people than you. Wherever you look someone appears to have their act more together than you.

Of course you can look the other way and see people who don't have it as together as you. Personally I think it is good to look in both directions and then come back and take a good look at yourself. Enjoy what you have that is satisfying, good enough, and pleasurable to you. Envy a little if you need to and regret that you don't have what they have.

Envy is not uncommon. Most people have some. Along with some resentment and admiration. Sometimes you can look at what someone else has accomplished and wish you had their fortune or you may see another's creativity or wealth or staunch good looks and wish you had some of that. That is fine. Feel the envy. Just like anything else. But don't dwell on it. Come back to your life and your reality and do what you can to make yourself more at peace with what you have around you. Comparisons usually come up short and rarely take in the whole picture. That person may have something you wish you had, but you probably have something they wouldn't mind having.

No one wants to walk around with a lot of regrets.

Everyone gets to have some. You just don't want too many. Especially when it comes to parenting your child.

Parents regret the missed opportunities, the paths not taken and the paths taken. The regret I hear the most is not spending more time together as a family or alone with your child. At some point most of the parents I speak with tell me that it all went by too quickly. One day their child was comfortably sitting in their lap and the next he is getting ready to graduate.

Whatever regrets you have at this point in your life cannot be undone. How much you want to regret, how much you want to blame yourself, be upset with yourself and punish yourself is up to you. I don't really want to interfere with that, except to say try to make the punishment fit the crime. And remember criminals get reduced sentences for good behavior.

Most of the things you have regrets for are over and done and all you can do is have the regrets and hopefully learn from them. Holding on to your regrets may help motivate you to take actions in the future. It may also serve you to feel bad about yourself. A certain amount of feeling bad about your actions or inactions is fine. It doesn't hurt to hurt about previous actions. But at some point you need to invest more energy into moving forward and less in beating yourself up about the past.

Some of the things you regret cannot be adequately repaired, others may have a healing step that might be taken. If your child is alive and you are alive there is still time for repairs. If they are not alive or the situation cannot be remediated in some way there are avenues a therapist can help you employ to find greater peace within yourself.

Can you think of something right now that your child would most likely enjoy doing with you?

If there is "nothing" then you have dug yourself a big hole, but still a hole. Where there is a hole there is room for filler. Even if you can't really think of anything engaging that your child would enjoy doing with you at this time, come up with one thing he most likely would be willing to do with you.

Instead of thinking of a big ticket item that may or may not be within your grasp, try to think of something that would take a short period of time and can be done with whatever you have at hand. Is there anything you could do with your child in the very near future that would take less than 15 minutes to accomplish that you think your child might enjoy, put up with, or at least endure?

What is it? _____

What stops you from doing that? _____

Let's try to stop what is stopping you. Okay, I know he may not want to do this. He may reject you. He may not think of it as highly as you do. It could go poorly. You could have more regrets.

You could also have regrets for not putting yourself out there and taking the chance at having more interactions with your child. Letting your child know that you want to do something with him that you think he would like at least tells him that you want to do something with him. That is a good message for your child to know. And he needs to know how to say yes and how to say no to you and to others. What parents often fail to appreciate is that most teenagers would rather spend time with their friends than their parents. It is not about you per se. It is more that they have more in common with their friends. Plus, you are around all the time; their friends are not.

If you can think of something to do with him that can be done at home when he might actually be there it will make things easier. I often suggest making a salad. That doesn't take too much time, but gives you an opportunity to be next to each other, engaged in something somewhat together with the chance to talk about anything. Cooking together can be fun, and it is especially fun if it is done by the people who usually don't do it.

Things may not work out well and you might end up wishing you hadn't done anything, but really do you want to start with that mindset? Be careful of self-fulfilling prophecies. If you go into this thinking it is going to go south you might inadvertently subvert the whole process so that it doesn't turn out well. You might have your doubts and fears, but try to muster as much hopeful enthusiasm as you can.

Don't expect your enthusiasm to be met in kind. He may be hesitant. He may say not now. He may say it is a stupid idea. He may hurt your feelings. Even if whatever you do is met with total rejection and humiliation, your child will know you tried to reach out. In whatever ineffectual way you approached him and invited him to join you, he got the message.

Hopefully it won't be that bad, but if you a) emotionally prepare for the worst anything else is an improvement and b) make this a campaign and this is your first foray. If at first you do not succeed…

One other thing about the salad idea. Don't make him go to the market with you. That is too much. Just tell him that one night this week you want to make salad together. Ask if there is anything in particular he would want and then go get what you need. Make sure it won't spoil right away as he might not join you the first night you ask. Ask again. And again. Then make it yourself and try something different.

One easy thing for parents to do which is actually a gift to your child is to start telling him stories about you that you haven't told him before. Learning about your life is something best heard from you. Many grown adults regret that they don't know more about their parents' lives from before they were born. Fill them in.

You could walk the dog, read a blog, watch YouTube, or any other things that might serve to give you some time together. It doesn't have to be a big production. You can just walk into his room and tell him a story and then leave. Easy in. Easy out. He will think you are weird, but he may just remember the story.

You may walk into his room and he may sigh and ask you to leave. Leave and try again another time. You will have other opportunities. Don't let your agenda to share more with him get in the way of you honoring his space.

Just walk out of the room and say, "Sometime later I want to tell you something. I think you will like it." It is usually good to throw a little teaser in there. Of course, he may be let down later when he hears what you have in mind. But, as long as you didn't oversell the tease it ought to pass muster.

When you say, "You might like it," that might get him to want to hear you out. Or not. Either way the seed has been planted. Sooner or later he will want to hear what you have to say. Unless he forgets, which teenagers do.

Don't take that too personally. If he doesn't approach you within a day or so try again.

Keep on trying.

You don't want to regret that you didn't spend more time with your child because you didn't reach out.

45

WHAT IS THE OPTIMAL BALANCE OF DISCIPLINE AND PRAISE?

When I taught a clinical skills course in graduate school I had a student that for her final paper wrote a syllabus for my class. I don't remember exactly how it went, but I used it for years. It was better than the one I wrote. She started it with: "You probably have learned by now that David…" and she went on to list a few things that might have become apparent to my students even in the early stages of taking my class.

I mention that now because you have probably learned by now that I don't have the exact answer to what is the optimal balance of discipline and praise. It is a misleading chapter title and yet I think it speaks to concerns that many parents have.

Discipline and praise are actions that parents take to help shape their child's behavior. Parents used to also use the word punishment but that word has gone out of favor, although the line between discipline and punishment can be hazy. Punishment's purpose is to punish. Discipline can include some punishment but its intention is to create learning and possible opportunity to redo something or make it better. We can all learn from aversive conditioning where something is so toxic you learn to avoid it. So yes if you have a very heavy-handed punishment it could prompt someone not to repeat the offense. But statistically speaking, that is a second tier option. Why go that route when there are more effective interventions you can make?

Some say spare the rod and spoil the child. Others say you can never get too much praise. According to Jill Stein, author of the bestselling sociology textbook *The Real World: An Introduction to Sociology*, there is never enough praise. While I agree with her I would also say there can be too much discipline.

It is probably best for me to go on record now and say as often as possible I would like you to come to consensual avenues to remediate situations that do not carry the onus of you punishing your child. I am not so sure parents really want to be in the business of dispensing punishment. Consequences, yes, but not punishment. The world deals out enough natural consequences that are punishing that you don't have to take on that position.

Parenting is a guidance system. While providing heavy negative consequences for actions may make you feel like you are engaging in best practices, that is not what the research says. While people will avoid certain things because of the negative consequences, we approach more things because of the positive consequences. Negative reinforcement works, it is just that positive reinforcement has a richer upside.

That doesn't mean you need to entirely abdicate your disciplinary actions. It just means that if you want to teach your child how to lead a more productive life, you would do better to find some things your child does or can do that you can positively acknowledge. You can take away privileges when things don't go as you would like. Just see if you can find five times as many ways to reward other actions. That reward usually doesn't need to be anything more than a "well done" with an occasional upgrade.

Like most things with parenting, these are things you learn, relearn, and learn again on the job. You can never fully evaluate how good a job you are doing because you have only the up-to-the-moment results. You can feel good in the moment and that is about the best you can do. Yet you won't know the long-term effects of your parenting until your child is out of the house and well into living on her own. You can only hope that the behaviors your child has that you value will continue and the ones you are not so keen about will evaporate. But it could go the other way. So you do what you think it best, observe the immediate results, and modify your actions as you and your child mature.

Any number of actions by your child can activate your "I need to do something about this" gene. A hopefully lesser number of actions will prompt your "there needs to be some serious consequence" gene. There may be times when you speak with your child about something she did that you do not feel good about. She may not agree with you and have little or no remorse. She might even get defiant and upset at you for bringing the subject up.

When your child reacts to you and behaves in ways that do not please you, I would prefer that you keep the focus on the matter at hand. Don't get lulled into a sidebar argument. It is easy for parents to get upset when their child speaks disrespectfully to them. It is not that I don't want you to be upset, I just want you to deal with first things first. You can focus on the disrespect later. Right now, don't try to get back to the main issue by throwing a punishment on your child to try to stop her from behaving rudely to you. Just keep going back to whatever unresolved issue needs to be addressed: "As we were saying…"

Unfortunately I have witnessed a parent tell a child, "That's another week," every time the child interrupted till she was looking at four months of being grounded. I prefer you dodge that dart and keep your attention on the matter at hand. That will probably stop her interrupting just as fast if not faster than the hurling of consequences.

We all have different trigger points when we get called into action. Usually an action has to be pretty serious to warrant a punishment/discipline consequence, but one person's serious could be another's not so serious.

Most times when a parent thinks they need to talk with their child they begin with some version of: "We need to talk." I like that opening because of the "we." Some parents say: "I need to talk with you." That works as well, as you are stating a fact and speaking up about what you need. Not surprisingly, "you are in trouble" is not my preferred opening as it points the blame. I would rather hear her side of the story before I did any blaming and even then I would go another way. Why not start with as open a mind as you can have?

Discipline and consequences are activities designed to eliminate unwanted behavior. When your child does something that you do not want repeated you have options about how to proceed. Much like a judge in a courtroom you can impose various sentences. The key is to "make the punishment fit the crime" and not only discourage your child from a repeat performance, but have her learn something that will assist her going forward.

We put people in jail to punish them for something they did and hope that the punishment will be harsh enough to inhibit them from doing the act again. The Bureau of Justice Statistics publishes yearly the national rate of recidivism and it is usually around 60%. Of course your child is not a criminal and your home is not a jail so this is not exactly an apples-to-apples example. But one thing I pull out of those statistics is that punishment alone does not do a lot to prevent a repeat performance.

If parents can structure their consequences so that their child learns something positive, it will increase the likelihood of her not doing the same action again. Certainly, being grounded for an extended period will keep your child from wanting to get in trouble again. But if you can think of something positive she can do that will help her learn, you and she will get bonus points. It is not easy to craft consequences that have learning options, but if you can it is worth a try.

Here are a couple of dos and don'ts that are easier to accomplish:

- Don't lecture her for more than a few minutes. Repeating yourself over and over is not going to increase the effectiveness of what you are saying. Say it once, and then ask her to repeat it back. If she gets it right, you are done. If she missed it, go back and forth until she does get it.

- Don't announce a consequence when you are upset. There is no immediate need to declare the consequences. Give yourself some time to think things over.

- Do ensure whatever consequences you create are realistic enough that you can be assured they will be followed by you and her, unless something significant has occurred.

- Do consider a consequence that has within it a chance for her to earn back her privileges sooner.

- Don't make community service a part of any consequence. That will only make her associate helping others as a form of punishment. Doing community service ought to be something that is fulfilling. The rewards of helping others are evident in the faces of those you help. Save your community service activities for other times when the full value of being of service can be realized.

- In the same vein, don't force her to do homework or write thank-you notes or any of those things that can be internally rewarding if handled well.

Many parents have their child wash their car, pull weeds, or do some extra chore. For a lot of people these are enjoyable things to do so you don't really want to frame them as consequences, yet adding chores or things to do around the home is a common ingredient in a lot of consequence packages. If you can teach her a more efficient way to accomplish these things, you have given her something positive to take away. But don't expect her to hold these chores in a positive light as she grows up. Although sometimes in doing these activities she can discover the inherent joy in them. But not often. And usually not in the moment. And not so she would tell you.

I would prefer the consequence be that if she does something that raises concerns, we need to talk about it. I don't want talking to be perceived as a negative thing. Yet I do believe hearing each other, gaining an understanding of what is going on, and supporting each other is the core of family.

A lot of parents take away social media, computers, phones, TVs, and other things their children like. I am not a big believer in this, but parents often feel online access strikes most at their child's interests.

I prefer not to take things away. If I were going to take something it would be her freedom. I would have her stay home. Grounding has been around for a while and also seems to strike at the heart of most teenage lives. But there are a lot of children that would be home anyway, so this isn't really a heavy consequence for them. And, once again, I don't want to make being home a negative thing.

Basically, the only thing I would take away from my child is my approval of her behavior. She will know I do not approve of her behavior because I have asked to speak with her and may be imposing some discipline on her. A parent's lack of approval weighs heavily on a child. She wants your approval. Not as much as she wants her own. But yours is right up there.

Some parents like to offer rewards to their children for acts well done. They give the child money if she gets an 'A' or pay her for doing good deeds. The difficulty with this has to do with what you are actually teaching your child. You are teaching her to do something for the external reward and not the internal reward.

For most children the self-satisfaction of getting an 'A' is sufficient reward. Once you start to add an external reward for something that is inherently internally rewarding you are shifting her pleasure from something she feels about herself to something outside herself. You want her doing things because she enjoys doing them not because you are paying her.

Certainly most of us enjoy the rewards of money for work done. Many of us would not be doing our jobs if we didn't get paid for them. But we all have done things where we didn't get paid and found them to be very rewarding in other ways. Why not save the paydays for those tasks that can be less internally rewarding?

Okay, you say. My child does not like math. I pay her to get good grades otherwise she would just flounder. If I don't pay her, she won't work hard.

So you say. To which I say, really? Are you sure? I would sit down, have a talk with her and tell her, "The money for grades is now a thing of the past. If you want to earn money we can think of other things for you to do, but from now on that money is going to a tutor if you want one, or to my retirement fund. I will help you in any other way I can to get a better grade in math."

Then I would let her flounder for a while to prove to me that the money thing worked and I am wrong. Then I would find some way to reward her for many of the other things she is doing well with words of praise and maybe something else she values. In my case it would be a trip to her favorite ice cream place or bookstore.

Parents are loathe sometimes to let natural consequences work as they don't like to see that GPA slip. As much as parents worry about this, so too do their children. Offer to help. Call the school for help and see what you can do behind the scenes to help her with her math. She wants a good grade every bit as much as you, but may not necessarily show you. The more you can be in the background and leave the issue of her and her grades between her and her teachers and school counselors, the better things will be around the home.

Unfortunately this is not easy for parents. In an interview in 2015 with NPR's Anya Kamenetz, Jessica Lahey, a middle school teacher and writer for the New York Times as well as author of *The Gift of Failure*, said: "After three years of research and a lot of soul searching, here's where I've ended up. Kids are anxious, afraid, and risk-averse because parents are more focused on keeping their children safe, content, and happy in the moment than on parenting for competence. Furthermore, we as a society are so obsessed with learning as a product — grades, scores, and other evidence of academic and athletic success — that we have sacrificed learning in favor of these false idols."

Students now "do" school to get good grades and are less invested in learning than achieving. These are widespread tides that any single parent is going to have trouble swimming against. Letting your child learn from her mistakes and trusting that those mistakes will benefit her is not an easy task. Our desire to keep our children safe and content undermines their ability to weather the storms that lie ahead.

Learning how to balance praise and discipline/punishment is a life-long task we all need to learn with our child and ourselves. Day to day, moment to moment, the ratio of praise and penalty shifts.

Many parents feel that if they praise too much they will spoil their child. If they tell her it is great that she gets a 'B' she won't try for an 'A'. They think praise leads to satiation.

Other parents like to focus on the B as evidence of her not living up to her potential. They chide their child and let her know the B was not good enough. If she had applied herself more she could have done better.

Where do these lead?

Praising too much might lead to complacency. Applying yourself more may lead to better grades. I can't argue with either of those beliefs. Yet I can point out where an overemphasis on those approaches can set your child back.

A child might relish and be satisfied with the praise she gets for a 'B', but chances are she will like the praise and want more of it. The teacher knows when students are faltering and when they are picking up the pace. Usually that teacher's remarks will be more forthcoming as her grade improves and the lesser comments will accompany any downturn. I would want to give positive recognition a try before I did anything else. See if praise alone will help motivate her. If it doesn't do the trick and if you think she is capable of more you can suggest to her that while it is great she got the 'B', maybe if she invested more effort she might get a 'B+' or even an 'A'. Just realize that this insight you have has not escaped her as well and you are just pointing out the obvious which tends to be greeted with a blank stare.

Remember, effort is the key. That is the part you really want to reward. If you just point out that the B is not good enough she will carry around the belief that she is not good enough. But, when you add that if she put even a little more energy into it you believe she will do better, well, she just might give that a try. Effort is something she can control. And we all like control.

Many people walk around feeling not good enough. They know they could do better if they focused more but they are unable to generate a sustained effort. Often their fear is that even with sustained effort they may not be able to achieve what they want for themselves. So, instead of pushing forward with a growth mindset they close their mind and their heart to trying. Ultimately the fear of not being good enough inhibits their trying and further cements them in not feeling good enough. Once you have a base belief that you are not good enough it takes a lot of concentrated effort to overcome that ingrained belief.

Most people feel not good enough about something. You are not that handy or good with numbers or you can't sing worth a damn. People have regrets about those paths not fully taken or not able to be taken. One way or the other, people make a measure of peace with those unfulfilled aspects of their life. The trick is to not let not being good enough in one arena stop you from excelling in another. You don't want those pervasive, not-good-enough blues. As Carol Dweck reminds us, we are all mostly average at most things

I would rather you bypassed sharing your thoughts that your child is not good enough and put your energy into supporting whatever positive efforts you see. That encouragement and praise will yield better results than you pointing out her deficiencies. Children can feel not good enough without you adding to the parade. Every day at school your child encounters someone smarter, more attractive, more athletic, and more together than they are. She can compare herself all day long and come out on the losing side more than once.

Of course, there are areas where you are going to think she is not good enough. Be it math, creativity, courtesy, or saying thank you with actual appreciation when you do something for her. I am not saying that you can't talk about these matters. I am saying you need to be careful in how you approach these issues. I would want a lot of "I wish you would say 'thank you' like you mean it" rather than "You aren't any good at thanking people and being appreciative."

Once again, if you choose to point out somewhere where her efforts are not meeting your expectations, you also need to make sure to point out a bunch of places where her efforts are plenty good enough. Don't exaggerate or pretend her efforts are better than they are. Find the places where you genuinely think she is good enough (not perfect) and let her know. If you cannot find those places, call a therapist.

46

FRIENDS & SOCIAL LIFE

For the most part, the calls I get from parents of teenagers fall into four categories:

- Drugs/alcohol

- Stress

- Concerns that their child is having too much of social life

- Concerns that their child is not having enough of a social life

Drugs, sex, and rock and roll are in the chapters ahead. Stress was a topic of the previous chapter although we will revisit it here as well. This chapter is mostly about friends and social life.

Your child will feel stress about many of the things you stress out about—relationships, school (read: work), his body, health, plans, and whatever else comes along. Of course, you probably don't have to worry about getting into college and taking the SATs or ACTS. But you have your annual review, your boss, your partner's opinions, and your worry about your child's test scores and his getting into college.

Your child may handle stress in a similar or dissimilar fashion as you. You may know when he is a little stressed and you may not know. You probably know when he is very stressed. But some teenagers try to hide the degree of their stress from their parents.

He may want your help and he may not. He may ask for your help and reject it. He may reject your help and be a little comforted when you provide it. You never fully know how your actions are received.

If you see him looking stressed and ask how he is doing he may share some of what is going on or he may say "fine" and try to move along. I usually push back a little and say, "Really? What's going on?" If he doesn't want to get into it, I let it go. If he is stressed and it continues, I would hope that eventually he would tell me something. And, I would probably ask again in a few days anyway. I can be a nudge sometimes.

You can let him know you are happy to speak with him any time and hope that when needs to he will approach you. Often, aside from hearing what your child says and commiserating with him there is often not a lot you can do. But don't minimize the value of your listening, caring, empathizing, and letting him know you are there for him.

I remember one time my teenage daughter came home from school and was very upset at one of her teachers. She thought the teacher had treated her unfairly. I did my best to commiserate with her and then I told her I would be happy to go down to the school and beat the teacher up.

She kind of laughed at that as I hope you are now doing; she knows I would never go do that. But the offer that I would do that and wanted to avenge her wrongs I hope made her feel I was on her side and had her back. I also asked if there was anything she wanted me to do and she said not to do anything. So I honored that. I was tempted to call the teacher, but I knew that was not what she wanted. But that doesn't mean I didn't think about calling for some time.

I had a mother of a 9th grader call me up and tell me she he was worried about her son. He was doing fine academically, but he didn't seem to have any real friends. He didn't go out on weekends with anyone and while he wasn't depressed he knew he would feel better if he had some friends.

Could I help him out? I told her I would try.

As a counselor at a school I can talk with faculty and ask them to do some matchmaking. Almost all classes at times break into small groups and partner up for activities. Often I ask the teachers to see what they can do about putting a student in groups where he might have a better chance of making a friend without the student ever knowing.

The magic in the teacher matchmaking is the child never knows it happened. I have to tell you that I have seen this backdoor approach to friend-making work many times. Proximity breeds familiarity, which often results in friendship. If you happen to be a parent with lack of friends concerns contact your school counselor and see what they can do.

I should also mention that most times when parents call me they ask me not to let their child know they called. Which means bringing their child into my office for a chat is challenging. Which is why I tend to work a lot with the teachers and the parents as well as the students.

A lot of times children don't have the social skills to build friendships and learning by trial and error often deters them from keeping on trying. It doesn't take too many rejections to make you wary.

Parents sometimes find themselves in the position of coaching their child on how to make friends. These can be uncomfortable discussions as your child has to expose an area where he does not feel good enough and listen to you tell him what to do to feel better. Feelings can be very easily hurt and no matter how carefully you proceed it is hard for your child to walk away from these discussions feeling less stressed. At best maybe you gave him an idea about how to approach someone. At worst you further undermined his confidence and aggravated his stress level.

Ah, what is a parent to do?

You model interacting.

You are out with him in public and you interact with a salesperson, waiter, or fellow sufferer in the checkout line where you are all waiting. You do your friendly best to throw out a semi-innocuous question, which might elicit a response. Or you are at the dinner table and you say something provocative to get a conversation going. And you continue to endeavor to do your best to have engaging conversations with him just like you would want him to have with the people he meets.

Children usually don't ask each other, "How was your day?" They often begin their conversations in the middle. For example, "The Lakers totally blew it," is a familiar opening line in Los Angeles.

I also suggest to parents that instead of starting a conversation with their child with a question they start with a statement. "You wouldn't believe what my boss made me do today," might get you more of a response than "Did you do your homework?" Model for your child the art of the inviting statement/question. He might be able to learn how to lure someone into a conversation.

But...

You at your communication modeling best are probably not going to be able to upgrade your child's social life. This is something they mostly have to do on their own. Usually with some fumbling help from someone else. Almost all children in a school end up connecting with someone. Maybe they only talk briefly during the day and never connect after school but that may not be too different from some of the people you interact with in life.

Parents hear their child say they have no friends and hated school and didn't talk to anyone. That may be true, but more than likely there are some exaggerations there. Parents get secondhand information about their child's life at school and don't really have a clear sense of what their child's day is like at school. Which is why it can help to talk to someone at the school.

Having observed high school students for over 15 years I can tell you that it is very rare for someone to not interact with at least some of his peers outside a classroom. It may not be for long and he may walk around campus alone much of the time, but most children find someone with whom they can connect on some level. We all know it is rare to find someone who you connect with on many levels, so finding someone who at least share something in common with is a good enough start.

The tricky part is getting your child to reach out.

If he happens to be an extrovert it is easier for him to initiate a conversation because he is more naturally drawn to want to engage with others. Whatever wounds and hesitancies hold him back, his nature often overcomes his fear and he reaches out. A little more cautiously.

If he keeps reaching out and getting rejected it is time for professional help. There may be things he is doing either consciously or unconsciously that are making it too difficult for people to want to be with him. There is usually some self-defeating activity that can be brought to light and options found for more positively managing the issues at play.

Since a good portion of the population are introverts, who by nature are not very comfortable initiating connections, many children will prefer to be approached than to approach. They are more comfortable when approached, but still reluctant to share much.

"How do I get my introverted child to reach out?" That is a question I am asked a lot. The answer is simple—you don't. You can try some of the things I suggest, but even those are only going to make a marginal difference. Your child will inch his way forward and ultimately he will find people with whom he can connect. It is just harder for an introvert to meet an introvert than an extrovert to meet anyone. Which also means there could very well be an extroverted kid who will reach out to your child. You never know. An introvert and an extrovert may have different communication styles but similar interests.

Parents of high school students often suffer a lot when their child does not have much or any social life. They know their child is not happy with the situation and then can't think of any new way to make things better. These parents take some refuge in the awareness that when their child leaves home they won't need to witness the isolation as much and often that child without the company of his parents does manage to reach out and form some connections. In the meantime they hurt for their child's hurt.

Even though many children, like a lot of adults, are happiest alone, their parents think they would be happier if there was more balance. They want their child to be invited to an occasional party or a movie or anywhere. When there is an absence of other children reaching out to your child it is painful. When you see how challenging it is for your child to reach out the disappointment intensifies. That's usually when my phone rings.

Boys especially have a hard time asking another guy if they want to hang out or go to a movie. It just feels awkward. It flows a lot smoother when there is a group of kids and they sort of organically stumble into making plans. When your child is not in that group, making plans with another child requires reaching out and opening himself up for rejection. Some weekends it is easier to stay home.

One way to help your child develop social skills is to get him to see a therapist who also runs groups for children his age. There are groups that teach social skills as well as groups that are educational and therapeutic. Unfortunately, there are not a lot of therapists who do groups. If you can find one, and you like the therapist, then consider signing up your child. Your school counselor may be able to help you find someone, but sadly there are not a lot of therapists who offer this service. You might check your local university as they do sometimes offer these services to the community out of their Counseling Center.

Your child won't want to go, but if he actually does learn some social skills he will quickly see that the group is helping him. If it isn't, get him out.

You could also consider individual therapy to help build his confidence and interpersonal skills. I think that is a viable path. Often people start in individual and then move on to group or do both.

With any therapy or therapist you want to be diligent about picking the therapist. I don't have the highest opinion of most of the people in the field so don't be reluctant to shop around until you find someone you believe has the warmth, knowledge, and ability to help your child.

The other major group of calls I get concerns parents who think their child may be partying too much and not spending enough time focused on his schoolwork. I don't usually get these calls until grades go home for the first time or their child gets in some kind of trouble. Fear often is the motivator to get parents to call me.

Every parent has their own agenda for how well they would like their child to do in school and how much of his life should be spent socializing, going to parties, playing games or interacting online or engulfed in YouTube and Netflix.

My advice to these parents will not surprise you. I tell them to reinforce the behaviors they want by saying something positive when they see the slightest glimpse of them happening. I would dwell less on speaking to him about the things he is doing that you don't like and more time spent talking about the things you do like. Not that you can't frown and clamp down on some of his activities. Just try to keep the frown to smile ratio in check.

Social connections mean a lot to students and they invest much of their time in interacting with their peers. You don't really want to take this source of pleasure away from your child, yet if you feel it is undermining his ability to attend to his studies and other activities you may need to do something.

Parents often associate partying with drugs and alcohol. If those are your concerns the chapters on those subjects are ahead. Right now I want to focus more on your concern about the amount of time your child is devoting to social activities.

Natural consequences can often be a parent's best friend. If you child does something too much he will pay for it one way or the other without you doing anything. Yet, parents don't always have patience and tolerance for those consequences to take hold. They also don't want their child to have to deal with some of those consequences if they can help it. Most parents I know don't want their child to receive a poor grade that could affect his college choices. Or they don't want their child to drink too much and get into some trouble that will cause undue hardship. A little hardship along the lines of throwing up in the bathroom is fine; too much hardship is not so fine.

Parents don't want their child to suffer harsh consequences. They try to instill values and behaviors that will reduce their child's risks. As parents see their influence wane they usually lecture, discipline and worry more.

I don't think you are going to make much headway repeating your same concerns over and over with your child. I think you need to consider getting help from the school, maybe a therapist, and by approaching matters differently.

My advice is to let him be who he is in the social interactive domain of his life. It is different than when you were a child and the world is now a place of discovery and interaction that you never experienced. Let your child explore this territory. It very well may serve him in ways you will never know. Being online in one way or the other is shaping this generation in ways we have yet to fully understand. Like most things it will have elements of the good, the bad, and the ugly. I have often found the child that has few or no friends at school has a wealth of people he connects with online.

Certainly you need the recurring lecture about online safety especially when your child is a preteen. I am sure all schools are teaching online safety but that doesn't mean some home reminders are not necessary now and then. As your teenager goes into high school and starts to actively build his resume for college he needs to know those online posts never really go away and more and more colleges are doing searches on their applicants. I just tell the students to consider all their posts to be part of their admission packet.

However your child chooses to invest his "free" time is really up to him. Most likely you will think his free time ought to be spent focusing on more productive activities, but that too is a losing battle. You can expose him to new things, provide opportunities for exploration and let him know there is more to the world then the part he is focusing on, but chastising him is not an effective approach.

What he chooses to focus on is where he feels most comfortable. You don't want to take too much of that comfort away. Rather than clamp down, think about opening up. Open up other avenues for him. He won't take all those opportunities. You don't. But he will explore some. Perhaps not now, but if the seed you plant is viable it may take root later.

Whether your child has a small or large social life you most likely would enjoy spending some time with them that was more about enjoyment and less about oversight. I just wrote a letter to the parents at the school where I work about summer vacation. I acknowledged that those lazy never-ending days of summer of our youth no longer exist for our children to the same extent. Now, like the athlete that stays in shape in the off-season so too do many students now attend to their schooling year round. Summer school, which used to be exclusively for those who did not do well in certain classes, still functions in the same way, yet now there are courses at colleges that promise a college course on your transcript and a bit of the college experience. Summers are full of community service activities and resume-building.

I encouraged parents to remember the occasional joys of summer vacation and make sure their child got some of that. The non-scheduled days. The "what should I do?" days. The "hang out with friends" days. The "lose yourself in your iPad, cell phone, or another technological instrument of the moment" days. The "do something crafty or creative" days. The "I am bored" days. And, hopefully, the "family trip" days.

Even if you can't do family trip days you can do family time together activities. Something that might actually have the word "fun" attached to it. Of course what is fun for you may cause a less than welcome a response from him. But don't let that stop you. The goal is to spend time together. Some things are more fun than others, but the idea is to do something out of the ordinary where you all get to discover new things.

Doing things together as a family is a way to open vistas for everyone. Teenagers sometimes moan about doing things with their family; they would often prefer to be with their friends. Don't let that stop you from planning activities together. Just don't overbook your child's life and his need for unstructured time. Extended family vacations or time together is usually too long for him.

Most of the students where I work have much less free time than their parents did. They have activities they do before and after school. They have sports and theater. They are on club teams, taking lessons, getting tutored, and otherwise booked up. According to Denise Pope *(Overloaded and Underprepared: Strategies for Stronger Schools and Healthy Successful Kids)* the average middle school student spends 6.9 hours Monday through Friday on extracurricular activities. In high school that bumps up to 10.5. Plus after a day at school and possible after school activities they have to come home, relax, eat, touch base with their friends, do homework, and get to bed. Which is why most of them don't get a full night's sleep.

Almost a third of high school students study 3.5 hours a night. I am pretty sure when you were in high school that percentage was much lower. Students driven to do well often pay a high price in terms of their downtime. They don't have as much open space, play time, and just general "do nothing" time. It's no wonder with that work load that the pressures that drive a third of the student body have a ripple effect and create an ethos that is not best for all.

There is a lot for them to do in a day. A lot they are supposed to do well. A lot that will foretell what college they will be able to attend. The pressure is on.

Your job is not to add to that pressure. You need to provide the love, support, guidance, and model. You can't make your teenager do what he doesn't want to do. Well, you can. You can threaten him, entice him, or otherwise try to motivate him. But the trick of getting him to do what you want him to do is to see if you can't help him find within himself his own desire to do those things. If the things you want have no connection to what he considers important, your wishes will die on the vine.

If you can get your child to find the joy in learning and accomplishing goals, he will want to learn more and do more. The best way to help him find that motivation is for you to give him some positive attention when he is doing the things you want and to occasionally ask him how he feels about doing the things he is doing. When he gets a better grade from studying it incentivizes him to want to continue. When he studies hard and gets a poor grade it de-incentivizes him Which is when you need to step in and give him an extra dose of appreciation for working hard, and a bit of that old "If at first you don't succeed, try try again" speech. Then say, "Ugh. I'm sorry it didn't work out well. Hang in there."

SECTION 7:

HOME LIFE

47

THEIR ROOM, YOUR HOUSE

One thing I have learned about teenagers is they tend to generally be kinder to others than they are with their parents. Your friends will tell you things about them that you only wish you could experience. Your child helping out in your neighbor's kitchen, saying "thank you" and generally being on her best behavior is usually not something you see at home as much as you would like to.

On the one hand, it is comforting to know your child possesses these skills. On the other, it would be enjoyable if your child demonstrated them more when she is home. Hopefully you get glimpses and reminders of her past sweetness.

The good news is that somewhere in her twenties her behavior in your home will be better. But first she needs to move out. Once she is living on her own fulltime, your home is no longer her home in quite the same way.

Her room in your house right now feels like her room in her house.

Later on it will feel more like her room in your house—that is, if you have not converted it to some other use.

But right now your child's room is the place she sleeps in, dreams in, dresses in, plays in, and goes to when disciplined. When children talk about where they live they use the expression "my house" or "my apartment" or "my home." They also say "my bedroom." Just as your bedroom is your room, so too is theirs.

The kitchen and living room may be common areas or lean one way or the other, but most of us feel a proprietary right to our own bedroom. That is, if we are lucky enough to have one or even share one.

There is a time while you are growing up when your parents choose all your clothes, meals and plans for the day. Some children start being actively involved in those choices early in their lives and others take more of a back seat—some for all their lives. Most parents, while they may not approve of all the choices their child makes, usually hand over a good portion of the reins sometime in high school if not before. Most teenagers are picking their clothes, have a say in what they eat, and are making social plans on their own.

A task of parenting is to take those things you do for your child and have her learn to do them for herself even better than you did. Usually that doesn't happen right away.

In order to make that transition, parents need to let go. There is a lot of control that parents will eventually cede to their children. Sometimes that control is thrust upon a child, other times hesitatingly given, sometimes greater self-control is welcome, other times rejected, and other times it is fought over. Sometimes it is seized.

The exchange of power is a trial-and-error learning curve activity. Most parents would like to think that they have sufficient experience and skills to be able to handle most tasks better than their child. While that is certainly true when she is eight, it may be less true at sixteen and hardly true at twenty-four.

Bit by bit parents hand over responsibilities to their children. Wordlessly at times, your child will take over a responsibility and make it her own. She won't take out the garbage like you do, and most likely she will need some reminders, as perhaps you did once upon a time. For some parents letting go of control is a considerable challenge. Others are happy to relinquish it. Sometimes parents see their child start to make more life choices and they are proud and happy to know she is engaging life in a more active manner. Sometimes parents witness the actions of their child and can't sleep at night.

When your child starts to take over some responsibilities there very well could be an initial decline in how well something gets done. It is easy to point out where your child is not doing something as well as you or as well as you would like. Yet you know that ounce of criticism is going to yield pounds of displeasure. Like any other beginner she is not going to be as good at something the first time as she will be after more experience. See if you can hold your judgmental observations to yourself and support her steps into independence when you can.

While handing over clothing choice issues may not be easy for some parents and provides moments of consternation, the stress shrinks in comparison to having your child become their own chauffeur. Watching your child drive off at night to a party has kept many a parent counting the minutes till their child is safe back home in her bed.

Parenting provides numerous opportunities to engage fear and loss in ways you do not experience elsewhere. A parent's love for their child is different than any other love they will have. Many parents will unhesitatingly tell you they would throw themselves in front of a bus to save their child. Parents make sacrifices for their child they might not make for others quite so willingly. Because parents love their children so much, the stakes on most everything are high.

Parents don't want their child to fail. They know their child will fail at various points and both parent and child will need to learn how to deal with that failure. The richness of life in all its majesty and all its tragedy is hers to discover. Trusting and believing that your child will navigate the harshness of life and find a rewarding enjoyable life is an up and down thing. There is no certainty with what your child will have to face and how she will fair.

Hopefully, one certainty she can hold is that your love and your home will always be there for her.

Which is why I believe you need to let her do what she will with her room.

Just like she needs to be able to choose her own clothes, make her own friends, and otherwise begin to take a foothold in the world, she needs to be become the ruler of her own universe.

Or at least her room.

With limits.

But still, more control.

Most parents want their child to have a natural confidence in their own ability to create a comfortable environment. As she increasingly takes over the choices of what is on the wall and how the place is painted you may become less comfortable in her space. The room you created and designed is now under new management. Her goal is not your comfort with the room but her own. The child's room you created now needs to become her own room and reflect her own interests.

She will eventually need to go out in the world and have a place of her own. To make that transition easier for her you need to let her know that you recognize her ability to be her own interior designer. She may or may not trust herself in this area. Your trust will support her as she builds her own sense of style.

If the process of guiding and supporting your child into adulthood requires your child to take on responsibility, why not let her room become truly her room? She is not going to get into a lot of trouble with decorating her room, but she may gain some assurance in her ability to govern her world.

The pictures you put up may be replaced by posters of things/people you have never heard of. The objects on the floor may include more clothes or items than you would like. The smell may not appeal to you as the often-closed door limits the circulation and the scents of youth are different than yours.

Basically you need to let go and look (and smell) the other way.

Tell her anything she does in there is okay except a few things. I might say no structural damage, no animals without beforehand discussion and mutual agreement, and respect for the fact that this is still also your house.

Many parents hold firm lines about curfew, homework, substances and other matters. I don't have a big issue with standing firm on those matters that you see as being of critical concern. But I would have you question whether the control of your child's room is really that important an issue in the overall scheme of things. If it is, so be it. But…really?

For those of you who have someone come and clean your house or if you are involved in cleaning up your child's room, I think it is fair to ask your child to also make her room available to cleaning. If she balks I wouldn't pick that battle to fight. She has to live in it. Hopefully sooner or later she will clean it or let someone else help out.

It is her room. Yes, it is "your" house. But it is also "our" house.

If you happen to own the house and today it is legally yours, probably some day it will be legally your child's house. Today's landlord is tomorrow's dependent senior adult.

I was once told that you cannot give someone power; they have to take it. I think there is some truth to that, as power requires an exchange. You can give it, but if they don't take it you are back where you started.

Give and/or take.

A parent can tell a child that she can decorate her room in whatever ways she wants just as long as it passes some basic decency rules. In order for the child to assume that responsibility, she would need to exert her power in some fashion. If she says, "I don't care. You decide," she is abdicating the power. But she also made a decision and that decision-making is the empowering element. Even if her decision is to relinquish power.

The more we are able to make decisions the more powerful we feel. Even if the decision is to have someone else make the decision.

In most households children increasingly take on a more participatory role in decision-making. Just like you, some of the decisions she makes will turn out to not be the best for her (or you). One just hopes in the long run that things work out well and today's hurtful lessons will help build a better tomorrow. While you don't want your child to flounder, you would much prefer she flounder while she lives with you than when she is out in the world on her own.

You can support and help get her through the rough patches of life much easier now than you will be able to later. So let her have more responsibility, make more decisions, have more poor choices, make more mistakes and learn from them while you are still on watch. All of which requires some hope, some luck, and some patching up.

There is a lot of hope involved in parenting. There is a lot of watching your child exceed your expectations, and disappoint you as well.

Regardless of the ups and downs, parents need to attend to helping their child believe in her ability to make good choices. You do this by letting go of those places where you have made the choices and letting her have more say in what happens in her life.

From the moment a child calls out to you to tuck her in bed, until she slams her door and tells you to stay out, parents and children are involved in the exchange of power and decision-making. From the moment she wants you to read to her a story for yet another time, to the moment she yells at you to leave her alone, you are involved in the push and pull of whose will will be done.

There will be power struggles and differences of opinions. There may be arguments and hurt feelings all around. Those moments of friction are part of life. Learning how to respectfully navigate through those skirmishes is an ongoing process. While I wish you a minimum of these contentious interactions, I don't worry about them too much as they are familial growing pains. Maybe you are not ready to hand over some responsibility to her but you can convey to her that when you both agree she is ready you fully believe she will be able to take good care of herself in all ways. Just because this is not that moment, it does not mean the moment won't come, and when it does you know she will be able to handle it. She won't like this as she thinks she is ready now and your refusal reflects your true beliefs about her abilities. You might want to think about that.

I happen to think handing over power to her when she feels she is ready for it is usually an esteem-building action. You don't need to do it all the time when she asks, but I would generally say yes more than I would say no. If you do say no to her try to figure out what she can realistically do so you can say yes about something. Give her hope and a roadmap.

Eventually your child will move out and have her own home and family and your rules and parenting guidelines will be a thing of the past. You hope your responses over the years have helped shape her to be a caring human being who will be able to create her own loving family. Do unto her as you would hope she would do unto your grandchildren.

Whether you give your child 100% control over her room or just a little more than she has now, the goal is the same—build her ability and confidence to successfully navigate the world.

48

HOMEWORK

Growing up I always thought school would be so much better if you did not have homework. In fact, when you start going to school they don't give you homework, which sort of lulls you in. Initially school is a place to go to be with other kids, learn, and play. It continues to be a place for those things, but they change the ratios and add on homework.

Most parents want their children to do well in school and see it as a passport into a better future when hopefully they will get a good job and once again have no homework. (Although I think we all find that after work we come home to various kinds of 'homework' to do.)

The statistics change year to year but the trend continues that the more schooling you have the higher your income. If you happen to have a teenager and are reading a self-help book chances are college entrance and college affordability are concerns in your home. Which most likely means the subject of homework has probably come up a time or two. I would be willing to bet there have been some arguments about it and it may even have become a sore subject in your home. It has in many.

There was a point when it was very necessary for you to help your child with his homework and there is a time when your assistance will be on a "will call" basis—which means hardly ever. Most parents find that aside from nagging there is not a lot of practical assistance they can provide to teenagers. What and how students learn now has distanced itself from when you were in school. While you may remember some of what you learned, chances are your way of handling an assignment is not "the way the teacher taught us to do it."

Most parents have become obsolete tutors who are not dependable to know the "right" way to do something. I have unwelcome memories of trying to help my 6th grade daughter with her math and being told in no uncertain way that my approach was wrong and I was not helpful. Ouch. The only good part of that memory is that I did take solace in her growing confidence in herself. The fact that it came in part at my diminished value was a lesson I was to learn over and over again.

The tricky part for parents is knowing and accepting when and how to move on. For most parents the end will be sooner than they want. No matter how wonderful you are as a tutor, guide, helper, or corrector, your child will increasingly seek to avoid your help. Even when you both know you have valuable help to offer.

Sure, there are some assignments your child will have that you know they can do "better" with your help. If you rewrote that English paper, or at least made some significant edits or corrected those math mistakes, he would get a better grade. Or more correctly said, you would get a better grade. Which might help him get a better GPA which might get him into a better college which might help him get a better job which might help him have a better life.

Or will it?

Children grow up with their parents being their helpers. You help him learn the alphabet, how to dress, how to eat with a utensil and how to approach a homework assignment. As your child grows up your role as a teacher/helper diminishes. Losing that esteemed position can be rough, but by the time your child is a teenager you have seen most of your advice, teaching, mentoring, and offers of assistance limited to being a chauffeur, chef, ATM, or nag.

Here is something I overheard a parent of a 9th grader tell his son after watching a basketball game in which his child had taken some ill-advised shots as well as some very well positioned ones: "When you do it the way I told you, it works. When you do it your own way, it doesn't."

What do you think of that statement? Do you agree with it?

It is probably true at some basic level that the father had told him not to take those ill-advised shots and maybe had shown him how to shoot that well-positioned shot. But, I wonder, what is the lesson he is teaching his child?

I talked with someone who knew this parent and they told me he basically says those kinds of things all the time to his son. That didn't make me feel good so I asked the parent if he would come and speak to me. In my role as the school counselor I spend a fair amount of time talking to parents about parenting and an equal amount of time talking to kids about dealing with the parenting they are receiving. In this situation I talked with the boy, then the dad, and then both together. I would have talked with the mother too, but she was deceased.

When I spoke with the dad I told him I had overheard his comment and wanted to speak with him about it. I asked him what his goal was in saying that. He told me he wanted his child to learn the right way to do things. On the basketball court there are right and wrong things to do and if you want to win you had better learn to do things right. That was true on the court and it was true in life.

While I could nitpick with that, I am willing to concede there is a good amount of truth to that statement. I told the dad I believed he was doing his very best to help his child be his very best and I could see how well their efforts were paying off. His son was a very good basketball player. I wanted to talk with him about different ways to help someone get the most out of their ability. I didn't want him to stop what he was doing especially if he thought it was effective, but I wanted to have him consider some other ways of accomplishing the goal.

I have found that when it comes to parenting skills I have one thing I do not want parents to do and a bunch of things I would prefer they didn't do. The law which I support does not want any parent to verbally, sexually, and/or emotionally abuse their child. Sometimes it is hard to tell when an act crosses over the line. The legal guideline for counselors is if you suspect something you report it and let others be the judge. My guideline with this is if you think you might be close to being abusive, stop. Do something else you know is not abusive. If you don't think you are being abusive, but are not completely sure, ask the person who you might be abusing and take their word for it. Then call your school counselor and get a second opinion as your child may not feel safe enough to tell you his truth.

I didn't think this parent's words fit the detailed description of emotional abuse, but others might hear it differently. I told him I preferred he did not tell his child that the father's way was the right way. There is an absolute to that message that I don't think serves him or his child. The father might think he has a better way or a more effective way, but circumstances change and there are individual differences that affect outcome. What might be right for him might not be right for his child. What might look like a better or right way in this moment may not be true in another.

I doubt there is as much to be gained from pointing out how not to do something as there is in pointing out how to do something. I suggested to the father that he take those moments that his child did things the "right way" and focus on those. Build from strength.

We spoke about the larger end goal. Yes, he wanted his son to be a better basketball player and that was a shared goal they both had and one I was happy to support and help achieve in any way I could. And, he spoke of another goal that I think all parents have for their children, and that is that his child be able to live a meaningful, fulfilling, enjoyable, healthy, happy life.

The father and I had a few more meetings and talked about his and his son's relationship on and off the court. He told me how his father had taught him and what that had been like for him. He acknowledged that he had a tough time with his father and he wanted his son to be closer to him than he was able to be with his father. He knew his child did not like how he was coaching him and that things were not going that well between them. He was uncertain how best to approach his child, but as things had gotten worse with his son he had gotten tougher on him. His son was losing confidence in himself as a basketball player and the father was losing confidence in him as well.

I could tell the father was hurting and unsure about what to do. One thing the father and I discussed was how to instill confidence. How do you do that? Wouldn't it be great if we all could just bump up our confidence level 10%-20% and not have a concomitant increase in our arrogance? I asked the father how he had gained his own confidence and he told me he built it step-by-step with hard work. He could tell as he spoke to me that he would need to do the same with his child. I suggested that one thing he could do to help build his son's confidence would be to let go of the idea that he knows the "right" way. The father's belief that he is right means the child has to look to the father to know what is right. You want the child to be able to look within not without. Just like Carl Rogers thought we all had the answers to what is best for us within us, I wanted the father to consider that so too might his child have that wisdom.

I suggested he let his son know what he thought was the "best" way to do something and then ask the son what he thought was best. That was too much for the dad. He could switch right to best, but asking his son's opinion —well, he wasn't ready to do that.

I then suggested to the father that he say what is best, and on those occasions when he sees his son doing that or close to it, he could say, "That's great. I can really see you trying and doing your best."

He kind of agreed to that and in his own way I am sure he found ways they both could be right. We all have to work within in our value and belief systems. Hopefully, we all want what is best for our children and can share with each other how best to help in those efforts.

Let me ask you, when you stumble and make mistakes, what do you want others to do?

_____

_____

I don't know how you answered that. Perhaps some combination of compassion, valuable feedback, and encouragement. Sometimes you might just want them to say and do nothing.

Whatever it is you would want, don't make the assumption that your child wants his mistakes and failures dealt with in the same way. Many people make the mistake of giving other people what they themselves want. If you would want encouragement you would be apt to give that. It makes sense. But, just because you might want to be treated one way does not mean everyone wants to be treated the same way.

It helps to ask.

I think teenagers get sufficient negative feedback from their peers and teachers that they don't need a lot from you. When it comes to schoolwork and homework they usually know they could be more diligent, but also know they are doing as much as they can handle. If they get a poor grade or you happen to find out that they are not doing so well, it is not an optimal time for critical feedback or some version of, "I told you so," or, "If you did it my way it would have worked."

You can ask how he feels/thinks about it. What he wants to do about it. How can you best be of assistance?

Usually those questions are interspersed with other less well-intentioned remarks that promote drama and ill will among all. School and all related topics become touchy items. School is your child's primary life away from you and he enjoys having that separate existence. When everything is good at school and the reports back are positive parents tend to hover less. When the news isn't so good, parents intrude more.

A parent needs to learn how to support their child when he falters and when he succeeds. Parents need to continually adjust how they interact over doing homework, going out, having sex, applying for college and everything else. Your calibrations will hit and miss, but the demonstration of your love and respect can be pretty consistent. One way to show your love and respect is to limit your "Have you done your homework?" or "Have you finished your college applications?" By the time he is in high school the homework question ought to be coming out of your mouth no more than once every few weeks if at all. If you are checking or talking about homework nightly or multiple times a week you have problems, but I don't need to tell you that.

You need to consider weaning yourself away. I know your fear is that if you don't nag the homework will not get done.

My guess is that by this time the continual checking has served its purpose. Your monitoring to make sure the job is done can be a Band-Aid, but in order to foster the kind of responsibility you are seeking from your child you need to back off. It may feel counterintuitive, just when he needs heavy structure and restrictions. I am suggesting you have taken over the responsibility of getting his homework done and not only will he rebel against that, but it is moving things in the opposite direction of the one you want to go. You want him more responsible and you less. I know doing less is not an easy step to take. So maybe just take a small one, but a noticeable one.

I had a student tell me once that he was on his way to his room to do his homework when his mother asked him if he had done his homework. He told me he turned around and went back in the living room and watched TV. I have told that story many times to parents and students and I can't tell you how many students nod their heads and say, "Yeah, I have done that."

If you need someone to nag them about their homework call their teacher. Then if your concerns persist call a school administrator. They might be able to help. You aren't.

Remember teen years are the rebellious ones. The more you give him to rebel against the more he will rebel.

Rebellion is not always something you know about right away. Sometimes kids rebel out of sight and maybe you get to hear about it later. If and when you do hear about it you usually don't like it and want to do something about it. Before you take any action, you might want to reflect on how you may be part of the problem. I know you don't like me saying that to you, but it is true.

Families are systems. They function as integral parts. You do this, they do that. If you change what you do they change what they do. It is pretty simple. At least in concept, if not in execution. You can be part of the problem or part of the solution. Or some of each.

Therapists are big proponents of natural consequences. If your child does not do their homework he goes to school and he "pays" for not doing it. Sometimes, he can fool some of the people. But we know, the more he doesn't do the more he eventually will pay.

Which is when parents get squeamish.

They don't want their child to get a lesser grade. That is not the price they want their child to pay, but it is often where you first notice your child's shift in behavior. They were a B+ student and suddenly they are getting C's. When parents get wind of that they feel a need to clamp down and get their child back on track. How to do that is the tricky part.

When you take a step back and look at children as primarily spending their time in their home and in their school you can begin to understand that they have two primary arenas for self-discovery. They learn their role at home and their role at school. They learn what they can and can't do at home and they learn what they can and can't do at school. And they learn that you have less control over what they do at school then you do at home. So school often is where you notice their first steps into independence. That and time out of the house on their own.

Parents may know the grades, the clubs, and some of the friends, but they never get the full picture. Just like your child doesn't fully understand your day neither do you understand his.

Children have a complete identity at school that parents never fully appreciate. You don't know how your child behaves in the classroom, with his teachers, with his friends, and with the other people at his school. In that space away from you your child can begin to understand himself separate from you. You may have told him that he is smart or stupid or this or that, but there are other voices at school that will also play into how he comes to view himself.

Parents know they have little or no real control over how their child behaves at school. They can lecture, plead, threaten, cajole, or do whatever they think will be effective. Ultimately your child learns you don't really have much power over this part of his life. Yes, you can take away all his privileges and restrict his activities if he doesn't do things the way you would like. His willingness to accept consequences might be easier for him to handle than the consequences he fears were he to do things your way.

School is a child's second testing ground for his place in society. He learns at home where he stands in the structure of your family and he learns at school where he stands in relation to everyone else. The more you oversee him and the more you are telling him you don't trust him, the more he will be prone to push back against you. It can be a vicious circle. He starts to flounder, you jump in, he either resurrects himself or flounders some more, you either back off or oversee more, to which he might distance himself even more from you.

Teenagers are prone to more black-and-white thinking about people. They often initially see people in simplistic terms—theater person, brainiac, athlete, robotics geek, and the ones with fake IDs who buy alcohol. There are myriads of social groups and sub groups and everyone earns a description in the yearbook for "most likely" to be or do something.

Some students have very little to do with school and others come early and stay late. Some hate it, others love it, and most make the best of it. Certainly most students would like something about their high school experience to be different. And most people feel that way about their lives.

On the one hand you want to have curiosity about your child's day and hope he will share something real with you. On the other hand, you want to get out of the day-to-day management. You want to let him know you trust his ability to navigate his way and deal with and rebound from anything that doesn't go his way. He will figure out how to make the most of his math class and is welcome to come and talk with you anytime.

As I mentioned before parents don't mind natural consequences except when they might hurt their child. They don't want their child's behavior to hurt their chances of getting into a good college. So they call me, they call others, they ask about the homework, they question their child's activities, and they put a strain on their relationship with their child. All because they want what is best.

Parents have a very hard time accepting it is best for their child to not do well. They get afraid that any downward trend is heading in the wrong direction and there is no telling where it will end. It is a good thing to be concerned about. You don't ever want to do harm. Yet, it is not easy knowing what is and what isn't truly harming. Parents listen to me encourage them to back off a little and they nod their heads, but very often they end up asking about the homework within a week. Oh well, a step at a time. 10%. That's what we are aiming for.

I have heard from many students that when they argue with their parents it leaves them in poor shape to focus on their homework. Their agitation and stress interfere with their concentration and focus.

I had some parents ground their daughter for a month so she could focus on finishing her college applications. They took the child's phone when she got home and basically told her to stay in her room and work. The girl stayed in her room, fumed, and came to me the next day and told me she got "zero" accomplished.

I called up the parents and asked them if they wanted to come and talk about it. No pressure. No requirement. Just me offering to assist them in whatever ways I could. I make a fair number of calls to parents in response to "issues" I hear their child is having. I hear about whatever is going on most often from teachers followed by the child and increasingly from friends. I call up, relay what I have heard, and ask if they would like to come in and talk about it. Most do. Some don't.

These parents came in and we talked. I asked them what they thought was going on and what they wanted. They felt at a loss for how to motivate their daughter to take care of the business of college applications. The deadline was approaching and she kept saying she would do it, but she kept not doing it and they kept getting more worried.

Her grades were not as solid as they would like but they had come to accept that they were what they were. What parents come to learn is that whatever the grade point average, tests scores, and extra-curriculars there is a college for every child. Maybe not their first-choice college, but one where their child will get a good education if that is what she desires. The fact that their child was not becoming more of an activist for her own future drove them to take extreme actions. They didn't like clamping down on her, but they couldn't think of anything else that might be any more effective at getting their child through the application process.

I have probably heard more variations of the college application blues than I have any other parent concern. It beats out drugs/alcohol and sex. Not by much. But by some.

I eventually made some recommendations to them. I told them their daughter told me that she thought they did not trust her. I wanted to repair that trust. They could ground her for a month if they wanted, but they could understand that within that action is the belief that left to her own devices she would fail at the task of getting into an appropriate college. Whether they kept their restrictions intact or not, I thought their primary task was letting their daughter know they did trust her to get things done and that she will be fine.

Sure they don't have conviction. But they do have responsibility. They need to help their child feel better about herself when within less than a year she will be heading off into a world where parents play a very small part. But more on that later.

I suggested they tell their daughter that their worry is what gets them to clamp down and they really want to trust her to do the applications and will do their best to back off. I also told them that since they probably would not feel all that comfortable backing off entirely they could check with her teachers and college counselor and find out how she is doing. If she was doing well enough, stay away. But realize she won't be doing things perfectly to suit their needs. She would be doing things well enough to suit her needs. But I told them, if there was too much slippage for them to manage without confronting her, to speak to me first so we could put our heads together about how to proceed.

I didn't hear back. Sometimes I do. Sometimes I don't.

The single most effective thing you can do to help your child with his homework is to have the expectation that he will do it, that he will work hard in school, and that he will be able to build for himself a meaningful, enjoyable, and valuable life.

Expectation and trust are hallmarks of most meaningful relationships. When you marry and exchange vows to be there for better or worse, for richer, for poorer, and in sickness and health, there is an expectation and trust that the union you forge will survive the challenges it faces. While it doesn't always work out that way, it is the foundation upon which the relationships are built. And so it is with your child.

See if you can find that expectation within you. Not the hope that he will do well, but the belief that your child does want to live the best life possible. Michael Thompson, PhD and author of *The Pressured Child: Helping Your Child Find Success in School and Life* writes: "Children want to feel successful."

It may be hard when observing your child's actions to believe he wants to be successful. Yet even his rebellious moments are prompted by the desire to be successfully rebellious. Your job is to figure out how to manage your worry in such a way as it gives opportunities for your child to be successful in ways more to your liking. When your child is not performing as you would like, the task is to help build his confidence and feelings of success, not to punish him into worrying about performing.

You want to tap into that basic desire he has to succeed. When you add a layer of restriction and distrust it makes it harder for him to focus on what he really wants. Often he would just as soon rebel against you. It may not be the smartest move, but I imagine we all can find times in our life when instead of doing what was best for us we wanted to push back against an intrusive force.

Why not let him choose what he thinks would be best? You can set a time in a couple of weeks to monitor his progress. He probably won't do as well as you might hope and you probably will check in on him before you said you would. If he is doing better than he was, acknowledge that and back off again. Even if that sock is resting on the hamper and not in it. The more you recognize his achievements the more he is going to be invested in them.

It is not a foolproof plan, but when it comes to homework why not back off 10%-20% and throw in 10%-20% more positive comments about his efforts? And, if it doesn't improve matters, sit down again with him and the counselor at his school.

One other thing about homework. Students now have more of it than you did. They also have more activities outside of school than you did. Time management is a skill they need to learn way earlier than you ever did. Some students are able to organize their days, assignments, and obligations fairly well. Some students, and they tend to be boys, lose track of their assignments, clothes, and other obligations. You will agonize about this, complain about it and eventually (hopefully) call your school counselor. While we get less of these calls in the high school than in earlier years, we still have students who are late bloomers in the organizing of responsibilities department.

When I was growing up in New York my mother used to tie a string to my gloves and run it up the sleeves of my jacket to lessen the chance that I would come home without them. That was a pretty effective strategy and when I walk around cold climates I do notice there is a collection of abandoned gloves on the streets. It seems I was not the only one who left the house with two and came home with one. Devising strategies to help your child be more accountable requires a degree of creativity on your part along with a good dose of patience. However forgetful and unorganized your child may be, your school counselor has probably run into similar issues before and may be able to help you out with some strategies.

49

WHAT ABOUT THEIR BODY, THEIR LIFESTYLE, THEIR CHOICES?

This chapter is about nutrition, weight, physical activity, sleep, tattoos, piercings, and the overall care and maintenance of the body. I think it is fair to say that when it comes to how we treat our bodies most of us have a pretty good understanding about what is "good" for us and what is "bad" or "not so good" for us.

The more challenging part is not so much knowing what to do that is "good" for us; it is actually doing it.

Surely we could all learn some more about what "experts" in their fields think. Knowledge is power and if you learn how bad something is for you, it increases the odds of you not doing it. It doesn't bring them down to zero, but the more you know the more informed your decision-making.

Of course, we all have witnessed what is considered healthy today not being considered healthy tomorrow. Still, given the choice you probably are better off following expert advice. Even if the experts were always right and you knew every "good" thing to do and every "bad" thing not to do, most people would still mix in some of the bad.

I guess the issue is how much you mix in and what exactly you are mixing.

The Center for Disease Control and Prevention has guidelines for what they consider healthy. According to them more than half of us aren't doing as well as we ought to be doing. They are not talking about mixing in some ice cream now and then along with a couple of drinks on a Saturday. They are talking about doing things that may more directly cause you to shorten your life.

If you are in the half that knows they are doing well—congratulations. I am sure many of you also know you could be doing even better.

If you are in the half that is not doing so well—maybe we can do something about that. Once again you can aim for 10-20% improvement. Maybe that is all it would take to get you to the other side of the equation. If it would take more than a 20% improvement to get you in the healthier half, you might want to reach out for some assistance.

If you want to improve your healthy living choices or that of your child or partner a good place to start is by acknowledging that you don't do as well as you could and they probably don't do as well as they could. They are imperfect just like you, except differently. Usually when someone is less well behaved in an area where we are pretty solidly behaving we tend to be judgmental. If they are excelling in some place where we don't do so well, we tend to look the other way.

I imagine that if you (or your child) are like most of us, you know certain behaviors/activities that you could realistically do that would be healthier. You can also probably cite some good enough sounding reasons why you don't do those things you know at some level would make your life better. You could also put out some rather flimsy excuses.

We all can explain ourselves and usually justify our actions. Sometimes it just boils down to, "I don't want to do it. Period. End of story." However we explain our own choices, most people know at some level they could do a better job if they really wanted. Their impetus to take steps in a healthier direction has not yet reached the action level.

For the time being let's just think about your body and lifestyle.

Is there a part of your body, health regime, and approach to life that you would like to improve?

_____

_____

_____

Is there a part of your child's body, health regime, and approach to life that you would like to improve?

_____

_____

_____

What do you think keeps you from doing something to take better care of yourself?

_____

_____

_____

What do you think keeps your child from taking better care of herself?

_____

_____

_____

Any comments?

_____

_____

_____

Certainly how you take care of yourself is going to be a primary influence on how your child takes care of herself. Parents may say, "Do as I say, not as I do," but the net effect of that is your child learns early about hypocrisy and how it is practiced. Most children start life doing as their parents do. They eat the food you serve, accompany you on your errands, and will lay down on the floor next to you when you do your stretching exercises. Then they start to branch off on their own. After which, the challenges start.

Parents often have wishes for their child that the child does not perfectly match. You may have hoped your child to be a great athlete, brainiac, entrepreneur, movie or rock and roll star, or just be nice to you. You may have wanted her to have a better physique, be more assiduous about her appearance, or be more conscientious about what she puts into her body. You may have hoped she would excel in positive ways and not get in any trouble as defined by you. And why not? You're her parent. You want the best for her.

Children don't usually completely match their parents' hopes. They score better in some areas than others. They exceed expectations in some ways and disappoint in others. They are your children after all, no longer your dreams. How you manage the reality of your child and the loss of your hopes will play a significant role in how your child thinks you perceive her.

I had a student tell me he never felt he was good enough because he knew his mother was disappointed he was not as talented as she wanted him to be. He too wished he was more talented in the ways his mother wanted. Whatever other talents he might have, he knew no matter how "successful" he was in life he would never feel good enough for his mother. I lamented that with him. I also told him not to compound the issue by also not being good enough for himself.

His mother was not wrong for being disappointed that her child did not have the talents she preferred. But she wasn't helping her son by being so transparent. Whatever amount of disappointment she might have experienced she needed to outsource. She could mourn the loss of her dreams and get as angry and disappointed as she wanted with someone else. With her son I encouraged her to focus on the things he did and the way he behaved that pleased her. Unfortunately the damage was done. But she could stop trying to shift the pendulum. I also recommended she went to therapy and worked on her disappointment so it did not burden her and him the rest of their lives.

We all have feelings/thoughts about our children. Some we share out loud, others we try to hide. Some of those thoughts/feelings make us happy and proud. Others trigger different emotions.

What you do with those feelings/thoughts varies. As a therapist I would want you to know what you think/feel about your child and then decide what to do about it.

Here are some questions to consider:

- What do you think/feel about your child's body?

_____

_____

- What do you think/feel about your child's weight?

_____

_____

- What do you think/feel about how and what she eats?

_____

_____

- What do you think/feel about her physical activity?

_____

_____

- What do you think/feel about how she carries and presents herself in the world?

_____

_____

- What do you think/feel about her emotional, mental, and spiritual life?

_____

_____

- What do you think/feel about how your child spends her time?

_____

_____

- What do you think/feel about your child's school life?

_____

_____

- What do you think/feel about your child's social life?

_____

_____

- What do you think/feel about her relationship with her other parent?

_____

_____

- What do you think/feel about her relationship with her siblings and relatives?

_____

_____

- What do you think/feel about her relationship with you?

_____

_____

I imagine not everyone wrote down that they felt great about everything. But I am sure some did. Lucky you. Enjoy your good fortune. And let's see if we can help you feel even better.

For the rest, there is always the serenity prayer: "God grant me the serenity to accept the things I cannot change, courage to change the things I can, and wisdom to know the difference." Whether you believe in God or not, those are wise sentiments to follow.

How you think/feel about your child will influence how you interact with her. If any of your answers to those questions prompted a level of concern on your part I would hope you would get yourself to a therapist and share your concern with them. I think most of us know when we are out of balance. Sure, we all can get upset about certain things, but for the most part our responses fall within a fairly well agreed upon range.

When you can realize your thoughts/feelings about something are out of the ballpark of your other responses you might want to go talk with a therapist so you can gain greater clarity and insight.

Most parents have wishes for their child in terms of body piercings, tattoos, and other matters of bodily changes. Let's consider the example of the parent who would not want their child to get a tattoo ever, but certainly not until she was over 18 and it was easily covered and small. If you were that parent and your 14-year-old child told you she wanted to get a tattoo you might not be eager or willing to give your approval.

How you don't give your approval, how you discuss or argue the issue, and how you come to a resolution are the kinds of life skills parents teach their child without ever really thinking about it. How you deal with the circumstances that life presents is a lesson in itself to our children. If you are calm about most things, so too will your child be when she encounters challenging times. If you lean towards loud drama, so too will your child.

So while you might wish your child was not so emotional your behavior most likely is influencing her one way or another. She very well could be a youthful edition of you or she might have experienced your makeup and chosen to take a decidedly different path. Sometimes if parents are too even-keeled a child may want to raise the emotional level to get a rise out of them.

In my Relationship Training Manual books I wrote about how men have traditionally driven women crazy. I gave an example of a man who doesn't raise his voice when his partner gets upset. Often his lack of overt emotion prompts her to overemphasize her emotion in order to get a reaction out of him, at which point he says, "Please dear, calm down, let's talk about this in a rational matter." This only inflames her more.

I mention this dance that couples often do, because your child may very well play a version of that dance with you. Your calm-headedness may drive her crazy just as easily as raising your voice will upset her and either prompt her to underplay her emotions or get her to go toe-to-toe with you.

To some of her actions you will have well thought out responses and to others you will blurt out reactions. There are no assurances that how you react will help/hurt your child. Your well-balanced response could head her south. Your overly emotional or stoic response may trigger her in positive or negative ways.

Unfortunately, I can't promise you that if you respond in loving open ways all will be well. You would hope someone who wrote about relationships would at least be able to give out some assurances. All I can say is your better behavior increases the odds of her better behavior.

Parents are left with hunches, instincts, gut-reactions, and impulses. You can also talk to other parents, listen to would-be experts, read self-help books and do all you can to be the best parents you can be. And then hope for the best, let go and move on.

I have no idea if you child should or should not get a tattoo or belly button piercing or the like. I have my personal preferences as a father and I shared those with my daughter and asked her, some might say pleaded with her, to wait until she was a little older to make her decision. I didn't threaten consequences. I just shared my feelings/thoughts and asked her to share hers. Then I said some version of, "I am sure you will do what you believe is best," and mostly left it at that. I think I also threw in a beseeching look.

The technical name for that is 'stalling'. Put off for tomorrow what you hope will be gotten over by tomorrow.

I don't know of any research into what happens when parents are able to get their children to hold off getting tattooed or pierced until later, but I would guess most kids wait and then do it. Which means there are some kids who move on to other things. The odds might not be great, but at least there is a chance.

Certainly the research on alcohol consistently finds that the longer children wait to experiment with alcohol the fewer problems they will have with it. I would imagine that might hold true for holding off on altering your body, but I don't know. What I do know is if you have opinions on these matters you need to make sure your child clearly knows them because you have directly spoken about the issue with her. Don't assume she would know what you wanted. Even if you are 99% sure she knows you want, when you speak with her it will be 100%.

When/if you think your child is gaining weight or not taking good care of her body many parents wonder if they should say anything, and if they do decide to say something, what they ought to say. Men have been taught to not speak with women about weight and women have been taught that you can never be too thin. What are parents taught about how to approach issues of weight with their children? Probably not much.

Whatever you say make sure you are not saying it when you are cranky, upset, or otherwise out of balance. Bring your calm, casual self to this conversation, because chances are whatever you do it is going to be "wrong."

Wrong because no matter how caringly and articulately you may share what you are thinking/feeling, your child's feelings most likely will be hurt. That, in and of itself, is not a bad thing. Feelings get hurt all the time. Because weight and body image is a sensitive and very personal matter to everyone, practically anything anyone says other than an A grade compliment is likely to inflame an already open wound. Sadly, very few people feel totally good about their body. Most everyone would change something if they could—or if it were easy. And, of course, some do.

When sore wounds get open it is not easy to walk away feeling better. When someone points something out about you that you don't feel all that good about it does rub salt on an already established wound. That doesn't mean you don't bring the subject up. It just means handle with care.

Sometimes you can have a conversation and everyone feels heard and understood and you come away feeling closer than when you started. Sometimes that happens. But not that often when you are talking about weight.

So should you not say anything about her weight, body, or desires to decorate her body?

No, if you want to something to say something, say something. But don't hold out much hope that what you say will make a positive difference.

It may. Which is hopefully why you are saying something in the first place.

There is not much chance you are going to be able to change your teenager's mind about most things. You might be able to get her to delay her decisions about a tattoo or be willing to consider taking steps to build a healthier body. But, if you are continually pointing out her poor health choices, you have already lost the battle. These are conversations you have occasionally, not regularly. Harping on a behavior will most likely extend the behavior rather than extinguish it.

You may recall that if your child was wetting her bed past the time you thought she ought to stop your doctor most likely recommended that you didn't make an issue of it. Sooner or later she would stop. That thinking didn't stop with bedwetting. It is a pretty solid approach for many things.

Share your point of view about your child's lifestyle choices and she will either incorporate it in her actions or she won't. If she wants help she will ask for it. If she doesn't ask, you can offer now and then, but as your child ages, the decisions about her body are more and more hers to make.

When they say to pick your battles, I suggest you put weight on the list of things to not fight tooth and nail about. I would save my battleground actions for matters directly related to her immediate health and wellbeing. If I thought my child was on a direct path to causing serious harm to herself then I would actively intervene. Of course, some people will think five pounds over ideal weight is too much and some people will think fifty pounds over is not that much. We all approach life through our own belief systems.

If your child's weight or desire to do something to her body is weighing on you and you "have" to say something, there are some things you can do that have a better chance of having a positive result:

- Don't start anything. Just listen to your child until you hear her say something about her weight, body, or decorative arts. If you can find even a tangential opening, that is usually the best way in.
- Begin (and pretty much end) with a question. Say something like, "I heard you say such and such about your body/health. What is going on? What do you think/feel about that?"
- Let her reply.
- Whatever she says, reflect it back. If she says, "Fine," you can say, "Fine."
- You can throw in a little question mark at the end if you want, but don't add your own two cents.

See where she takes the conversation. If she seems to want to talk about it go for it. Be curious about how she thinks/feels and respond to what you hear her say. Be a listener and maybe even a sympathizer, but not a lecturer. Save that for another time. If she seems to want to avoid the whole thing, let her. You want her to have a sense of power about the subject. And, if something is a real issue it will come up again and again, so don't feel like you need to push it in the moment. You will get other chances.

Body issues are lifelong issues. You are not going to resolve them in a day. If she brings her weight or issue up in some way, use that as an opening for being curious. Not as an opportunity for you to harangue her.

Parents sometimes feel starved for conversation with their teen and when a chance occurs they often try to weave in this, that, and the other thing. You will be better served by short talks. If your child learns she can get in and out of conversations with you she is more likely to want to enter into them.

She will say something another time and maybe you say something that time, but first ask her to expound on her thoughts/feelings. Let her know you are paying attention and, if she keeps bringing it up, that you are open to talking more about it. If she knows you are open to talking about something when she is ready, you can consider her mentioning the subject an invitation for your greater participation. Just tread lightly.

If she is having some issue with her body, chances are you are too. It is a lot easier for you to listen to her speak about it and support any of her thoughts that resemble your own. If she is to take positive action on her lifestyle it will occur over time with lots of twists and turns in the road. You are in this for the long haul. Try not to be overbearing. Trust that if something continues to be a major concern for her, she will have the ability to take care of it. Believe in her. It will help her believe in herself.

I am a believer in yearly physicals. For you and your children. Since weight issues usually do not happen overnight you could hold off on addressing them and wait until it is time for her annual checkup. I would call ahead to her doctor and let the doctor know my concerns and ask the doctor, if they share those concerns, to please talk with her. If you can get the doctor to convey the message you don't have to worry about a rebellious backlash against you.

If I had written this book twenty years ago I could have gotten away with not writing anything about the various ornaments and decorations people now have decided to use to enhance their look. I know when my young adolescent wanted to have her navel pierced it caused quite a ripple in my house. On the one hand I wanted my child to be able to keep current with social trends. On the other I didn't want her to do anything she might regret later on (while I would regret it right away).

My basic approach to her was, "You can do what you want when you are 18."

That didn't go over so well. So, after much discussion, we came up with an embargo of anything that was not easily reversible. I lost out on the pierced belly but was able to forestall any illustrations that would have threatened my outdated sense of propriety.

Generations do clash and as parents you want to be sensitive to your child's desire to do things that will give her a certain level of peer acceptance. That said, you also need to guide her through her early years so she doesn't make too many decisions she might later regret. You want her doing something because she wants to do it, not because others are or because she is rebelling against you. Her actions need to come from a comfort she has with who she is and what she wants.

Which is why I came up with the easily reversible bottom line until she was 18. She didn't totally love that guideline, but she was willing to adhere to it. While she wanted me to fully trust her good judgment, she also realized I wanted her to acknowledge my good judgment—at least for a few more years. Maybe I was providing that 20% of cognitive functioning that wasn't fully hers yet.

Often as parents the best we can do is to let our children know our wishes. We hope they will follow the core ones and not get in too much trouble when they veer off course.

50

SOCIAL MEDIA

By the time you read this there will be some new device, game, or interactive activity that is consuming more of your child's interest than you might desire. Needless to say, your children are spending more time connected to digital technology than you ever were.

Jill Stein, PhD, a sociology professor, told me she had her students go a day without electronics and not only could some of them not do it, but others said, "What's the point?" One student said if she couldn't go out and take pictures of what she was doing and immediately post them, she might as well stay home. Another said that if he wanted to read old news he would look at a newspaper. Times have changed.

How this generation is being influenced by technology is not something most parents can fully comprehend. The idea of not going out if you can't take pictures and post them probably is not something most parents would ever consider. Certainly the idea of not going out if you couldn't post pictures is not widespread, but it is spreading.

Of course, when you were a teenager you might have been less electronically connected, but you did spend your time doing something. It might have been reading extra material for school and doing community service, but chances are you idled away some of your adolescence. Most likely there were elements of what you were doing that your parents were less than keen about.

The big question to me is: Are the activities and the time spent doing them harming your child in some way we (you) ought to be doing something about?

Unfortunately that question is not so easy to answer, but let's see what we can do. First, let's acknowledge the value of time spent listening to music, watching videos, playing games, interacting with friends known and World Wide Web users both known and unknown. Time spent in any of these activities can be beneficial in ways too numerous to list and not so beneficial in critical ways.

Parents often have concerns about their child's exposure to pornography and violence. Given the amount of time children spend online it is not surprising to learn that children start watching porn as early as six. Parents sometimes block certain access for children and have porn talks long before they have sex talks. Younger children usually respect the boundaries set by parents, but as they grow up, more and more they want to set those boundaries themselves and find ways to get around the ones you have established.

That doesn't mean you don't talk with your child about your thoughts about his watching sexually explicit videos or playing violent games. Sex and violence are part of life and sooner or later he will be exposed to it. You can tell him there are parts of sex and violence that he can learn about now and parts you are going to restrict till he is older. Then, of course, you need to be able to explain to him what you think is appropriate for him now and why you think some other things are not. Parents usually are not adept at explaining sexual concepts to children and often let their awkwardness lead to avoidance.

Let's focus on sex, violence, and social media. Whatever guidelines you may have on the Internet and social media, by the time your child becomes a teenager they are going to have close to full reign. Some parents can hold a line, but most children can find a way around it once they decide to push back. By the time their child is in his mid-teens most parents reluctantly cast a blind eye on their child's Internet content. Trying to monitor and restrict access becomes one of those battles that increasingly loses importance as the skirmishes shift to the amount of time he is spending online rather than where his focus is aimed. If he can't watch porn at your house he will do it at someone else's. If he can't play games for endless hours at your house he will do it elsewhere.

I am not encouraging you to give up the fight, but I would like you to consider what battles you want to fight with your child. If his usage of social media or time spent gaming or online troubles you, then certainly you need to address it. I just don't want you to have a long list of grievances so that you spend the majority of time with your child trying to rein him in. You might want to take a look at what is on your list of grievances. I don't know is an appropriate number of issues to have with your child but if that number is more than three you might consider paring down. You don't want your grievance conversations to take up more than 20% of your actual conversations.

I have heard many a parent lament about the amount of time their child is online and how little time he spends doing homework or being with his family or engaging in something more meaningful (to the parent). I have had parents worry about their child being addicted to online games and I even have had students tell me they were addicted. In those situations I have recommended therapy with cyber addiction specialists as one does not want to be ruled by addictions.

Of course, almost all the people in this world who excel have done it at the expense of balancing their lives. Often those that do most things in the "correct and proper way" (whatever definition you want to use) don't excel to the degree of those that specialize. Like it or not.

You listen to most Olympic stars and they can speak to you about things they had to sacrifice in order to achieve their goals. Every four years we reward that, but most days we worry if our child isn't spending too much time devoted to this activity. I think we all know that in order to excel people need to invest time and energy. Malcolm Gladwell in his bestseller *Outliers: The Story of Success* posits that it takes 10,000 hours of focused work to obtain mastery at something. It's when parents can't see the value in how their child is spending his time that issues arise. If they thought the time spent would manifest in great success they probably wouldn't worry so much. But when your child is playing violent video games into the wee hours it is hard to feel confident in the upside.

It doesn't really matter what the child is putting his energy into, when it starts affecting his performance at school most parents push back. It is sort of akin to when you have a drinking problem. It really doesn't become a "problem" until it starts to affect your work, health, or home life.

We can discuss as long as you want the pros and cons of doing well in school. We can point to those who have done well in school and not so well in life and those who have floundered in school and prospered in life. The general truth is that those who do well in school tend to do well in life, but just because the statistics point that way does not mean it is a given.

I have known students who squeaked through school with spotty attendance while spending considerable hours glued to their console that went on to successfully create programming and content for various online enterprises. I have also known students who paid little attention to school who also pay little attention to work. Their parents worry about their ability to support themselves. Just like every other parent. When parents have a hard time seeing how their child's behavior will lead to any viable future, my phone rings.

My generic advice to parents is to encourage your child in those areas that hold his interest. I think we all know that areas that once held interest do not always continue to hold interest. I imagine we all know some toy/game/thing that your child had to have which soon became yesterday's news. Parents need to be cautious about getting into a pushing match with their child. The grievances prompt you to be more aggressive with your child and your child will either flight or fight. If they push back you have the makings of a pattern. A pattern that you need to break. Some fights are best walked away from. The message to send to your child is that you support his engagement in life. While what he is doing might not make you as pleased as you would like to be, the fact that he is putting effort into something and being rewarded in some fashion is a necessary life skill to learn. My experience with teenagers tells me it is rare for the 19-year-old to like what they did at 13. There is a pretty high turnover rate when it comes to interests and technology. Teens like to be on the cutting edge and be involved with the new thing. I would tend to let your teen's interests run their own course and not interfere that often. When you get more involved and restrictive with his interests it adds another dimension. A dimension most teens are keen on challenging which then escalates the focus on the issue. Layers upon layers often prolong matters.

That ought to not stop you from making your views and values known and heavily suggesting he bring some more balance into his life. As I have said before, don't just berate him for what he is doing that you don't like, but find the times that he is doing the things you like and acknowledge those. Tell him what you want and hope, and when he does anything closely resembling that, acknowledge it. Make sure you bite your tongue and do not point out his falling short more than you point out his moving in a direction of your liking.

Most of the students I have known who devote hours a day to social media tend to socialize with other kids who are doing the same thing. As long as they aren't scheming on doing harm, I think the networking and socially interaction are valuable skills to learn. Often that socially awkward child who doesn't have many friends in person is able to make connections online and develop those into friendships. The skills he learns from interacting with others online will serve him as he goes forth into the world.

If you do think your child is too insular and you have concerns about his welfare by all means reach out for help. I would start with the school counselor.

I do think parents are well served by talking with their child periodically about their concerns about Internet usage and if they would like there to be some general limits on activity. I do fully expect that whatever parameters are established, many children will eventually cross over those parameters. That is part of their job description. I just hope that if you mostly set the guidelines together, he won't need to cross over too often or too far. But, he is a growing child and parameters can be both comforting and confining. If he does cross over too far and you find out about it discussions will follow. Feelings expressed. Consequences discussed. Negotiations reinitiated.

I can't tell you if the reason he is not staying within the guidelines is because he is upset with you and thinks the restriction are unfair, or if he is rebelling because they really are unrealistic. There really isn't anybody that can definitively answer that for you, but there are plenty of people you could talk to who would be willing to weigh in. I might first ask his friends and their parents.

Parents sometimes want to keep their challenges to themselves and not share them with other people. That is too bad. Most families go through the teen years with some conflicts and hearing other parents share their responses and approaches can not only make you feel not so alone, but you may hear something that will help you out.

Call the other parent, a friend, the parents of a friend of your child, a school counselor, a therapist, or even your own parent. Ask for feedback and suggestions. Ask them to meet with you and then with your child. Then maybe ask them to meet with both of you together.

If you try all those options and none are helpful, keep reading parenting books until your child has moved out and is living on his own.

When girls and boys first get involved in the Internet/social media parents worry about their children becoming prey to pedophiles. Later they worry about identity theft, financial scams and what their child's digital foot print looks like. Since a large part of every parent's duties are to protect their child, there is a heightened level of concern when his activities occur without your immediate oversight.

Children can be lured into promising situations that are dangled in front of them. They are not much different than you in that way, except you hopefully are better at being able to discern the dubious entries. Most children now get involved with social media long before they become teenagers so it is very important that parents are exceedingly clear about the guideline for online use. I am not going to list the necessary safeguards you should have in place as that is a fast-evolving field and it is not really my expertise. I don't want to endorse any particular company but if you search for "Internet child guidelines" you will find some very helpful material for you to consider.

Since schools are using iPads and your phone is your communication center there is so much activity on your child's devices that it becomes increasingly harder to monitor what exactly he is doing. And who really wants to be in a detective role with their child? Once you have an overt presence in his online world, you are telling him you don't think he can manage himself responsibly. If that is true then perhaps it is a necessary action to take, but I would want to provide him opportunities to be able to demonstrate that he can be responsible.

I veer away from these kind of policing actions as they indicate a level of distrust I would not want a child to experience. Yet, there are times when parents lose trust in their child and feel a responsibility to create stricter limits. So be it. Just make sure that the restrictions given out as punishment can be resolved in a timely manner and you create a pathway for him to rebuild the trust.

Parents care/worry about their child's physical health, emotional life, social life, school life, home life, and any number of other concerns that pop up. There is your usual day-to-day level of concern as well as your "drop everything and attend to this" level of concern.

Let's say you have more than your usual level of concern about something but not the alarm bells ringing level of concern. In this case we are talking about social media, but we could just as well be talking about alcohol, drugs, schoolwork, or anything that is causing your concern to start to move up the scale. Once the time you are usually thinking about something starts to multiply, it is time to talk. I am a big believer in talking about things when they start to heat up as opposed to when they get hot. It is a lot easier if you can nip things in the bud.

One reason to deal with things sooner than later is that extra level of concern is something you will not be able to hide; your stealth is not always as effective as you might think. You may think you are fooling some of the people some of the time. And you are. Just not all the time. You very well may start acting a little differently towards your child. Perhaps in subtle ways that you may not even notice at first.

Your child will sense your disapproval and yet not always be able to discern what exactly it is about. While you may want your child going around with some vague sense of your disapproval, the prolonged downside of that can be far worse. A child can interpret that disapproval as you not liking him. Once he thinks you may not like him, he may double down on whatever it is he may also not like about himself. He may start doing things to punish himself for not being more likeable to you and him.

I was taught to think you may not like the behavior but that doesn't mean you don't like the person. Sometimes you can separate out what someone does from who they are. Sometimes not. You may have a friend who smokes and you don't like that, but that doesn't mean you don't like *him*.

Better to just tell let your child know what you don't like and also tell him that while you don't like this behavior he is doing it has nothing to do with you not liking him. A child can understand that difference and accept it. He may have a teacher he likes, but he doesn't like the homework load the teacher hands out.

Parents want their child to know that there are certain things they disapprove of and do not want their child to do. Most parents disapprove of lying, bullying, cheating, and an overabundance of whining. When they experience too much of these behaviors they usually let their child know both indirectly and directly.

Every parent has their own list of behaviors and beliefs that they do not condone. Most parents don't want their kids to smoke, whether or not they smoke themselves. Conveying your thoughts/beliefs about smoking or anything is an ongoing part of parenting.

When it comes to cigarettes, political party affiliation, and religious beliefs, most parents want their children to be like them and get upset when their child differs. Most children usually hold their parents' values about these matters until they get into their teenage years and often then they begin to challenge authority and want to have their own thoughts and values honored. Most still follow, but many veer off.

There is a difference between when your child veers off in their use of social media and when he decides to practice another faith or join another political party. Parents don't usually call for help when their child proclaims differing political views, though they usually get into heated debates. Parents sometimes call when their child is devoting "too much" time to social media. Parents usually get on the phone when alcohol/drugs or school issues come up.

Here you are one day with a certain general sense of concern about something and the next day that concern has had a bump up. You worry off and on about your child getting into drugs and/or alcohol. You see a picture of your child online taking a hit on a bong or perhaps the school calls about a drop in grades and that prompts a greater level of attention.

Once you find yourself thinking about what your child has done and how you are going to deal with it, you have gone from "what if" to "what now?" Ideally you buy yourself some time to reflect on your possible future responses by yourself and with your partner. Other times you catch your child in the act and you are called upon to respond in the moment.

Parents get disturbing news and immediately go into the "what am I going to do?" mode. I prefer you hold off on doing anything. As a therapist I tend to like people to reflect on how they think/feel before they act. But there are times when you are going to feel compelled to take action before you can fully reflect on much of anything. While I do think there are times that call for spontaneity, I don't think that call always needs to be answered right away. See if, when you find that picture of him taking a bong hit, you can't allow yourself the time to consider these:

- How do you think/feel about what you have learned?
- Why do you think/feel that way?
- What are the values and beliefs that you have that are being challenged by this event?
- What are you worried about?
- Why do you think your child has done what he has done?
- What does he need/want most from you now?

There may be any number of other questions that you might want to ask yourself before you speak with your child. As I have mentioned before people often feel an emotional urgency to deal with something right away, but the truth is often there is no real immediate need to fully deal with the situation. You can give yourself time to reflect before you have your talk with your child. Yes, you want to deal with this sooner than later, but sooner doesn't mean you have to do it *now*. You usually can buy yourself some time to reflect before you act. A little separation time after an incident often allows for some cooling off. Cooler heads usually prevail. Or at least arrive at an agreed upon workable solution faster.

Needless to say there is a difference between stumbling upon a bottle of beer in your child's room and being concerned he may be spending too much time on the Internet, but the way to handle them is basically the same. Whatever concern you have, you need to talk with your child. Notice the words "talk with," as in "discuss," as in not "talk to" or lecture.

- There needs to be back and forth in this discussion.

- There needs to be close to calm voices.

- There needs to be truth.

- There needs to be empathy.

- There needs to respect, caring, and concern.

This discussion usually begins with some form of "we need to talk" and ends when a mutually agreed upon outcome is reached. If you can't reach that point, take a break, but before you do make a set time to resume. Keep doing that until you get something you all can agree on.

Worst case, you bring in a third party.

Most parents are able to talk with their child about something he has done that bothers them and come to a good enough resolution. Since your child is your child and you have legal and moral responsibility to raise him well, your vote usually counts more. As he gets older and older your vote counts less and less. But unless your child emancipates himself, you are the responsible one until he is 18, if not longer.

If you come to an "agree to disagree" resolution and your child leaves grumbling because he thinks you are being overly harsh, you may want to consider revisiting the subject down the road when everyone has had more time to reflect and see how things have proceeded. Even if everyone is in agreement it doesn't hurt to check in a week later and see how everyone is doing. Progress check-ins help most endeavors.

Sometimes everyone gets frustrated with the negotiating process and just wants to come to a resolution. Everyone half-heartedly agrees just to be done with the conversation. That is okay, but if everybody is just mostly on board I would make sure to revisit it sooner than later.

As I mentioned in an earlier chapter, usually when you ask a child what he thinks the consequences for his actions should be, he will come down harder on himself than you would. In which case you can be the lenient one. Certainly many a child has suggested the consequence be nothing or extremely minor and the parent has had to say that avenue is not acceptable.

Basically you want everyone aiming for having the "punishment meet the crime."

If your child hasn't really misbehaved in a status quo altering way you may want to limit the consequences. Perhaps he is online more than you would like and you don't want to discipline him for that, but you do want him to cut back on the activity before it does have a significant effect.

You may be afraid that if you are too lenient he will keep doing what you don't want him to do. That certainly is a possibility. If he can get away with this, he may want to see if he can get away with this plus that.

Before you try to nip something in the bud by over-disciplining try to talk your way to an understanding of boundaries. Letting him know what is not okay with you at minimum puts him into a position where he will have to make a conscious decision to overstep the boundary.

You can always say that if he is not able to stay within bounds you will have to take more serious actions. It helps if you can clearly outline what is and what is not acceptable to you. Letting him know some acceptable items gives him some room for play. Maybe you only allow him access to social media two hours a day, but you might make allowances for weekends and holidays. That doesn't always stop the undesired behavior, but it can help slow him down and keep him closer to the line.

It can be challenging for parents to clearly outline their boundaries because they may not really know them as this could be new territory for you. You can say no sexting, no R-rated picture-sending, no this and no that, but there will usually be some escape clause that a child can find. Some parents get around the naming of specific things by saying: "Don't do anything that you suspect I am not going to approve of. If you're unsure that I would approve, ask." That gets to the heart of the matter and puts the onus on the child to acknowledge his parent's limits. It is not foolproof but it can help.

If he continued to do something that was against my wishes I would need to let him know that I was upset that he wasn't honoring what I want. I would also need to listen again to why he is doing what he is doing and its value to him. We may not see eye-to-eye, but hopefully we can respect each other's points of view.

I am a believer in a family's ability to come to satisfactory solutions that are acceptable or at least mostly acceptable to all. I believe in explaining and sharing and working together. If I thought there ought to be some consequence for a behavior I would ask my child what he thought and share what I thought and let him choose his course of action. Certainly as your child matures he can take on a more responsible role in the decision-making, but I would still hold this approach much if not all of the time with all children.

As your child grows up with you he will learn your values and mostly adhere to them. Especially if those values include the empowerment of all. I had a father tell me recently how proud he was that his daughter was strong and independent. Of course, he added, that did not always make things easy, just preferable.

Having ongoing conversations with your child about the things he does that please you and the things he does that displease you is part of parenting. Parents often call me because they are not having a sufficient amount of real conversations with their child. I tell them no matter how unconnected to their child they may be, the repair route runs the same for everyone. Keep trying to engage. Consider different approaches, but don't let your child's lack of enthusiasm for speaking with you stop you from speaking with him. Just try to make sure the bulk of those conversations are about the weather, popular culture, something funny or weird that happened to you, and anything else that has nothing really to do with the "issues" you have.

In large part, parents' concerns about what their child is doing have less to do with what he is doing and more to do with how what he is doing is impacting other parts of his life and his future. Parents usually agree with me that if their child was keeping up his grades, his social life, and family life, it is hard to argue that his time and involvement in social media is hurting him. Parents and their children just don't agree on what keeping up all those things means. Parents can usually point to some things they want him to be doing better. Plus they point out that there are things he could be doing that might be more enlightening and beneficial to him.

Hard to argue with that.

But, come on, don't we all spend time doing less than meaningful things? Sometimes we all need some downtime.

Social media is the way this generation communicates and connects with the world. They need to be literate and active in social media as it is the link to their future—just like when you were a teenager and needed to be knowledgeable and conversant about whatever was happening in your social world. It is just that your world was way smaller.

51

HOME LIFE AND AREAS OF RESPONSIBILITY – FORMERLY CALLED 'CHORES'

I don't like the word 'chore' because it sounds like something you have to do that you don't really want to do. I think everyone in a household needs to do different tasks to help with the running of the home. I prefer to call those things areas of responsibility. Not that the name change all of a sudden makes you want to do it. It is just that areas of responsibility, while they encompass things you might not want to do, can also include some things you like doing very much. Why call something a chore and automatically enter it in the "Don't want to do" category when you can call something a responsibility and have a chance it might be viewed differently?

If you prefer to think of these tasks as chores please just substitute the word when applicable. Especially for those areas of responsibility that may feel more like chores.

Regardless of whether you call them assignments, undertakings, jobs, tasks, or duties, everyone who lives in a house who is old enough to help out ought to help out.

While this book is mostly about parenting teenagers if you happen to have a younger child or if you are just embarking on doling out assignments I suggest you start with something you think will be as close to enjoyable as you can get. You want your child's first responsibilities to be positive. If you start her off with the heavy lifting she is likely to generalize and have a negative attitude about helping out around the house.

When I grew up Saturday mornings had some loosely devoted time for everyone to do something or other to help out around the house. Often music was playing and there was a lighthearted attitude about the whole thing. If everybody was doing something it just felt like a natural way to go.

If you are cleaning windows while someone is eating bonbons and watching TV it doesn't make for good worker morale.

When I had my own home I wanted to follow my parents' routine, but Saturday mornings seemed to get away from my family. We ended up with a little Saturday morning clean up, but as my daughter grew up activities pressed hard on that time slot. We all tended to have our own areas of responsibility that we took care of on our own timelines. Mostly.

Often a parent's timeline is different than their child's. Sort of the same thing when you have a roommate and one of you wants to do the dishes right away and the other after they pile up. The job will get done, but there can be annoyances along the way.

Getting your child to do her task in the vicinity of your tolerance usually requires some nagging and some patience. Balancing the two is not always easy and the scale seems to teeter up and down.

Some time at dinner when everyone is basically okay and the conversation is lagging throw out this question: "What does everyone think the definition is of home and family?" See if you can get people to weigh in. It can be a very informative conversation and be the catalyst for many things. One thing you are hoping the discussion will promote is the idea of everyone helping out in the maintenance and running of the home. We all have a part in the making of our home and family is one of the concepts I would want to make sure got spoken.

Because soon after that comes the conversation about areas of responsibility. I am hopeful that within the framework of these tasks you can take a step toward improving your relationship with your family and continuing to build your home in a way that makes you all feel good about yourselves and each other. See if you can infuse activities with a sense of them being community service to the family.

When you give your pep talk include the concept that you are a family, you all share this living space, you all do things to help make your space together as good as it can be. Then you put on Sister Sledge singing *We Are Family* and hand everyone a dust cloth and you all can do some dusting in the living room. It's a skill set your child will have to learn sooner or later, might as well learn it on your shift.

You might be reluctant to address some of these things right now, but let's take it from the point of view of what you would really like.

In your best dreams about how you would like your family to interact, what are the tasks around the house? What would you like to be more shared?

_____

_____

Perhaps there are things your parenting partner does that you would like to be more involved in?

_____

_____

What are the things you do that you would like others to be more involved in?

_____

_____

Of course the rest of your family may or may not agree with your list. They may have a list of their own. In fact, here is a plan to follow. Ask everyone to write up their own list of tasks around the house with a short explanation. Announce that there will be a family meeting at such and such time to share lists and discuss the topic of tasks around the house.

You may or may not have the gumption to call that meeting.

I want to encourage you to be the new sheriff in town on this matter.

You have the power in your family to call a family meeting. In fact, everyone in your family has the power to call that meeting. Families ought to have periodic family meetings aside from their more casual interactions. Yes, most things can be handled at the dinner table, but now and then calling a sit-down "let's talk" meeting can air certain tensions and allow things to get unblocked.

You can ask everyone to come to the meeting prepared to discuss the topic of tasks around the house. What they think needs to be done and how they would like to see them handled. You can give some examples: food needs to be brought in the house, clothes need washing, house needs cleaning, etc.

When it is meeting time thank everyone for participating. Suggest a few ground rules for the discussion and then have everyone read their list. If they haven't written it have them say it.

Ground rules:

- No interrupting.
- No snickering, comments, or asides.
- Everyone reads their list with their explanation of the task and we don't talk until everyone is done and then I will give some more ground rules. Thank you very much. Let's begin with the youngest or if you don't want to begin we can work our way through the rotation until someone wants to start.

Be the note taker.

Write down every and I mean every task that people have so you have a master list. Make sure you don't put anything on the list that wasn't said out loud. Ideas have to be voiced before they get written on the master list. Write them down as they speak them; don't substitute your language for theirs even if you think you have a better name. Everyone will hear them discuss their list and will be able to refer later to the item as it was presented.

When everyone has read their list you say:

- We are now going to discuss the tasks. People may want to amplify the explanations, ask for clarification or share their thoughts and reactions.

- No criticizing, minimizing, or otherwise downgrading any item on the list. Keep those snarky things to yourself. Or later on behind my back (joking).

- No name-calling, blaming, and discussions about past performance.

- This list will change with time, but today is a start for us all to have a better understanding of how we all want to contribute in the family.

- Set a goal to combine items on the list that were held in common or have a lot of overlap.

Later on you will write down who is going to do what.

Even later on you will be the arbitrator.

And even later on when people forget to do their task you will have it all written down. That doesn't count for a lot, but it does count. Especially if the tasks assigned are done in such a way that everyone is in agreement, even if it is somewhat but hopefully not a lot reluctantly.

Everyone is going to have opinions and things to say about each other's lists and what is and what isn't a task. I would do my best to guide people away from editorializing. I would also point them away from categorizing tasks in terms of degree of difficulty or value to the realm. Taking out the trash usually is not something that most people love doing, but for most people it beats cleaning the bathroom. The idea is not to list the tasks in terms of desirability.

The goal is to get an agreed upon list of tasks around the house.

Some families have doing homework, paying bills, and grocery shopping on the list. Others have getting to bed on time, cleaning your room and walking the dog. Others have practice piano, pull the weeds, and wash the car.

It really doesn't matter what is on the list. Everyone will have opinions and a good part of your job is managing the discussion so it is actually kind of an eye-opening event as to how people see the things that go in to maintaining a home. All tasks are necessary. Some hold different places on the hierarchy, but all need to be respected.

I just spoke with a young mother who told me she would do anything around the house if her husband would do the laundry. In her eyes he is a wiz at it while she loathes it. It is hard to compare the relative value of tasks, so don't even try. Just list them.

Being a sports fan may have influenced what I would do next.

Once you have a list that includes everything people mentioned and you've highlighted the ones everyone agrees on, you can ask around if anyone has anything to add. When that is done, if you have a copier available, make everyone a copy of the master list.

Then you can follow this approach.

The first stage has each person go over the task list and circle twice any item they want to do. Then put one circle around any they would be willing to do. Next to each item put either an "A" if they want to do the task alone or a "T" if they want to do it with someone else.

Then I would have everyone take a turn and read one thing on their list. After everyone has shared one item, if no one else wants said item, it is theirs to do. In cases where multiple people want to do the same thing I would ask them how they would like to resolve it. Most of the time they ought to be able to decide between themselves. If they can't decide in a couple of minutes, the item goes into the second stage. As people read their list of tasks they want to do, other people can cross that task off the master list with a notation next to the task of who is going to take it on.

I would continue until everyone had listed the items that had two circles. Some people will have mentioned more things than others. Don't worry about it. Everyone now has a list of what tasks are being handled and by whom as well as which ones have yet to have their fate determined.

The second stage is for everyone to look at their single circled tasks and read those aloud. After everyone has read theirs go around again and have the first person pick one item off their list that they would be willing to do and double circle it. The others can cross it off their master list.

Continue going around with people picking one item off their list until someone gets to the end of their "Willing to do" list. All the remaining tasks will go into the third stage unless someone feels strongly that they want to add some item(s) on their "Willing to do" list and usually there is no complaint about that. If there is you can talk about it. If you can't resolve it send it on to the third stage.

The third stage is to have everyone write down who they think has the least attractive list. Maybe everyone votes for themselves or you have no "winner," but if someone does have the list the fewest amount of people would like they get to be #1. They also need a round of applause. Later, they can play the martyr card, but for now make sure you acknowledge and thank them for carrying the least compelling load.

Then I would vote for #2 and so on. If there is a winner, fine. If not, we have to find some way to pick straws, play Roshambo, or otherwise determine an order. Whatever order you decide is best right now may not be the best when you need to do this again.

When you have an order you have a draft.

#1 gets to pick first. They can have whatever item on the list but they need to take one and circle it on the master list and everyone else crosses it off.

Then #2 goes and so forth.

If you get to a final round where there are not enough tasks for everyone you start with the last number and work your way forward.

Now, this is not a perfect system. There are many variations you can have on the draft and allotment system. You may not want your child to have as many unattractive tasks as others. If you think the list they volunteered for is sufficient you can leave them out of the draft. Or you can have them in it for a round or two.

Since people have noted which tasks they would like to do with others some of the tasks on the list may be shared and as such count on more than one person's list. There is no perfect way to handle the distribution of household responsibilities. You do your best to do it in a fair and respectful way and that is the lesson you are teaching. Homes need to be maintained. Home dwellers need to help out.

I am sure you can find ways to adapt this to your family that work for you. The goal is not so much to divvy up responsibilities but to continue to build a sense of family. There ought to be joking, sympathy, empathy, and an attitude Sister Sledge could sing about.

There needs to be some level of acceptable responsibility with each task but you ought to operate under the assumption that these are tasks you all agree on and you all are expected to do your part to help the house run smoothly. Some may be daily tasks, some summer tasks. There will be disagreements about frequency and how well a task was done, but save that bickering for later. When you have this conversation you want to do your best to have it end well.

Later on you will need to revisit it and deal with the day-to-day operations.

There will be bumps in the road. Deal with them when they happen. You may end up doing more than your share of the tasks. You probably do already so this may not change that. But, what you hope it does is make your family more cohesive.

A child may take on the responsibility of taking out the trash. In some households that involves a lot of reminders, while in others the child is completely on top of it. Those lucky parents get to worry about other things. In those houses where reminders are necessary and there are judgments about the quality of the work, there need to be more meetings. Sorry.

Even when everything is running smoothly periodic meetings will need to take place to review and revise the responsibilities. At those meetings it is critical to listen to what your child tells you about the task and to work with her to refine the job or find ways to support her to do the task at a mutually acceptable level.

There is doing the job and there is doing the job well.

If your child tells you your level of expectation is unacceptable to her and you let her know that her level is unacceptable to you there is an impasse.

Instead of putting your foot down and basically saying you are doing it my way because I am the parent you might consider asking your child what she thinks would be a reasonable way to resolve the impasse. Resolving impasses is a skill your child needs to learn and you are going to be the one modeling how to do it.

If you just yield the power in these situations that is what your child will learn. Most likely she will adopt your methodology. In the world and with you.

If you roll over she is likely to take that approach as well.

Sometimes you just can't win. Even when you work out a mutually agreeable pathway there is a chance she will opt for other approaches in her interactions.

Still, I aim for mutually agreeable.

To find those mutually agreed upon pathways you often need to develop your patience and flexibility skills as well as your ability to dwell in the uncertainty. If your child's level of acceptable task-doing is significantly different than your own and you can't come to a satisfactory agreement right away you may want to table the discussion for a few days. You might dwell on why this is so important to you and what lesson you want to teach your child. You might also remember successive approximation and consider acknowledging the pros of what she does and not the cons, or at least balancing it out.

If there is no immediacy you can consider various solutions. There is no way of knowing if your solution is the best one for you and your child and there is no way of knowing if it isn't. You do know the future is uncertain. Whatever resolution you forge will say as much about your relationship as it does about the task. Even when something needs to be decided immediately, you can always commit to actively considering other ways to work out the differences between you.

Allowing issues to be unresolved is anxiety provoking and you don't want to extend situations any longer than possible. Yet you also want time to reflect on a conflictual situation and try to find a better resolution. Just searching for that resolution is a positive thing and valuable role modeling. Uncertainty often resolves itself if left to brew.

Allowing uncertainty and the lack of resolution to have a place does not mean avoiding or neglecting the impasse. You need to keep engaging in discussions about finding a workable solution. But you do not always have to rush to resolution. You can say let's think about this and come back to it tomorrow or later. Remember, unresolved issues remain in our thoughts.

Sometimes these impasses never get resolved. Other times they can take way longer than you would like. Even when there is little agreement and possibly some building resentment there still need to be periodic meetings to discuss how things are going. Even when things are not going well and meetings may be uncomfortable, still have them. Maybe shorter ones. Maybe less frequently, but people need the opportunity to talk about what is and what isn't working for them in the home and with the family.

You may need to agree to disagree for some time and see if you can't collaborate on a quasi-acceptable solution for the time being. Sometimes if you tone down the task and cut it into more bite size pieces you can find a good enough resolution.

Sometimes a decision needs to be made in a timely manner and you need to come to it by such and such time.

Deadlines usually help people get to solutions. Whether you like it or not, knowing something needs to be done at a specific time forces you to make a decision.

You can always claim the parental fallback position that if an agreed upon resolution has not been reached by such and such time we will do things this way for the next _____ weeks and then re-evaluate it.

Once tasks are assigned, shake hands, hold positive thoughts and move on. Things will not follow perfectly, but they will shift.

Have a follow-up meeting in a week to have everyone report on how things are going.

Keep doing that until it isn't helpful any more.

Good luck.

52

DIVORCE AND SINGLE PARENTING

Needless to say, divorce and single parenting are far greater subjects than I can satisfactorily cover in a chapter. While I want to address some of the significant challenges involved in raising children when you are divorced or a single parent, what I really hope to do here is to provide you some support.

Certainly no single parent can be both a mother and father so right from the get-go you are not going to be able to provide a framework of parenting that you would in a household with two parents. Instead of your child having another parent to go to or you to have someone handy to run things by, you are basically playing one on one. And when you have multiple children not only are you outnumbered but you are also acting without backup the majority of time.

So, first and foremost—cut yourself some slack. You can't be all things. No matter how great a job you do, there are just some things you will not be able to do. For instance, you can't really give a second opinion. You can't really be the other person your child goes to when he needs a level of comfort you cannot provide. You can't be the other parent that he goes to when he fails to get some headway with the stricter parent.

The list goes on and on. Dwelling on the list can very easily prompt you to think you are not doing a good enough job. Indeed you would not be doing a good enough job if your job was to be two people. Fortunately, your job is not to be the best mother and father. You don't need to be the strict one and the lenient one. The good cop and the bad cop. You just need to be you. That is, ultimately, the lesson you want to teach your child so making your peace with your strengths and limitations is a service to you both.

Often single parents think they need to provide a more traditional family for their child. Yet that is placing a value on having a "traditional" family that does not really bore scrutiny. Most of the research on traditional families suffers from not having more socially accepted forms of parenting for comparison. People are biased to believe traditional families are best because that is what historically has been the prevalent model. As more and more people explore alternative methods of parenting the value of non-traditional families may prove to be even more successful. We all certainly can point to people who have come from traditional families who we would just as soon avoid entirely.

Some couples are heterosexual. Some are homosexual. Some couples have a lot of relatives who are in the house often. Other couples have few. Some couples have friends who hang out. Some couples live relatively isolated lives.

Some single parents choose to have a child on their own. Some have multiple children. Some have a large support network and others less so.

Some divorced or widowed parents live most of the time with their child. Some single parents rarely live with their child. Some single parents have other people who play meaningful roles in their child's life. Other parents play a larger role in their child's life.

So many options. Who is to say what is best? You do what you can with what you have.

An important thing to remember is that while you can't be all things, you will be a model for your child in self-sufficiency. He will see you handling your life in responsible and not so responsible ways. He will learn, as you have learned, to manage to get through the day and past the challenges. He will also learn from you that he doesn't have to be all things and he will have good days and not so good days.

While living with someone else might shore up some areas, every couple, like every person, has strengths and areas of weakness. While you want to strive to improve those strengths and weaknesses you don't want to let your imperfections get in the way of you modeling to your child that you will find a way to make things work out. And, when you can't figure things out or keep all the balls in the air, you ask for help. Just like you would want him to do. Asking for help is a sign of strength, not weakness. Regardless of what you may think.

Not a lot of people get married with the idea of getting divorced or widowed. Not a lot of people decide to have children with the idea of raising them alone, although more and more people are choosing that option. Whether you are married, living together, have a partner, or have some other arrangement, when you have children they are yours until the end of time.

Even in the best relationships with the other parent, the emotional ties you have are often not as strong as the one you have with your child. As much as you might love the other parent they are not of your body. Shared blood being thicker than water, most parents would go to lengths for their child that they would not for their partner. Although for many people it is a close call—especially during the teen years.

When relationships falter a parenting partner can choose to be less close to the other parent. First they emotionally withdraw and then they often physically withdraw. That distance can manifest itself in divorce, separation, or some other arrangement that involves less mutual parenting and more individualized parenting. Even when they are living together, parents often confer on big issues and deal with day-to-day, moment-to-moment issues without consulting their partner. Needless to say, when parents decide to break up their relationship it is going to affect how they parent their child. It is also going to significantly affect their child.

We all know divorce is one of the most traumatic experiences in a child's life, which is why a lot of parents choose to wait until their children are older before dissolving the union. Depending on the quality of the relationship that may or may not be a good decision.

Parents need to teach their children to stick some things through even though the going is rough. They also need to teach their children when to say uncle. As with most relationship matters there is no right or wrong or good or bad. There is just this consequence and that consequence.

Sadly some people become single parents because their partner dies. There are few things in life more painful than losing a partner or a parent. The emotional and behavioral reverberations extend through your lifetime. There are stages of mourning that everyone needs to go through and significant adjustments in living that occur. As difficult as a divorce can be on all parties, losing a parent is usually much harder on everyone.

There is a wealth of material on families having to deal with death. It is another one of those subjects that I can't begin to cover satisfactorily in a chapter let alone a paragraph. I'm sorry I am not giving it more attention as I know there may be people reading this in that situation. I encourage you to find support in as many ways as you can get it. The support I want to offer now is about the continuing job of parenting that must go on whether the other parent dies, you separate, or some other action is causing you to parent primarily alone.

Not having that other by your side when decisions need to be made often causes insecurity. Am I doing the best thing? What would my partner have said and done? Am I being one-sided? That doubt can undermine your confidence. Which can lead you to be wishy-washy or overly strict. It is hard to know if you are doing the best thing as the proof is in the pudding that has yet to be made. You can't fully predict how something you do today is going to affect your child tomorrow. But, certainly you can see how it is affecting him now and you can respond to that.

All parents know what the Beatles sang—we do get by with a little help from our friends (or family members and various others).

Reaching out for support—be it finding someone who can babysit or getting a massage or speaking to someone at your child's school—is something every parent, single or not, can do. It is not easy for some people to ask for help. If you are one of those people who thinks they need to be more self-sufficient so be it. It is important to be able to handle what life hands out. And yet, it is also important to let others give you a hand. Yes, you may have some IOUs to fill, but helping others as they have helped you is not such a horrible thing. When you reach out to someone you can share whatever shame or embarrassment you might have for not being able to do everything. If you are fortunate enough to not be one of those people who feels guilty asking for help, consider who modeled that for you, and thank them.

If you are one of those people who finds it extremely hard to reach out for help, please reach out to a therapist and ask them to help you get over your resistance for asking for help. Enjoy and appreciate what you can do for yourself and add to the list your ability to ask for help as something else you can do. Reaching out for support is good modeling for your child and will give you resources to assist you with raising your child. While you might think asking for help is a sign of your own inadequacy and weakness others may see it as a sign of your realization that you too are not perfect.

Let's focus on parenting while you are in the process of changing or have changed the living conditions with your partner.

First and foremost, there is a message you need to say to your child, yourself, and your former partner over and over again in many ways: We will always be a family. Whether we live together, whether we marry other people, regardless of what happens in our lives we will always be a family. When called we will be together to support each other in whatever ways we can.

Personally I think you ought to read that last paragraph again as it is one of my strongest beliefs. Once a family, always a family. No matter what.

Now there is some wiggle room in there when you say you will support someone in whatever ways you can because your level of support may be zero. I would hope that would not be the case, but in those cases where parents separate on the worst of terms, I believe there needs to be a common understanding that "our" children will always be "our" children and "we" will always be their parents.

Despite how you may think/feel about each other when called upon you will do your best to unite to best serve and support your children. If your level of support is closer to zero than it is to 100 you need to be in therapy. If it is closer to 50 than to 100 you still need to be in therapy. You need to get at least a C in support before you can consider yourself passing over the bar. You may grade yourself one way and your ex another, but this is one of those places where you need to be honest with yourself. If your partner thinks you deserve an F and you think you get a B, then you need to go talk to someone who does not entirely have your side so you can get a decent second opinion.

When/if you find yourself in a stage where your anger at your partner supersedes the best interests of your child you need to be in therapy. If you are in therapy, you need more.

Parents who use their children to hurt their exes are hurting everyone. That is not good for your self-esteem, for making things better with your ex, or for the welfare of your child. If you are unsure that your anger is having a ripple effect then it probably is. This ought to be something you are pretty clear about. If you're not, ask your ex, your child, and your therapist.

When you are building a life away from your child's other parent you will not always like what the other parent is doing. You may disapprove of things the other parent does with your child. You may not like what they say about you to your child.

You may not like to deal with the other parent about your child. Yet for the wellbeing of your child you need to endeavor to maintain as positive a relationship as you possibly can. If you hadn't noticed by now I am a believer in once you have children, your life is no longer about you. It is about your children and helping them take the family torch that you are handing them and make a better life for themselves. If you are not doing that, you need help.

I know it is easy to say to behave in the best interest of your child and it is not always easy to do. I don't know if anyone gets a perfect score, but you do want to aim for the honor roll. If anything is worth putting in the extra effort, it is rising above your hurts and helping your child. Belittling your ex, calling them names, and making your child make choices between the two of you are not things your child needs to experience. Besides, it is not going to do anything to improve your relationship with your child. He will see you demonstrating the worst of your dark side and eventually want to distance himself from you.

If the priority is the welfare of your child some of the battles you may find yourself engaging in are really not worth it. I'd prefer you say uncle and fight fewer battles. Save your conflicts for those things that really matter.

Students come in and tell me that often they hear their separated parents arguing. They also tell me that they have multiple conflicts and arguments with one of their parents more than the other. I do hear from parents that the reason they have more arguments is because the other parent doesn't adhere to the "mutually" agreed upon parameters of parenting. Whether you are a single parent or not, there is usually one parent that gets the brunt of their child's anger. That privilege can shift over time.

I am sure you consider most of those conflicts necessary and important and they very well may be. I would just suggest you don't need to have the same argument over and over again. If you are in perpetual argument mode you are modeling a form of relating that I would like you to reconsider. If you do need to argue with the other parent do it in private and don't share it with your child. Don't try to get him to see your side.

Yes, the other parent has a markedly different relationship with your child. One you may disapprove of and not condone. While there certainly are important differences to continue to try to iron out, do you really need to make a big deal out of what time your child comes home from being with the other parent or how many days spent with them this week as compared to you?

If you are going to fight those lower level battles, what are you going to do when the other parent wants to move or their new spouse wants to adopt or they have decided to change religions and want to raise your child in a way that is completely against your beliefs? I'd save my battles for the gut-check issues.

Consider the benefits of compromise or letting the other parent have their way in most of the day-to-day issues. What really are the losses and what are the gains? Your child is a teenager and soon he will be out on his own. Learning how to deal with different situations is a large part of what life is about. As much as we may want to protect our children, sheltering them may only hurt them more. The more exposure they have to reality the better job they can do of handling it. Yes, shelter your younger children, but by the time your child is in his mid-teens, sheltering can be experienced as being overbearing and prompt his rebelliousness.

Don't let your anger and frustration with how the other parent interacts with your child get in the way of you taking the higher ground. Don't let your anger and frustration at how the other parent interacts with you get in the way of conducting yourself with respect and care.

Be the role model.

Usually if you are involved in some perpetual discord you need to explore your own motivation. I am sure there are some things you will always rally against and if the other parent is involved in some illegal or immoral activity you do want to stand firm. But, if you continue to argue over logistics perhaps there is a personal reason that is underscoring your involvement. Once again, please consider if your actions are really in the service of your child or if they are serving your own issues.   At that point you are not part of the solution. You are part of the problem.

Even if you believe it is entirely the other person's fault.

You need to be a problem solver not a problem perpetuator. Interact with the intention of resolving things in the interest of what is best for your child.

Unless your child's other parent is evil in some overarching, non-redeeming way, it is important for your child to have a relationship with them. One that doesn't require your editorializing. Letting your child be with the other parent will allow him to form his own opinion. The more you chime in about the other parent the more your child will need to defend them and close you off. If your assessment of the other parent is accurate your child will discover that for himself.

Regardless of whether you initiated or objected to your relationship with the other parent shifting, you were a participant in the dissolution of your family as your child knew it. It doesn't matter if you think the other parent was 100% responsible. Your child, and the rest of the world, will most likely see it differently. Your child, other family members, and friends may not say that to your face, but the majority of people think that this leads to that which leads to this which leads to that, and so forth. In other words, there is usually responsibility to be handed out to everyone.

Initially it does not matter if everyone is better off after the dissolution; when families first separate the child's world is thrown into disarray. Unless there is a high level of abuse going on most children want their parents to stay together. The family unit as your child knows it is a big source of his sense of security in the world. Unless there is considerable abuse, he feels safest surrounded by his family in familiar places.

Many a parent has had their heart broken listening to the wail of their child as he expresses his dissatisfaction at the breaking up of the household. No parent wants to hurt their child. Yet their own lack of happiness in the partnership causes them to decide to try to remedy their situation. In doing so parents know their actions will hurt their child. They take this action in hopes for a better future for all. Yet many a parent has anguished about dissolving a relationship because they know the hurt it will cause to the one person they really don't want to hurt.

Whether you believe breaking up to be a pro or a con or both, it is unsettling. Those times when your child is unsettled are times you need to endeavor to be as settled as possible. That is not always easy when your own world is in upheaval. Yet when going through transitions you need to dig deep and do your best to be a consistent reliable source of love and support for your child.

We all need to weather storms. We all have known slippery footing and we have all fallen. Which is why at the very core of your relationship with your child is making sure he knows you love him, will always love him, will always be there when needed and believe in his ability to land on his feet. Even when you are having difficulty keeping balance.

You consistently convey that message and he will know it in his heart and mind. That will give you a little more room for slippage. Not a lot more, but at least your child will know your love even though you are not dealing with things as well as he or you might like.

But, he sure would like you to get back in balance as soon as possible so he can count on you. As would you.

Most parents can't explain their leaving a relationship in a satisfactory enough way because the parent's reality is not the child's. He is welcome to a different opinion. Don't push him to understand your perspective. You need to allow and validate *his* perspective.

When/if your child gets mad at you for separating, let him. You need to honor his truth and let him know you are sorry that your actions have hurt him and you will do your best to help him through. He is going to have a range of feelings and he needs to be able to feel safe with you to express them. Don't let your fragility get in the way of being able to acknowledge and support his reactions to your separation.

There is no really good statement to tell a child about divorce. Couples divorce because one or both parents are not adequately satisfied in the relationship and think they can find a better path. Hopefully that path will also be better for all.

If you are choosing to leave a relationship you need to explain why to your child in as honest a way as possible. The closer you are to being truthful the more likely he is to understand. Needless to say there are going to be situations when you are hesitant to tell the truth. If your partner has been unfaithful your anger may prompt you to want to share that truth, but, in fact, it is usually not their unfaithfulness that is prompting you to leave. It is more likely you are leaving because of betrayal and a lack of trust. That too would be hard to share as you do not want your child to not trust the other parent, although in the moment you may want to throw him or her under the bus.

In those situations where you are challenged to share the truth, you can point to the differences in the relationship that may have prompted the unwanted behavior. Usually sufficient differences arise in a relationship that prompt unfaithfulness or any other action that may hasten the path to dissolution. Try to explain to your child why those differences which once were more tolerable have become sore points. These discussions are fraught with landmines and are best discussed beforehand with a therapist or trusted friend before shared with your child.

As best as you can explain the why of a breakup, most children will not be able to fully grasp the justification for ending the family as they know it. What they can more fully grasp is how you feel. You want to share how you feel about ending the relationship. Your child needs to see your sadness and any other feelings you have about ending the relationship. This will help him put his feelings in some perspective.

Certainly at the onset of a separation emotions can be very raw. Many a parent has cried themselves to sleep and been tested to put on a brave face. I don't think you need to pretend that everything is fine, but I also don't think you need to make your emotions the centerpiece of your relationship with your child. His welfare may be contingent upon your own. Letting him know you are upset, sad and afraid is okay, but try not to make it a daily occurrence. He needs to know you will be okay. Even if you are emotionally overloaded, try to throw in some "everything will be okay" statements.

 If you have any positive thoughts about your (and his) future he needs to know that as well. That will help ground him and give him a sense of security about going forward. Maybe even some hope.

If you have a fair amount of fear, try not to over-represent it to your child. He needs to have confidence in your ability to carry on. Even if you are not that confident this would be one of those times I would try to put a solid foot forward even if I was not feeling so solid.

In psychology we talk about feeling your way to a new set of actions and acting your way to a new set of feelings. In many a therapy office, a client will share their emotions in hopes that unburdening their pain will clear the way to moving forward. In other offices, clients are encouraged to act a certain way in hopes that the longer you act that way, your feelings may shift. Acting confident about being able to get your life back on track will help you and your child rebuild your lives.

If you have been widowed you need to spend time with your child explaining how this happened, how you feel, and what is going to happen. While this is similar to a separation this loss also encompasses so many more variables. Children fear for their own lives as well as yours. They worry about things that they were not so focused on before.

Widowed parents need to remain stalwarts of their child's life. Sometimes children move away from the surviving parent for fear of future abandonment. They don't want to get closer and suffer more pain if and when a loss occurs. Other children cling more and need more assurances. As a parent your job has not changed. You need to let your child know you are there for him. Yes, his other parent "deserted" him and he may be scared you will leave him too. He may not believe your assurances, because truthfully you cannot guarantee them. Don't let that stop you from giving them and demonstrating your dependability. This is not the time to say you will pick him up at 5:00 and show up at 5:30.

Whether you are a widow/widower or divorced, children often blame themselves. They can find reasons why their behavior may have influenced events. Children sometimes even feel that if they had not been born then the stress on the family would be such that everything would be fine. Do your best to repeat over and over again that the events had nothing to do with them. This, whatever this is, was going to happen regardless of them. They don't always fully believe you, but don't let that stop you from trying to convince them.

Even if the extra financial and emotional burden of having a child may have led to the demise of your relationship, it is not fair to put that on your child. You chose to have this child, even if you did not directly choose to do so. There have been many decisions made along the way by you and your partner that have affected all your lives. Do not let your child believe that his existence is the reason for your difficulties.

Whether you are mourning the loss of a partnership or a partner in your life, you and your child's lives are forever altered. As emotionally upsetting as these events are they do provide opportunity for you. You can endeavor to travel through the turmoil in close connection, learn new ways to be in the world, and form an even closer bond.

Sometimes when there is a personal loss, people, like animals, want to isolate themselves and lick their wounds. We all need time alone as well as time together to heal the wounds of loss. Do not overly fret if your child wants more time alone. At the same time, don't let them completely hide themselves away from everyone.

It is important to let your child know you are there for him and to make time to be with him. It is also important to give him space to find his own way. I would keep a distant close eye on him. Just like you, he needs to rebuild his own life. Let him have room to mourn the loss of the family unit. Just make sure his alone time is of his choice and you are not distancing yourself from him. Just as he might be afraid to get closer to you for fear of losing you, so too might you be afraid of getting closer to him. Don't let this fear get in the way of you having a meaningful and active presence in his life.

53

CHILDREN WITH SPECIAL NEEDS

I suppose we all are children with special needs. How each of us deals with our needs and gets them met or dealt with when they are not met are big time issues. That, however, is not what this chapter is about. But, it is in the mix. This chapter is about children who are now labeled as having special needs.

Every few years the voices of influence shift who and what is a special needs child. There is a good chance that by the time you read this the term "special needs" will be considered prejudicial and there will be a new vocabulary for those children who are born or develop in such a way that the insurance companies and medical practices will consider them out of the mainstream. There is no comforting way to speak about these children as a "group" or "type," yet schools and support agencies need to have these children designated in some way so that the families and service providers can be financially supported for the extra attention these children often need.

That paragraph probably offended some and made reasonable sense to others. Regardless of the political and personal approaches there are children who parents and schools believe need extra help. Our elected officials, judges, doctors, other professionals, and service providers may or may not agree about who, what, where, why and when. Yet most agree all children need help. As with most things there is a continuum and when it comes to being a "special needs" child we are talking about a small yet significant amount of the population. According to the Department of Health and Human Services in 2011–2012, 19.8 percent of U.S. children under the age of 18 had a special health care need, representing 14.6 million children.

Our country is not exactly built so that everyone has equal access to "necessary" support. We don't have a mostly agreed upon set of legislations that provides optimum care for all who need it. Some people don't believe in providing much support while others fight for more. We all know the wealthiest among us have choices that many others don't have or won't get without major struggles with schools, workplaces, and insurance companies.

Some parents invest time, energy, and money in getting the best professional help for their child whenever they sense their child is not behaving in the way they think she ought to be. They take their daughter to a therapist because she doesn't have any real friends or an educational therapist because she has learning differences. These parents are proactive and have the means to provide everything from music lessons to tutors to anything else that would help their child live a better life.

Other parents want to do all those things but are limited in their options. They may not be able to afford to take their daughter to the Mayo Clinic or have tutors in three different subjects or have a battery of exams to determine what is going on with her. .

Parents do what they can to support their child. Financial and other limitations do not need to put a limit on the amount of love, care, and emotional support that a parent can provide. Let us not underestimate the power of having a high degree of loving support. Certainly being able to afford any actions to help your child is advantageous. Yet if it is not embraced with a high level of love and care the external help may be less beneficial.

If you child has been labeled by someone a "special needs" child or as having a "learning difference" or put in a special class section, she often spends some time feeling like a second class citizen. Whether she has been teased, bullied or just observant, she comes to realize the differences between herself and the majority of kids. Those differences are not always perceived well by her or others.

Parents have to devote much love and attention to all children, yet I think we all can agree that certain children require considerably more effort and test a parent's love, devotion, and patience. Parents of children with special needs have their own special needs. If you are one of those parents, please reach out to those around you and ask for help, guidance, support, and whatever else you need.

Having a child that is different, however they are different, demands more from us. Yes, we are all different, but some are on the further end of the spectrum. From the moment the parent discovers their child is going to be out of the mainstream they know they are going to be dealing with a lifetime of challenges the people next door will never fully understand.

Not a lot of people have envy for these parents. Yet, in many ways, they often report that they feel the most fulfilled.

When children are at a disadvantage they want to believe their parents can make things better. So do their parents. Making things better is what you did when she was an infant and cried. You fed her or changed her and that mostly took away whatever pain she was feeling. You held her till she fell asleep in your arms, often when you yourself were exhausted and your tank was close to empty. There was a time when you could heal most of her woes and soothe her.

Having the power to soothe your children soothes you. That soothing gets harder as she gets older. For you and for her. But don't stop trying.

By the time you have a teenager you may find some of your soothing powers have vanished. For both you and her.

Almost all children feel different from their peers at some time. They may feel special and unique or they might feel not as good as others. Or some of both. The prolific author Stephen King captured a mostly universal truth when he said: "Let's face it. No kid in high school feels as though they fit in."

There is a point in your child's life when she finds out she is different and there are plenty of times she is reminded that she is different. Unfortunately these often occur during a developmental stage when she would prefer not to be different. As children mature, "different" gains greater appeal. But it is always a matter of how different and how that difference is perceived by others and self.

More different than you want to be is not a good place for anyone, let alone a child.

More different and not a lot you can do about it is also not good for a child. It doesn't matter if she is the small one, tall one, fat one, thin one, smart one, or not so smart one. Most children want to belong to the group and to do that you need to be within a few deviations from that norm. Sadly, most children's social groups don't include kids that differ too much. Children tend to be friends with people like them. Often "special needs" children seek out others whose differences keep them out of the mainstream and it is within that group they can have a sense of membership. Sadly, while the connection feels comforting, it is not always a group to which they totally want to belong.

I had a client once refer to herself as "damaged goods." She had a hard time loving herself, thinking of herself as being not good enough. Try to steer your child away from that mindset and more towards one of acceptance. Along the way to that acceptance you may run into those Kübler-Ross stages of denial, anger, depression, and negotiation. Just make sure you keep your empathy flowing as you aim for acceptance. Many a disadvantage has been turned into an advantage by a parent's nurturance and focus on the positive.

How to love, support, care for and nurture your child when she may be feeling like there is something "wrong" with her and she is more different than she wants to be is often a one-step-forward-one-step-back thing. You say something soothing today. You say basically the same thing tomorrow and your child barks back at you. You quickly learn that route is not always the best route. But you are not sure what the difference was between yesterday and today.

Many days are filled with hurtful reminders of her differences. Standing by while your child is hurting and knowing that there is nothing you can come up with to do directly to help the situation is painful for parents. We don't like seeing our children hurting. Yet, there are times when the world treats them in such a way that the only thing we can do is to give them the room to feel their pain and let them know we are there when they want us. Listening to your child ache with pain wrenches your heart almost as much as theirs.

Often when you approach a teenager to talk, their opening remark is they don't want to talk about things. On the one hand you want to respect their wishes. On the other hand you may have a deep-seated belief that it is better to get these things off their chest and out into the open.

So, you try to encourage them to speak to you. Here is a route I might take:

- "Honey, I know you don't want to talk and I want to respect that. Yet I also think it would really be helpful if we could talk. Preferably now, but if not now, soon."

I try to say what I am thinking and feeling. Although there are times I moderate it, I do aim for being as truthful and respectful as possible. If I have judgments and opinions I try to keep those to myself. At least at the beginning when I am hoping to engage her , not push her into a defensive mode.

Being somewhat of a nag I would probably say something one more time before I let it go. Maybe it would sound like this:

- "Honey, I would really like you to talk with me about this. Come on."

I would say that last part gently. Definitely not threatening or too whiny. Just gently nudging.

Then if she didn't want to talk about it I might say:

- "Okay. Let's drop it for now. But I really want you to come and talk with me about this soon."

Many teenagers are eager to talk, although they often don't show it or really know it until they get started Sometimes you just need to get past that initial knee-jerk reaction. One of the tricks therapist use is to say your request and then be quiet. Let the onus of responding be on her. If you can quietly wait with an inviting look on your face many a teenager will open up. Not all, not always, but the warmer the invitation the more likely she is to open up.

When a child shares her concerns with her parent it is an important moment in the relationship and requires full attention. Regardless of the content, the fact that she is sharing her internal life is something that others parents will envy and something for which you can be grateful. It is especially gratifying if your teen will talk with you about real issues, since as children grow they increasingly bring fewer personal matters to their parents.

Whether she comes to you or you try to engage her once she starts to open up, it can either bring you closer or create more distance. Truthfully, you're the one who needs to take responsibility to bring you two closer. She is the vulnerable one who is sharing. You need to honor that sharing and whether you like or don't like what you are hearing, your end goal is to hear her and be there for her. You don't have to do anything right away other than listen and love her.

There are many opportunities during the day for kids to get wounded. A passing look from someone, a careless remark, or an intentional putdown can all wear down your child's spirit. Often you won't hear from them and sometimes parents would prefer not to hear all their sorrow. It weighs heavily on everyone. Yet, I encourage you to inquire about how her day has been as often as possible.

Asking how her day has been may yield some results, but often you are greeted by a minimalistic response. If you want to try and get her to open up you might try some of these avenues.

Instead of saying, "How are you?" say, "It is good to see you. You look ____." That usually elicits some response.

Instead of saying, "How was your day?" say, "A strange/funny/scary/weird/sad/unusual/boring thing happened to me today," then tell the story. That can hold her attention for a few minutes. Make sure it is a few-minute story and not your long, drawn-out version. When you are done you can pause a moment to see if she has a response and if not then you can ask her about her day.

Instead of asking your child to share something, you share something. One person's sharing often begets another's. But with teenagers it usually isn't a 1 to 1 ratio. You don't always want to go first, but if you aren't getting much of a response asking her about her day you might want to opt for sharing more about yours. You will probably get more by sharing something that happened to you than you get by just asking her what happened to her. Sometimes you give a little to get a little. Sometimes it doesn't work.

There was an article in the *Huffington Post* in 2015 by Liz Evans: *25 Ways to Ask Your Kid "How Was School Today?" Without Asking Them "How Was School Today?"* Liz Evans also wrote a companion article: *28 Ways to Ask Your Teen "How Was School Today?" Without Asking "How Was School Today?"* Check out those lists and see if you could use some of the suggested prompts.

Finding meaningful ways to engage a teenager can be difficult. Some parents join a club with their child or walk the dog or share a YouTube video. Others find their own overlapping areas of interest. Hopefully every parent eats with their child a few times a week if not more. If nothing else you can talk then about the food. Common experiences are the easiest topics of conversation for people to join. Weather can at least elicit comments when it gets into the extremes. Your task is to find and/or create those common experiences. It can often be easier to empathize about the weather than her trials at school.

This chapter is about children with special needs. 'Special needs' basically implies there is going to be an extra degree of attention paid to the welfare of your child. Not that all parents don't put in an extra degree of attention. It is just that when your child gets off that mainstream course most parents are called to even greater action.

I read a blog written by a special needs parent where she talks about being tired, alone, jealous and scared.

While there is some research to support special needs parents feeling fulfilled, there is an awful lot of evidence that the author of this blog is not alone. All parents need support as do all children. If you have a special needs child you already are aware of the network of support available to you and most likely have availed yourself of some of it. No matter how much support you get, I suspect at the end of the day you too feel like the writer of the blog.

54

PROBLEM-SOLVING TIPS

You ever notice that when you are driving with someone it is often easier to get into a conversation with them? People tend to be more comfortable in the car than they are at the dining table. I know it is hard to get your children to not listen to their headphones or to turn down the music when they are in the car with you. Sometimes you can ask him to just sit quietly with you and maybe even talk for a minute or two. Just a minute or two, then he can get back to his devices.

I will tell you why it can be easier to talk in the car than in the living or dining room. You are facing the same way. While you can make some eye contact, most of the view is straight ahead.

Lots of therapists will tell you how important it is to make eye contact. I agree with that. But, it is also easier sometimes to have a conversation when there is less eye contact. In the car you are not so focused on the other person and more able to focus on yourself and what is ahead of you.

I took a workshop at Esalen in Big Sur and one afternoon our facilitator had us walk out to the lawn and pair up. At first he had us interact face-to-face and then side-by-side. It was much more comfortable for everyone when we stood by the side of our partner. He told us that if we were having a conflict with our partner it would be beneficial if we stood alongside them and pointed to our problem as if it were out there in front of us both rather than between us. Instead of having the problem between you it became something out there that the two of you needed to face together and solve.

I have shared this idea with a lot of people over the years and found this simple shift in where you place your body has helped many families. Sit by the side of your child and when you describe the issue at hand, gesture so that it seems the difficulty is out there in the world rather than between you. You can point ahead of you into space and say something like, "We have this disagreement and you want this (then point somewhere) and I want that (and point some other place) and I am just not sure how best to resolve this. What do you think?"

I have a short video of this on my website if it helps to see this as opposed to reading it. If you want to live it or something like it, you might want to go to Esalen. It is one of those places I think everybody needs to visit some time in their life. Check it out.

. . .

. . .

. . .

I will give you the answer in a little bit. In fact, I will give it to you right now, but I just want to write a few sentences first and then slip it in the middle of the paragraph so maybe if you did try to figure it out you didn't see the answer right away. The trick to solving this is that you have to think outside the box. Most people draw the lines within the dots and it just doesn't work that way. You have to take a line and extend it outside the box. Once you do that you are on your way to solving it.

The lesson to be learned is that in order to solve the problem you need to think outside the box. This is worth considering when you are thinking about your relationship with your child. When something arises that is problematic it usually is out of the norm. The usual status quo has been broken. To fix it you might need to look outside the box that may have helped create it. Have an open mind about having a resolution that involves everyone doing things differently.

Usually the worst thing that happens is the new thing you try doesn't work, which is pretty much where you were when you started. Hopefully you won't let one false start keep you from experimenting. Don't put unrealistic expectations on yourself that if you do something differently with your child it will make an immediate positive difference. It may. It may not. Maybe one positive difference is you could feel better that you tried something new. You may want to modify what you did going forward or keep trying.

It can be akin to when you have a behavior that you would like to stop. If you bite your nails and would like to stop. Or if you procrastinate about doing certain things and would like to get them done in a timelier manner. Sometimes people can go cold turkey and completely reverse those and other behaviors, but usually changing a behavior takes time and effort as well as steps forward and steps backward. When you aim for changes, aim for the long run.

If you are having a "problem" with your child you may focus on him changing his behavior and shaping up. While that might work now and then, you might want to consider the problem to be related to the system that birthed it. Perhaps there is something in how your family is functioning that is affecting your child's behavior? Maybe. Maybe not. But if there is a problem why not take some time and ask your family how each one thinks things could be improved going forward. It is a "we got into this and let's get us out of it" kind of approach.

Aim for a "win/win, good enough/good enough, sleep well/sleep well, wake up looking forward to the new day" approach. If the members of your family don't know how to make that happen ask everyone again. And again. And keep asking until you find a mostly agreeable resolution. Then you can call it Positive Resolution Lecture #27.

SECTION 8:

RAMPING IT UP

55

YOUR CHILD'S SEXUALITY

Most parents are not eager for their children to become sexually active. I remember talking to a teacher at a Waldorf school who encouraged parents to keep their children innocent as long as they could. There is plenty of time to deal with life's realities, she noted, so you might as well let your children indulge in their naiveté.

For many parents this is manifested when they consider admitting to their children that there is no Santa Claus per se. I throw in the per se because I think Santa Claus really exists in your heart and you can endeavor to keep that part of your heart open. Most parents want to allow their children to believe in nursery tales and happy endings for as long as possible. Most parents get around to admitting that Santa Claus may not be all that they said he was long after their children have already figured it out.

In fact, in many homes children ask their parents to be honest with them and tell them if Santa Claus really exists. Parents get torn between wanting their child to trust their word while at the same time wanting to keep their child in that innocent state as long as possible. This dilemma is actually a significant point in a child's developing relationship with their parents.

Most children start off believing in the omnipotence of their parents. As children grow up they realize their parents are human. Make mistakes. Are disappointing. And are not always there for them the way they would like them to be.

Just like everyone else.

They also learn that their parents, the very ones they ought to trust the most, lie to them.

Once they figure out you are lying to them about Santa Claus or any other fairy tale they begin to realize that you may not be fully trustworthy on other matters. Their awareness begins to shift as they increasingly realize they are not going to be able to entirely depend on you.

Yet, they also know they are too young and unable to fully take care of themselves.

It is a cold splash in the face for all of us when we realize we need to depend on others who are not entirely trustworthy.

As for Santa Claus and most other things, when people want the truth they end up going to Wikipedia. Which we also know is not entirely dependable either. What and who your child goes to for the truth hinges on many factors. I probably don't need to remind you how much of your sexual activity and concerns you brought to your parents. Nor do I need to remind you how much your child doesn't bring to you.

It is probably a safe bet that your child is about as forthcoming to you about her sexual life as you are to her about yours.

How and when your child will begin to explore her sexuality will come in her own time in her own way. There are approximately 15% of all 15-year-olds who have lost their virginity and about an equal percentage who lose theirs after 21. Any way you look at it, by the time your child is 21 she most likely will have lost her virginity. Whether she lost it to a person of the same sex or a different one, happily or not so happily, she is now on her own interactive path discovering what her sexual life will be like.

Just another series of things for a parent to worry about. Will infectious diseases and pregnancy be involved? Do I need to take her to a doctor? Have a sex talk? Do I condone what she is doing, approve of it, encourage it, or ignore it?

Your child's sex drive goes into higher gear during her teen years. Certainly some teenagers, as well as some adults, have little interest in sex. Others have the pedal to the metal. For most teens, whatever attention sexual matters garnered when they were 12 has been left behind. Whether teens are sexually active or not, the talking about it, the viewing of it, the texting/sexting/posting/tweeting and anything elseing about all matters sexual surrounds the world of teenagers.

You can try to encourage her exposure and behavior or slow it down. Your opinion about her sexual involvement while mattering to some degree is losing influence every day. Soon, if not already, it doesn't really matter at all except to raise your blood pressure. Your best-intentioned efforts to help and guide her will mostly be heard, attempted to be adhered to and then disregarded. Her sex drive, just like yours, is influenced by a lot of things, but most likely not her parents' wishes.

Even if you tell your child that sex is dirty and that to think of it in any way is to sin, her desire and drive is still going to make its presence felt. In many ways the more anyone tries to hold down yearnings the more they are going to keep coming back and demanding attention. That doesn't mean you can't contain your desires, it just means that vigilance will be involved. But when it comes to your child's desires even your vigilance won't stop her longing and interest in exploration. And, ultimately, I would think most parents do want their children to have a wonderful sex life. They just don't want to think about it. Just like they would not like to think about yours.

Sooner or later children will learn how interested they are in sex and with whom they are interested in having sex.

For some the answers for those are clear. For others it can be murky.

For some it can be a smooth and fun exploration. For others it can be a bumpy road.

Many parents would prefer their child were heterosexual. Many parents just want their child to be happy and in love with someone who treats her well. Many parents lovingly support their child's explorations without judgment.

Some parents want to stop their child from becoming gay. Some parents disown their gay children. Some parents don't want their child to explore their gender identity. Some parents don't want their children to be sexually active until they marry or at least are close to it. Some parents throw their kids out of the house for their sexual behavior.

I realize people have deep-seated feelings about sex and all the various ways it makes its way into our lives. I also realize there are moral, political, and social issues involved in this discussion so I might as well just state my case.

I believe a child needs to discover her sexuality with the same amount of love and support you give to her exploring all other avenues of her life. Sexuality is a big part of our lives and culture. I hope you would want your child to be able to find where her heart and body feel at peace.

If your child becomes sexually involved with a man or a woman or both and you are not happy for her, then find a way to deal with your unhappiness without imposing it on her. If your child wants to explore changing her gender identity, support that discovery, but hold off on any elective surgery till she is of legal age to make this decision. If your child loves someone from another religion or race or place, be happy because your child is in love.

When you are not happy about what your child is doing tell someone who is not involved. When your beliefs get in the way of your child's love of life, you need to focus on you. What is getting in the way of you fully supporting her? What are you afraid of? Worried about? Can you see that your concerns are more about you than her and that she might benefit from having her own experiences?

Whatever concerns you have, however justified you may or may not think they are, I encourage you to work them through with others long before you consider imposing them on your child.

While I would like to believe that parents can withhold their sexual values, just like Santa Claus or the tooth fairy, your child will know how you feel about her sexuality. She will know because she knows you as well as anyone does. She has seen you over the years. Your tells have shown. Parents share their values about sexuality just as they share their political beliefs and their ideology about money, people who are different, and any other strongly held viewpoints.

Your child knows how you think/feel about her sexuality.

If she has never gone on a date, she knows how you feel.

If she has had too many dates for your liking, she knows how you feel.

If she has dated someone you liked or didn't like she knows how you feel.

She knows you.

You just don't know and trust her quite as well as you would like.

If you have strong feelings about what she is doing you know you won't be able to keep them to yourself and you are going to have to share them. Many parents just blurt out a bottom line and walk away—"Remember your safe sex lecture" or "I don't want you doing anything I would not approve of." Hopefully you would pick a semi-decent time to actually talk with her about how you think/feel about her sexuality and how she thinks/feels about how you think/feel. You can have your declarative statement, but make it a *part* of the whole, not the whole.

Whatever time you pick it won't be a good time. Things will either be going along fine and you don't want to ruin it with a heavy discussion, or things are not going well and you don't want to pile on. There is no good time. Some are better than others. Like when you have open time ahead and when everyone is sober and alert.

When that conversation comes, it would help if you could lay out your fears and concerns without blaming or inflaming. It also helps if you bring your empathy and care.

Before you launch into your lecture, but right after you say, "We need to talk," you ought to say something along the lines of, "I want to hear how you are doing and I would like to know more about what you are doing and how you are feeling about your social/sex life." Of course, once you say that she most likely will not want to say anything. Don't let her reluctance to talk stop you from being upfront about the agenda for the discussion.

I tend to think when you are going to have "talks" with anyone it helps if you can get the other person to go first. But you can't always do that as sometimes you are overflowing or they want to get a better handle on your agenda before they react or they just don't want to tell you. Once you let your child know the topic of the discussion, she might anticipate the direction things are going and say something preemptive. "I didn't do anything" is often heard. Other times she just might clam up.

You don't have to start by getting everything off your chest. Unless you are so fired up you can't hear what she has to say and are just going to rebut anything she says. In that case, you might as well start and unload.

That won't bode well, but when you are considerably upset you probably aren't going to manage a two-way conversation. Say what you have to and then be prepared for either an argument or her shutting down.

When either of those two things happens you might as well let her get what is bothering her off her chest or let her storm away and follow up when things have simmered down.

Most times when you want to have a "talk" she is not interested in going first. If you are not fully charged up you ought to be able to get things started a bit more smoothly. If you are charged up you will probably charge in. If you are not charged up you can start by explaining your concerns and why you want to speak with her. While your hope/wish is that she behave exactly as you want, you might want to consider an end goal that she respectfully engages you in a discussion and you both do your best to honor and respect the other's position. That might be all you can reasonably expect and that itself is not an easy thing.

When you share your concerns, make sure you aren't holding back something to purposefully nail your child. In that case you are having an interrogation. Which, for me, is vastly different than a discussion.

There may be times when your talk's purpose is to get a confession so that you can know what your child is doing. I would approach those talks differently. I would share my concerns and fears and then I would say my exact purpose for this talk and that I really wanted her to tell me the truth about what is happening with her. Then I would listen and hope she would be forthcoming. And, I would refrain from punishing her for doing what I asked and telling me her truth. Unless I didn't want to hear any more future truths.

You may not get the truth, the whole truth, and nothing but the truth. But, once again, I refer you back to you and your parents. Maybe you were in that small percentage of children that tell their parents pretty much everything about their lives. In that case, I am sorry, but your child may not be as close to you as you are or were with your parent. Which, you know, may or may not be a good thing.

Listening to what your child tells you may not be easy. It requires you to pay attention. Not just to her words, but to how she is impacted by what is happening for her. You want to be empathic as she is sharing a very private aspect of her life. If you had to turn around and tell her exactly what you have been doing the last few months with your sex life you might not find that an easy conversation to have either.

For the vast majority of people their sex lives are very private matters. Most people are very picky about who they tell and what they tell. Very few people share their full experiences and thoughts about their sex lives with anyone. Asking your child to share some of her sex life with you is intrusive. If you don't think so just go out and ask your parents, friends, or boss.

As a therapist and counselor I want people to get past the story and into how they think/feel about what is happening in their life. I ask them questions such as:

"What is it like telling that to me?

"How do you think/feel about what you said?"

"How do you think I think/feel about that?"

"What do you make of all that?"

"What do you want to do about it?"

I ask those questions because the person has come to me asking for help. They want to understand why they are doing what they are doing. More importantly they usually want to do some things/feel some things differently. I ask those questions to help them figure out what is going on with them to open some pathways to moving forward.

I am also aware that whenever we tell anyone anything we are acutely aware of the other's reaction to what we say. We look closely to see how the person is judging us. We see a reaction and are quick to judge the reception we are receiving. As a therapist I endeavor to be encouraging and supportive of the sharing itself more than what is being shared. That said, when I ask people what it is like sharing something with me, they can often point to something in my response that either encouraged them or discouraged them. I have learned as a therapist that sometimes other people see something that is not there because of their history. I have also learned that as much as I want to stay neutral, my own thoughts/feelings are often more apparent than I think.

As a parent listening to your child share a usually embarrassing and difficult subject, I encourage you to aim for being more tuned in to appreciating her openness than to reacting to her story.

When you are talking with your child about her social/sexual activity she probably has not come to you for your help. Although that happens at times, but more often than not it is your concern that prompts these conversations. Prying into her very personal world is best accompanied by permission. I might say something like:

"I know this can be hard to talk about, but I really want to understand what is going on with you. I may ask some personal questions but that is only so that I can have a clearer understanding of what is happening in your world. I am your parent, after all, and even though you are becoming an adult and are more able than ever to take care of yourself, I am still doing my best to help you make your life as good as possible. So, please, let's just talk about what is going on and I will try to be sensitive to your privacy."

I usually start most of my conversations that are going to get into personal material with this question that is difficult to answer in the negative: "Is it okay if we talk about ___?"

Hardly ever will someone say no, so you will likely have their general permission to go forward. If they do say no you can ask, "How come?" and follow that road.

It is a bit manipulative, but what the heck? We all need to be able to pull out some manipulative skills now and then.

If the story your child shares is one that meets with your disapproval there are going to be fissures in the relationship. No parent wants their child to be doing something they don't want them to do.

Occasionally you can forbid something and that works.

Other times you can forbid it and she will go behind your back.

Sometimes you can dissuade her and that works.

Other times she will just continue to do what she is doing but keep it better hidden from you.

Sometimes you can explain your reasoning and she will agree and follow your guide.

Other times you can explain yourself till the cows come home and it won't make any difference.

These discussions are laid with minefields and it is hard for most families to talk about their child's social and sexual development without having some explosions.

Hopefully they are not big ones. But they can be.

Which is why it helps to proceed with the best intentions of loving your child and doing your best to model the behavior you want in how you conduct yourself in emotionally laden territory.

One other thing about sex drive and sexuality.

How you are sexually when you are 10, 20, 30, 40, 50, 60, 70, 80, 90, and a 100+ evolves.

So will your attitude.

You might not want to take a hard line stance when you know things are going to change.

56

THE ABCs OF SEX, DRUGS, AND ROCK & ROLL

A

Pretest.

Before we begin this chapter in earnest let me ask you some questions before I ask you some more questions and answer some. Let's go back in your life to when you were the age of your teenager. Think about your own sex, drug, and rock and roll life at that time. Use a few words to describe your:

Sex Life

_____

Drug Life

_____

Rock & Roll Life

_____

Reflect on your list. Were you happy at the time with those words? Were you doing what you wanted or not? How come? How have things turned out for you? How do you think your experiences have influenced how you are now?

Have those words shifted for you or remained the same? Would those still be the words you would use today to describe you? Want to fill in what those words are today?

Sex Life

_____

Drug Life

_____

Rock & Roll Life

_____

Got anything to say about that?

_____

_____

Chances are some of the words remain and others are different. Maybe a little. Maybe a lot. Maybe you are happy with how things are now. Maybe you were happy then. Or maybe not so much.

Any thoughts about how your responses are the same/different?

_____

_____

Now think of a few words that describe your child's:

Sex Life

_____

Drug Life

_____

Rock & Roll Life

_____

Got anything to say about that?

_____

_____

I asked you to take this pretest to point out to you that your own history might affect how you view your child's development. You may or may not have done something you regret and you don't want your child to make the same mistake. Or maybe you were very content with you own sex, drug, and rock and roll teens and want your child to have a similar experience. Either way, your words and attitude reflect your own experience. When you consider what words your child might use to describe their sex, drug, and rock and roll life, you may be comforted or dismayed or both.

Most people's sex life, drug life, and rock and roll life evolves. We learn as we get older that there are physical restrictions nature provides that limit our actions. Not only do we become more risk averse as we age, but our bodies no longer have the elasticity or endurance they once possessed. One somewhat dismaying finding is that teens rebound quicker than adults from having had too much to drink or lack of sleep The last hangover you had which prompted you to promise to quit or cut back may not be as much in play when you are younger. As we age, our bodies and the responsibilities of adulthood and parenthood shift our point of view and recalculate priorities.

As you most likely have evolved so too will your child. By which I mean his experimentation and investment in partying shall also pass. That said, you might not feel like relying entirely on the passage of time to moderate his usage. Some heavy involvement in your child's life might be required if something goes south with his partying.

Parents worry their child may harm himself in any number of ways. Certainly sex, drugs, and rock and roll have hurt many people.

And helped many people. Like a lot of things they are a crap shoot.

I don't know if you are comforted or not by the words you put on your list that match the ones for your child. If you acted out and did a fair amount of drugs, had your share of sexual encounters and were a groupie, would you be happy if your child was the same or different?

Many parents want their children to be better than they were as children. Parents know how their own experiences with partying shaped them. They often don't want their child to have their negative experiences, but at the same time they want their child to be able to enjoy their positive ones as they once did.

Sometimes it works that way. Often it doesn't. Children have their own reactions to their world. Your job is to help your child find his own solid footing as he takes on these challenging issues, not follow in yours.

More questions.

If you had your choice:

When would your child have a first kiss?

When would you have your daughter lose her virginity?

When would you have your son lose his virginity?

When would you have your daughter have her first alcoholic beverage without your knowledge?

When would you have your son have his first alcoholic beverage without your knowledge?

When would you have your daughter have her first experience of getting drunk and throwing up?

When would you have your son have his first experience of getting drunk and throwing up?

When would you have your daughter have her first experience with marijuana or some other drug?

When would you have your son have his first experience with marijuana or some other drug?

When would you have your daughter go to her first concert without you?

When would you have your son go to his first concert without you?

When would you have your daughter go to her first music festival without you?

When would you have your son go to his first music festival without you?

And lastly, when would you prefer your daughter or son got in trouble with any of these activities?

Any observations you want to make about your answers to those questions?

_____

_____

As you have gathered by now I am big on self-reflection. So, even though I want to weigh in on those questions, I really want you to think about your beliefs, hopes, and expectations for your child and for yourself as well. I want you to reflect on what you do when your responses come true and when they do not.

Chances are that sooner or later all those items are going to happen to your child. My guess is you don't really want your child to get into any real trouble for doing any of those things. Especially if your child is doing what you basically condone. If he does them earlier or to a significantly greater degree than you are comfortable with, you might want him to face some real-world consequences to slow him down. Yet for the most part we want our children to explore the world and know what is out there and yet not be harmed by that exposure.

We can dream can't we?

And we can hope our kids do as we would wish.

But we know better.

Your child is going to get involved in life in his own way in his own time and there is not a lot we can do about it.

But we can do some things. Both to guide him and soothe us.

Is there really a right or wrong time to lose your virginity, get drunk, and play loud music that your parents don't like?

Parents would say some times are better than others.

Kids would say they know when it is the best time for them.

Parents would say we want to trust you, but it is an act of faith.

Kids say, trust me.

Parents say I want to, but I am scared you will not be able to handle it (whatever it is).

Kids say how will you know I can handle it till I get to handle it?

Parents say I prefer you handle it when I feel ready for you to handle it.

Kids say I may or may not wait for your blessing.

Parents say I know. I didn't wait for my parents' blessing either.

Parents can put restrictions on their children, make threats, and do their best to restrict their children's access to sex, drugs, and anything else. But where there is a will there will be a way. You know it, I know it, and they know it. And we all know that for most everyone, sooner or later there is a will.

So, let's start with these facts. 96% of children will at some point in their lifetime become sexually active. Most parents would prefer their sons to be sexually active before their daughters and most would prefer it happened in the context of a relationship.

When I ask students about having a "sex talk" with their parents most say they didn't really have one. A few say it was very awkward and not educational. And a very few say it was valuable.

You have already read through a chapter on sexuality so I don't want to go over all the terrain again. We all know talking about sex in an open and honest way is a challenge for most. Talking about the various aspects of sexual behavior with your child can be awkward and uncomfortable. But don't let your ineptness at a task you rarely do stop you from giving it a try now and then. One lesson you want to model for your child is to not let being ill at ease in a situation deter you from facing it. Throughout life there are times we all feel tongue-tied and self-conscious. You can point out to your child that even though it is challenging for you to talk about these matters you are glad you both are able to get through it. Whew.

As a parent I had to deal with sex, drugs, and rock and roll issues with my daughter.

Let's start with sex.

On the one hand I wanted my little girl to be my little girl until she got married. On the other hand I wanted her to have experiences in relationships and love to better prepare her for the trials and tribulations ahead. I wanted her to love her sexuality and to enjoy it as much as she enjoyed other aspects of her being. I wanted her to have a wonderful life in as many ways as possible and then some.

I don't remember all the details of our "sex talk." I know it was more a series of mini-conversations, comments about interactions we saw in the media or the people we watched going about their lives. If we would see a couple kissing in a restaurant I might say, "Looks like they are having fun," or if the couple got hot and heavy I might say, "Find a room," or any number of things. Over time she would learn what I approved of and what I didn't.

The message I tried to convey was I wanted her to have a great sex life. I actually did sit down with her once and have a very brief conversation where I succinctly shared my value system. I told her that sex can be one of the most exciting, intimate, and enjoyable activities we ever get to have. I wanted her to take pleasure in and love her sex life. And I would hope it would come in the context of a great love life. I would never want her to have to be drunk or high to have sex. I would never want her to do anything that she did not want to do. I would want her to enjoy her sex life to the fullest in the context of a love that she felt fully able to share. Lastly, I said I would think all this and more would come to her when she felt secure enough, mature enough and able enough to bring it into her life.

That is the message I gave her and have been sharing with parents for many years. I have to admit it: I like it. I am sure others can add and improve on it and I hope they do. Hopefully you do as well. I put it out there in the same way I put out the rest of the book—in hopes that it will stimulate your thinking and approach to your relationship with your child, partner, and most everyone else.

I am a believer that the more we share what we think and feel, the better off we are. I know 100% openness may not be the best number, but I think it is close. And yes, my daughter listened to me, made some vague "okay" comment and that was that.

57

THE ABCs OF SEX, DRUGS, AND ROCK & ROLL

B

But what about drugs and alcohol?

Your child has either not yet had a drink or tried a drug or she has. You may or may not know the truth of what she has and has not done. You may think you know the truth or you may not be too sure.

Let's consider all the options. But first let's focus on you.

What exactly is your position on your child and drinking? What would your alcohol lecture sound like?

_____

_____

What exactly is your position on your child and drugs? What would your drug lecture sound like?

_____

_____

What age would you ideally want her to experiment with drinking and drugs and how would you prefer she include you and these things in her life?

No matter where along the pipeline you already are with your child, you need to reflect on your present position and not your ideal position. You thoughts on your child's experiences with drugs/alcohol may be the same now as they were when you were her age. Or your views may have evolved. Or you may have had one view, but now that your child has embarked on her own path your view may have changed.

Of course, whatever position you have today may change tomorrow. But for now, I encourage you to read this chapter and then sit down with yourself and then with your parenting partner and talk about your beliefs, wishes, and hopes for your child regarding alcohol and drugs as well as sex and rock and roll. Then sit down with your child and find out her thoughts as you share your own.

You may be reading this with the full conviction that she has not done anything (yet) or with the complete knowledge that she is past the "experimentation" stage and into the "more regular than you may like" stage. It really doesn't matter if your child is 12 or 30, sober or not, as long as you are her parent you have at minimum an emotional investment. Worrying about your investments is a time-honored activity, be they emotional or financial. There are plenty of adult children who now talk to their own elder parents about how their parents take care of themselves.

Your child, perhaps like your parents, may not listen or follow through, but don't let that stop you from speaking your mind. Just don't do it too often as your talking about it all the time makes it an even bigger issue. It is not that these issues don't deserve ongoing consideration. It is more that putting a large focus on them means you are not focusing as much time on other matters with your child. Instead of dwelling on a sore subject, invest your time in finding ways to connect with your child in more mutually enjoyable activities. While that won't necessarily put the brakes on her partying, it will probably do more good than your harping.

When you share your thoughts/feelings with your parenting partner you may or may not be able to come to a common understanding. Having significant differences will make it hard to impart a clear message to your child. If you are like many couples you may agree about certain aspects and be not so much in agreement about other parts. I recommend you spend time coming to an agreed upon approach to having your "drug/alcohol talk." Find those things you can agree on and share those items. Once again, instead of having a convoluted extended talk, consider an ongoing series of brief topics that are more easily digested.

Even if you and your partner disagree considerably your child will benefit from hearing each of your points of view. You may not want your child drinking until she is in college, while your partner thinks it is okay under certain conditions in high school. Ideally you resolve this behind closed doors, but often these differences come out either overtly or covertly. Every child I have ever spoken to could pretty accurately sum up their parents drug/alcohol policy in a couple of sentences. See if you can do that too.

You can model having differences and accepting and respecting each other's point of view. You make your case. They make theirs. You can point out where you agree and disagree. Then you tell your child you trust her ability to make good choices for herself. Then you add that she is encouraged to speak with either one of you whenever she wants about this or any subject. Then hope for the best.

We know that even when parents come to an agreement about how to parent, it is the rare case when they each approach their child in the same way. One will be more lenient, one stricter. We all have nuanced values that only come into view when being called into action. You and your partner will hopefully agree on the big-ticket items and have manageable differences on the rest. Even when you both promise to hold the same position it is difficult if not close to completely impossible to perfectly overlap. Something is usually sticking out around the edges.

Parenting is, after all, a shared activity, not a cloning.

Every teenager will quickly learn who the more lenient one is and that is where she will go more often than not and do her best to work that leniency to her advantage. Which is a life skill you actually want her to learn, although maybe not always enjoy when it is being practiced on you.

Lest you spend a lot of time bemoaning the differences between you and the other parent, let me just remind you that your child needs to be able to discern between differences. She needs to learn how parents resolve the differences in their values. She will certainly have encounters with her friends where there are differences in values and having observed how you manage those disparities will help her when it comes time to address her own.

You wanted her to wait to drink and your partner said there were acceptable occasions in high school when it would be okay. Now she is in high school and has a DUI. Or both you and your partner thought she should wait for college to experiment and now she has a DUI. Or you both said there were no acceptable times now and then she gets a DUI.

You never know. DUIs happen. Calls from the police station happen. The hospital, the Dean of Students, or your child's best friend's mother calls. You hoped your child would behave in one way and it turns out she behaved differently. If you want to think of behavior in terms of misbehaving and behaving, you might say your child with a DUI misbehaved. She knew better and yet she did it anyway. That seems like a reasonable definition of misbehave to which we all can relate. Knowing better and doing better is not the same thing. We all have misbehaved, but when it is your child and drugs and alcohol are involved the axis at home shifts.

Jane Nelsen, Ed.D. wrote a classic parenting book called *Positive Discipline*. Nelsen cites research about why children misbehave. She found that children who misbehave basically have feelings of inadequacy and want attention, power, and revenge.

Of course, most of us have misbehaved a time or two and I don't think we would necessarily use all those words to describe our motivation. If you are willing to consider that perhaps some or all of those words may be dwelling in your child, then you might want to consider some additional ways to interact with your child to prevent the feelings associated with those words from flourishing.

I know when relationships are strained it can be hard to have the simplest of conversations, let alone constructive interactions that promote a sense of wellbeing for all. Yet your role as a parent does not let you off the hook for continuing to pursue those pathways.

I imagine we all have moments of feeling inadequate. Moments when we want attention, power, and occasionally revenge. These feelings alone don't cause us to misbehave.

Lots of times teenagers have no idea why they aren't doing what their parents want them to do. They tell me all the time they just felt like doing something and they did it. They don't know why. They knew better, but they did it anyway.

You can endeavor to let your child know your values and do your best to not infuse her with a sense of inadequacy. She gets that enough growing up without you reminding her. Be her cheerleader, not her deficiency expert. Give her positive attention and include her in decision making and she won't feel powerless and need to be revengeful.

Easier said than done. Especially when you and your partner have vastly differing views. If you can't come to a general understanding of what you want to tell your child, go to a therapist. Don't let any festering resentment toward your partner get in the way of you doing your best parenting. If you need help, get it.

You can point out what you want, what you are not pleased with, and your expectations. You don't want to deprive your child of attention. You want her to feel seen and valued. You don't want to have her feel that she has no say in what happens in your household. Increasingly, she needs to gain a sense of power over her life. She is on a learning curve and you need to help her build her confidence in her developing skills. Do not point out her inadequacies at the expense of building her strengths. Let her know you believe in her and point out when her abilities are growing.

The research about alcohol and drugs can help you with making decisions about what to tell your child. The easiest fact to absorb is that teenagers who wait longer to experiment with drugs and alcohol have fewer problems with those substances in their adult life. So encouraging your child to hold off would seem a reasonable request. It reduces worry for you and exposure for them. Of course, worrying about future consequences is not a big motivator for teenagers.

How long you would like your child to hold off is up to you. Most parents mention 18 or "when you are in college." While I certainly think it might be a good idea to put some concrete time or number out there, the message I would want my child to hear is that the longer she holds off the better the chances she won't have problems with these things. Just share that fact with her. Don't embellish it. Just let it stand for itself. There are some others you can throw in, but you are not going to convince her by facts alone as teenagers tend to think they will be able to avoid dire consequences. You might be able to convince her by your conviction. Ultimately she will do what she wants to do, as will you. But knowing how important something is to you can be influential.

I would hope she could grasp and appreciate the delay message along with the others she hears and try to rein in her curiosity and desire to see what all the fuss is about. But alcohol is so related to having a good time in our culture that it is hard to imagine why most people wouldn't want to check it out at least once. Statistically about 22% of women and only 11% of men consider themselves lifetime abstainers. It is very challenging to not try something when you go to a party and a significant percentage of those in attendance are drinking and seemingly having a good time. Although I have had many students tell me they have observed some pretty stupid behavior at parties that did influence their desire to get that drunk.

It is hard to get solid statistics on drug use because more people lie about it than they do about alcohol. According to a 2015 Pew Research Center poll, almost half the adult population of the United States has tried marijuana and a recent Gallup poll found that about 50% of teenagers today have tried it before graduating high school. I think it is safe to say that by the time your child graduates high school she has had the opportunity to drink and do drugs. Whether your child chooses to partake depends on a few variables.

It is close to impossible to predict who will and who won't experiment with drugs and alcohol in their teen years. There are some resilient factors that put a teen at less risk. If a child has positive role models and friends, a strong family unit, parental supervision, high parental expectations, no experience of loss or separation as a child, high self-esteem, does well at school, thinks before she acts, and feels negative about the effects of drugs, she is less likely to experiment. Less likely, but not entirely unlikely. Which is why parents worry. No one is assured smooth passage. Plus not a lot of people fit all those criteria.

From my vantage point many parents would settle for their child drinking or taking drugs if their child didn't have "problems" with them and get in trouble. Since there is no guarantee about what will happen when you drink or take a drug—which is part of the appeal of both—parents usually prefer a cautionary approach. Wait. Wait. Wait.

It doesn't hurt to throw in some understanding as well: "I know other kids are doing this and it will be tempting and it is not easy saying no when others are saying yes. Yet I hope you will say no for now and save your experimentation for when you are older."

If you have strong feelings about substance use it is important that they be shared. Your convictions and expectations will help your child say no when both her internal and peer pressures kick in. Sometimes it is wise to hold back on those things that you don't really feel strongly about so your child can find her own way without your influence. Others times you want your beliefs to be clearly heard and understood. If you don't ever want your child doing heroin then repeat the message and expectation from an early age so that wish gets deeply embedded. Don't assume she knows that, even if you are pretty sure she does. Just hearing it now and then can reaffirm it in her mind.

You may have thoughts about the physical/emotional/spiritual harm that may come to your child from imbibing before her mind and body is more fully developed. There is a lot of research that can support the harm that drinking does to the brain. Not only are teenagers more likely to have future issues with drugs and alcohol, but the earlier they start using the more harm they are inflicting on their mental function. Unfortunately they don't experience the long-term brain damage in the moment so they don't have a lot of concern about it.

Whatever your beliefs about experimentation and whether your child does or does not do drugs/alcohol there needs to be an overriding value that I would like you to consider ingraining in your child, your partner, and yourself: Do not do anything that will harm you or another. The Hippocratic oath that physicians take includes the promise "to abstain from doing harm." I think that is an oath we all can take. Your child needs to know that if she is going to drink or do drugs, she can't drive or have anyone else drive who has had even the smallest amount of alcohol or drugs.

- She needs to know to be with people she trusts in places she can get help if needed.
- She needs to know that with drugs, alcohol, and most anything else there is use and there is abuse.

Therapists often distinguish between use and abuse. We can go back and forth about which is which, but I would think the bottom line rests within each of us and is measured by the quality of our lives. If your child chooses to drink or use drugs, hopefully it would be to enhance her life in some way and would not become a negative force in her life. Certainly many people will argue that any use is abuse and for those people there is a clear path.

Most people start off their journey with alcohol and drugs in a positive way after a vomit or two and continue to have it in their life and find pleasure with it. Others start off on good footing and discover that the drug or alcohol has more control over their life than they do and bad things start to happen. You never know when you are starting out which path you will take. According to Paul Thorn, "Everyone looks good at the starting line."

What one person may consider a fine balance another person may consider abusive. One person's enough can be another's too much. You need to make sure your child knows your definition of use/abuse. More importantly, you need to know hers.

When your child moves out of your home and has her own living space I imagine you would not be surprised if she might have a bottle of beer and/or wine in the refrigerator. She might have some weed tucked away in dark place. Many parents hope their child would partake now and then in a responsible way and enjoy themselves. Others prefer abstinence. Whatever your vision is, your child needs to hear it.

Right now your child is living with you and most likely under 18 and you are charged with her wellbeing. My own belief is that any use before she is of legal age is abuse and if you condone her usage then you are being abusive to her. It is a harsh stance and I don't make a lot of them, but this is one where I find too much physical and social evidence that points to the dangers of partaking in substances before your body is more developed. Condoning your child's usage or turning a blind eye to it is not the kind of responsible parenting that I can support.

If your child, to the best of your knowledge, has not had a drink or taken a drug, you can share your expectations with your child with the hope that she will pretty much follow your prescription. Of course it is easier for everyone to be optimistic when you lay that picture out when your child is younger. Every now and then when something happens in your collective world you can share pieces of your values and expectations to help guide her behavior. But remember, when you talk to your child about substance use you want it to be a discussion, not a lecture.

Whether you are encouraging your child to steer clear of or postpone her drug and alcohol experimentation, or you have found out she has imbibed, you are going to need to have ongoing conversations. It is akin to advertising. Advertisers don't just buy time for the Super Bowl or Academy Awards—they sprinkle their ads all over us.

If you listen to a lot of adolescents talk you will see their discussions are choppy and multitasked. They rarely dwell on subjects. The lectures you give them are probably more focused and overbearing than most others they encounter. They are used to staccato. You speak to them like old monophonic speakers while they are used to the multiplex.

I don't encourage you to speak to your teen like the social media she engages in all day. I am suggesting you don't need to dwell on things as long as you do. You want items to be open to ongoing discussion. You want your child to speak to you about what she sees and hears in her life about drugs/alcohol. You want to swap sound bites, stories, and glances. Questions about what she thinks and what she believes can elicit more information if they are not followed by rebuttal. If you ask your child her point of view, you ought not to punish her for sharing it.

Just as you want her to hear and respect your beliefs, you might want to consider giving her the same courtesy. While you ideally might want her views to be the same as yours, it is unrealistic to expect her to have the same world view.

Most likely her view of the world is different than yours. Who knows? It might even be more realistic. You might even be able to learn and benefit from hearing her take on how things work. She does have a better pulse on what is happening in her generation than you. And probably knows what is trending in a lot of arenas where you are clueless.

Discussions are about an exchange of ideas and experiences. If the conversation only flows one way, you can't expect the other person to have much interest in it. Hold on to the goal of having an exchange with your child where thoughts/feelings are shared and people feel understood and valued. And, hopefully, occasionally agreed with—she to you and you to her. Find those areas.

As much as a parent may value discussion, they often want to end that discussion with some rule of behavior. Parents are comforted by the structure that a rule provides and hope that by being clear about the guidelines their child will be more apt to stay in bounds. Many parents might be comforted to know what percent of teens follow their parents' rules and how best to structure a rule so that it is followed. I have looked for those studies, but have not found any worth sharing. I do know there are more effective and less effective ways to present and frame the "house rules" and I am happy to point those out to you.

Rules are more likely to be followed when fully understood and mutually agreed upon. We might not all like paying taxes, but we get the idea of why they are important. We may disagree on how the monies are spent and how much is taken, but a healthy majority of people follow the rule and pay their taxes. Not necessarily just because they want to.

If you are going to lay down the rule "Do not drink or take drugs," it will help your child to follow that rule if she can understand why you made it. While it would help, you know it won't guarantee anything. We can guarantee that not everyone will follow the rules. If there is anything we could all agree on, it is that somebody somewhere is breaking some rule. And maybe that someone is us.

If you are going to be making rules with your children there are several points to consider:

1. How are you going to know if she breaks the rule?

2. What is going to happen when you find out she broke a rule?

3. What will the consequences be for breaking the rule?

4. Are you going to be able and willing to enforce the rule?

If you are pretty clear about your answers to those questions and have shared that information with the other parent and they are basically in agreement, you ought to feel comfortable enough to speak with your child and establish the rule. If you are going to make a rule do it when everyone is sober and focused and you have time to discuss things through. Realize that once you announce the rule, your child will react to it and possibly make a counteroffer. Listen and consider it before you reject it. Possibly find a meeting place.

Parents are often hesitant to establish rules, because they know the odds are good the rule may be broken and then they will have to follow through with the consequence. In my experience, parents rarely completely honor the terms they set. Slight differences in parental opinions get chipped away at as your child continually renegotiates with possible scenarios that make good sense. The strict measures that were in place can lose clarity as circumstances come into play. Consequences usually end up becoming more and more lax. Which is fine. It just teaches your child that the initial terms you set will be negotiable down the line. Which frankly makes sense as you don't know the circumstances surrounding a future incident.

If your child continues to misbehave, those consequences increase. If she behaves well the consequences usually decrease. Since your child will eventually want to go do this event or do something that has been taken away from her, she will be talking with you. Teenagers, like most of us, talk about something when they want something.

Take advantage of her coming to you to talk. Often parents complain that their teens don't talk with them. Seize this moment and make these conversations not only about privileges and, "If I do this can I get that?" Your child wants something. You can take her willingness to engage you and use it to speak about school, friends, the world, or anything else you want. She is talking to you to win you over to her side. To do that she needs to demonstrate some listening and engaging skills. Not a lot. But some. Plus, you can restate your values and expectations which she will probably be happy to repeat for you rather than have to listening to you say them again.

If you child comes home obviously drunk and you have a "no drinking" rule, by rights you ought to impose the consequence that you went over when you first talked about what would happen. Yet when you first spoke about the rule the conditions in your child's and your life were one way and now they are another. Perhaps time has altered how you would like to deal with the situation. When you laid out the rules to your 14-year-old they might have been applied somewhat differently than when your child is 16. Or not.

I like flexibility. It is easier for me.

Some people like things black and white and that is easier for them. Things are right or wrong, good or bad, and when this happens that happens. There is some comfort in those "this or that" positions, yet for me so much of life is gray and ambiguous that often I can't comfortably rest with yes/no. I am more of a "this, that, and the other" kind of guy.

Certainly you need to make decisions about how to respond to your child coming home drunk, but if your feelings/thoughts are mixed, that could affect your consequence.

If your child came home drunk you might have consequence A.

If your child had driven home drunk you might have consequence B.

If you child called you and told you she was having someone sober drive her home because she had too much to drink you might have consequence C.

Circumstances yield a story and that story influences what follows.

Therapists usually place more emphasis on the process of events rather than the content of them. Content (the what) is certainly important and can be of critical relevance. The critical fact is that your child is drunk. Yet, how you deal (the how) with that content (the what) has significant bearing on the quality of your relationship. Often you cannot control the what, but you have direct control over the how. If you child comes home drunk there is not much you can do about the 'what' of that, but there is a lot you can do about how you deal with it.

When you are not in crisis and are just sitting around talking, you model a way of interacting that will serve you when you get to that coming-home-drunk scenario. The more you can learn as a family to share your feelings/thoughts and respectfully listen to others' feelings/thoughts, the sooner you will be able to resolve differences when they arise. When a crisis occurs, the day-to-day skills will once again serve you. Regardless of how you respond to a situation it will eventually get resolved and people will move on. You just want to do your best to try to get your family to work together to find satisfactory resolutions to the challenges you all face. Not everyone will be happy all the time. But if everyone feels heard, understood, and thinks things are basically fair, it is a lot easier to get along.

Remember, the bottom line is the health and welfare of your child. You want your child safe and usually home in her bed or sleeping over at some friend's or relative's home.

Most parents want to get in one last word before their child heads out into serious party country. One thing you might want to say is that first and foremost you want her to be safe at home at the end of the evening. You would prefer she came home sober, but if by some chance she is not going to be coming home sober, she needs to ensure she gets home with someone who is sober or that she sleeps over at the house of someone you trust.

Where I work the kids have Uber and Lyft on their speed dial. While these services are not yet as regulated as some might like, it does usually work. Hopefully by the time this is published Uber, Lyft, and their competitors will be more licensed and there will be a greater level of confidence you can have about the driver's safety records. While there may be some issues about how your child gets home, safety is still the bottom line.

If she needs to call you to get that ride home, you want her to call you. You don't want her trying to get home when she is under the influence or driving with anybody who is anything but sober. If she needs a ride she can call you. No lectures. No reprimands. Just a ride home. Followed by a discussion in the morning.

I know I have mentioned coming home safely before and I may very well again, but it is one of those lectures I think you need to repeat often enough so that your child rolls her eyes and can finish your sentences. When she can do that, you both can smile at one another and you can try to have a restful evening.

Making your expectations for your child's behavior known is an ongoing activity. When you are with your child in the car and you pass a liquor store you can say something akin to, "When you are 21 and decide to go buy your first bottle of wine you might want to go to a wine store and not a liquor store. They will help you with your selection and you won't just pick something because you saw it advertised somewhere."

Of course, if you say that, you are condoning drinking wine. But you are also putting an age to it.

If you are watching TV and someone is drunk you might say, "That's something I never want you to do. If you are going to drink when you are an adult try to keep it under control. I don't want you to be that person and hopefully you don't either. Do you?"

I tend to think parent/child lectures need to be short. You sprinkle their life path with your expectations, not cover it.

One cluster of expectations I have said over and over to my child and urged every group of parents to share with their children involves driving. They go like this:

- Don't ever drive when you have any amount of any substance in your body. One toke, one sip, one anything gets you out of the driver's seat.

- When someone tells you they are fine to drive, don't let them drive unless they are 100% sober. Remember the one toke, one sip rule.

- I want you home safely. Call me and I will pick you up any time any place.

An accompanying sidebar lecture that I have mentioned often to parents centers on the concept that if your child calls you, the consequence for her being under the influence is significantly less than it would have been had you found out on your own. You need to get your child to believe that if she calls you she won't be severely punished. If you come down too hard on her she won't call you. My recommendation is you make the consequence minimal and be thankful she is home safe and sound. You can have a talk about what happened in the morning.

Wanting her not to drink or do drugs is nowhere near as important to you as wanting her to be healthy and safe. If she calls you for a ride don't bust her chops. Yeah, maybe discipline her the next morning when everyone is sober, but make sure that consequence is considerably less than it would have been had she not called you. Make sure she knows she is being rewarded for being responsible about her safety while at the same time disciplined for breaking a rule. If you don't make the reward sufficiently rewarding, she probably won't call you next time.

Be thankful it wasn't a call from the police, or worse, the hospital.

Home safe and sound is the goal.

58

THE ABCs OF SEX, DRUGS, AND ROCK & ROLL

C

Suppose you find out your child has used substances. Maybe you found paraphernalia in his room or you got a call from the police station or someone told you that they knew your child was doing something. Your reality gets shattered and you realize something significant has happened in your child's life. Once you find out your child has been caught doing something you probably hoped he wasn't doing you are called upon to exercise your parental duties. You now need to step up to the plate and respond.

When something "bad" happens to your child you are flooded with thoughts/feelings. Your life gets out of its usual balance. Big emotions get elicited. The dominos start to fall.

You may be mad at your child. Or scared. Or sad. Maybe even some glad thrown in. Whatever emotions you have, you need to do something, and chances are you are going to lead with your emotions. While that is not necessarily a bad thing I do think it is worth taking a breath before you plunge in.

As a therapist I usually recommend that when something elicits considerable emotion, try to talk it out with someone else before you get into it with your child. It doesn't always work that way as things often are thrust upon us, but when it is possible make sure to get those immediate emotional reactions out in safer environments. Many are the car rides to the police station, hospital, or party that have been full of venting. Angers and fears need to get expressed. Certainly your child needs to hear them. He just doesn't necessarily need to hear them right away at full strength.

See if you can get some of that emotional jolt off your chest with the other parent and lighten your own load a bit. We all need to know when our actions upset others. Just as we need to know when our actions please them. When your child has done something to upset you he will know soon enough, but hopefully you can share it with him in a way he can understand and respect. Save the uncensored full-volume version for your partner. Just don't blame them.

Talking beforehand won't take away all of your emotional charge, but it may dull the edge. That will help when you speak with your child as he will be able to feel your emotions yet also be able to hear your attempts to resolve the situation in the best way possible. I remember long ago reading that there are two symbols in Chinese for crisis. One is danger and the other is opportunity. While few people like a crisis, most would agree that it does provide the chance to consider going forward differently. While this incident may not seem like a gift, it may turn out to be a needed opportunity.

Hardly anybody likes to get caught doing something they ought not to be doing. There is as much direct learning through the shame and embarrassment in being caught as there is in the parade through the consequences.

When you have to face your child after he has done something "troubling" it is not easy conveying upset while at the same time letting your child know you still love him, care for him, and want the best for him. You have to put on your best parent game face. You may want to remember this basic tenet of parenting: I want my child to have the complete and thorough knowledge that I love him and always want the best for him.

Even in trying times. Especially in trying times.

Here you are at a significant, complicated, emotional, and challenging point in your child's life. You want your child to have the baseline security that comes with knowing you will be upset with him but in no way does this affect the love and care you have for him. This is a bump in the road that will be managed, learned from, and moved on from.

Whether it be on the drive home from the police station or in the living room, I would prefer you refrain from your "I am upset with you" rant and instead begin with:

1) How are you?
2) Tell us what happened…

Listen before you leap.

If, indeed, your child's welfare is of utmost importance, then asking how he is doing is a pretty good way to show that and start the conversation. It conveys the kind of bottom line message that I would want my child to know (especially at moments like this): I care about how you are.

When your child does something than lands him in trouble it is not about how your life is now ruined. It is about his life and how he and you are going to learn from this and move forward.

Before you rant it helps to know what exactly you are going to be ranting about. The fact that you know something happened was the starting point, but there is more to the story. I would want to hear that story first from the person who lived it. You can always rant. Many parents think they own that right or at least could be forgiven if they got carried away. I have nothing against ranting just as long as it doesn't include name-calling, blaming, threatening, or otherwise compromising your family's ability to trust you and your good judgment.

If your rant seems out of proportion to the event your family members are not going to want to be sharing their truths with you for fear of your reaction. That is why I suggest getting all the information before igniting your rant. Once you know what happened you can better calibrate your upset.

You want your family to trust you to be able to "appropriately" handle situations. The more you fly off the handle, make accusations, and make it all about you, the less anyone is going to want to do with you.

Listen to what your child says, count to ten, breathe slowly, and then speak your truth.

I had a student email me and tell me that his father had once again railed against him for something he did and he was grounded for the two weeks of spring vacation. I wrote him back and commiserated and asked him what he thought he could do. He wrote back and said there was nothing he could do. His father had sworn at him, told him he was a "stupid asshole" and was impenetrable. When the dust settled and he had apologized to his father, he told me his father had never once apologized for anything he did. The student wanted to meet with me when the break was over and I wanted to meet with him and the dad. But first I wanted to hear more from the boy.

I mention this because I would hope you are not that father. Some people find it difficult to apologize and some people do halfhearted apologies. If you ask your child how your behavior affects him and what he thinks about your parenting you might find in his response some things that you genuinely feel sorry for causing. Telling your child that you think he is a "stupid asshole" is something I cannot condone. I know adults who can readily recite the damning words their parents have thrown at them. Those wounds do not easily heal and an apology is not going to erase them, but at least it helps the healing process instead of prolonging it.

Trust means different things to each of us. Often when parents think about trust and drugs/alcohol they think about trusting their child to behave "appropriately" according to whatever standards have been put forth. Rather than entirely putting your trust in his behavior, try to invest your trust in two other things as well:

1. Know that whatever happens he will be able to survive it, learn from it, and go forth in a better way.

2. Know that whatever happens to your family, you will be able to talk about it in a caring, responsive way and come to a good enough resolution.

Parents worry about their child when he does not do the "appropriate" thing. They can be disappointed in choices their child makes. But please do not ever fully let go of believing your child will be able to do well in the world, and never fully stop conveying that belief to him.

Parents need to convey the trust that says "I believe in you" in deeds as well as words. More than ever when those beliefs are challenged.

Go find your inner best parent and pull him out and let your child know that even though this moment is not a pleasant one, you believe in your family's and your child's ability to build on this and make things even better.

I know this trust is not easy to give. Because we all know our children, partners, and friends are not always trustworthy. People don't generally do everything just the way we would like. They do things the way they want to do them.

Hopefully we like it. But not always.

Yet even though it is not easy to give your child 100% trust, you want to aim high. As your family teeters through the teenage years your assurance and trust may vacillate. Do your best to hold on to your belief in his ability to live a valuable, meaningful, and enjoyable life. Maybe not on your terms, but on his.

I know parents have doubts and fears. As do children. I think you can share the doubts and fears with your partner and therapist.

You share the belief with your child.

Teenagers stumble and fall like the rest of us. They tend to be more prone to experimenting with life than their parents so their mistake rate is higher. But we all make mistakes. It is just that as a parent you usually don't have your parent around to point them out.

An unusual thing happened to this present generation of parents. Unlike their own parents, they are highly invested in their children liking them. If you go back two or three generations the notion of your child liking you would seem foreign. Yes, they wanted their children to respect and honor them, but liking was more something the parent bestowed than desired.

Now parents often are hesitant to take certain actions or follow through on consequences if they think their child will be upset with them. Many parents endeavor for a more peer-to-peer kind of relationship with their child—albeit one where they clearly hold the ultimate power cards.

Children have more power over how their parents treat them than their parents ever had. Parents care less what their own parents think of their parenting than what their kids think. Grandparents, while usually adoptable as babysitters, rarely have their "how to parent" opinions implemented except when other options continue to fail. Even then, parents are keenly aware of how their child thinks/feels about the interactions and are considerably more responsive to their reactions.

Parents often talk to me about wanting to dole out some consequences for perceived misbehavior but fear their child will punish them if they are too strict. A common reaction when someone takes something away from you is to want to push against them. It doesn't matter if the consequences fit the crime, most people don't want to have to face the consequences. Especially if they are harsh. The harsher they are the more you can expect your child will not be happy with you. Parents need to learn to be more accepting of having their child displeased with them for actions taken.

Hardly anyone likes it when people are displeased with them—especially if those people are your family. A parent's actions will at times hurt their child. Just like other people's actions hurt you. People hurt people. Intentionally and unintentionally. It is part of the formula. Parents need to find a level of acceptance with their child being upset with them with the knowledge that time will help heal the wounds. Maybe tentatively at first, but hopefully better than ever in the long run.

Young children enjoy liking their parents. They value their caretakers. They grow up comfortable with you, knowing you better than anyone, and looking up to you. By the time they reach their teen years the bloom has come off the rose. They have come to know you more fully. Like everyone else there are some things about you they like more and some they like less. Your tenure on the pedestal has expired.

There is no right/wrong or good/bad about wanting your child to like you. I suspect like most things it has pros and cons. If you are on either end of the spectrum it is probably of more concern. However much you want your child to like you there are going to be times when you do something he will not like. He certainly will do things you don't like.

As your child moves through his adolescence he will seem to care less about your liking him while you often care more about him liking you. As our children grow our relationships with them evolve. As they gain independence and move away, their interests in being liked shift to their friends while you long for the days when he snuggled up in your lap.

There is a time when a child is fully dependent on his parents and ultimately a time when he is no longer dependent. There is time when parents are independent from their children and a time when they often become dependent themselves. It is summarized this way: You become your parent's parent and they become their child's child. I would like to give someone credit for that phrase, but that wordsmith has gone unknown.

There will be times you may need to choose doing the unpopular thing because you think it is the best thing. It is difficult knowing your child is upset with you and not liking you, yet it is more difficult knowing you may not be doing what is in your child's best interests. Of course, it is not always clear what is in your child's best interests, which is why it can help to not act in haste so you can repent at leisure.

Remember, when life hands your child a setback it helps if you don't hold it as your own personal setback. Your child's life is about him. Don't trump his issues with your own. Save yours for another time. And hopefully, another place.

When your child is up against some dose of unwanted reality your job is to help him get through it. Not to add on to it. Yes, your emotions will be as triggered, as will his, and most likely you will bring those into the mix. Just try not to have them dominate. This is the moment your child needs you most; don't desert him by upstaging him.

Yes, his life certainly affects you, but as much as it affects you, it affects him more. As much as we all think life is about us, it really is about you and your child.

I am hesitant to suggest the following because I don't particularly want to get the other parent in trouble. But I think it is worth the risk.

The next time you have an emotional flare-up that trumps your child's, I would like you to ask your partner to seize the moment. I would like them to remind you with a glance that you need to take a backseat and attend to what is happening with your child. They can give you a subtle heads up without drawing attention to the fact that you have stepped over the line.

Remember, if you ask for this feedback, don't punish the messenger.

If you don't want this intervention and/or think your partner has their issues and would throw the flag at you because of issues between you, don't share this with your partner. But, if you want to put some effort into improving your interactions with your child (and family) consider asking for the feedback and reflecting on it. Later when the dust settles you can ask your child for some feedback on how you handled matters. He might not tell you the truth, but he might. Either way it helps to ask and listen. Not rebuke. Listen.

After your discussion with your child, ask the other parent for feedback on how you handled the situation. Just listen to their feedback and your child's and incorporate it any way you can. If you took the emotional focus away from your child your partner ought to be able to point that out to you. Rather than defend yourself, try to just understand how your interaction looked to someone else. The goal is to find ways to respond to your child (and your partner) that don't take the focus away from them, yet allow room for you.

Yes, you can have times when the conversation is mostly is about you. You can have times when it is about how you think/feel about what is happening to your child. Or anything in your life. You can have times when you all share how you think/feel back and forth. But you also have to let there be times when it is about your child and how you are going to support him.

When you ask your child how he feels and what happened you listen to his reply. You ask questions for clarification. You might be empathic here and cranky there, but the initial goal is for you to hear what he has to say about what happened. Hear his story, hold off on your emotional reaction and then ask, "What do you want to do about this?" Not, "Here is what I think ought to be done about this."

Once again, it is not about you. Let him problem-solve and see how he would like to resolve the situation. He needs to build his problem-solving, resolution-making skills. Give him a chance to exercise them. If he has gotten himself into some kind of trouble ask him how he would like to get out of it. This empowers him, teaches him responsibility, and shows your trust in his good judgment.

You may completely disagree with his solution, but it is always good to hear the other person's position before you state your own. When you ask him how he would like to resolve the situation he may not be ready to answer this question as he still may be absorbing what is happening. It is fine to give him time to respond. Yet, encourage him to come up with a next step. Thinking about next steps will help move him (and you) into resolution mode.

Usually when children are asked to suggest the consequences for an action gone wrong they put up more punitive damages than adults. In part because they don't think it will come to that and in part because they think with stronger consequences facing them they actually might toe the line.

You might find your child's ideas reasonable and accept them or you may want to suggest alternatives. If you happen to think his ideas are too light you can offer a heftier suggestion. If you think his are too heavy you can suggest a less harsh consequence. That not only makes you a reasonable parent and increases the odds of your child liking you, but it also models finding an agreed upon compromise, a skill that will serve him throughout his life.

While I was interning at a residential treatment center for teenagers, I learned a valuable lesson that has served me throughout my career. There was a meeting in the living room involving all the boys and girls who lived there as well as the counselors. During the meeting, one boy got up without permission, walked out, and went into the backyard to have a smoke. Since I was the new counselor, one of the more experienced counselors told me to go to the back door and not let the boy back in. So I stood in the doorway and watched him smoke his cigarette. He finished, walked up to me in the doorway, and started to head in. I told him they had asked me to tell him he could not come back in. He barely looked at me and kept walking into the house.

I realized as he brushed by me that I was unwilling to physically restrain him. So in he went. I learned then not to make rules I was not willing to enforce.

Like most things, an ounce of prevention is easier to handle than a pound of cure. Sitting down with your child when all is basically good, going over your sex/drugs/alcohol concerns and talking with him about possible scenarios can be of considerable assistance when/if something unwanted happens.

Here are some reminders:

- If you're having a discussion about possible future consequences for actions, don't establish iron-clad ones that you will not enforce. That will only undermine his respect for what you say. Do what you say you will do, and don't do what you say you won't.

- In order to make that follow-through easier for you don't create "If you do this, I am doing that" scenarios. I think it is easier to just say there will be consequences that are appropriate to the situation which hopefully we can agree on, but if not, so be it. Together you could think of some different situations and how they might play out. Ideally you reach some fairly well understood and agreed upon parameters. Realistically, you make the final call.

- When your child offers a consequence for his behavior think it over. Maybe it is acceptable as is. If you think it is too harsh or too easy, you need to offer other consequences that you think are more likely for everyone to follow through on.

- It is not the end of the world if you say that if he breaks curfew without calling he will be grounded for two weeks and then change it to one week as it does show some flexibility on your part and you can reward his behavior by reducing the time he is grounded. They do that in the prison system. It is okay. I have done it. Yet, I would say there is no need to overly reward desired behavior. It is expected. If he does things above and beyond, that could be more deservedly rewarded.

- That said, we can all benefit from being acknowledged and appreciated for just showing up. Some days that is a much harder proposition than others. You don't always need to go above and beyond to be appreciated. We all can use some positive reactions to our everyday, regular selves. No doubt about it. We all can use some of that. Even when we are serving time for having misbehaved.

- When it comes to helping your child resolve a challenge in his life you need to not be stingy with the reward/praise/acknowledgement. Following disruptive incidents, many parents are blaming and shaming. While I would prefer you shared the blame/shame with your therapist I imagine some of your upset will seep out in one form or another in the aftermath. Which is why you also need to throw in those positives.

Just because your child is in the doghouse for something he did does not mean you don't engage lovingly, playfully, and seriously with him. From the moment you know your child has done something of serious concern to you, you are in repair mode. You and your child's daily routine has been broken and a degree of crisis has descended upon you. As upset, confused, and dismayed as you may be, you also need to attend to the care and welfare of your child. You can huff and puff as long as you want but it isn't going to make it any better until you stop venting and start repairing and getting your relationships back on sound footing. Remember, this crisis is also an opportunity.

Once you get caught up with your child in a sex or alcohol/drug incident it can overtake your household. When you discipline a child you do it with the intent that it will teach him a lesson. You want to be careful what lesson you are teaching. You don't want to teach him the lesson that you are an unreasonable, overreacting parent. You want to teach him that you are an engaging and loving parent who wants to be able to continue to discuss what happened and go forward until this doesn't really need to be talked about any more. You want everyone to learn from this and speak together about what is going on. You want to take the opportunity of the crisis and build a closer-knit family unit that can take heart in knowing you resolved matters together and came out the better for it. That actually happens. Not all the time, but enough that you would want to aim for it.

59

WHEN YOU GET A CALL

Parents live in dread of getting a bad call. Be it a call from the school that your child is not doing well or a call from the police or the hospital. Parental anxiety shoots up when they hear a school administrator's voice or the phone rings late at night.

Whatever general amount of worry and concern you have for your child multiplies when you get unwelcome news. No one wants to hear that there has been an accident or your child is being held at the precinct or the school would like you to come in for a meeting. When those calls come your body tenses and you can feel your life teetering.

However severe or slight the news may be, it will upset the stability in your family. Maybe a little, maybe a lot. Any unwelcome event will prompt a reaction which may very well have significant emotional and behavioral consequences.

Many parents consider the oversight of their child to be their life's primary work and when an event goes awry their equilibrium can go tumbling with it. Depending on the severity of the phone call, your life as you know it may be forever altered.

Dr. Kübler-Ross was an early pioneer in the study of loss and grieving. She developed a five-stage model that has become the industry standard and which you may well know. In its simplest form her theory suggests that when there is a death or some other fateful event occurs, people react with denial, anger, bargaining, depression, and acceptance. Those reactions don't necessarily occur in that order, but usually they do mostly occur. And just since you went through one stage doesn't mean you won't go through it again. And again.

I think her theory fits many circumstances. It doesn't have to be an extreme event. You could get a call from the school about unexcused absences or a call from the doctor that says they want to take more tests.

More often than not when there is some kind of loss involved you touch on those five stages. The loss may be physical; your child may have injured themselves. The loss may be psychological; you may get a call that your child has been skipping school. A loss of innocence can trigger your entry into those Kübler-Ross stages as can the loss of a loved one. You find an empty liquor bottle in your child's closet or sneak a look at her phone and see she has been sexting. Basically, people go through those emotional stages when something happens that causes them to lose the status quo.

In the minutes and days ahead as you react to the call and embark on whatever actions you take it may help to run these questions through your thoughts. Ask yourself:

How am I in denial? (Not that one would fully know.)

How am I angry?

How am I sad?

How am I bargaining?

How can I find a level of acceptance?

You can ask yourself those questions and allow yourself to search for answers. Even though you may have a quick response, you might want to challenge that and spend some time considering how you are managing your way through the stages. There is no right or wrong. As Kuber-Ross said, you flow from one of these states to another and back again. Sometimes you barely touch on a stage while others may affect you in myriads of ways.

You may find yourself upset, angry, and afraid. Then not want to think about it. Then maybe think if you do this then maybe such-and-such will happen. People deny and bargain in various ways. Just as they come to acceptance on their own terms. Most people bounce around. Spend more time in one place than another and eventually get to a semi-reluctant level of acceptance.

I mention the stages as a way of normalizing your reaction to disturbing news. You might slam the phone down and swear, you might cross yourself and pray, you might start crying or grab the keys and start driving. There is no right way to initially act to a jarring phone call. When life hits you in the gut you react from the gut.

Allow yourself to react in whatever way you do. But depending on the urgency of the situation remember there are other people involved and you probably need to do something. And it is probably better to do something that is not self-destructive or otherwise destructive.

I had a client once speak with me about what the bottom line single issue was that kept him from having the kind of life that he believed he could achieve. He told me it came down to the uncomfortable fact that he didn't trust himself. He didn't believe he could build himself a rewarding life. His self-doubt held him back because he wasn't able to take the necessary risks to move things to another level. He was afraid to say what he really felt and thought to those close to him for fear they would abandon him. He was a people-pleaser at the expense of doing what he really wanted to do.

He did not believe in himself because he didn't think his parents ever believed in themselves or him. They lived closed-off, compromised lives and were not encouraging or supportive of him as he grew up. They did not foster a sense of ability in him and he thought that was because they didn't have much sense of their own ability.

Whether or not you trust your own ability to be a parent in the best of times and/or the worst of times, you need to keep your focus on the real bottom line—your child's health and wellbeing. I don't use the word 'always' much, having been taught never to say never and always because most things are not that absolute, but when it comes to parenting I think you always need to act from a place of concern about your child's safety, health, and wellbeing.

When that call comes, no matter how upsetting it is, if your child is alive be thankful for that. You don't want to get that other call that brings to an end all your dreams of the future. If her life is not in jeopardy be thankful for that. If it is, there is a whole other world you are about to enter that is drenched in those Kübler-Ross stages.

If her life is not in jeopardy, the next bottom line is you want your child to come out the better for this experience. You want her to learn from it, gain from it, and grow from it.

So don't do anything that is going to affect that bottom line. You don't want to leave your child with the thought that she is unable to manage herself well.

Even if she just didn't.

You want her to know she made a mistake. People do that all the time.

You want her to know she will need to deal with the consequences of that mistake with your support.

You want her to know you believe in her ability to handle herself better in the future.

You need to make sure she knows those things. If you don't believe them, you need to go find a therapist to help you all out.

As upset as you are for what has happened, once you get that call you are dealing with the consequence and healing stages. Not the blaming, belittling, and bemoaning stages.

I work at a school where I get to call parents when their child raises our concerns or gets in a certain kind of trouble. I have made calls about attendance, drug use, eating disorders, bullying, harassment, and threatening behaviors. But that was last week. I also call when faculty members are worried about a student's wellbeing or a student walks into my office and tells me she is not feeling the way she would like to feel.

Things most often happen this way. I am told about something a child has done that concerns someone on the faculty or administrative side of the school. I am not the "because you did that you are going to have to do this" discipline person. I am the "because you did this, you need to speak to me to help figure out what is causing you to do this and what you can do to make things better" person.

If the student was involved in doing something that the school responded to in a disciplinary way, someone else makes those calls and asks the parents to come in. When they come I often pair up with the person who is going to be handing out the consequences. I get to be the good cop and try to hold the family's emotional hand while they go through the disciplinary process. Often that process includes some follow-up time in my office.

I get called in solo when someone at the school hears something about a child regarding their welfare. Things like a student was drunk and passed out at a party over the weekend or hasn't been eating lunch and may have body image issues.

Sometimes I hear that a student might have a drinking problem or is missing a lot of school. It does not matter the source or the veracity of the claim. Once I hear it, I need to act on it. I am not a detective or a judge. It is not my role to ascertain the truth. It is my job to help the student and the family find their truth and deal with it in an effective manner.

Most often, I have the student come to my office and I tell them what I have heard and ask them what they think/feel about it. Then I shut up and see what happens.

Once they respond and we talk about it, I tell them one of us is going to have to tell their parents what I had initially heard along with their response. Once their parents hear what happened, the family can deal with the situation and I try to support them in whatever ways I can.

In all my years of doing this, very few students ever wanted me to talk with their parents. I have had students beg, plead, threaten, cajole, and cry a lot of tears about their parents having to hear what I heard. Whether what I heard is true or not, most students would rather their parents did not know and they assure me that if there is any truth to the matter they will take care of it. I am happy when I hear they think it is an unsubstantiated rumor. I am happy to hear they think they can take care of it. And I still need to call their parents. If what I heard is untrue the parents need to know that untruths are being spoken about their child. If it is true and their child is engaging in risky behavior, they also need to know.

I am the messenger. Between other students, faculty and the influx of social media, administrators at a school often learn things about a child that the parents don't know. It is not the school's job to pass along every little thing they hear. Certainly there are legislated matters that need to be shared such as someone being a threat to themselves or others, but there is a lot more gray area than there is black or white. When it comes to the gray, I use the baseline: What do I think a reasonable loving parent would want to know? It is not a perfect measure, but it has guided me pretty well so far. In situations where I am unsure or barely sure, I ask others.

Sometimes those calls start like this: "Your daughter is in my office and I asked her if she would prefer to talk to you or have me speak. She wanted me to start. She isn't in any trouble with the school, but we heard that she has been drinking 'excessively even on school nights.' I don't know if that is true or not, but since we heard it, I wanted to make sure you heard it as well. If there is anything I can do to help, I am here to offer whatever support I can."

Things take off from there in any number of directions.

Before I call the parents I first talk with the child. I tell her what I have heard. I don't embellish. I just tell her and then ask her to help me understand what happened or what is going on. I also tell her that what I am telling her also needs to be shared with her parents once I am done talking with her. They usually take it all pretty well, until I get to that last part. They don't always like that and I can't blame them. But I know parents want to know.

Once the student and I are done going over her response to what I have heard and she has exhausted her pleas that I don't immediately call her parents, I ask if she would prefer I or she call her parents. I say I am going to tell her parents exactly what I told them plus anything else they want to suggest.

I prefer students talk with their parents about what happened, but I also know that once parents hear what happened they will want to speak with me and find out what the school is going to do about it. If the school called because their child was on a school trip and was caught drinking alcohol they might worry about whether she was going to be expelled and what would that mean and how would it damage their child and isn't there something we can do? Most times, when I call, the school has no consequence as these are more personal issues. Sometimes I tell the student the consequence is that they have had to speak with me and we have to call her parents. That often is consequence enough.

While I don't often make the really bad calls, I am usually there when the parents come in to talk with the person who is going to be delivering the bad news. My job is to help the family understand the school's process and do my best to support them when the going gets rough.

Having done this for some time, I usually have an inkling of the range of consequences the school will consider. I also know that before the school decides anything the family needs to be heard and given a chance to respond to the circumstances. If the student was drinking at a school event there is a "no tolerance" rule; in those cases the student usually needs to leave the school for a period of time. How long can depend on how the student responds to the situation. But before the school makes any declarative statements they want to hear from the family. That doesn't usually change anything too much, but it's helpful to have as much information as possible before making decisions that could seriously affect a child's life.

Along the path to resolution families often go through those five stages of loss with me. Whatever occurred caused a loss of the awareness that was present before the event. Day-to-day reality has shifted. It is not easy being a parent when your child has done something that challenges her status at a school or anywhere in her life.

I have seen parents strongly defend their child's actions and I have heard parents call their child stupid. Regardless of the situation almost all parents want their child to learn from the situation and come away stronger. Some welcome a form of discipline to help "straighten out" their child. Other parents want a warning and nothing on their transcript. They don't want their child hurt by their mistake and yet also realize this could be a teachable moment.

Very few parents want their child punished "too much." But one person's too much might be another's too little. I tell parents that while they would prefer their child not to be in trouble, it is usually better for these things to occur while the child is living in their home as opposed to living away. That isn't much of a silver lining but it does put things in a certain perspective. While parents feel decreasing influence as their child ages, there is even less influence once she moves away. Your last best chance of helping turn that mistake into a positive is while she is still living with you.

Whatever consequence the school puts forward, another task on the parent "to do" list is to teach your child how to navigate misfortune. Blame, shame, and scolding are not conducive to an overall positive result. You need to have ways to express your dissatisfaction, hurt, upset, and hope for the future without damaging your child's confidence in her ability to go forward in a positive manner.

You don't need to raise your voice, call her names or be abusive. You can tell her you are hurt and upset. You can express those reactions in your own words. Just as you need to let her talk about what happened, how she thinks/feels about it. Then you need to talk together about what you are going to do moving forward.

We all know that shit happens. It is going to come and you are going to have to deal with it. You can do things to make it worse and exacerbate the situation or you can do things to improve things. Usually you do both. Hopefully one way more than the other.

Certainly when that call comes from the police and there is lawbreaking involved, there is a whole other level of concern. Parents hope for the future welfare of their child. Arrests are not a welcome part of that hope.

Most parent calls from the police about teenagers have to do with driving under the influence or being under the influence in some way or some other infraction of the law. They usually don't involve what most would consider gateway activities to a life of crime. Most people don't equate DUI with criminal activity. Until someone gets hurt and then it is a much more serious situation.

Regardless of the "crime" a parent's role is to be the believer and supporter of their child.

If the call is from the hospital it is entirely another matter. When life is in the balance, priorities shift. I often tell parents that having my child home and healthy at the end of the day is a good day and one for which I am grateful and thankful. When your child's health is not perfect your life is significantly affected. You think, you worry, you plan, you do this and you do that, and you worry some more. And you hope.

Hope is healing. Sometimes you have to dig deep to find it. If you can't find it, find someone to help you carry the burden. Without hope, life becomes pretty grim.

60

FAMILY TIME

While I am not overly knowledgeable about how our ancestors in the Stone Age went about their parenting, I imagine that when they got to eat it was probably more of a family event than it is nowadays. Many of the teenagers I speak with eat more meals by themselves than they do with their parents. I only have anecdotal stories to back me up here, but when I ask parents if they eat with their children more or less than they did with theirs most parents tell me they eat far fewer meals with their children.

There are numerous studies that point out that the children who have more meals with their families learn language earlier, are better readers, and get better grades in school. The icing on the cake is a study from Children's Hospital in Cincinnati which found that children who ate dinner with their families at least five times a week were the least likely to take drugs, feel depressed, or get into trouble.

I think most of us would agree that family dinners are a foundation of family life. Having time to be together and talk about the events of the day, how things are going, and whatever else pops up bonds a family together. Even the outbursts and arguments link family members together. It is that "for better or worse, good times and bad" thing. Families go through them all together.

Less family meals usually results in less closeness. When you miss opportunities to be with your children there is a gap of experience that eludes you. The more of those opportunities that are missed the more of your child's life that is not shared. Shared experiences bring people together. Good, bad, or ugly those experiences get stored in the "we" collection. We have all reminisced with people about the good and the bad times.

The sharing of food is a traditional communion time in people's lives. We join together at birthday parties, weddings, funerals, and most other occasions. While I want to encourage you to prioritize taking the time to eat together, I really want to encourage you to talk together. Eat and talk.

Even when you are in a hurry and standing up eating over the sink, there is opportunity to speak together. Something parents of teenagers often don't get enough of. Parents often don't have viable entry points into their child's life and can feel left out. When you are eating together you know your child is going to be there for at least a few minutes and you can eat and talk which is usually easier than just talking.

Having your hands and mouth occupied makes it easier to communicate because it is less stressful. You can always pretty easily say nothing because the fact that you are eating gives you a fallback position. You can always say the reason you are not talking is because you are focusing on enjoying your food. Which is not a bad thing.

When you are eating there is greater comfort and acceptance of silence than there is when you are just sitting around the living room and talking. Plus the intake of food is a stress reliever in and of itself. Feeding satiates hunger and that satiation affects mood. Maybe not a lot, because we all have had heated arguments at the table, but usually that argument is a little less extreme than if the food were not present.

While eating can provide an opportunity for talking, other activities that you do together can also be a springboard. Whether you are sitting at a baseball game or making dinner together it is easier to talk around what you are doing when the whole focus is on the conversation. If you aren't eating with your child you can find something to do together and have snatches of conversation. One thing you could do together is some "chore" around the house. If dishes have to be washed, one can wash and one can dry. If leaves are to be raked, use two rakes. If sheets are to be switched, grab an end.

I want to suggest a family activity that I learned from Michael Thompson, PhD whose books, if you have yet not read, you would be well served to check out. This activity is called the Family Table. Michael was told by some parents about how most nights the family would eat dinner together and then after all the cleaning up was done the family would come back to the table with their various after-dinner activities. The children would bring school books, iPads, and their phones. The parents would bring a book or magazine or their laptops and everyone would fill the next period of time together at the table involved in their various activities. Sometimes there would be cross talk and other times things would be silent.

Many of the families where I work have fewer dinners together than they do apart. Most people know having meals together does bring a family closer. And many people know that doing activities apart is necessary and sometimes invaluable. Regardless of how often you eat together you might consider proposing some after-dinner table activity. It is akin to when families used to adjourn to a family room and just hang out together. It doesn't really matter what room you hang out in after dinner. Spending some time close to one another even if you are not all doing the same thing is a bonding activity. Sure, it is best when you are all watching TV together or looking at a YouTube video or collectively engaged, but even a little family together time does increase connections. And, I know most nights your teen will probably prefer to be in his room and his world.

However our predecessors defined their home life, my guess is your present home life is not exactly like it was when you were growing up. Generations evolve and how your parents created their home, while influential to you, is probably something you have adapted to suit your values and needs along with those of your partner.

You may have never actually stopped and thought about your own personal definition of home life. Chances are things just evolved on their own without much conscious thought. When you were dating the other parent you may have talked about raising children and religious/spiritual beliefs along with stories of your own parents' upbringing of you. As your relationship developed, a shared way of doing things evolved. Your thoughts about childrearing that were voiced are now put to the test of experience.

There are ways you do things differently than your parents that you like and there are ways you have built your life that you might wish were more like your parents. The values and atmosphere of your household growing up influences what you bring to your own home which then has to blend with what your partner is bringing. When you reflect back on what you wanted your home to be like, there are probably some things that are just the way you hoped (give or take a little) and some things you wish were better. There were probably some things you may have thought that now you see differently and some things you never anticipated or thought about.

Can you think of some ways your home life now is as good as or better than you had wanted?

_____

_____

_____

Can you think of some ways your home life now is not what you had hoped?

_____

_____

_____

Most people can find the pros and cons of anything. There is a lot of gray in life. You see other families and how they are raising their children and it is hard not to do some comparing and contrasting. You get a glimpse of some other child's life and you note the differences between him and your child.

Their child is doing something you wish your child were doing. Many parents see those differences and blame themselves and or their child. Some parents ask the other parents what they are doing to help their child do such and such. Sometimes those parents can teach you a thing or two. Sometimes their child is just more talented in one area than your child. That usually doesn't feel good, especially if you had hopes for your child that now need to be tucked away.

Every parent is continually learning how to parent. Just like every child is learning now to be a child. All our roles evolve with us. Whatever shape your home life is in, it will continually evolve. Your goal is to help it improve.

I imagine your parents conveyed a message to you that they hoped your life would be as good as or better than their own. Parents want their children to "succeed" in life and make things even better for themselves than they were able to provide. Parents want their children to enjoy, value, and participate in life in more fulfilling ways than they are able to achieve.

While many children have grown up and been able to expand what their parents created, there are many grown children who believe they have not been able to do as well as their parents. One may have done better financially but may lack the sense of security that their parents felt. Others may enjoy the greater freedoms they have found, but miss the pace of life their parents had. As with most things, evolution brings its own pros and cons.

You could also be happier and living a better all around life than your parents. Or the same. Or any number of variances which you may or may not compare and contrast. Comparing yourself or your child or your family to anyone else is a mixed proposition. You can always find the better and the worse. Which mostly makes you feel better and worse.

I come from the "accept what is and do what you can to make things better" school of thought. I don't like to invest a lot of time in recrimination, blame, and beating myself up. I certainly can get disappointed when I look at someone else and wish my life were a little more like theirs, but rather than dwell on it I like to note it, throw in a brief pep talk to myself, and endeavor to learn from it and do better going forward. Sometimes getting from the disappointment to endeavoring to do better can take longer than other times.

Let's get back to you and your child.

How are you building the kind of life you want for him?

Are you as close and connected to him as you would like to be?

_____

Are there elements of your relationship with your child that you wish were better?

_____

Most parents would acknowledge that they would like an even better relationship with their child. Who doesn't want their close relationships to be as flourishing as they can be? It doesn't matter if it is with your child or anyone else. We all want our relationships to be as good as they can be.

There is no shame in wishing things were better. There might even be some shame or lingering guilt if you didn't try now and then to do something to improve things. Since I have no interest in having you feel ashamed or guilty, let's focus on something simple you can do to improve your relationship with your child.

Keep in mind that your relationship with your child is going to be a long-term one.

That's it.

You may or may not stay close with your child's other parent, but your child will always be your child. When you think about 5, 10, 20, 30 plus years from now I imagine you would still like to have a meaningful relationship with your child. Keep that in mind as you go through the ups and downs of your relationship. You are in it for the long haul.

It is important for parents to let their child know that they will always be there for him and will always love and care for him. You can discuss what that means when you get down to the details, but don't let the small print get in the way of delivering the larger message. I am your parent. I will always be your parent. And I will do whatever I can to help you make your life as good as it can be.

I am sure we have all had the experience of hearing ourselves say something and realizing it was a direct quote from one of our parents. That may not exactly be a conversation with your parent, but it means you are carrying them with you and bringing their values to your child. That can be a "for better or for worse" thing. Either way parenting is a long haul operation, generation to generation.

Parent/child relationships are the most sustaining of any relationships. Not necessarily the best. But the longest. So remember that these teen years too shall pass. While you are doing your best to guide your child through remember he is one of the people you want close by when you blow out your birthday candles.

I do believe the greatest gift one can have in this life is a child. The relationship may not always be what you want it to be, but from where I stand, loving that child for the duration of your life is the best part of being alive.

SECTION 9:

COLLEGE BOUND AND OUT OF THE HOUSE

61

THE COLLEGE APPLICATION PROCESS

Before we get into this chapter let me confess that I work at a school were 99% of the graduates go to college. There is an expectation that students and their families have that everyone who goes to the school goes to college.

Since only 75% of high school students graduate high school and of those that graduate approximately another 75% attend college, needless to say, my professional experience is skewed. As such, what I have to say about the college application process may be of greater benefit to those parents who hope/expect their child will go to college. While a lot of college application process is applicable to the job application process there are considerable differences. Parents of high school students are much more likely to be involved in the college process than they are in the finding work process. Which means there is a greater likelihood of conflict.

One other thing to start things off.

Given that over a third of Millennials are living at home after college, helping your child transition to college may be one of several transitions you will play an active role in as your child builds her life. When your child heads off to college you never know when she will be regularly sleeping in her bed again. The statistics for completion of college differ for fulltime and part-time students and public and private schools so it is difficult to give a reliable percentage of students who start and finish college, but if pressed you could put it at around 60%. Which means some of your children may be coming home sooner than you thought.

For many children in America, going to college is something they want to do. They look forward to it. College is when education gets meatier and the parties get wilder. Before they go to college most high school seniors will tell you that they expect college to be among the best years of their life. Looking back, many adults agree.

Students usually don't enter high school with the idea that it will be among the best years of their life. Although, I think for many it ranks right up there. It is just that the expectation isn't as high and there are lots of grown-ups with horror stories. Many adults, looking back, consider it among the worst times of their life.

Because going to college is held in such esteem there is a lot of pressure that accompanies the whole process known as college admissions. Some might say it starts at conception as I can recall hearing of a parent who enrolled her fetus in a highly regarded nursery school as a first step towards getting into a prestigious elementary school, middle school, high school, college, and life.

Since I work in a high school I am going to start there. I work at a school that, like a lot of private schools, has college counselors whose jobs are to help students get into the college that fits best. College counselors talk about the fit; parents talk about the best.

I am not a college counselor but that doesn't stop parents from talking to me about the role they should play in the process. And it doesn't stop me from responding.

Basically I tell them that at the end of high school their child will be heading off to college and will, at that point, take on a substantially larger role in the running of her own life. There will be no curfews, no parents asking if she has done her homework, no attendance taken in some of her classes, and little structure. Their child will be much more responsible for her own life.

In the last years of high school, a parent's responsibilities include assisting their child to develop her ability to manage freedom and responsibility. You don't want there to be too big a leap from senior year to freshman year. As a student leaves high school and enters college the familiar structure, safety net, and rules of behavior slip away. The increase in independence and how to handle it are among the first lessons she will need to learn. Often not without some bumps in the road. Which is why any lesson-learning she can gain while she still lives with you is good college prep.

Parents have a lot of anxiety about the college process. For many families, this is their child's first step into big-time decision-making. There will need to be choices made about what schools to apply to, what tests to take, what schools to visit, what essay to write, what application to send early and a host of other tasks that are at once comprehendible and overwhelming. Only to be followed by which college to attend.

Most parents that went to college applied to a few schools and there was nowhere near the competition there is today. Now students are applying from all over the world and most students send out at least twice as many applications as their parents did. Each year you read that college acceptance rates are getting lower and lower. Which makes more students apply to more places, which makes more schools more competitive. Throw in people from around the world who usually end up paying more tuition and therefore are more financially rewarding to colleges and you have a growing formula for uncertainty and stress.

When parents know there is a big task to do that has many moving parts, they have learned from their own experience to be anxious and not procrastinate too much. When the task really needs to be done by your child, who you increasingly have less power over, the uncertainty is multiplied. Parents know their kids. They know if their child will handle the whole thing herself in a proficient and highly competent manner. They also know if their child will drag her feet over the whole thing and maybe not get the task done without their stepping in and doing some heavy lifting. Or so they believe. You never know.

Parents tend to have more anxiety about the whole process than their children because they have less control. Their anxiety is infectious and spreads to all around them. Seniors tell me they have more arguments with their parents over the application process than they did in the rest of high school.

It's understandable. The pressure is on. There is a timetable. There is competition. And lots of tasks to worry and argue over. Plus there is all the uncertainty:

- There is the uncertainty about which classes to take and which tests to take.
- There is the uncertainty of choosing where to apply.
- There is the uncertainty of being able to write a compelling essay and complete the application process itself.
- There is the uncertainty of being rejected or accepted.
- There is the uncertainty about making the best decision about where to go.
- There is the uncertainty of next year.

But there are certainties, too:

- There is the certainty that there are more colleges out there than you will ever know about.
- There is the certainty that there are good colleges out there that you will never apply to because you don't know anything about them.

Right off the bat you know you are not going to be doing a thorough job. You have to trust your college counselor, your child, and yourself to be able to find the most appropriate colleges to apply to. If everything turns out okay, everyone is happy enough. If things do not work out as hoped there can be a lot of recriminations. It is a challenging process filled with way more uncertainty than certainty.

There is also the certainty as the year progresses that this is the last year of your child's childhood as you have known it.

I tell parents to let their children decide as much as they can handle. If parents are not comfortable with their child going to school outside the state they need to say so. I have had parents say they would not pay if their child went here or there. While I don't like that stance, I can accept it. If you hold strong beliefs or have direct demands you are best served by putting them out there early and not have your child bump into them when the stakes have gotten higher.

Just be prepared for a backlash.

All I can tell you is the stronger your position, the stronger the reaction may be.

Which has pros and cons.

You may not welcome your child's response to you, but you may be proud of yourself for demonstrating standing up for your beliefs. You may also be proud of her for standing up for hers.

If something is important to you or non-negotiable you need to get it out in the open early in the process. If your finances limit your options, explain the available options. If your values limit the places you will support your child attending, let her know what you would support. The sooner your child knows the parameters of her choices the easier it will be for her. I have had students tell me they appreciated the limits their parents put on their choices as it made things easier, and while they might have preferred more options, they didn't really mind the ones placed on them.

While I favor flexibility and entrusting your child with much of the decision-making, I know there are parents who have strong beliefs. I had a student tell me that his father told him he needed to get a finance degree so he would have a job when he graduated. His mother told him she wanted him to go to her alma mater which was a pretty prestigious place and it didn't really matter what he choose as his major. I, of course, asked him what he wanted to do. He told me he had no idea.

There are a couple of issues here that are hard to unravel. On the one hand, these parents want to give their best advice to their child. On the other hand, they want to empower their son to trust his ability to make decisions. I don't fault these parents for sharing their values as their hearts are in a good place. I did, however, speak to them about how they were going to build their son's capacity to trust his decision-making ability. The father told me that if his son just went the route he suggested then he would be able to turn over the rest of his career decisions. The mother told me that she knew her son would find happiness at her alma mater, which the father said was fine except they didn't have a finance degree and the one business degree they offered was not that well regarded.

I asked them what would happen if their son opted for a different college and major entirely. They both told me they thought he would be making a poor decision, but they would continue to love and support him. I told them to make sure they also conveyed that message to him, but might leave out the poor decision part because perhaps they weren't seeing and valuing their son's values as much as they wanted him to value theirs.

Differences of opinions come up all the time between parents and children. Sometimes parents enforce their position. Other times they are more willing to concede the decision.

This father had a belief that finance is a secure path to take while the mother believed the name and network of her alma mater will pave the way to success. What is missing in the discussion is what the son likes, values, believes, and wants for himself. From my experience most high school students don't know what they want to do for their career, but they mostly want to have a job they like that earns them a good living. Since that goal is obtainable from many directions I tend to lean towards the "Honey, whatever you do I know you will do it well" direction.

I had a senior tell me that his grandfather and father had both gone to Harvard and his father told him that if he wanted to have a successful life he too should go to Harvard. The boy told me he liked his father's big house and fancy car, but he didn't need those things. He wanted a different kind of success that didn't necessarily translate into a larger income and more prestigious degree. Even though his grades might very well have gotten him into Harvard, he elected to apply other places.

I have told that story to parents. Then I asked them if they were that child's father would they be:

A) Disappointed?

B) Happy?

C) Both disappointed and happy?

D) Other?

Most parents lean toward C but it is not a runaway. Parents want their children to be successful. Parents know what has worked for them and try to pass it along.

Children follow suit on some things and go their own way on others. While going to Harvard had meaning and value for the father and grandfather it doesn't hold the same place for the child. He does want to be successful. But in his own way. Most parents I share this story with like that the student wants to create his own path and worry about it because it is unfamiliar.

Parents also know that what a child holds to be true while she is in high school may change as she gets older. It is akin to the Winston Churchill quote: "Show me a young conservative and I'll show you someone with no heart. Show me an old liberal and I'll show you someone with no brains." While I do not entirely agree with that sentiment, I do think it speaks to people's values shifting as they age. That said, I am not sure there is lot of value in forcing your child to do something she really does not want to do. Maybe down the road she will thank you, but along the way it could be a rough passage.

The message is the same whether the child goes to Harvard or anyplace else: I love you, believe in you, and I will support you.

Children need to establish their own worth and identity.

High school is a critical stage in human development that we all go through. We have to discover our own competency in our most grown up state to date. We know we will get other chances later on, but in high school there is a lot of focus on how things feel right now. As you get older you might look back at the drama level in middle and high school and think it was ramped up, but when you are in the midst of it, it all feels very real.

As much as students need to think about their future and get involved in planning for their future, for the most part they are prisoners of the moment. This moment in your child's life is one where she will need to marshal her energies in ways she has never done and actively begin the process of leaving home. Having your trust will help her. The increasing responsibility and freedom you give her translates to trust and helps build her confidence for the future.

Parents and students conflict about the level of parental involvement in the college application process. I have known parents who were totally hands off and ones who pretty much did everything. At my school, our college counselors tell a story about a parent who filled out their student's application to one school but made the mistake of putting her own name on the application.

Frankly I think you need to speak with your child about what level of involvement she wants you to have and then do your best to honor that. Since many parents have difficulty fully trusting their child to handle the whole process I think it wise to set up check-in dates every other week in the fall of senior year and a few times in the second half of junior year. I would try to keep the word 'college' out of my discussions before then.

Your child may complain when she knows in advance that she will be sitting down with you and going over where she is in the process, but it is usually helpful. Having scheduled appointments serves to combat procrastination, although many a child has waited till right before the appointment to do their work. As long as she does it by the appointed meeting time I would back off and just remind her about the next appointment. If she is basically on course, congratulate her. If she is behind, ask what you can do to help. Then do that. Try not to jump in when not asked.

62

CHOOSING A COLLEGE

As I drove around one day I heard Jim Rome, the sports commentator, talking about the conflict he had with his father over where he was going to college. His dad wanted him to go to a school in Tucson and he wanted to go to one in Santa Barbara. On the one hand, he thought it ought to be his decision since he was the one who was going to spend four years there. On the other hand, his father said as long as he was paying Jim was going to go to Arizona State. Jim didn't relay exactly how the final decision was made but he ended up at the University of California in Santa Barbara. Lucky him.

There often is a difference between where parents want their children to go to college and where the child wants to go. With difference of opinion comes conflict. A little conflict can be a positive thing. A nagging, perpetuating clash of wills can get to the point where most everyone in the house would rather be someplace else.

The sanctuary that is your home can be invaded by what we used to call "bad vibrations." Which is the opposite of what the Beach Boys sang about. What was once a comforting, pleasant place to rest can become overrun with tension. People can get hesitant about how to approach each other and every overture is an invitation to injury. You never know what you are going to say that is going to set someone off.

Welcome home.

Senior year, especially the fall, is when I get the most phone calls. Everything gets heightened. Grades mean more. Little moments become big dramas. The application clock keeps ticking. My phone keeps ringing.

I do an exercise at meetings for parents of seniors where I ask them if their child knows what school they would like their child to attend. Most of the parents raise their hands and acknowledge that their children most likely know what they want. I follow that up by asking if they know the school their child most wants to attend. Fewer hands go up.

Much of the time that is because the child doesn't know or is reluctant to tell them.

What do you think is the situation in your family? Do you know where your child wants to go to college and does he know where you hope he will go?

_____

_____

Most students know one, two, or three schools they are interested in before they start their senior year. Some know exactly where they want to go before they enter high school. Some don't want to say these schools out loud. Others bandy it about. Some wear sweatshirts proclaiming their interests.

Many students don't know a lot about the colleges they are interested in aside from the name, a few people who went there, how their athletic teams fared, and perhaps some other noteworthy item.

Often, students and parents want to talk to our college counselors and ask what the counselor thinks would be a good fit. They know the list they have in their heads is forged by personal interests and connections and they don't really know a lot about the college landscape. Parents find out along the way names of colleges they never heard of that might very well be an excellent choice for their child.

Where I work the parents and students log in to the website Naviance.com. If you are not familiar with it, schools use it to help students gather information about colleges, fill out forms, make applications, and otherwise monitor their college process. Starting in sophomore year, students log in to see if their grades and test scores match up with other graduates who got into the various colleges they are interested in.

Parents tend to like to be able to monitor their child's activity and see if he is doing what he tells them he is doing. Kids tend to not like that. My compromise position is for parents to use Naviance as a reference and explore various colleges. Parents can look for schools throughout the world and see if their child's test scores, grades, and extra-curriculars would match the school's acceptance criteria. I think parents ought to stay away from looking at what their child is doing. But, like that open drawer in your child's room, it is hard not to look in.

Most of us can name some of the Ivy League schools and the ones with well-known athletic teams as well as our local schools and a few places we know for various reasons. There are more excellent colleges whose names you don't know than ones you do. Most of us have no reason to know the names of colleges because we aren't buying anything from them, selling anything to them, or hear much about them unless something goes wrong.

Until maybe we have a college-bound child.

Sometimes you get flyers in the mail. Other times you notice you are paying more attention anytime the subject of college crosses your path. Whatever you do, it really would help you and your child if you all would consider opening your minds to the idea that there could be an excellent match for your child that you do not know or barely know about. While name recognition matters to some people more than others, getting the most out of your college experience matters to all.

Choosing a college is a bit like choosing a lover. You can't meet everybody in the world and then decide who you want to love. You get to meet some until you decide to love one.

There are just too many choices. Too much to know.

Even if you knew everything about every school and your child got accepted to all of them, it still comes down to practicalities, values, who gets to make the final decision, and how that decision will be supported.

You love a school because it has a great reputation. Your child loves it because it is in Santa Barbara. Who gets to make the final choice? The one who is going or the one who is paying? Or has paid for most everything so far? Or who thinks they know best?

The college application process is a contained universe where your child can only learn so much before he has to make a commitment to apply somewhere. Which schools he is going to apply to is your child's first big decision. He knows what you want, he knows the names of the more well-known schools, he is aware of how little he knows about the vast college universe. He also becomes increasingly aware as he goes through the process that he has a lot of control over where he decides to apply. He comes to realize he doesn't have to apply some place if he doesn't want to. Unless you stand over him and force him to push send or you fill out the application yourself and send it in, chances are if your child does not want to apply somewhere he won't. As frustrating as that is for you, it makes him feel powerful. And usually a little scared too.

Most students apply to some of their parents' choices for schools and some of their own. There is a cost in time and money when doing applications, so families need to decide how much they want to invest in the application process. Since there are no guaranteed results students tend to be guided by the one third application principle—one third of the schools are a stretch, one third are good possibilities, and one third ought to be close to a slam dunk. If you want to go to a certain college, why not aim high? But you want to make sure you end up somewhere.

Certainly the name of the college you attend and the people you meet at college will assist you in transitioning to the next stage of your life after college. And yes, it very well could land you more interviews if you go to Harvard than Unknown U. Statistically it has been shown to have some small yet significant economic advantage having a degree from a prestigious college. Yet there is not much solid research regarding any real quality of life difference between the vast majority of people who graduate from colleges you have never heard of and the ones that usually come to mind. So apply where you want and go where you can and be happy. It is college after all, the last big blowout before adulthood becomes a bigger issue.

The application process is a parent's introduction to another chapter in learning just how much it actually costs to raise a child. You knew it was going to be expensive but might not have realized just how expensive. Unless you have a lot of wealth, supporting your child's college application process and costs of visiting or otherwise learning about schools is expensive. Worse yet, it is just the tip of the iceberg.

For most parents the cost of rearing their child is more than they spend on anything else with the possible exception of their home.

I don't know a better way to invest your money.

I am fortunate in that the school where I work is able to provide college counselors so the students are actively supported throughout the process. The counselors meet individually with students and their parents to assist in creating a list. At the high school where my daughter went to school she had to create her own list and got very little support from the school counselors.

When I see the level of support my school provides it makes me upset that not all schools are able to provide the same range of services that can help students get the most out of their school years. I appreciate that there are plenty of pulls on where tax monies ought to be spent and how much we ought to pay in taxes. For my money, education ought to be at the top of the list.

If you are not fortunate enough to have your child in a school where they provide a high level of support you might consider having your child and you talk to someone outside the school about the college application process. It doesn't have to be a paid educational consultant although it is a flourishing business. It can be a parent who has been through it before or anyone else who is not emotionally invested in the decision.

Most parents I talk with say with varying degrees of conviction that they want their child to go to whatever school he wants. Some have qualifiers. Some not. There is always a percentage who want their alma mater on the list or a well-known school whose name resonates with them. Others want their child close. But most want their child to go to the college of his choice. So long as he does sufficient research to be able to make that decision based on more than a name or sport or location.

There is no correct amount of schools to have on the list. I have heard students apply to as many as 23 and as few as 1. At my school most come in with 8-10 applications divided between what their parents want, what they want, what they really want, what they are willing to accept, and one wild card.

Whatever school is last on the list is still on the list and needs to be valued because that is where you might end up going. "Love your list" is what our college counselors say.

I don't know if you can love 8-10 schools from afar. I'd go for loving some and hoping to love the rest if need be.

I tell students to be happy if they get into their first choices and sad if they don't. Celebrate your wins, mourn your losses, and move on. Be willing and able to open your mind and heart to the rest if need be. You never can tell what the future holds, but you will be there to help it unfold. Wherever you go, you will be able to make it a valuable and enjoyable experience. And if it isn't, you can transfer.

63

A FEW MORE WORDS ABOUT THE COLLEGE APPLICATION PROCESS

I don't need to tell you that there is a lot of pressure to get into a good college. The better student you are, often the more pressure to get into a more prestigious college. With an increasing interest around the world in attending American colleges and there not being a lot of new colleges added to the marketplace it is difficult to know who colleges will accept. There are many valedictorians who applied but were not accepted to Harvard. If they can't get in there is not an abundance of hope for rest of the student body.

I wonder when American students will whet their appetite for foreign universities. It is only a matter of time. I personally might aim for those countries where there is a better quality of living than our own. That way, even if your child elects to stay in the area she went to college in, at least it will be in a country with a better prognosis than our own.

Since looking outward is probably not going to happen any time soon, and since there doesn't seem at this time to be more demand than there is supply of colleges, high school students usually focus on getting in to the "best" college they can. In most cases best means most well-known. Unfortunately, most of the students in the top half of the classes aim for a small amount of schools. That drive to be in that select group does more than create a high level of stress and uncertainty. It also causes students to think about what they could do to make their resume stronger. They could take a harder course, do more community service, and be active in something aside from social media. It also can get your child to consider cheating at school, exaggerating her accomplishments, and otherwise straying off the ethical path.

Most students I know rarely cheat, bend the truth only a little and, like most everyone else, expand the boundaries on their ethical behaviors on occasion. That said there are some statistics that say less than 5% of students have never cheated. Sadly there is a significant level of social acceptance of the behavior. Some students tell me their parents encourage them to embellish experiences on their applications. It is not always easy for a student to stay the course when her parents encourage her to exaggerate and she knows other students who are cheating and massaging the truth to get ahead.

It is not unlike athletes who take banned substances to get an edge or someone in business that misrepresents herself on her resume. Most all of us feel some pressure to get ahead and that pressure can sometimes manifest itself in behaviors we prefer to keep secret.

I don't want to get on a high horse here, and I am certainly not here to judge you. Yet I do want you to take a few moments and reflect on your role in promoting, encouraging, and supporting your child's progress toward future goals. If you encourage her to fudge the truth in some way be prepared for her to continue to adorn the truth in ways you may never know.

Situational ethics is something many people justify. People tell themselves, "It is okay to cheat here and now because it is not really that big a deal, but I would not cheat over there because that is not right." You rationalize your position to allow yourself to proceed without too much burden on your psyche.

I am not a purist. I know people fabricate the truth. I certainly have. I just want to remind you that you are a role model. Just since you say it is okay to misrepresent yourself on a college application does not mean your child won't take that situationally ethical stance and apply it elsewhere. And, more than likely, eventually at you.

Her lying to you is not the worst thing; you probably have lied to your parents, boss, and others on occasion. I would just aim for having those occasions be occasional.

I have a theory about people that get ahead in the work world. I certainly don't think it is a hundred percent true, but from my experience I have yet to meet the person that did not do something unethical to get ahead. Maybe you looked the other way when somebody did something or you told a partial truth or you did something that you knew in your heart of hearts was not "right." I don't like that people feel the need to compromise their higher values and I am not surprised when they do. As a parent I think you don't want to encourage your child to bend her truth or look the other way. I also don't think you need to shame her when she does. Because, really, fabricating the truth is a life skill you don't want to get too good or practiced at, but you do want to be able to do well enough when called upon.

Most people exaggerate the truth now and then and explain circumstances to their best advantage. While it is not ideal, it is usually not harmful. Yet I think there is a line between stretching the truth on occasion and teaching your child that they are not good enough as they are.

Each time we misrepresent our truth we are in essence saying our truth is not good enough.

Certainly some truths are better than others. An A on a test is usually better than a B. Unless you cheated in some way to get that A, in which case I am not so sure that take away is better.

If you child received B's that could be a major accomplishment which resulted from hard work. I would celebrate that. If she got the B because she did not really apply herself I would want her to possibly lament that she did not work hard enough to get an A, but I would also want her to know that her B is plenty good enough. A B will take her to some college where other students with the same B's are attending and she will enjoy that she earned her placement. Plus a B in high school does not mean one will lead a B life. It just means she was a B high school student in the grade department. In other areas of high school life she may have earned other grades.

If she is not happy with her academic grade point average, she can consider new ways to apply herself so that perhaps in the future things will be different. Your job is to let her know if she decides to apply herself more fully you believe she will get what she wants. Once again we are talking about effort and your conviction that with greater effort one usually achieves greater results.

As I have mentioned, most therapists are going to come down on the side of natural consequences. You eat the dessert and savor its flavor and bemoan the extra weight. Weight gain is the natural consequence of overeating. You don't need a lecture to learn that. Usually in school the more you apply yourself the better you will do.

If your child chooses not to do something to enhance her resume over the summer she needs to be prepared to face that consequence. She can relax and enjoy the time off and appreciate that choice, and acknowledge that had she applied her efforts in other directions, other options might have presented themselves. The student that worked over the summer loses the relaxation of the summer off but gains some experience and attention by admissions officers. Although I am sure there are admissions officers who place value on taking the summer off. Or at least I hope there are.

Many students I know manage most of their college application process with little input or pressure from their parents. Their parents trust them to handle the process. Well, that trust is conditional as it usually involves the help of a college counselor and an occasional scheduled check-in now and then, along with an intrusive dose of periodic prodding.

Some parents have to hold their children back from working too much. I get more than a few parents in my office lamenting that their child is a workaholic and all they can do is sit back and wonder and now and then whisk their child out for some ice cream. Most parents wish their child did more. Parents share with me many differing methods used to motivate which basically fall into the stick and the carrot. The reward that will be forthcoming versus the negative consequences which will arrive. Each has its day. I am sure you know by now which approach I favor.

Regardless of how you try to encourage and motivate your child, by the time she is in her mid-teens your influence has been severely diminished. Parents come to me and tell me they have taken everything away and grounded their child to the end of eternity but it is not making any difference. I remind them that Albert Einstein said the definition of insanity is doing the same thing over and over again and expecting a different result.

Then I quickly say something to let them know I don't think they are insane. They are just exasperated parents of teenagers. It is called watching your child grow and behave in some ways you wish she didn't, but feel powerless to affect. Welcome to the club.

Some parents yell, threaten, restrict, plead, beg, and otherwise attempt to get their child to put more effort into her college applications or schoolwork. But most parents learn as their child ages that despite their best efforts to get their child to do what they want about school and related activities, their efforts are not going to yield much.

At some point you need to evaluate if the gain your child receives from your input is worth the strain on your relationship. If your relationship with your child is significantly deteriorating and she does not seem to be stepping up her activity level, maybe you need to try a different way. You can still have input and involvement in her life, but perhaps you need to consider new avenues.

If you are having an uncomfortable amount of conflict around the college process you probably need some outside help. It might be a school counselor, a therapist, family friend, movie, book, or video on YouTube. You can't tell where the influence will come from, but usually you know when your influence has sufficiently dwindled and your frustration has expanded, it's time to unburden yourself on someone other than your child and the other parent.

There is not a lot of joy in beating your head against the wall. Rather than find yourself in continuing skirmishes, see if you can bring in some other voices. Find someone who you can basically trust and ask them to speak with your child. Ideally your child never knows you initiated this. Realistically she usually does. Don't let that stop you.

Share with this other person what you want for your child. Ask if they can help you in some way. They may agree with you and be able to help out. They may not agree with you and decline to help. At best they won't do things exactly the way you want, but perhaps they can have a conversation with your child that you really are not able to manifest.

Since you went to them for help you might want to take into consideration what they have to say to you if not your child. You never know. They might be able to suggest something to you that will help you out. You may get defensive when someone's remarks point out that what you are doing may be part of the problem. Okay, be defensive. But also open yourself to the possibility you could learn something that would help you out. Pathways to discovering new ways to enhance your life abound. It is allowing yourself to travel down them that can be challenging.

Sometimes in life you just need to surrender to what is. Acknowledge a truth in your life. You don't need to give up trying to improve matters. You just need to admit that what is happening is indeed happening, and if you want to make it better, you are going to have to do it. Surrender to that truth. Acceptance is the key, even if it means admitting that what you are doing is not really working the way you had hoped.

Let's pretend you are single and you are at a party only for single people who are looking to meet someone with whom they could have a relationship. Everyone is asked to form a big circle. You look around the group and are asked to pick the 10 people you are most interested in learning more about. Then you go up to each of those people and ask them if, based on all they know about you at this moment, they would like to go on a date with you. Yes or no.

Some people might get 10 positive responses. Some people might get none. Most people would get some. What would it be like for you once you asked them and waited for their reply? I would think for most people there would be some nervousness and some excitement.

When your child applies to colleges, most likely some schools will be interested in her and some won't. And just like you, she will be nervous and excited while she waits. It is not easy to declare your interest in a college and then wait for that school to accept or reject you.

Tom Petty sang that the waiting is the hardest part. I mostly agree with that. The unknown is usually more frightening. Of course, there are times when the waiting is better than the knowing, but even when you get bad news you can strategize about how to proceed while you lick your wounds.

I find that students are so relieved when they finish their applications that the initial stages of waiting are a relief. They know approximately when they will hear and they need to bide their time. They slink into senioritis. They have trouble motivating themselves and begin thinking about the end of high school.

It is a bittersweet time for most.

As the time to hear from schools approaches and as their peers begin to hear, the stress level gets ratcheted up.

Then the letters come, except they are mostly online posts now. There will be something else when you read this as colleges now find the act of acceptance a time of promotion. It is hard to believe that what was once a form letter in the mail is now becoming a tailor-made presentation. It is akin to the senior girl who came to me recently wanting help in trying to figure out how to ask a boy to the prom. It wasn't that she was nervous about him accepting, she was nervous about how great her presentation of "the ask" was going to be. Gone are the days when you just swallowed and walked up to someone and asked. Now you have to make a production of it and get it out to social media instantly so people can comment on it.

Most adults don't have that kind of social stress anymore. Thankfully.

Children can get pretty beaten up in this process.

Rejections, even the ones you thought might come, still hurt.

You get rejected, your friend gets accepted.

You get accepted, your friend gets rejected.

You are surprised and upset that someone else got in and you didn't.

You are relieved you got in and they didn't.

Tough territory to navigate.

Parents need to be available to comfort and celebrate.

This is a poignant time in your child's and your life.

Feelings are delicate and easily bruised.

If a child gets rejected there really is nothing you can do to make it better.

Except to love and be there for her. Let her know you love her just as much regardless of where she goes to school.

Do not make her rejections about you and your disappointment. Don't have your emotional drama trump hers. If you are hurting about her rejections, siphon off the majority of your emotions elsewhere. Save your empathy and commiseration for her if she will have it. You can cry with her but not as loud and long. Cry for her sadness, not yours.

Never tell her she got rejected because she did not do something well enough. She is already thinking that. You don't need to pile on. You don't need to be the critical judge. Be the good, loving, supportive parent who believes in her and knows that everything will be okay.

This is when I bring in the big guns and sing some Bob Marley. I am not the best singer, but these are the best lyrics: "Everything is going to be alright, everything is going to be alright." I would sing it over and over until she tells me to shut up. Then once more.

Most students I speak with worry about just getting accepted to one of the preferred colleges on their list. Then they worry about getting into any of the schools on their list. Once they get one acceptance there is a big exhale, especially if it is in the top cluster. If an acceptance comes from the bottom of their list they wait to hear from all the top ones before opting in. Other students sweat it out waiting to hear good news from anywhere.

There are countless scenarios. All with a portfolio of stress. Even the best news often brings on its own stressors. It is a rollercoaster year in the lives of most families.

Students weigh their decisions on your interests and desires as well as their own. They know you favor certain schools even though you mostly tried to keep your wishes to yourself. They know what you want. They have a growing awareness of what they want. Sometimes your wants and their wants do not line up. There can be conflict as not everyone has the same priorities. As I mentioned earlier, if you have something to say about where you child goes, that is best spoken earlier, but if you haven't said anything now would be a good time or consider keeping your thoughts perpetually to yourself. Throwing a monkey wrench into the mix at the last minute is not recommended.

How important is it to you that your child goes where you want her to go? However you answer that, I encourage you to share your answer directly with your child. Otherwise you will just do it indirectly and it may not be as clear as you or she would like it to be. Put your cards on the table, whatever they are, and then let your child decide what she wants to do.

While I would prefer your child have total control without negative consequences from you, I know that is not always the case. To minimize any negative impulses you might have if she doesn't do things your way, you might as well say: "If you do this, I will do that." Just make sure you are very clear that you know what you will and won't do. If you can afford so much, say so. If you are going to be emotionally challenged to have her far away, say so. Let her know what you prefer and what you can live with. You may not want her three thousand miles away, but if that is where she thinks she will be happiest, you can let her know if you can deal with it. If you can't, well, I would like you to see someone to help you out, but if that is your bottom line truth so be it.

I have had parents tell their child that if she went to college outside of Los Angeles they would not pay. I have had parents tell their child that if he majored in anything but business they would not pay. I have had parents tell their child that if she went to college out of town, they were going to move there. I was not happy to hear these statements, but it was important for the children to hear these truths out loud. They needed to know the consequences of their choices and what their parents would and would not support.

Hopefully, you have these conversations well before applications are going out and not when admissions are being handed out. Once your child knows your position, she is going to be left with making up her mind about which school to apply to and attend. Usually there are pros and cons about every school and your thoughts will weigh in her decision as she balances things out.

This is your child's big decision and she wants to make it a good one. Your stated trust in her ability to make a good choice goes a long way to helping her confidence. But it still doesn't make the choice easy for some students. I had a student tell our Psychology class she was afraid that whatever she decided she would second guess herself. Another student said he tried to never second guess himself. She asked how he did that. He said, he just did that. I don't think she was sure if that was helpful or not. She told me later after class that a bunch of her friends had talked with her about second-guessing and their own concerns.

One year a student came to class and said he could not decide between two colleges. I asked him to leave the room and come back in and announce to the class, "Guess what. I am going to go to _____," then leave the room and go outside, take a moment and come back and say, "Guess what. I am going to go to _____." He did that. Then I asked him after he said both those schools if he had a clearer idea of where he wanted to go. He said he thought so. I asked the class if they knew which school he wanted to attend and they all agreed on which school he really wanted to go to.

The class could feel the greater excitement he felt about the one school over the other and he was able to experience it as well. Usually a person knows which school they want more than another, yet they can be afraid to say it out loud. Especially before they are accepted.

I remind students about the 80/20 decision matrix. You can randomly ask yourself multiple times during the day, if you had to choose, which school would you attend? If 80% of the time you are picking the same school, that is a solid enough majority to make the decision. If your child really feels unable to make a decision I would call the school college counselor or your therapist and have a sit-down conversation. Let her list her pros and cons to an unbiased person who can help sort things out.

There will be students whose path is clear and students who are uncertain about where to apply and where to go. This is their first big-time decision and they want to get it "right." I tell them that wherever they go they will make it right for themselves and if they can't they can go someplace else. Depending on which study you believe, 30-50% of college students transfer from one school to another.

From the moment a high school student starts thinking about college until the day they begin college, they are also dealing with saying goodbye to their youth, their familiarity and their home. Each step of filling out applications, waiting to hear and deciding where to go is also a step away from home. When you get cranky about how she is doing you might want to consider that her steps forward are being met with her having to say goodbye to you and her life as she knows it. Sometimes you need to drag your feet in that process.

64

GRADUATION

Some people have wonderful memories of high school and others not so much. Just like your experience had its ups and downs, so too has your child's. He probably had some dreams about his high school experience that came true and others that didn't. He may have had unexpected moments of triumph and unforeseen moments of defeat.

As with most things he will come to grips with what it is, what it might have been, and what it never was.

The end of senior year is a bittersweet experience on many levels. It is something most high school students can't wait for, and yet as it unfolds, many wish things would slow down.

As excited and nervous as seniors are about what lies ahead, most are also happy and sad about saying goodbye to high school, their childhood, and their home.

Whether you are moving from kindergarten to elementary school, elementary school to high school, or high school to college or real life, each transition comes with some sadness, celebration, and concern about the future. Finishing high school and transitioning to college or work wins the award for most emotionally challenging.

I have parents in my office most of the year welling up about saying goodbye while at the same time stressing over where their child will end up. I had one mother come in, stride directly to the tissue box and grab a handful. Senior year is a very emotional year for your child and you.

In the next chapter I want to talk about letting go, but in this one let's talk about holding on and making the best of the moments you have with your child.

A former student and I often write each other and wax about life and share how we are doing. I told him a story about a moment I had that was very special to me. I knew in the moment that I wanted to always remember that moment so I told myself to look around, take everything in, and remember. I wrote to him about it because I no longer could remember what I saw, but I could remember being there and wanting to remember. He told me that what I really wanted was the memory and not the picture.

I mention that to you to suggest you do want to attend to your memories. Take selfies and post Instagrams all year long to keep you company now and down the road. Try to have more family meals and time together, although the closer you get to graduation the harder that may be. The truth is he would rather be with his friends than be with you. It is not because he loves you less, it is because he figures you will always be there but his friends are going to disperse. This is the end of his school adventures with his friends and if he doesn't hang out with them now, when will he? You, well he can catch you later.

When you are able to grab some time with him, here is something you can do with your graduate and the rest of your immediate family that will hopefully help fill your memory album whether you take selfies or not.

Let's start with what you can do right before graduation.

Give your child a graduation in your home with your immediate family about a week before his school graduation. Everyone will be making a graduation speech. They can write them up and read them or do it spontaneously. Everyone will be speaking even if it is just to say, "Congratulations." Hopefully people would say more but it is up to each family member to decide.

As you read this, graduation may be some time off so here is something you can do now that will attend to how things are in this moment and how they will be going forward.

Give your child a graduation ceremony in your home now. Everyone will be making a graduation speech. They can write them up and read them or do it spontaneously. Everyone will be speaking even if it is just to say "Congratulations." Hopefully people would say more but it is up to each family member to decide.

You may have noticed there is no difference between doing this the week before graduation and doing it today. Today's graduation speech is to acknowledge your child for having graduated from yesterday to today. Just like everyone else he needs to be commended for showing up and being here for another day. In fact, we all need to be celebrated for this. So either continue to go around and give speeches for everyone or focus on one person today and set the date for the graduation party for someone else.

This may seem a bit awkward to do and you certainly can amend this in any way. The idea is to spend time as a family acknowledging the accomplishments and contributions of each family member. Do it informally or formally. I tend to like traditions and ceremony but I also know spontaneity works well and you don't want to find yourself bound by tradition.

We learn new things every day and are indeed graduating to a new day with new information. I don't think these graduation ceremonies need the full on pomp and circumstance. They just are an opportunity to acknowledge the efforts of one another. Whether you do this daily, weekly, monthly or occasionally, there are things that have happened that may not have gotten their due in the moment or are worth re-visiting. This is a time to acknowledge achievement and effort.

In most families there are plenty of occasions when your interactions are focused on less positive matters. Even if less than desirable things may be happening in your teen's life, so too are items worthy of positive recognition. Sometimes they are harder to uncover, but I bet if you try you can pull some out. Remember, at graduation ceremonies you don't hear anyone reminding the graduates that they need to go to their room and do their homework.

65

LEAVING HOME

For most parents taking their child to college and leaving her there is an emotionally challenging event. Personally, having my child leave our home to go to college was the worst part of being a parent. Our sacred duty as parents is to prepare our children to make it in the world and to let them go and wish them well. I know that. But I don't have to like it.

The day my daughter started college I put a lot of effort into carrying boxes and bags and trying to be of good nature. But as her room got set up and her mother and I became less needed it was all I could do to not cry. I knew my daughter didn't want me to tear up as my tears usually trigger hers and that wasn't what she wanted on this day. Her mother and I saved the bulk of our crying for when we were back in the car and could freely sob. We sat in that car a long time before heading out to get some comfort food.

Many parents feel emotional whenever they think about their child leaving home. Having your child move out of the house is very much a bereavement. The way of life you have known for so many years is coming to an end. For some that may also bring great relief and a rebirth. For others it will bring emptiness and loss. For many it will evoke a range of reactions and actions.

 Even if your child is moving down the block, things are going to be different in the home. Some prefer not to talk about it. Some prefer to talk a little and then put it in the back of their minds. Others want to dwell on it. There is no right or wrong here; I just want you to talk about moving out now and then with your child.

I had a recent graduate's mother come visit me after she dropped her daughter off at college. She told me she thought it would be a good idea for her family to take a two-week road trip that ended at her daughter's college. She said it ended up being a good news/bad news kind of situation. It wasn't emotionally difficult leaving her daughter at college because by the time they got there everyone hated each other. Road trips can do that to you.

I had another parent tell me the parting words his mother gave him. As she walked away down the hallway filled with students and parents, she waved goodbye and said in a voice too many could hear, "If you get her pregnant you marry her." (Who says kids don't listen and remember what their parents say?) He told me not only does he vividly remember what his mother said to him, but he was teased about that throughout college and to this day with his close friends. But, he admitted, he *had* been careful enough along the way to be able to marry first before impregnating anyone.

Regardless of how you feel about taking your child to college, let this be about her. Don't let your emotional neediness get in the way of giving her an encouraging send-off. Don't stay longer than she wants you to. Remind her you love her, believe in her, and are there for her any time she needs you. Then bravely smile and leave.

Save your big emotional discharge for when you are not with her. Sometimes she needs you to be emotionally resilient. This is one of those times. Don't let her entrance to college be overtaken by your need for her to see your demonstration of how much you care. Let her know you will miss her and you will be fine. Even if you are unsure.

The fact is, your child will ultimately move out. It starts early, with those first nights away, and continues in spurts as children slowly but surely move away from their parents. Your job is to reassure her and yourself that all will be well. As Gabe Dixon sings: "All will be well, Even after all the promises you've broken to yourself, All will be well, You can ask me how but only time will tell."

I had a former student now in college tell me that her mother always cried a lot every time she returned to school from a vacation. Each year it got harder instead of easier. The amount of time between return visits increased and a growing awareness took place with both her and her mother that at the end of college there might yet be another move. Maybe back. Or maybe to another city or state where she might build a permanent home.

This college student told me her mother's sadness made it harder for her. She thought about staying closer to home to comfort her mother, but realized that might not be ultimately in her best interest. She was torn. On the one hand she too was sad when she left and missed being closer to her mother, but she also wanted to build a life of her own, and she wanted her mother to be happy for the life her daughter was building.

Other children have told me their parents make the coming and going easy and still it is painful for them to leave. When it comes to coming and going, I would much prefer to be meeting my daughter at the airport than saying goodbye to her. Plain and simple, it is sad when she leaves. We always embrace and usually cry because we don't like being so far away from one another. Yet as great as the pleasure I derive from being with her, the love I have for her finding her own path and building her own wonderful life is greater. Not by a lot. But by enough.

Whether you are going to celebrate or mourn when your child leaves home, it will happen. Between this moment and that one, you have some time to consider your hopes and plan for what you are going to do. Just as your child goes through a college admission process or a job application process, so too must you address what you are going to do after she leaves.

I tell parents that as soon as their child starts the college application process, they too need to start their own next-phase process. In addition to bugging their child about how she is doing with her college applications, they need to be bugging themselves about what they are doing about their next phase. A child's graduation is also the parents'.

You need to plan for your future. Which, it turns out, may include your child moving back home. In 2012, even with the economy improving, a record 36% of Millennials lived in their parent's home. While this may be due in large part to the economy, in a study by Clark University a large percentage of parents said their grown child lives with them because "we get along well" and not just because of finances. As the economy improves the percentage decreases, but it doesn't get down to zero and you never know on which side of the percentages you are going to end up.

In most families relationships improve after the child leaves home and they continue to improve as the child gains more distance and greater perspective. When your teenager becomes 25 she will interact with you very differently than when she was 17. Most parents report better relationships with their children after college than during high school. This is mostly due to the fact that when children move away from their home and get some distance from their parents, they start to see their parents more as individuals and not just parents.

We all learn from our experiences that living with people is not the easiest thing. It is a lot easier visiting a friend for a few days than it is to live with them. It will likely be this way with your child. So, even though you may get into heated situations while your child is a teenager, try to keep some perspective on the long-term. Build your relationship now so it can sustain itself and grow.

When your child does head off to college or moves out of the house there will be new questions for you to consider:

- How often do you call/text/Skype/write?
- How often do you send a care package? What ought to be in it?
- When do you see her again? How soon is too soon to make plans?

The situations keep evolving.

You are now involved in redefining your relationship. Not that one is not always redefining their relationships. But this time you are doing it from afar. How much space do you give your child? How inquisitive ought you to be?

Not that long ago you knew much more about her friends, classes, and activities even though you complained about not knowing as much as you used to know. Now you have to deal with even more uncertainty. Many parents have a high level of interaction with their children through high school. Even though that level might continue or taper off only a little once their child moves away, they still come out with less information.

Parents are left to worry more and know less. Or know less and worry less. For those who like certainty and want a greater degree of control, the uncertainty can be unnerving at first. See if you can find other ways to settle your nerves than to reach out to your child. Restrain yourself in her direction, but open yourself to others for support. Trust that no news is good news or at least not bad news.

"Don't worry about what you don't know" would seem to be a good motto to try to take to heart. And, when and/if the shit hits the fan, you will find out and deal with it then. In the interim, hope she is enjoying herself and engaging in activities that serve her well.

Trusting that everything will be alright is not always an easily accessible road for parents, but it is one that bit by bit finds its way into your life. Most parents always have a level of concern/worry about their children, yet absence does provide a shift. At first, not knowing might cause more worry, but the lack of daily contact does give way to your thoughts receding.

When a child leaves the home, parents can devote a certain amount of time worrying about her wellbeing and being sad about missing her. Whether you have one child and now you have an empty nest or have several child and one less in the home, the process is the same. The attention that went to that child now gets dispersed differently.

Some children go off to summer camps or do activities away from home over the summer, but for most families, college is the first extended time the family has away from one another. Be it going off to college or leaving home to get a place of her own and a job, no one really knows how it will go. Sure you will worry about her. You don't really know how well she is handling herself. You can hope and wish for the best, but you have to rely on your child to make her way without your direct support. Much like you had to trust her when you dropped her off at kindergarten, you know you have to trust her to make her way in the world. And, when she needs you she knows how to find you.

You know she is not going to do things perfectly. At times she might want to give up. She might even want to come home. Or move someplace else.

You don't know the future. All you have is your trust in your child's ability to make her way. Whether that trust is great or small you have to rely on her as your parents had to rely on you. And, if she seriously falters she will let you know and you can help her out in whatever ways you can.

Once she leaves home there will be a lonely, empty place in your home and heart. Your job now is to accept that hole, honor it, and refill it as best you can.

You might want to listen again to Allan Sherman's "Hello Muddah, Hello Faddah."

I have a bad news/good news item to share with you. A survey was conducted in 2015 looking at people's life spans and when they are happiest and when they are not. Want to guess where the high and low points might be? As you might guess, those college years rank right up there on the happiness scales. People are more carefree and the newfound freedoms take the burden of pleasing others off your back. Plus, the worry about getting into college is behind you.

It is not all downhill from there. There is some good news ahead. But first, let's deal with the bad. Turns out, right around age 50 things bottom out. There are a few reasons for that. First, you have to deal with your own midlife crisis and make peace with what was, what is, and what most likely will never be. You can mount plans and attend to your bucket list which do plant the seeds for the future. But in the moment, your own midlife crisis is accompanied by your empty nest and together those bring the low points in many people's lives.

But, let us not forget there is also good news. It turns out that as people age beyond midlife things pick up. People gain greater freedom to do what they want to do and those therapy sessions begin to pay off with a greater acceptance and appreciation for what life is now about.

I don't expect this will be much comfort as you confront your empty nest, but at least it foreshadows that while a good portion of your life's work is over, there are rewards ahead.

SECTION 10:

WRAP IT UP

66

TESTING YOUR LIMITS & BOUNDARIES

It goes without saying that your children will test the limits of your endurance and boundary lines will get crossed. I became uncomfortably aware of this when my daughter was two. She started to cry and then sob until eventually she was inconsolable. Everything I tried only inflamed her and there was nothing I could think of to help calm her down. The more I did or didn't do, the worse things got.

Two realizations became clear to me.

First, I was going to need to let her go to her room and find her own way out of her tantrum.

Second, my patience was close to wearing out. I was concerned that if I didn't find relief soon I might do something I regretted.

Before I regretted my actions I took her into her bedroom and told her I would be in the other room and she could come out any time she wanted. Then I left and tried to compose myself, hoping she would do the same.

My limits had been tested. How I did on the test depends on who is grading. As a teacher I am always rooting for people to get good grades. Myself included. I also know not everyone gets good grades on everything all the time. While we all might want to be honor students, sometimes a passing grade is good enough.

Whatever your current grade point average, there is another test on the way for you to raise or lower it.

Children are supposed to test their parents' limits. They are also supposed to test their own limits. Not just with you but with the world at large. How they fare with you will go a long way in determining how they fare with the rest of the world.

It is an inherited obligation of the next generation to move things along. While we all can mourn the good old days and wish for parts of it to return, evolution is real. We don't have to argue the origins of humankind to acknowledge that people today do not look, live, or act like people did centuries ago.

If you were living back in those cave-dwelling days and were the age you are now you would already be grandparents, having lost children along the way, and would be very close to your own demise and not reading a self-help book. And your kids and grandkids would be testing your patience along with the wild beasts that lurk outside your cave.

Children have always been tasked with taking the world their parents gave them and finding their own way forward. To do that we all have to do things differently than our forbearers as the world is no longer exactly as it was. Even those parents who wish their child would follow in their steps probably can admit there are things they would like to see their child do better than they did or do. In order for that to happen, children need to act differently which can lead to pushing tolerance and boundaries.

I often ask people if they would like to marry someone 100% like them. I have yet to find the person who thought that pairing would be ideal. Of course, that doesn't stop you from complaining when your partner doesn't do something the way you like it done.

While most parents would like their child to have their better qualities, they would also admit they would like their child *not* to have all their qualities and maybe some others they don't have. Unfortunately you don't get to choose. You can try to influence your child's behavior, but your child is the one who is going to have to make his way in the world. He needs to adapt ways of being that work for him, not just for you.

As he goes through trials and tribulations in his life, he will rub up against your comfort zone. He will test your patience, fears, beliefs, and loving ways. It is not personal—well, not completely. It is evolutionary.

How did you test your parents' patience, fears, beliefs, and loving ways?

_____

_____

Perhaps you were the apple of your parents' eye and never caused a ripple. If so, you can stand over there with that very small group and look over at the rest of us. While you're there you might reflect on how being such a "good" child has affected your life. My guess is, like most things, there are plusses and minuses.

For the rest of us who didn't always perform up to our parents' wishes, perhaps you have/had a challenging relationship with one of your parents. Maybe your differences aggravated your relationship or made no real difference in terms of the love and support you felt. Chances are you were less of a thorn in their side than your child is with you. It's that evolution thing. If it is any consolation, their kids will probably test them more as well.

Of course, some of you tested your parents more than your child tests you. Perhaps in pushing away from your parents' beliefs you established your own values which today provoke much less rebellion. Whether your child actively rebels against your wishes or is mostly content, chances are he is not going to adhere to your desires 100% of the time. Whether your child tests the limits a little or lot, you are going to have moments that test your limits.

Most parents who have multiple children will tell you how they raised their children differently. Their parenting style evolved as they aged and had more experience. Usually parents are more lenient with each additional child and aren't looking over their child's shoulders quite so much. Often a second, third, or fourth child can do things the parents would never have allowed their first child to do. If the first child had tried the same thing, they would have pushed their parents' limits and their parents may have clamped down. Years later what was once tested is now scored and the bar has been raised (or lowered).

Much to the chagrin of the older child.

Just because you can intellectually grasp that your child needs to learn how to test limits, doesn't mean you enjoy it when they are challenged. Since so much of parenting is about facing each situation on its own context, there is a constant need to be aware of what you truly want and believe.

Your child may want greater degrees of independence and freedom before you are ready to cede them. He may say things that hurt you, do things that upset you, and want things you have never had to consider allowing.

You respond by instinct as there really is no right or wrong way to handle most situations.

There is your being ready or not ready. And there is his being ready or not ready.

There is your now or later. And there is his now or later.

It is easy to say midnight is the curfew and hold to it most of the time. But does that mean you never fluctuate from midnight? Isn't one of the things you need to teach as a parent how to hold the line as well as when to make exceptions?

Think of a child who wants to play guitar and bugs you to get them one and then when you do he takes a few lessons and decides he is not really that into it.

On the one hand a parent needs to teach their child that even though something is difficult you need to stick with it. Yet they also need to teach their child that just since they start something does not mean they have to finish everything they start.

How long to stick it out and when to let it go are not things you can exactly define. Many a parent has stayed in a relationship too long and maybe not given another one more of a chance.

If you have a guideline/rule and it has been broken, is that because the line was not well enough established and needs to be rethought? Or because what once was valid is no longer? Or some other reason entirely?

Children do need their parents to set boundaries as it provides them comfort and structure. At the same time they need to rebel against that and stretch those boundaries. Sometimes it can be helpful to them for you to hold the boundary even though they protest.

You are modeling standing up for what you believe. Listening to another point of view and yet honoring the established structure. They need to learn how to do that.

And they need to learn to respectfully push back against that.

You need to teach them about making exceptions and about holding the line.

A perfect balance is elusive and I have not met a lot of people who only have success stories in these arenas. If this were a clear and easy thing to do you would not have read this far into the book. Parenting is an art form after all. Not a science.

Whose will will be done?

Eventually it will be his.

You will never have as much power as a parent as you have at this moment.

And, you have less now than you ever had.

You are going to have to learn how to hand over the reins and how to manage your own loss of power. This means that when your limits/beliefs/values are challenged, think of how you can grow from this rather than how you can limit his growth. You might even think about how you can both grow from the challenge.

Yes, you may say "No" to him now. But, eventually your "No's" will hardly matter at all.

Rather than fight the challenge head on, find ways to discuss the underlying fears, values, and desires and see if you and your child can't learn more about each other's perspectives. From that knowledge base it will be easier to reach decisions for both of you.

"How can we best resolve this?" is a question you can ask multiple times.

When boundaries are crossed they need to be addressed. If your child has transgressed against something that he knows is a "rule" in your home, you need to discuss it with him.

- Why did he do what he did?
- What did he want?
- Why didn't he talk about it first with you?
- What does he think ought to be done about it?

When boundaries are crossed, especially if they were basically understood and agreed upon, then something is out of balance and needs to be addressed and mutually resolved.

Perhaps the boundary needs to be rethought.

Perhaps new consequences need to be discussed.

Perhaps new guidelines need to be created and hopefully agreed upon.

Life always tests us.

It was Bette Davis who said, "Old age ain't for sissies."

Neither is parenting.

She also said, "If you have never been hated by your child, you have never been a parent."

67

DOES YOUR CHILD NEED TO LOVE YOU ALL THE TIME, SOME OF THE TIME, OR MOST OF THE TIME?

I mentioned earlier that this generation of American parents is the first that really wants their children to like them. I can tell you from working with a fair amount of parents this is much more of a concern than I can remember it being when I grew up. Of course, I was a child when I was growing up and didn't see parenting through my parents' eyes. Regardless of whether we want to be liked more or less than our parents did, the issue for you to consider is: How important is it that your child like you all the time?

It doesn't take long for new parents to find out that despite their best attempts at being a "good" parent there will be times when their child rails against them. There is some way that you are interacting that annoys, bothers, upsets and displeases your child. Even if yesterday the same thing got you some positive feedback. There are no guarantees you aren't going to do something to upset her.

A teenager can roll her eyes at you in ways that clearly let you know what a loser you are. She can also assemble words that can let you clearly know how little value you hold in her life. When she is displeased with you, she will usually waste no time letting you know. I know you will say/do something, uphold a "rule," not let her do this or that, and she will clearly communicate that she does not like you in this moment; it will not feel good to hear.

How long can you endure her being upset with you? How well you can handle that?

What you do about her reaction to you depends a lot on your own ego structure. The more you genuinely like yourself the easier it will be for you to accept others not liking you so much.

No one—well, very few people—like others to be upset with them. But if your insecurity runs deep you will be more prone to want to quickly make peace and reassure yourself that you are indeed loveable. If you basically feel loveable it is easier, not easy, to let others be upset with you. Whether what you said/did with your child was on the money or not matters less than your own comfort with yourself. Even parents that know they did the "right" thing can quickly change their position when their fear of their child not liking them starts to mount.

I know parents that have not only reversed their position on an issue, but have tried to buy back their child's love. One parent told me that after his daughter gave him the cold shoulder for a few days he not only lightened up on her curfew, he bought her a car months earlier than he had planned. He got a hug out of it from his daughter and a frown from his wife.

Letting your child have the room to be upset with you and not having to make peace right away is a gift you can give her that only costs patience. Being able to withstand another's dissatisfaction is a life skill she too will need to develop. Learning how to gracefully accept that someone you care about is upset with you can be uncomfortable, but don't let your discomfort undermine you.

Most of us don't like it when someone is upset with us and most of us don't like being upset with someone we love. Yet there is value for each party in allowing that angst to brew. When people are upset they spend time dwelling on what is bothering them. While that dwelling can take all manner of directions, as a parent I would want to direct myself and my child towards including some time reflecting on how this disharmony provides opportunity. Opportunity to reflect on what you believe and want and how your interactions with others enables and disables you from getting what you want.

When you tell your child she can't go to a party over the weekend, more often than not she will be upset with you. She may plead, bargain, cajole, and argue with you. She may walk away disgusted with you and mutter some not-so-nice comments on the way. Nobody wants someone else telling them they can't do something they want to do. She has good reason to be upset.

If you quickly go to her room and offer some compromise or immediately cave in you have taken away her time to be angry. She needs to dwell on why you said no, what she might have done to get a yes out of you and what she could do to change your mind. Or perhaps she will think about ways to get herself to the party without you knowing. All of these are problem-solving skills she needs to develop.

When your discomfort at the disharmony causes you to try quickly to make things better you have deprived her of this self-reflective time You may be relieved to see her anger disperse, but unless you think you handled the situation poorly I would prefer you give her some time to brood and come up with a plan. She is going to hear plenty of "No's" in her life; she needs to learn how to respond to them in creative healing ways.

Once someone is registering an 8, 9, or 10 on their own personal 1-10 Richter upset scale, you need to be prepared for a prolonged cooling off period. Usually the greater the upset the more time a person needs before they can open up their heart and mind.

Of course, there are some hurts people endure after which they never are able to fully open their hearts or minds again. But unless you have slammed the door and sworn off communication and meant it, there is going to be a coming back together.

Maybe slowly. Maybe not as close as before. Maybe slowly at first and closer later.

For most skirmishes that occur around the house the cooling off periods ought not to extend to days. I personally aim for trying to at least make a move to mend bridges before bedtime, unless of course you are having your argument at bedtime. I just want to make an appearance within 24 hours so the ice is broken and reparation talks are underway. As the parent I think it is incumbent upon us to make the first move.

Some parents, when they think their child has been disrespectful or they know their child knows they are in the wrong, will hold out for the child to make the first move. That is fine if it happens in a reasonable amount of time, but you don't want to get into power struggles with your child. Especially when you don't have to.

This is one of those places where I would say pick your battles. If you are going to have power struggles—and you very well may have some along the way—is this where you really want to make your stand? If it is, so be it.

Even when you want your child to extend the olive branch you need to keep yourself available. Don't slam the door and go in your room. If your child reaches out to you to make peace, welcome her intention. Even if she comes just to plead her case some more, at least she is engaging you. That engagement over differences is a valuable component of a loving relationship. It is when your child disengages herself from you that you have a higher level of concern. With engagement there is hope for settlement.

Personally I would prefer to make taking the first step a non-issue. Which means I often take the initiative. Most often it would be more than an hour and less than a day.

In the eventual discussions I would say that I would have liked it had she come forward first.

She might say she wasn't ready.

I would say, "Well, hopefully sometimes you will be ready before me."

She might ask for more time as our temperaments are different and she may need more time to cool off.

I would try to honor that.

I have a general "house rule" where if a person knows in their heart that they screwed up or the other person's perspective is the better one for now, then they ought to be the first one to step forward. I would add that often when you have disputes one person does something and then the other person reacts and things go back and forth. Often both of them are not behaving in the best way. In those situations I would also want the one who started it to be the one who takes the first step.

Unless the other person took a really nasty last step. In which case, may the worst offender please stand up.

If this is a going to be a "house rule" you impose you need to make it clear to everyone in your home and allow for input and modification. Any "house rule" will have a better chance of being followed if all hands are on deck.

However it gets spoken, all parties should know we are in this relationship thing together, so let's endeavor to make it as good as possible and not quibble about who puts out the olive branch first. Unless you think the other person is considerably more at fault—say in the 80/20 range. In those cases there needs to be some discussion about conflict resolution and why the olive branching can't be better shared.

When it comes to your child being upset with you, please consider that supporting your child not liking you is one thing your child may eventually like about you.

Letting your child not like you, be upset with you, disappointed with you, or otherwise displeased with you is a gift. It is one I don't want to have to give all the time. But I do want my daughter and everyone else's children to know it is okay to be disappointed and upset and to voice that dissatisfaction. Let your child know you can take it. Not enjoy it. But handle it.

In a mostly respectful way.

The more freedom you can give your child to experience life in all its emotional, physical, and spiritual beauty, the greater appreciation she will have for life. Let her learn what it is like to be disappointed and try again. To come up against obstacles and find ways past them. To live within structure and find ways to expand that structure. To be upset with you and know things will simmer down and the closeness and love you share will still surround you.

You don't want your child to be afraid to feel and show her displeasure. You want her to be able to acknowledge it, accept it, and find ways to resolve it. You also want her to know there are times when you are of a firm mind and will not change your position and there are times when you are able to hear her concerns and modify your position. Most of all you want her to learn that you are not afraid of her anger, her sadness, her disappointment, or any of her emotions. You are able to hold her emotions just as you held her when she was a small, vulnerable bundle in your lap.

68

ONCE A PARENT, ALWAYS A PARENT

Parenting is a lifetime occupation. Once you get the job you keep the job. Even in those horrible instances where parents lose their child, that does not stop them from having an ongoing relationship with their child. Just because someone dies does not mean your relationship with them ends. It just moves into a different realm.

As I have mentioned, parenting is a sacred trust. Not everyone gets to be a parent.

Every parent knows that what you think about parenting when you don't have children is significantly different than what you experience when you are a parent. Others can talk, think, and write about it, but living it is where the magic rests.

Your life as a parent has transformed you in ways you didn't fully grasp. You no longer are the person you were before you had children. You are forever changed.

With that transformation comes a covenant with life.

Not every parent takes on the full vow of parenthood and in truth we all make our own vows. Most of which are never fully spoken or fully realized until time reveals them or someone asks.

So I am asking: When you conceived your child and thought about being a parent, did you have any vow you made to yourself, your child, your partner, your God, or the universe? Is there some deeper level of commitment you have to love your children that helps define you?

_____

_____

_____

You may not have fully lived up to the vows you made, just as many people do not fully live up to the vows they make when they marry. We mostly all start with the best of intentions and then do our best to live up to them.

What you will and won't do for your child differs from parent to parent. Most parents will do things and feel things for their children that they don't feel and do quite the same with anyone else. There are bonds that connect family members that don't exist with others. Blood is thicker than water and the blood of a parent that flows to their child often runs thickest of all.

There are people who believe you should love yourself above all others.

There are people who believe you should love your spouse above all others.

There are people who believe you should love your children above all others.

There are people who believe you should love none above others.

There are people who believe you should love your God, your country, your sports team, and your pet above all others.

We can all believe what we want. We are fortunate to live in a country that promotes individual beliefs. Yet what we believe and what we do day to day don't always walk arm-in-arm.

Whatever the priorities of your love and however much you fulfill them, if you have a child there is someone on this earth who is a direct descendent of you and your forbearers. There is someone on this earth who is of you and who will carry forth your heritage.

For some, that holds a level of pride and responsibility. For others it doesn't mean that much.

If being connected to your forbearers does happen to mean something to you and you want to honor the lineage of your family, be sure to make efforts to convey those values, stories, and heirlooms that carry meaning for you. Whether you are sharing a funny anecdote about a grandparent or aunt or uncle, you are sharing your family history and giving your child a sense of what it has been to be a member of this clan. I encourage you to have those talks with your child.

I remember a day when my mother walked me around her house and told me what she wanted me to know about each item of importance to her and each item she wanted me to save. I didn't like that conversation because I knew it meant one day my mother would die and I would inherit her life. Yet it was a meaningful conversation to us both and we repeated it in various forms over the years. Like some other emotionally challenging discussions, those conversations made us cry, laugh, and grow closer together. I am grateful for them and thankful she took the time to let me know what was important to her.

Have I respected everything she told me in a way she could respect? Probably some things more than others. But like many parents, I have found myself talking to my child and heard my mother's voice.

Most people don't want to talk about their own death, let alone to their child. While I do think it is something you need to do, I also know that for most people there is a lot of procrastination. While there may be no apparent rush there also is some rush because you know you never know. I think it is easier to share what is meaningful to you in your life with your child in casual conversations throughout your lifetime. Until you feel brave enough and think your child is ready, you can save telling him, "Let's sit down and talk about my will and the things I think you ought to know on the occasion of my demise. Whenever it is."

Just don't wait too long.

I remember being at a Jackson Browne concert with my teenage daughter and when he played *For a Dancer* I told her I wanted that song played at my funeral. She looked at me with a pained expression and later told me it was weird and she could never hear that song again without thinking about what I said. That was okay with me. Not great, but a step in the process of shifting generations. I also knew that when I died she would play that song and we would be connected in that moment. Now, I hear that song and cry and think of the love I share with her. Those tears mean a lot to me.

While that was a direct "when I die" comment, there are many more stories you can share that have nothing to do with death but everything to do with what have been hallmarks of your family's history.

If you want to get an early start on this I recommend connecting your child with the articles around your home in storytelling ways. Everything you have has a story. Some worth telling. Some not. Some forgotten.

While you still can remember the stories, sprinkle anecdotes into your conversations until you hear, "Not again. I have heard that story too many times." Then you know your work has been done.

You are the historian of your family. Share your oral history. If you are inclined you can write up the stories or go around to the pictures you have in the house and stick a note on the back that explains it.

When you are home together and something organically comes up, you can weave in the "I would like you to keep this item" comments. Your child will learn what has meaning to you and when the time comes he will be inclined to keep the ones with the most meaning.

Not always, but mostly.

Just like you have done.

Or haven't.

Just as you will always be your child's parent, so too will he always be his parent's child.

If you live long enough you may become your child's child and he his parent's parent. It doesn't hurt to keep that in mind. You may want/need him sometime to be there for you in ways you were there for him. Chances are he will interact with you with the same level of TLC you have given him.

As a parent you can only do your best and know it isn't perfect.

You may wish you had done better.

You may wish that your relationship with your child was better and you may wish you could have done some things differently.

Just as your relationship with your parents was not perfect, neither is yours with your child nor his with you. It is a relationship after all.

Until the moment you die, you have the ongoing ability to continue to do your best and let your child know you want things to be as good as they can be between you, and as good as they can be for him in his life away from you.

Love your children as best you can.

Love you as best you can.

Love your life as best you can and do your best to be gentle to yourself and others as we all learn how to live on this earth in peace and harmony.

POST SCRIPT

I don't know what percentage of self-help book readers make it to the end of a book, but if you are one of that group let me thank you for having plowed through the entirety of this book. If the book has sparked any interest in the subjects I have discussed, please come visit my website. The website contains my blog along with my current thinking on various subjects. Both the blog and the website are interactive.

I welcome you to share your thoughts and stories.

Certainly some of the statements I have made may have prompted you to want to challenge me, discuss it with me, or take something to another level. While I am happy when someone agrees with me, I also am happy when they take the time to point out another way of looking at things. Let's continue to learn together.

DavidUngerPhD.com

ACKNOWLEDGMENTS

In order to feel eligible to write a book about parenting teenagers I needed to have fathered a child and gone through the process myself. My daughter, Marissa, has been my best teacher. I have learned innumerable lessons about love, caring, and respect from "growing up" with her. So, first and foremost thank you Marissa for letting me discover my favorite word—dad.

Next on the list is the professor of sociology who helped edit this book for me and found ways to engage me in the material that helped make the book clearer to me and hopefully to you as well. She also has gotten the hang of loving me and being my partner in life. Thank you, Jill.

There are students, former students, and parents who have spoken with me and with whom I have learned how to be a helping hand. I want to thank you for your honesty, trust, and willingness to open your lives to me.

I am lucky that the Head of School who hired me still signs off on my checks. His ongoing support and encouragement has helped me grow as a counselor. Since I work in the Upper School (high school) I am fortunate to have a supervisor whose work ethic has prompted me to work more than I ever have, learn more than I ever have, and experience a level of support for which I am truly thankful. Thank you, Tom and Peggy.

I think most authors know that someone else has basically written what they want to say before and most likely said it better. In my case that would be Michael Thompson, PhD who has consulted with more parents and schools than probably anyone. I couldn't reread any of his books before I wrote mine because I would have thought, *Why bother?* In his book *The Pressured Child*, he stated, "...what a parent can provide is easy to name and often difficult to implement, attention, resources, space, time, experimentation and faith." I have tried to provide those to myself, my daughter, and all the others my path has crossed as I have walked in his footsteps. Thank you, Michael, for your inspiration.

As the book headed into the stretch run Michelle Josette helped with the final editing and Grady from Damonza.com did the art work. I want to thank them both for sprucing things up.

Last but certainly not least are my colleagues and friends. My colleagues are the ones whose hands-on work makes the school a better place every day. They are invested in learning and they are as good a group of teachers as you will find anywhere. Special thanks to Dirk and Ray for making school so much fun. My friends take the time to talk with me. About real things. In real ways. Usually with a lot of humor and always with a lot of love. I am gratefully indebted to Marsha, Steve, Liz, Olivia, Aaron, Joaquin, Patty, Jeff, Lefty, Mary, and Stuart. Long may we run.

13821802R00228

Printed in Great Britain
by Amazon